Cool Careers For Dummies, 2nd Edition

Shortcuts to a cool career

These careers offer many of the benefits of a prestigious career in a fraction of the time and cost. Here are a few examples:

The Long Route	The Short Route
Doctor	Physician's assistant
Lawyer	Mediator
Psychologist	Personal coach

For more, see Chapter 2.

Three not-pushy ways to land a job

- Ask a friend to call employers he knows on your behalf and say, "I've just heard that (insert your name) may be available. She's terrific. You should get your hands on her while you can."
- Join online discussion groups. Megalists of them are at www.topica.com and www.list.com
- Sign up at "push" Web sites such as monster.com, which deliver on-target job openings right to your e-mail box.

For details and more not-pushy strategies, see Part III.

Three musts for successful self-employment

- Realize that you may need less capital than you think. Choose a service rather than a product, start your business at home or at a government-subsidized small business incubator, avoid hiring help, and resist the temptation to buy expensive furniture and equipment.
- Do a mini-business plan. It will help you decide whether a business is for you, and provide a blueprint for your success.
- Use the marketing methods you're most comfortable with. The best method is useless if you won't use it

See Chapter 20 for much more on going solo.

How to convince someone to hire you instead of someone with more degrees

Write a letter that . . .

- Says something like, "I deliberately chose to upgrade my skills without going back for another degree because I knew I would learn more of value."
- Describes what you did and what you learned.
- Ends with something like, "I believe I chose substance over form, but now comes the moment of truth. Will you interview me?"

For a model letter, see Chapter 7.

Five ways to make any job better

- To get what you want from your boss, figure out whether he or she is persuaded by facts or feelings.
- Propose to do a project you'd find fun.
- With coworkers, trade tasks that emphasize your weaknesses for tasks that use your strengths.
- Would telecommuting or a change of schedule make you happier? Pitch it to your boss.
- Even if you're a clerk, think like a CEO. Think of cool ideas to improve your workplace or the bottom line. Get credit — bring your ideas up at a staff meeting.

Chapter 19 has much more on making any job better.

Cool Careers For Dummies, 2nd Edition

Cheat Sheet

33 great careers most people wouldn't have thought of

Attorney specializing in outer space issues

Audiologist (a master's-level job with doctor's prestige)

Biological weapons deterrence specialist

Celebrity personal assistant (assistant to the stars)

Child-life specialist (helps chronically ill kids adapt to life in the hospital)

Counselor to college-bound athletes

Dating coach

Foley artist (creates movie sound effects)

Graphologist (handwriting analyst hired by police, FBI, and so on)

Holographer (makes holograms for festivals, trade shows, and so on)

Hydrologist (collects and tests water samples from mountain streams, glaciers, and so on)

Locksmith

Mediator

Muralist (for freeway underpasses, eyesore buildings, and so on)

Neon sign maker

Newborn photographer (takes pictures of newborns, moms, and dads in the hospital)

Nurse anesthetist

Perfumer

Prosthetist (makes artificial limbs)

Restaurant menu designer

Robotics engineer

Rock band photographer

Special occasions cake baker

Sports information director (provides info to the media on a college's sports teams)

Shyness coach

TV show casting director

Venture capitalist

Virtual reality computer programmer

Volcanologist (studies volcanoes)

Enologist (winemaker)

Web content finder

Work-family manager (helps companies create more family-friendly workplaces)

Chapter 2 has scoops on these plus hundreds more great careers.

Six cool career Web sites

Wanted Jobs (www.wantedjobs.com). This site simultaneously searches 350 employment Web sites, 3,000,000 jobs, to find good fits for you.

Monster.com. 500,000 easily searchable job listings, a great online resume creator, plus tons of great advice. New sections for freelancers and executives. Also see flipdog.com. It contains many thousands of jobs not listed on Monster.

Wetfeet.com. Insider information on dozens of careers and industries and on hundreds of companies. Vault.com is similar.

About.com (www.about.com/smallbusiness). A wealth of self-employment support, both written and human.

Google (www.google.com). The biggest search engine: searches 1.5 BILLION Web pages, fast!

The Riley Guide (www.rileyguide.com). Links to hundreds of the best career sites.

Copyright © 2001 Wiley Publishing, Inc. All rights reserved.

Item 5345-3.

For more information about Wiley Publishing, call 1-800-762-2974.

For Dummies: Bestselling Book Series for Beginners

Praise for Cool Careers For Dummies, 2nd Edition

"A career guide that REALLY works — thorough, reliable, and amazingly helpful."

> — James C. Gonyea, nationally recognized career guidance
> expert; Host: Gonyea Online Career Center on AOL

"Whenever you have the opportunity to get career advice from Marty Nemko, you've got to listen. He's terrific!"

> — John Lucht, author of *Rites of Passage at $100,000+,*
> *the Insider's Guide to Executive Job-Changing and Faster*
> *Career Progress*

"If you don't have a career coach, you must invest in *Cool Careers For Dummies*. It both brims over with information and offers solid, nurturing advice. Whether you're going to get that first job, considering a career change, or leaning, not leaping, into self-employment, *Cool Careers For Dummies* has something to offer. Technology and demographics will shape the 21st-century labor market, and *Cool Careers For Dummies* is one of the key resources that will make this market easier to navigate."

> — Julianne Malveaux, Economist and Syndicated Columnist,
> Washington, D.C.

"If you think you're doomed to boring jobs, you haven't read *Cool Careers For Dummies*. This essential, ingenious book provides hundreds of thought-provoking ideas for jobs you would actually love. The authors also provide clear, step-by-step directions for making your dream job a reality."

> — Bob Goldman, Syndicated Columnist, "Work Daze"

"Finally, a book where career idealism, realism, and practical career manage-ment advice come together. Loaded with great ideas to help you select, plan, or change your career. Whether you are starting your own career, are in a corpora-tion, a profession, or your own business, this is a read to succeed."

> — Kent Black, formerly Group Vice-President,
> Drake Beam Morin, Inc., the world's largest
> career transitions consulting firm

"Highly recommended for anyone confused about choosing a career or wonder-ing 'what's next?,' *Cool Careers For Dummies* takes the mystery, fear, and drudgery out of getting ahead!"

> — Mary-Ellen Mort, Project Director, Job Smart,
> top-rated careers Web site

"If you're looking for work that gives you more than just a steady paycheck, *Cool Careers For Dummies* is a great place to begin your search. The straight-talking authors first provide an unusual array of 500 career possibilities and then offer useful advice on how to land a job in the area you choose. It's a fun read that may be of invaluable help in making one of life's big decisions."

> — Jack Kahn, Director of Program Development,
> PBS-TV *Nightly Business Report*

"Cool Careers For Dummies provides a fast-moving, humor-filled tour through questions about careers, including self-employment, job interviews, determining one's interests, creating opportunities, and making decisions."

> — Dr. Robert A. Scott, President,
> Ramapo College of New Jersey

"Whether you're looking for a job or want to switch careers, Marty Nemko will show you the tricks you need. His thorough knowledge and direct style have helped thousands of my listeners."

> — Ronn Owens, Talk Show Host, KGO, San Francisco

"Cool Careers For Dummies is a breath of fresh air! It guides readers through the career planning process in a new way and provides lots of interesting, practical suggestions that really make a difference."

> — Marilyn E. Maze, Career Software Designer, ACT, Inc.

"Anyone who dreads the 9-to-5 rut will embrace *Cool Careers For Dummies*. It offers readers the options they need to find the right career, the guidance to get there, and the inspiration to do it."

> — Dave Murphy, Career Search Editor,
> *San Francisco Examiner*

"A lively, irreverent, funny, and really helpful book for all those millions of people who are trying to figure out a new cool career. It's jammed with good advice and lots of new possibilities, and it sure takes the sting out of a difficult process."

> — Ann Sparks, Program Director, Alumnae Resources, San
> Francisco's largest career development organization

"Extra-strength resources to continually relaunch your career search . . . cool!"

> — Jeffrey Taylor, Founder, The Monster Board, a leading
> employment Web site

"I wanted to make a change but was clueless about where to even begin. *Cool Careers For Dummies* walked me through the process step-by-step and inspired me just like my own personal counselor — all with a touch of humor. I also found the career scoops divided into categories invaluable. So much information at a glance!"

> — Natalie S. Gifford, Katy, Texas

 ™

References for the Rest of Us!®

BESTSELLING BOOK SERIES

Do you find that traditional reference books are overloaded with technical details and advice you'll never use? Do you postpone important life decisions because you just don't want to deal with them? Then our *For Dummies®* business and general reference book series is for you.

For Dummies business and general reference books are written for those frustrated and hard-working souls who know they aren't dumb, but find that the myriad of personal and business issues and the accompanying horror stories make them feel helpless. *For Dummies* books use a lighthearted approach, a down-to-earth style, and even cartoons and humorous icons to dispel fears and build confidence. Lighthearted but not lightweight, these books are perfect survival guides to solve your everyday personal and business problems.

> *"More than a publishing phenomenon, 'Dummies' is a sign of the times."*
>
> — *The New York Times*

> *"A world of detailed and authoritative information is packed into them…"*
>
> — *U.S. News and World Report*

> *"…you won't go wrong buying them."*
>
> — *Walter Mossberg, Wall Street Journal, on For Dummies books*

Already, millions of satisfied readers agree. They have made For Dummies the #1 introductory level computer book series and a best-selling business book series. They have written asking for more. So, if you're looking for the best and easiest way to learn about business and other general reference topics, look to For Dummies to give you a helping hand.

Wiley Publishing, Inc.

5/09

Cool Careers
FOR
DUMMIES®
2ND EDITION

**by Marty Nemko and Paul
and Sarah Edwards**

WILEY

Wiley Publishing, Inc.

Cool Careers For Dummies,® 2nd Edition

Published by
Wiley Publishing, Inc.
909 Third Avenue
New York, NY 10022
www.wiley.com

Copyright © 2001 by Wiley Publishing, Inc., Indianapolis, Indiana

Published by Wiley Publishing, Inc., Indianapolis, Indiana

Published simultaneously in Canada

For general information on our other products and services or to obtain technical support, please contact our Customer Care Department within the U.S. at 800-762-2974, outside the U.S. at 317-572-3993, or fax 317-572-4002.

Wiley also publishes its books in a variety of electronic formats. Some content that appears in print may not be available in electronic books.

Library of Congress Cataloging-in-Publication Data:

Library of Congress Control Number: 00-112136

ISBN: 0-7645-5345-3

Manufactured in the United States of America

10 9 8 7 6 5

2O/SR/QV/QT/IN

About the Authors

Marty Nemko has several cool careers. As a career counselor, he has worked with 1,600 clients. His column appears in the *Los Angeles Times* classified section, on monster.com, and in the Sunday *San Francisco Chronicle,* right above *Dilbert.* He's in his 13th year as producer and host of *Work with Marty Nemko,* on a National Public Radio affiliate in San Francisco. He is the host of a nationwide PBS pledge-drive special, *Eight Steps to a Better Worklife* and a repeat guest on many TV and radio shows. He has been the primary interview source for dozens of articles, including in *The New York Times,* the *Washington Post,* and *The Wall Street Journal.* He attained a Ph.D. from the University of California, Berkeley, and subsequently taught there. He does find a few moments for hobbies: He loves to play basketball and play romantic songs on the piano.

Paul and Sarah Edwards are the award-winning coauthors of 13 other books, including *Home-Based Business for Dummies* and *Changing Directions Without Losing Your Way.* Their books, which have sold over a million copies, guide people in how to live the life they want to live while doing work they want to do. They cohost the weekly radio show *Working From Home* on the BusinessTalkRadio.Net. They are columnists for *Entrepreneur* magazine and have been named Speakers of the Year by *Sharing Ideas* magazine. Occasionally their show, broadcast from their California mountain home, is enriched by the barks of Billy, their toy Manchester Terrier.

Ask the Authors

Phone or in-person career counseling: Marty Nemko's office: 510-655-2777.

Self-employment information: The Edwardses provide a wealth of ongoing information at www.workingfromhome.com and www.simplegoodlife.com.

Dedication

Marty: To my parents. As teenagers, they were wrested from their home in Poland and into concentration camps. After the war, they were placed on a cargo ship and dropped in New York City with no money, no family, no education, no English, but plenty of Holocaust scars. Despite it all, they succeeded. They are my inspiration.

Paul and Sarah: To our son, Jon, who followed his own career path. I, Paul, was told from Day 1 that I should be a lawyer. I followed the script and did graduate from law school but took the first chance I got to go in a different direction. I, Sarah, was told that my best bet was to be a teacher. I got the education I needed to teach but never spent a day as a classroom teacher. So we were careful not to push Jon into a career. The result is that Jon is doing something he likes: He designs computer games. We salute Jon for choosing his own career and for all the hard work it took to succeed.

Authors' Acknowledgments

To the thousands of career searchers who taught us much of what is in this book: the callers to our radio shows and especially Marty's clients.

To the book's wise reviewers: Jim Gonyea, career forums host on America Online; Marilyn Maze, director of career products for American College Testing; and the queens of online career searching: *JobStar.com*'s Mary Ellen Mort and especially *The Riley Guide*'s Margaret Riley Dikel for her review of the entire new edition. Special thanks to Dave Murphy, Marty's editor at the *San Francisco Chronicle*. No matter how hard Marty tries to excise every unneeded word, Dave cuts a few more — and it reads better.

To the other talented people whose ideas enrich these pages: Dan Blacharski, Christina Fox, Dodge Johnson, Lynaire McGovern, Dennis Miller, Monica Pataki, Jennifer Murphy, Neil Fiore, Julie Petrie, Michael Scriven, and Marty's dear friends, David Wilens and Allan Gold.

To my consigliere: august Doubleday editor emeritus Luther Nichols.

And thanks, Dr. John Jones, for your reassurances.

To the good people at Hungry Minds: Mark Butler and Kathy Welton for believing we were the right authors for this book, Karen Doran for picking up where they left off, Tim Gallan for his zen-like project editing, Norm Crampton and Neil Johnson for their responsiveness and light touch in editing the second edition, and Allison Solomon for handling administrative tasks with unusual intelligence and diligence. Special thanks to Clark Scheffy, who had to leave the project when U.C. Berkeley called, but first educated Marty on what works in a *For Dummies* book.

And finally, Marty wants to thank his wife, Barbara Nemko, for being the voice of uncommon sense.

Publisher's Acknowledgments

We're proud of this book; please send us your comments through our Online Registration Form located at www.dummies.com/register.

Some of the people who helped bring this book to market include the following:

Acquisitions, Editorial, and Media Development

Project Editor: Norm Crampton

Acquisitions Editor: Karen Doran

Copy Editor: Neil Johnson

Acquisitions Coordinator: Lauren Cundiff

Technical Editor: Margaret Dikel

Editorial Manager: Pamela Mourouzis

Editorial Assistant: Carol Strickland

Cover Photos: © Ziggy Kaluzny/Tony Stone

Reprint Editor: Bethany André

Production

Project Coordinator: Leslie Alvarez

Layout and Graphics: Angela Chaney-Granger, Jacque Schneider, Julie Trippetti, Jeremey Unger, Erin Zeltner

Proofreaders: Laura Albert, John Bitter, Nancy Price, Marianne Santy, York Production Services, Inc.

Indexer: York Production Services, Inc.

Publishing and Editorial for Consumer Dummies

Diane Graves Steele, Vice President and Publisher, Consumer Dummies
Joyce Pepple, Acquisitions Director, Consumer Dummies
Kristin A. Cocks, Product Development Director, Consumer Dummies
Michael Spring, Vice President and Publisher, Travel
Brice Gosnell, Publishing Director, Travel
Suzanne Jannetta, Editorial Director, Travel

Publishing for Technology Dummies

Richard Swadley, Vice President and Executive Group Publisher
Andy Cummings, Vice President and Publisher

Composition Services

Gerry Fahey, Vice President of Production Services
Debbie Stailey, Director of Composition Services

Contents at a Glance

Introduction 1

Part I: Find the Right Career for You, Right Here 5
Chapter 1: Searching for a Career: Jennifer's Tale 7
Chapter 2: The Cool Careers Yellow Pages 11
Chapter 3: The 25 Most Revealing Questions 135
Chapter 4: Integrating Head and Heart 145
Chapter 5: What's That Career Really Like? 151
Chapter 6: Finding the Courage to Commit 163

Part II: Getting Smart 173
Chapter 7: Degree-Free Career Preparation 175
Chapter 8: Degree-Based Career Prep 189

Part III: A Better Way to Land the Job 203
Chapter 9: What Really Works 205
Chapter 10: Creating Your Mind-Set 213
Chapter 11: The Right Resume in Much Less Time 221
Chapter 12: Finding Your Dream Employer 239
Chapter 13: A Better Approach to the Want Ads 251
Chapter 14: Getting Hired by Your Dream Employer — Even if
  They're Not Advertising Openings 267
Chapter 15: Networking Made Easier 287
Chapter 16: Interviewing Better 299
Chapter 17: Negotiating a Cool Deal (Even If You're Dealing with Scrooge) ...319

Part IV: Customizing Your Career 337
Chapter 18: 30 Days to a Good Job 339
Chapter 19: Making Any Job Better 351
Chapter 20: The Six Musts of Successful Self-Employment 371

Part V: The Part of Tens 387
Chapter 21: Ten (Plus Five) More Sources of Cool Careers 389
Chapter 22: Ten (Okay, 48) Extra-Strength Procrastination Cures 399
Afterword: Our Best Thoughts on How to Have a Happy Work Life 411

Appendix: The Cool Career Finder 417

Index 423

Index of Careers...431

Cartoons at a Glance

By Rich Tennant

The 5th Wave — By Rich Tennant

"So what if you have a Ph.D. in physics? I used to have my own circus act."

page 173

The 5th Wave — By Rich Tennant

"My sense is you're personalizing your resume too much."

page 203

The 5th Wave — By Rich Tennant

"When choosing a career I ignored my heart and did what my brain wanted. Now all my brain wants is Prozac."

page 5

The 5th Wave — By Rich Tennant

"We don't care where you see yourself in five years, as long as you can see where our clients will be."

page 337

The 5th Wave — By Rich Tennant

"I'm sure there will be a good job market when I graduate. I created a virus that will go off that year."

page 387

Cartoon Information:
Fax: 978-546-7747
E-Mail: richtennant@the5thwave.com
World Wide Web: www.the5thwave.com

Table of Contents

Introduction *1*

   What's New in This New Edition? 1
   How This Book Is Organized 2
       Part I: Find the Right Career for You, Right Here 2
       Part II: Getting Smart 3
       Part III: A Better Way to Land the Job 3
       Part IV: Customizing Your Career 3
       Part V: The Part of Tens 4
   Icons Used in This Book 4

Part 1: Find the Right Career for You, Right Here *5*

Chapter 1: Searching for a Career: Jennifer's Tale 7

Chapter 2: The Cool Careers Yellow Pages 11

   What Makes a Cool Career Cool? 11
   Using the Cool Careers Yellow Pages 12
       The categories 12
       The Yellow Pages' icons 12
       What price prestige? 13
   Work with People 14
       Bringing people together 21
       Sales-oriented work 23
       Other people-oriented careers 25
   Work with Data 28
       Scientific data 28
       Computer data 33
       Business data 36
   Work with Words 39
   Work with Things 44
       Artistically done 44
       Structured procedures 48
   Work with People and Data 57
   Work with People and Words 66
       Public speaking 66
       One-on-one 73
   Working with People and Things 75
   Working with Words and People 77
   Working with Data and People 83
   Working with Data, People, and Words 88
   Work with Data and Things 94

Work with Things and People 97
Other Things/People Careers 101
Work with Things and Data 106
Work with Things, People, and Words 112
Work with Data, People, and Things 112
Work with Data, Things, and People 118
Work with Things, People, and Words 122
Ahead-of-the-Curve Fields 123
Not-So-Cool Careers 130

Chapter 3: The 25 Most Revealing Questions 135
Making the Process Easier 136
Your Values 136
Your Abilities and Skills 137
Your Passions 139
Big-Picture Questions 142

Chapter 4: Integrating Head and Heart 145
Julie Finds a Career 145
Discovering Your Top-Choice Career(s) 146
Step 1: List your career musts 146
Step 2: Do the careers you picked satisfy your career musts? 146
Step 3: Do your career musts suggest other careers? 146
Step 4: Remember what careers excite you 149
Step 5: Pick one or more careers that might actually work 149
Step 6: Find out more 149

Chapter 5: What's That Career Really Like? 151
The Busy Person's Way to Check Out a Career 151
Julie Finds a Career: The Final Episode 152
Reading about a Career 153
Why read before phoning or visiting? 153
Best stuff to read 154
Using the Internet 155
Contacting People in the Field 155
"Okay, okay, but whom do I contact?" 156
What to say 156
Visiting a Workplace 158
What to do during a visit? 158
A virtual visit 159
After the phone call or visit 159
Getting Serious 160

Chapter 6: Finding the Courage to Commit 163
When You Don't Know Enough about a Prospective Career 163
When No Career Seems Attractive Enough 164

When You're Afraid You'll Fail 165
    Recognize that it's usually worth risking failure 166
    All your ducks needn't be in a row 166
General Inertia 167
    Compare your options against the status quo 167
    The Judge Judy technique 168
    Try out your new career as a sideline 168
    Give yourself a trial period 169
    Take an assistant position 169
    Choose more than one career 169
    Choose a less radical option 170
A Final Check 171

Part II: Getting Smart 173

Chapter 7: Degree-Free Career Preparation 175

Lousy Reasons to Go Back for a Degree 175
Good Reasons to Go Back for a Degree 176
Will the Piece of Paper Be Worth the Time and Money? 177
You U. — Often a Better Way 179
Convincing Employers to Hire You Without That Degree 182
Planning Your You U. Education 184
    Finding a mentor 184
    Figuring out what to learn 185
    Sources of courses 185
Lifelong Learning 188

Chapter 8: Degree-Based Career Prep 189

Choosing the Right Program 189
    Be sure you've identified your career niche 189
    Identify programs that train you in your niche 190
Finding the Right College or Grad School 192
    Getting in 193
    Getting into killer colleges 195
Finding the Money 196
Comparing the Deals 198
Making the Most of the School You Choose 198
    Make the effort to find good teachers 199
    Read first 199
    In class, stay active 199
    Choose your advisor well 200
    One-on-one 200
    Adapt assignments to fit you 200
    Don't take crap 200

Part III: A Better Way to Land the Job 203

Chapter 9: What Really Works 205
A Better Way to Land a Job 206
Be Real 207
The Keys to a Fast Job Search 208
A Computer is a Virtual Must 208
A Special Note 208

Chapter 10: Creating Your Mind-Set 213
Staying Up 213
You're going to the mall 213
Playful yet persistent 214
The truth option 214
Fake it 'til you make it 215
Breathe 215
Three balls in the air 215
Be in the moment 215
Get support 215
Finding the Time 216
Shrugging Off Fear of Rejection 217
You say you have no real skills? 217
It's all in how you think of it 217
What would God think? 217
The library book mind-set 217
The only game in which batting .050 is good enough ...218
The two gold miners 218
Rejection as a blessing? 218
What's the worst that could happen? 218
A tool for curing more deep-rooted fear of rejection ...219
Getting That Chip Off Your Shoulder 219

Chapter 11: The Right Resume in Much Less Time 221
A Just-Right Resume in Ten Easy Steps and One Hard One ...222
Step 1: Write your name and contact information 222
Step 2: (Optional) Write your job target 223
Step 3: Choosing your format: chronological,
attributes based or hybrid 223
Step 4: Pick out a specific resume to use as a model ...225
Step 5: Draft a resume that follows the structure,
language, and feel of your model resume 225
What accomplishments? 226
"I still can't think of enough accomplishments!" 228
"But I have no previous experience in that line of work!" ...228
Step 6: Write the education section 231
Step 7: Optional sections 232
Step 8: The personal section 232
Step 9: List your highlights at the top of your resume ...233

Step 10: Get feedback 235
Step 11: Stop obsessing and start celebrating 235
Your Electronic Resume 235
Want an Electronic Handholder? 237
Want a Human Handholder? 237

Chapter 12: Finding Your Dream Employer 239

Just What Sort of Organization Should You Work For? 239
Top six reasons to work for a large company 240
Top six reasons to work for a small company 240
What about start-ups? 241
No-nonsense about nonprofits 241
Working for the government 242
Self-employment 243
Finding Your Dream Employer 244
Creating your list of dream employers 244
Finding the right people to talk with in each organization. 247
Keeping track 248
Finding Out What That Organization Is Really Like 249
The public info 249
The inside info 250

Chapter 13: A Better Approach to the Want Ads 251

Want Ads: The Most Underrated Job Search Tool 251
How Much Should You Use the Want Ads? 253
Making Want Ads Work for You 254
Two easy record-keeping systems 254
The best ads to respond to 255
Developing an efficient way to screen a large number of ads 255
Posting position-wanted ads 259
A special way to use the want ads 259
Want-ad stress savers 259
When to respond to a want ad 262
The best way to respond to an ad 263
More ways to boost your chances 265
Saving Emotional Energy 266

Chapter 14: Getting Hired by Your Dream Employer —
Even if They're Not Advertising Openings 267

What to Write: Sample Letters 268
Approach 1: When you don't have relevant experience 269
Approach 2: When you have no experience, and you're
   open to lots of career options. 270
Approach 3: When you have directly relevant experience 271
Before Calling 273
Your quick human story 273
Cold feet? 276
Making the call 277
Getting through to the hirer 277

Walking In: Not for the Fainthearted 281
Do I Really Have to Write a Thank-you Letter? 282
    A model thank-you letter 282
    The worst-case thank-you letter 283
Going to Job Fairs 284
    Preparing 284
    At the fair 284
    Virtual Job Fairs 285

Chapter 15: Networking Made Easier **287**
How Much Should You Network? 288
Making the Most of Networking 289
    Ten things you can get from a networking contact 290
    Secrets of successful networking by phone 291
Are You a Reluctant Networker? 293
Extra Credit Networking Opportunities 294
    Attending conferences, trade shows, and workshops 294
    Getting active in your professional or trade association 294
    Striking up a job-finding conversation at a meeting or party 295
    Leading a workshop 295
    Joining networking groups 296
    E-networking 296

Chapter 16: Interviewing Better **299**
How Chava Triumphed over the Interview from Hell 300
    The big date 302
    Chava walks in 303
    The interview from hell 303
    Out the door 306
The Key Interviewing Principles 307
    Nineteen ways to create great chemistry 307
    Don't just say you can do the job — prove it 313
    Maximize the good part of the interview 314
    Golden opportunity: Is the employer unsure of
        the job description? 314
    If you sense you're a poor match for this job 315
    After the interview: Where the job is often won or lost 315
You Got the Job Offer! 317
Someone Else Got the Job: All's Not Lost 318
Facing Rejection 318

**Chapter 17: Negotiating a Cool Deal (Even If You're
Dealing with Scrooge)** **319**
Chava Negotiates with Scrooge 321
    The end of the interview 321
    Chava prepares 321
    The negotiation meeting 322
What Would Convince You to Give a New Employee a Fat Salary? 325

Before the Negotiation Session 326
    What are you worth? 326
    A dress rehearsal 327
The Negotiation Session 327
    Building chemistry 328
    Getting ammunition 328
    Getting the boss excited about you 328
    Popping the question 328
    Negotiating with an employment agency 329
    Benefits 330
    Stock options 330
    Twelve things every negotiator must know . . .
       and most don't 331
    If you're self-employed 333
After the Negotiation 334
    Learning about your new job 334
    Nine signs of a job that's right for you 335

Part IV: Customizing Your Career 337

Chapter 18: 30 Days to a Good Job 339
Day 1 339
    12ish: Lunch 340
Day 2 341
    8 to 11 a.m. 341
    11 a.m. to noon 341
    Noon to 1 p.m.: Lunch 342
    1 to 5 p.m. 342
Day 3 343
    11 a.m. to noon 343
    Noon to 1 p.m.: Lunch 343
    1 to 5 p.m. 343
Day 4 344
    8 a.m. to 10 a.m. 344
    10 a.m. to 5 p.m. (with a break for lunch) 344
Day 5 345
    8 a.m. to noon 345
    Noon to 1 p.m.: Lunch 345
    1 to 5 p.m. 345
Day 6 346
Days 7 to 28 346
Days 29 and 30 348
Secrets to a Smooth Career Change 348

Chapter 19: Making Any Job Better 351
How Chava Turned an Okay Job into a Cool Career 351
    Getting the lowdown 351
    Starting the sculpture 352

Recruiting her all-star team 354
Staying fresh 354
Moving up 355
Moving out 355
Seven Steps to Making the Most of Your Job 356
Making the most of your boss (and co-workers) 356
Keeping your job interesting 359
Keeping the workload moderate 360
Learning the smart way 361
Moderating your stress 362
Making the most of telecommuting 363
Winning at office politics 365
Will You Get Ahead? 367

Chapter 20: The Six Musts of Successful Self-Employment 371

But What about the Downsides? 372
Job insecurity 372
Insane hours 372
You're on a perpetual job search? 372
The Self-Employment Test: Is Independence for You? 373
1. Do you like being in charge? 373
2. Are you flexible? 373
3. Can you get things done? 373
4. Are you good at solving real-world problems quickly? 373
5. Are you persistent? 374
6. Do you communicate well? 374
7. Are you willing and able to market and sell? 374
Scoring 374
Six Musts for Hiring Yourself 375
A good idea 375
Putting your toe in the water 376
Your mini business plan 377
Have an entry plan that keeps the cash flowing 378
Acting like the CEO you are 382
Getting business to come to you 383
But What If I Fail? 384
You're Not Alone 385

Part V: The Part of Tens 387

Chapter 21: Ten (Plus Five) More Sources of Cool Careers 389

A Special Note 389
Lists of Careers 390
Create a Vision 392

Develop a Third Eye 392
Be Where You Want to Be 392
The Media 393
Personal Connections 394
The Dream Industry 394
The Dream Organization 395
Internet Searches 395
Imitate a Successful Business 396
Ten Ways of Creating Your Perfect Cool Career 396
Combine Two of Your Features 397
Seven Career Fantasies 397
Find a Need and Fill It 398
Randomness 398

**Chapter 22: Ten (Okay, 48) Extra-Strength
Procrastination Cures** **399**

Does Your Procrastination Really Need Curing? 399
So You Want to Stop Procrastinating 400
My System for Curing Procrastination 400
Cures for Excuse-Making 401
All-Purpose Procrastination Cures 407

**Afterword: Our Best Thoughts on How
to Have a Happy Work Life** **411**

Marty Nemko's Thoughts 411
Think twice about following long-shot dreams 411
In praise of the anonymous achievers 412
Balance is overrated 413
Want to succeed? Consider lowering your self-esteem 413
The Tough-Love Lecture 414
Work is work 414
Up is not the only way 415
Paul & Sarah's Thoughts 416

Appendix: The Cool Career Finder *417*

Index *423*

Index of Careers *431*

Introduction

• •

*F*ifteen years ago, I heard about a little-known career called child-life specialist. When children must go to the hospital for extended stays, they're
assigned a child-life specialist to help them adapt to living without their parents.

When I told my clients about this career, they were glad to hear about it, even
if they themselves didn't want to pursue it. It gave them hope that maybe a
cool career that they hadn't heard about actually existed for them.

That's what started me on my collection. Every time I hear of an interesting
career, I add it to my *catalog of cool careers*. I include unusual careers as well
as neat niches within the popular careers, for example, lawyers who specialize in outer space issues. Now my catalog of cool careers (See the "Cool
Careers Yellow Pages" — Chapter 2) contains more than 500 careers. I got
many of the self-employment ideas from Paul and Sarah Edwards, who have
written 12 books on the subject.

This book contains a quick scoop on each of the 500-plus careers plus the
strategies that my clients have found most helpful in choosing a career *and* in
actually landing a job. I developed many of these strategies because the standard career advice wasn't working for many people. And that's the book in a
nutshell. Its ideas have helped a lot of individuals find a cool career, including
many people who were quite stuck. This book is particularly valuable if you're
looking for your first real job, considering self-employment, or thinking about
changing careers.

What's New in This New Edition?

Although the first edition *Cool Careers For Dummies* received uniformly gratifying reviews, from the day the book was published, I have been working to
ensure that this new edition is even better. Nearly half the book has been
upgraded. For example, I've:

- ✔ Added 80 new, rewarding viable careers and dropped some that no
  longer measure up as *cool careers*. I've updated many of the previously
  profiled careers.

- ✔ Completely updated the "Ahead-of-the-Curve Careers" section. It's filled
  with ideas on how to get in on the ground floor of the next Big Things.

- ✔ Highlighted easy-to-transition-into careers that don't require long back-
  to-school stints.

- ✔ Revised "The Most Revealing Questions" so that they're even more likely
  to reveal what you really want in your career.

- ✔ Provided new guidance for career searchers who simply don't have an overriding passion or skill.

- ✔ Offered a busy-person's approach to checking out possible careers. Many of my clients say they don't have the time (or courage) for informational interviews.

- ✔ Updated the help sections for the many people who have a hard time making the final decision — "Yes! This is the career I want to pursue." I've upgraded the chapter, "Finding the Courage to Commit."

- ✔ Listed eight faster (really) ways to land a job. The impatient job seeker definitely appreciates these.

- ✔ Improved the advice offered on how to land a job when you don't have previous experience.

- ✔ Improved the help offered for job seekers who hate networking or have few people to network with.

- ✔ Included a section on *e-networking:* how to use the Internet to meet people who can help you.

- ✔ Added a brand new chapter, "30 Days to a Good Job," which shows what a successful job search actually looks like day by day.

- ✔ Beefed up the chapter about how to put fire in your belly, considering the procrastination that slows so many job hunters.

- ✔ Greatly enhanced the chapter "Making Any Job Better." Even more important than landing a good job is whether you make the most of it. This chapter now provides a step-by-step plan for making even a hum-drum job much better.

How This Book Is Organized

The chapters in this book are organized into five parts:

Part 1: Find the Right Career for You, Right Here

Whether you've never had a career before or want to dump your old career for a new and improved one, this part is for you.

First, follow your heart

Browse the quick scoops on the 500 cool careers listed in the Cool Careers Yellow Pages and simply pick out one or more that make your heart beat a little faster. If you don't feel like browsing all 500, there's a quicker approach. I've divided the careers into categories to make it easier to home in on the ones that are right for you.

Next, use your head

I ask you to list what's really important to you in a career. Don't know? Chapter 3, "The 25 Most Revealing Questions," will help.

Finally, blend head and heart

This part's *virtual career coach* simulates what I do with my private clients so that your final career choice makes sense *and* feels good.

Part II: Getting Smart

Choosing a career is one thing; succeeding at it is something else. Often, a key is to be trained well. In this part, I show you how to find the right career preparation for you and how to make the most of it. If a university seems right, I show you how to maximize your chances of admission and how to reap the maximum benefit from your back-to-school stint. But often, you can learn more at what I call *You University,* a custom mix of mentoring, articles, tapes, and live or online classes. I even show how You U. "graduates" can get hired over candidates with more degrees.

Part III: A Better Way to Land the Job

The standard advice — network, network, network — simply doesn't work for lots of people. They either don't have many contacts to network with or they're uncomfortable with schmoozing. This part shows you an effective way to land the job even if the thought of networking gives you the creeps and you don't have a 500-name Rolodex. For my clients with a tendency to procrastinate, this approach has been a godsend. And if you *are* open to networking, there's a chapter for you: "Networking Made Easier."

Part IV: Customizing Your Career

When you buy a suit, it probably looks just okay off-the-rack. To really make it look good, it needs to be tailored and accessorized. The same is true with your career. This part shows you how to make any job better by tailoring it to your strengths and by using wise approaches with your boss and co-workers. Another approach to customizing your career is to become self-employed. Chapter 20 takes the exciting but scary thought of being your own boss and shows you how to maximize your chances of success.

Part V: The Part of Tens

Many good ideas don't require long explanations. So here is where I plunk lots of good idea that are self-explanatory. Are 500-plus careers not enough? In the Part of Tens, I show you at least ten ways to find many more. Suffering from the heartbreak of procrastinitis? Stall no more. I give you ten (actually 48) extra-strength cures.

Plus we offer an Afterword with our best thoughts on how to be happy with your worklife — our favorite pages in this book.

Finally, at the very back of the book, just before the index, there's an appendix called "The Cool Career Finder" — a way for you to find careers in such categories as "Too much fun to be work" and "Make a big difference in the world."

Icons Used in This Book

Of course, I think every word in this book is golden, but there are some ideas I really don't want you to miss, so I mark them with one of these icons:

Your basic good idea.

Little-known ideas.

Avoid these common pitfalls and you probably won't bomb out.

This icon lets me brag. These are the ideas I'm most proud of.

Many people procrastinate on their career search if it's drudgery. So, over the past 15 years, I've kept track of approaches that are fun yet effective, and put many of them in this book. This icon makes sure that you don't miss them.

A key strategy you won't want to forget.

Part I

Find the Right Career for You, Right Here

The 5th Wave   By Rich Tennant

"When choosing a career I ignored my heart and did what my brain wanted. Now all my brain wants is Prozac."

In this part . . .

*L*et's get right to it. This part walks you through a proven, effective (and rather fun) process of finding a career that's right for you: from how to make the most of the Cool Careers Yellow Pages to finding the courage to say, "Yes! This is the right career. I'm going to go for it!"

Chapter 1

Searching for a Career: Jennifer's Tale

In This Chapter

▶ A little morality tale on career planning

· ·

Sure, some people come out of the womb knowing what they want to be when they grow up — the 5-year-old violin prodigy comes to mind. But most of us aren't so lucky — and we don't get much help.

Some parents tell you, "It's your life. You decide." Other parents go to the other extreme, expecting you to follow in their footsteps: "Hazardous waste disposal is a great career." Before you even learn how to tie your shoes, they're pushing: "Come on, let's visit Daddy's toxic waste dump."

In high school, you take a career test that asks what you're interested in. How the heck are you supposed to know? If you're like most teens, you spend most of your school life studying such career irrelevancies as the symbolism in *Romeo & Juliet,* quadratic equations, and the slave ships of 1628. After school, you play soccer, and you're forced to take piano lessons (a skill for which only your mother thinks you have talent). You spend summers at Camp Kowabonga, during which your career exploration consists of observing your counselor go postal. How in the world are you supposed to validly answer test questions about your career interests? It's little surprise that many high school students laugh at their career test results: funeral director, clergy, or the utterly useless, "You could pursue a wide range of careers."

Many students remain undaunted. They figure that career clarity will come in college. Trouble is, most colleges proudly proclaim that their courses are *not* for career preparation but for general education. Worse, college courses are taught by professors — people who have deliberately opted out of the real world. So, many college students' career sights are limited.

As college graduation approaches, panic often sets in and the same students who procrastinated endlessly trying to ensure that they made the perfect career decision suddenly force themselves into a choice, often based on very little information. Their entire reasoning often fits on a bumper sticker:

> ✔ "I want to help people, so I'll be a doctor."
>
> ✔ "I'm lousy in science and I like to argue, so I'll go to law school."
>
> ✔ "I want to make a lot of money, so I'll go into business."
>
> ✔ "I don't know what I want to do, so I'll get a master's in something."

None of the above would work for Jennifer. She was sick of school. So she headed to the college's career center where she was pointed to a career library and encouraged to "explore." That's inadequate guidance for most of us. She did, however, fall into a job. Her cousin was the janitor at Western Widget Waxing, Inc., and put in a good word for Jennifer: "She has always been interested in widgets." Jennifer wrote a letter to Western Widget Waxing, Inc., that began, "I believe I'm well-suited for a career in the widget waxing industry." She got an interview. She wore that conservative suit she swore she'd never wear and told old WWW, Inc., that ever since childhood, she spent much of her spare time waxing widgets. She got the job.

Within days of starting at WWW, Jennifer realized that widget waxing wasn't all it was cracked up to be. Now what? WWW's human resources manager told Jennifer only about options in widget waxing. "Well, Jennifer, you *are* on track to becoming a widget waxing supervisor, and down the road, I think you have the potential to become a waxing director." On seeing Jennifer's face go flat, the manager tried, "Well, you could join our sales department. Would you like to sell widget waxing? How about the accounting department? Shipping? Well, what *do* you want, Jennifer?" That was the problem. Jennifer didn't know.

In desperation, Jennifer decided to seek help from a professional — even though it used up the money she'd been saving for that vacation. "What's a thousand bucks if it can land me a cool career?"

Alas, when Jennifer showed up at her appointment with the career counselor, there were those tests again.

Counselor: Well, Jennifer, on the Myers-Briggs Type Indicator, you're an ENFP. That means you're an extraverted, intuitive, feeling perceiver.

Jennifer: So what should I do for a career?

Counselor: Jennifer, you can't rush this. That would be premature foreclosure. We need to review the results of the Campbell Interest and Skills Survey. You're an RIC. That stands for realistic-investigative-conventional. Let's interpret that.

Jennifer: So what should I do for a career?

Counselor: Well, Jennifer, use the information you've learned about yourself from the Myers-Briggs Type Indicator and from the Campbell Interest and Skills Survey, by exploring in the career library.

Jennifer: Noooooooh, not again!

Instead, Jennifer returned to Western Widget Waxing, Inc.

Too often, career counseling is like psychoanalysis: You gain insight into yourself, but your life is no better.

One day, Jennifer heard about a book called, *Find Your Career Joy While Doing What You Love and the Money Will Come While Your Flower Opens.* So off Jennifer trotted to the bookstore, and although daunted by the book's thickness and its 66 worksheets, she figured it was only $16.99 — the cost of two movie tickets. Such a deal. Jennifer bit.

Five years later, our hero was still on worksheet #4. Her mother, her friends, even her haircutter, were asking her, "Well, Jennifer, what *are* you going to be when you grow up?" Jennifer decided to get serious. She pulled out her aging copy of *Find Your Career Joy While Doing What You Love and the Money Will Come While Your Flower Opens* and actually managed to complete all 66 worksheets. This gave her a complete inventory of her skills, interests, values, job requirements, personality attributes, and inter-ocular focal length.

But doing all that still didn't tell Jennifer how to figure out which career fits best.

I swear I am not exaggerating. Even the best-selling career guides do not take you through that crucial next step: showing you which careers fit your skills, interests, and values. The guides state or imply that if you do all their worksheets, you will somehow divine your dream career.

Jennifer cried, and Jennifer stayed on at Western Widget Waxing, Inc. "Maybe I *am* meant to be in widget waxing," she told herself. She worked hard, and indeed the human resources manager's prediction came to pass. Jennifer became director of Widget Waxing. But she still wasn't happy.

Then Jennifer was sure she found a solution: the computer. WWW, Inc., benevolent firm that it is, bought a career-finding software program, and made it available to its employees. Jennifer was first in line. A couple of hours and voilà, 15 best-fit careers popped out. Some of the careers made sense but didn't excite her enough to make her quit her now-comfortable job at WWW to go back and get retrained for a profession she wasn't even sure she'd end up liking better. After all, Jennifer had become a director and was fully vested in WWW's retirement plan. A few of the generated careers did excite Jennifer, but they were careers that excite too many people — TV broadcasting, for example. So what if Jennifer would love to anchor the nightly news? So would half the continent.

Although Jennifer didn't know it, many computer programs often fail for another reason. They eliminate careers if the career seeker lacks even one ostensibly necessary skill or personality trait. In the real world, many careers don't have such rigid skill and personality requirements. Take book editors, for example. Some succeed primarily because of their aesthetic sense, others because of their feel for the bottom line. And aren't some editors introverts, others extroverts? Even if Jennifer was lacking a key attribute, if she found a career that excited her, she may well have been willing and able to put the energy into compensating for her weakness. But the computer program never gave her the chance.

Krishna Rama (*nee* Jennifer) now resides at the Harmonic Transcendent Monastery in Berkeley, California, hoping to find career nirvana through meditation.

All jokes aside (at least for the moment), despite taking career tests, plowing through fat career guides, and/or meditation, many people end up falling into their careers more by chance than by choice. Not a good way to ensure career happiness. There has to be a better way.

There is. Read on.

Chapter 2

The Cool Careers Yellow Pages

In This Chapter

▶ How to use the Cool Careers Yellow Pages

▶ All kinds of good careers

▶ Some not-so-cool careers

*T*he first step in finding the right career may be the most fun: browsing the Cool Careers Yellow Pages.

I'm especially excited about the Yellow Pages because it gives you a fast yet substantive introduction to more than 500 good careers, including many unlikely suspects. Scan the names of the careers, and when one intrigues you, read the short scoop on that occupation. Jot down the names of any careers that, based on gut feeling, seem like possibilities.

What Makes a Cool Career Cool?

Competition for a spot in the Cool Careers Yellow Pages was fierce. First, a career had to be either:

- A popular mainstream career
- A little-known niche within a mainstream career
- A little-known career
- A self-employment opportunity that appears to offer relatively high payoff with relatively low risk

I narrowed the careers down further by choosing only those that scored highest overall on these criteria:

- Potential to make a difference in society
- Potential for at least a middle-class income
- A good job market

Using the Cool Careers Yellow Pages

To make it easy to home in on the right career for you, I divide the careers into categories, but the career scoops are short and fun to read, so you may want to read them all just for the heck of it. Who knows? Your dream career could be in a category you wouldn't have picked.

The categories

A career can require skill with *people,* with *data,* with *words,* and/or with *things.* In the Yellow Pages, I categorize the careers accordingly. For example, the attorney scoop is in the "Words/People" category. Most attorneys must excel at using words and must also have good people skills. (See the Table of Contents for the complete list of categories.)

Puhleeze, don't treat a career's category as gospel. The individual job you land may be different. For example, one lawyer may mainly write contracts, in which case, he doesn't need exceptional people skills. Another reason not to take the categories too seriously is that many careers fall on the border between two categories. They could easily fit in another category.

So if you have the patience, ignore the categories and just skim the Cool Careers Yellow Pages from beginning to end. That way you won't miss anything. Don't worry; it won't take long. If, however, you want a shortcut, pick a category as a better-than-random starting place.

And speaking of shortcuts, the appendix of this book has 17 special lists of careers: for example, the careers most likely to impress your family, easy-to-transition-into careers, those that are too much fun to be work, those offering the surest routes to big bucks, and those likely to make the biggest difference to society. You might want to start by browsing the careers on one of those lists.

The Yellow Pages' icons

Sometimes, a picture is worth 1,000 words. Not so with these pictures; they're worth maybe three or four. Here's what they mean:

Careers marked with this icon have significant self-employment potential.

Each career's profile is accompanied by an education icon that lets you know the minimum amount of schooling you need to start out in that career. Many people in the field have more than the minimum, but if you have at least the amount listed, you have a shot at the job.

No degree required. Training may involve an on-the-job program, an apprenticeship, or a certificate program that takes a year or less.

 Some college required, usually a two-year degree.

 Bachelor's degree required.

 Master's or other post-bachelor's education required.

 Doctoral degree required.

 Careers marked with this icon are profiled in-depth in the *Occupational Outlook Handbook,* an authoritative government source available in most libraries, and online at www.bls.gov/ocohome.htm.

Careers marked with this icon are profiled in-depth in Paul and Sarah Edwards' *Best Home Businesses for 21st Century.*

To make it easy to find out more about a career, most of the profiles include one or more Web sites or books that can help you decide if that career is right for you.

What price prestige?

I hold some unusual views about choosing a career. They're in the Afterword. There is, however, one bit of iconoclasm that I should share with you right here:

 The Cool Careers Yellow Pages covers the popular professions such as doctor, lawyer, and psychologist, but as you know, those careers require years of graduate school. Many people in these fields believe that their education did not really prepare them for their careers despite the years of effort and its costing them what they might pay for a house. Before committing to all that schooling, know that many people find great career satisfaction and good income in similar careers that require far less time behind a student desk. Examples:

> ✔ Aspire to be a doctor? Physician's assistants and nurse practitioners realize most of a doctor's benefits: They command a good salary, get to treat patients, and because they rarely treat serious illnesses, most of their patients get well.

✔ Leaning toward the law? Consider becoming a mediator or paralegal: less confrontational work, fewer ethical temptations, and shorter training.

✔ Motivated to become a psychologist? Personal coaches not only train for a shorter time but because they deal with healthier people, they see more progress.

So in addition to the popular high-status professions (which *are* covered in the Cool Careers Yellow Pages), consider checking out the Yellow Pages' many other careers.

Okay, enough preliminaries. I've tried to make each career profile pleasant to read even if you're not interested in the career. So enjoy.

Work with People

Caretaking and coaching

Mediator. Traditionally, the way that divorcing husbands and wives avoid killing each other is by hiring two attorneys and letting the lawyers slug it out. That's expensive, adversarial, and often, just plain yucky. An increasingly popular alternative is to hire a mediator. Don't like divorce mediation? Tackle employment cases — before going to trial, most wrongful termination suits must be mediated. Lawyers generally are chosen to mediate complicated fact-centered disputes while counselor-types more often are used when emotional issues are at the core. Whether a lawyer or counselor, a really good mediator needs the listening skills of a suicide counselor, the patience of Job, and the wisdom of Solomon. But, not to worry, mediation can be a rewarding career even for mere mortals. *Mediation Information and Resource Center:* www.mediate.com, *American Arbitration Association Center for Mediation:* www.adr.org.

Geriatric Care Manager. Imagine that you had aging parents living in another city. They need help dealing with the HMO, finding someone to look in on them, or completing some paperwork. You want to keep them out of a nursing home. You'd help out if you were local, but you're not. The answer? Hire a geriatric care manager. *US News & World Report* tells of geriatric care manager Pat Gleason. She has dozens of 'adopted' grandparents. As she makes the rounds to private homes and nursing facilities in Texas, she is showered with hugs and kisses from clients she helps with the problems of aging. It may be a woman recovering from a broken hip who needs help making her home easier to navigate, or a widower having trouble rebuilding a social life . . . One job perk, she says, is free history lessons, such as the stories she heard from a 104-year-old about crossing the Oklahoma Territory in a covered wagon." *National Association of Professional Geriatric Care Managers:* www.caremanager.org.

Psychotherapist. This is a career to which many caring types aspire, but upfront, you need to know a rarely spoken truth: Many patients don't get better. That's why many people are starting to turn to personal coaches, who tend to focus on solutions rather than childhood causes. Nevertheless, for now at least, demand for psychotherapists remains solid. More health plans are covering psychotherapy visits, because it's tough to cope with life's ever-greater demands and because new therapies *are* more effective. For example, brief solution-oriented therapy, sometimes combined with new drugs, is rapidly replacing prolonged analysis of childhood angst. *About.com's psychology portals:* psychology.about.com *and Links:* mentalhealth.about.com. *Social Psychology Network (*www.socialpsychology.org*) has terrific links on all psychology specialties.* Jeffrey Kottler's book: *What You Never Learned in Graduate School: A Survival Guide for Therapists.*

(Neat Niche) **Relationship Acceptance Therapist.** Couples counseling apparently works best when it helps partners learn to accept each other as they are rather than trying to change each other. (This makes sense. How easy is it to make *you* change?) A study found that after just six months of acceptance therapy, 90 percent of couples considering divorce reported "dramatic" increases in satisfaction and none split up. Andrew Christensen's book: *Reconcilable Differences.*

(Neat Niche) **Sports Psychologist.** A golfer has trouble concentrating. A pitcher freaks out under pressure. Teammates hate each other's guts. Enter the sports psychologist, who frequently uses guided visualization and hypnosis. *The American Psychological Association's Division of Sports Psychology:* www.psyc.unt.edu/apadiv47/. Ken Baum's book: *The Mental Edge.*

(Neat Niche) **Men's Therapist.** The 1990s saw an increase in therapists for women and people of color. Now men are starting to seek counselors specializing in men's issues.

(Neat Niche) **Infant Mental Health Counselor.** This career emerged because more and more children are born with severe mental or physical problems, or into homes with parents ill-equipped to be parents. The infant counselor advises parents on how to bring up a challenging baby while retaining their sanity. *World Association for Infant Mental Health:* www.msu.edu/user/waimh.

(Neat Niche) **Money Counselor.** Some people hoard money, others spend it too fast, boomers can't discuss it with their aging parents. Enter the money counselor. In my favorite incarnation of this career, you first help your client understand the cause of his or her money problem and, in turn, develop a plan to cure it. Then, if the client is deeply in debt, you negotiate for the client, asking creditors for reductions in interest and penalties. Sometimes, creditors will even pay you a percentage of any debt payments you submit to them. *Myvesta:* www.myvesta.org, *National Foundation for Credit Counseling:* www.nfcc.org.

(Neat Niche) **School Psychologist.** This can be a great job: nine-month year, high status, moderate stress. Typical project: Johnny is doing lousy in school. What should school and parents do? In comes the school psychologist: Observe the kid; test him; pow-wow with parent, teacher, kid, and special education teacher; and write jargon-filled report. School psychologists may also do parenting workshops and screen students for gifted students programs. *National Association of School Psychologists:* www.naspweb.org.

Alas, programs for gifted students are being dismantled. Why do slow learners have the right to special, high-cost instruction, psychological and other services, but gifted students, with so much potential to contribute to society and who often flounder without attention, increasingly get zilch?

College Student Advisor. In years past, professors used to advise the students, but colleges have realized that professors are more interested and knowledgeable about their own research than about what courses Jill should take. So colleges now hire counselor types to advise undergraduates. Sometimes, it's just a matter of reviewing a transcript and suggesting courses, but with the amount of malaise that many college students feel, it often goes well beyond. *National Academic Advising Association:* www.nacada.ksu.edu. *National Clearinghouse for Academic Advising:* www.uvc.ohio-state.edu/Chouse.html.

Personal Coach. Do you like to help others but would rather deal with problems easier to address than reconstructing a personality? Personal coaching is some combination of goal-setting advisor, time-management consultant, motivator, sounding board, confidant, dream-builder, and etiquette instructor . . . everything but going back and discussing the childhood causes of one's malaise. The emphasis is on problem solving — what are you going to do to solve this now. A big plus for becoming a coach rather than a shrink is the much shorter training time. Online certification is offered through *Coach U:* www.coachu.com. *International Coaches Federation:* www.coachfederation.org. Laura Whitworth's book: *Co-active Coaching.*

(Neat Niche) **Career Coach/Counselor.** Here, I get to write about my own career. The part I like best is helping people make the most of their current jobs — I feel successful with nearly all those clients. Unfortunately, most people hire a career counselor to help them get a different job. And here I have mixed feelings. With students and new college graduates, it's still fine. I help them identify new options and develop a plan to get hired, and it usually works. But many older people come in wanting to change careers, and my success rate and that of other career counselors I've spoken with is low. Few people who say they want a new career end up willing to put in the time and effort necessary to make it happen. The third type of client wants help landing a job. I find this work a little boring because it's mechanical: cranking out a resume, and teaching them how to win the job-hunt game. More important, I dislike that part of my job, because I believe it actually makes the world a worse place: My task is basically to make my clients look their best to employers. That gives my clients an unfair advantage over uncoached candidates who may in fact be more qualified. All that said, there's lots that's great about my job. I work one-on-one in a peaceful environment — my home. I get to hear people's life stories — fun. I get to wear many hats: counselor, idea generator, marketer, cheerleader, chastiser. I improve people's worklives and often help them make a bigger difference in the world than they otherwise would have. If you want to be a career counselor, here's what it takes. You must be credible yet not intimidating and optimistic yet realistic. You must also be a perceptive listener, know a lot about the world of work, able to motivate people to act, and know how to use the Internet's myriad career resources. Private practice can work if you're willing to self-promote, especially if you pick a niche: teachers, lawyers, women older than 50, whatever. If you're averse to marketing yourself, some of the best jobs are at college career centers. The book that you're reading constitutes an introduction to my style of career coaching. An excellent book presenting a more traditional approach is Howard Figler's and Richard Bolles' *Career Counselor's Handbook. National Career Development Association:* www.ncda.org. *Career Services Kiva:* www.careerserviceskiva.com.

(Neat Niche) **Time Management Coach.** When someone asks, "How are you?" The answer is as likely to be "Swamped" as "Fine." Enter the time-management coach — the person who tries to help wring 25 hours from a 24-hour day. Many people and employers willingly pay for that kind of advice. Marketing tip: Conduct time-management seminars in workplaces. That generates a fee and helps you recruit individual clients. Start preparing for this career by doing the equivalent of writing a term paper. Read a few books and articles on time-management, do a Web search, and write down potentially useful strategies so that you have plenty of different strokes for different folks. Then do a few freebie consultations for friends. First book I'd read: Julie Morgenstern's *Time Management from The Inside Out.*

Time management is all about making choices; we can't do it all. The question is what to do full-bore, what to do halfway, what to delegate, and what to say no to.

(Neat Niche) **Parenting Coach.** Whether it's a newborn or an adult child who just moved back home, many parents worry that they're not good-enough parents. They don't want a therapist; they just want help in getting their pride and joy to not drive them crazy. You can market to individual parents, for example, by offering free seminars at Lamaze classes. School districts and social service organizations may also hire parenting coaches. *The Portal Group:* www.portalgroup.com.

(Neat Niche) **Shyness Coach.** Fifty percent of people say they're shy. Coaching them is an almost completely untapped market. You role-play stressful situations with clients, and help them realize that the worst-case scenario isn't so bad or so likely. *The Shyness HomePage:* www.shyness.com.

(Neat Niche) **Dating Coach.** L.A. dating coach Bart Ellis doesn't just talk with his clients, he sends them out with staffers on mock dates. The staffer writes a report analyzing the client's strengths and weaknesses as a date, and then Ellis reviews the results with the client. *Bart Ellis's Web site:* www.thedatedoctor.com. Competitor *John Fergus's Web site:* www.fix.net/~dogmag/john/home.html.

(Neat Niche) **Executive Coach.** Many executives are just a beat off. They're a bit too intense, too detail oriented, too something. Companies or the executives themselves hire coaches to help get them back into the rhythm.

Personal Organizer. With the paperless office the most incorrect prediction in history, our desks are piled high and our mailboxes are stuffed full. In addition, we're saddled with more material stuff than ever. So it's no surprise that the demand for personal organizers is soaring. Marketing tip: Contact HR directors at nearby businesses. Suggest that they hire you to do "organizing makeovers" for any employees who feel they need it. Since 1993, membership has doubled in the *National Association of Professional Organizers:* www.napo.net. Julie Morgenstern's book: *Organizing from the Inside Out.*

(Neat Niche) **Children's Personal Organizer.** Parents go nuts trying to get their kids to do their homework, organize their notebooks, and get themselves off to school in the morning. Wanna help?

Image Consultant. "Are you a winter, spring, summer, or fall?" As an image consultant, you may start by picking out clients' colors, but you'll probably move on to clothes and makeup. You may even play with body language, speaking style, etiquette, nonverbal communication, and business protocol. (Do you know the right way to shake hands?) Image consultants are popular because primping up one's image is a relatively painless way to get an edge at work and at play. The freshly divorced, for example, are often eager to present a new persona. Market your services by offering seminars for singles groups or for an organization's employees. Or convince a corporation's HR department to hire you to spruce up all employees who'd like an image assessment and upgrade. Neat niches: Singles older than 50, those who wear plus sizes, employees in a specific field. *Association of Image Consultants International:* www.aici.org.

Doula. The most exhausting period in many women's lives is labor and childbirth. Throughout, the *doula* is there to provide pain-decreasing techniques from breathing techniques to different positions, from massage to aromatherapy. Doulas also provide much needed emotional support for moms (and dads?). Some evidence suggests that doula-assisted births result in shorter labor, fewer Caesarean and forceps births, and less need for pain medications. Doulas of North America has seen membership grow from 85 in 1992 to 3,000 now. *Doulas of North America:* www.dona.com. *See also* www.childbirth.org/doula123.html.

Literary, Artist's, or Performer's Agent. Most artistic types aren't entre-preneurial. Left to their own devices, they'd hang out, practice their craft, and the checks would somehow arrive in the mail. The agent's job is to make that happen. Agents help polish the sample product, pitch it to prospective buyers, and negotiate the deal for 10 percent to 15 percent of the take. Why is being an agent a cool career? You get to pick out and then champion the tal-ented people you want to represent, work closely with them to ensure that their product is well packaged, and help your star reach as large an audience as possible. Plus, being an agent requires no formal credentials. Most agents learn the business as an agent's assistant or as a talent buyer — acquisitions editor for a publishing company, for example. *National Association of Performing Arts Managers:* www.napama.org. *Association of Authors Representatives:* www.publishersweekly.com/aar.

Social Worker. Many people and families just can't make it without help. A child is abused; an older adult has Alzheimer's disease; a single parent with eight children, on top of it all, gets AIDS. Few jobs are more intimate and human than the social worker's. Despite the frustrations and low pay, most social workers who make it past the first two years love their jobs. Even if they can't solve the entire problem, the small steps feel rewarding enough. Only half of all social workers work for the government. The rest work for HMOs, private agencies such as the Red Cross, or open a private practice, which in many states, requires a master's degree. *About.com's social work portal:* socialwork.about.com.

Employee Assistance Professional. Workers show up with more problems than they used to: drug abuse, prone to violence, in financial disarray, and with eldercare needs. Employee assistance professionals coordinate pro-grams dealing with these problems. On a positive note, EAPs may establish physical fitness programs, sponsor workshops on time management or career planning, and even arrange carpools. *Employee Assistance Professional Association:* www.eap-association.com.

 Victim Assistant. Imagine that you've just been assaulted. Upon reporting the crime — if you're fortunate — you're introduced to a victim assistant. This person provides you with emotional and practical support all the way through trial and is your liaison with the district attorney. Victim assistants work for social service agencies, courts, or in private practice. As a fairly new, growing field, credential requirements haven't yet been solidified, so entry may be easier than in future years. *Victim-Assistance Online:* www.vaonline.org. *National Association for Victim Assistance:* www.try-nova.org.

 Child Life Specialist. Imagine that your child is told she has a serious ill-ness and must suddenly move from home into a hospital for a long stay filled with painful treatments. The child life specialist's job is to help children adapt to living without their parents and to psychologically prepare them for scary medical encounters. Child life specialists also help ensure that these kids get an education and a bit of fun in their lives. *Child Life Council:* www.childlife.org.

School Guidance Counselor. The modern version of this job is much more complicated than dealing with kids kicked out of class for chewing gum. School counselors may coordinate sex education, health awareness, career counseling, and on-site social work services. And yes, counselors still spend a lot of time telling Johnny that he better shape up or else. *American School Counselor Association:* www.schoolcounselor.org.

Nanny. The training is short; the task is doable, often pleasurable; and you may get to work in an environment most people only dream about: a wealthy person's home. That's not a bad combination, even if the pay is low. If you're good with kids, you won't have trouble finding a job. With the increase in single parents, and with two-parent families working full time, even many middle-class people find that a nanny is a must. The key to enjoying nanny-hood is to get hooked up with a great family. Attending nanny school maximizes your chances. Why? Because many desirable families search for their nannies by contacting nanny schools. *American Council of Nanny Schools: 517-686-9470. National Academy of Nannies-800-222-NANI (6264).*

Child-Care Provider. How do you stand out amid all the child-care providers? One way is to teach kids something important that they probably didn't learn well in school. Science-oriented franchises include Little Scientist (www.little-scientists.com) and The Mad Science Group (www.mad-science.org). Computer-oriented organizations: Computer Tots and Computer Explorers (www.computertots.com). Prefer dance? With a Kinderdance franchise (www.kinderdance.com), you bring a dance and exercise program to local child-care centers. *National Association of Child Care Professionals:* www.naccp.org.

Personal Assistant. According to the *New York Post*, a typical day in the life of Olympia Dukakis's personal assistant consists of rendering a second opinion on a movie contract, dropping off her dry cleaning, picking up her dog's gourmet dog food, and suggesting ideas for marketing Dukakis's new salad dressing. Salaries range from $30,000 to $100,000, plus perks. What sort of perks? Well, this isn't typical, but Carol Burnett gave her assistant a Land Rover for her birthday. Of course, not just celebrities need assistants. These days, just about any busy person could use one. Niches: executives, college presidents, wealthy widows, and your run-of-the-mill busy middle incomer. Sometimes, the job may be more like an office assistant: word-processing a report, coordinating a project, handling the bookkeeping, but Beth Berg makes a good living with none of that. She started "Dial a Wife." She'll plan the meal, wait for the plumber, take Sara (and her friends) to ballet, perhaps plant your herb garden, even do the initial househunting. Sounds like a traditional wife, but she gets paid $40 an hour. Berg's first ad simply said, "Buy time." *Personal Assistants International:* www.igginc.com/iggi/pai/pai.htm.

(Neat Niche) **Virtual Assistant.** This is an ideal option for anyone who wants to take administrative skills home, for example, word-processing, database management, Internet searching, travel arranging, bookkeeping. Of course, virtual assisting is especially appealing if you have a disability or want a portable business because your spouse's career requires frequent moving. Your clients can be next door or on another continent. A *Newsweek* article describes being a virtual assistant as like an administrative assistant without a boss looking over your shoulder. There's no office politics, no commute, and you can tell a cranky client to shove it. *International Virtual Assistants Association:* www.ivaa.org. *Training:* www.assistu.com. *Jobs:* my virtualcorp.com.

Corporate Concierge. Marcia's concierge service, operating in the lobbies of residential and office buildings, helps inhabitants with the mundane tasks of life such as picking up dry cleaning, returning videos, and taking cars in for oil changes. Marcia can often get employers to pay for her services because they know that many employees sneak time off work to take care of life's necessities. In hiring Marcia, the boss gets full use of the employees and grateful workers as a bonus. *Articles:* www.bestuponrequest.com/resource.htm. *The National Concierge Association:* www.conciergeassoc.org.

Bringing people together

Personnel Recruiter. Forget about the image of the recruiter coming onto campus to recruit top graduates. Today's recruiter starts before jobs are even advertised. He develops ongoing relationships with the sorts of people the employer is likely to want to hire. For example, a company that uses Java programmers may routinely post tips and tricks on Java discussion groups on the Net to elicit positive feelings toward the recruiter. When a job opens, the recruiter posts it on the Web and sets up software to electronically screen applicants. Increasingly, he conducts interviews by phone, online, or even using a webcam. Job growth is fastest in temp agencies. *National Association of Personnel Services:* www.napsweb.org. *CareerXRoads (*www.careerxroads. com*). Recruitment Technologies:* www.netcruiting.com. Lou Adler's book: *Hire With Your Head.*

(Neat Niche) **Employment Interviewer.** You've been on the other side of the table: "Mr. Job Applicant, why do you want to work for this company?" (You think, "Because I'm desperate. I'll work anywhere." You answer, "Because I'm impressed with your fine line of products.") How'd you like a career in which *you're* the interviewer? Private employment agencies hire interviewers, sometimes without a college degree, to screen applicants, prep them for interviews, and then sell them to prospective employers. Don't like the selling part? Try working for a company or the government. Your job is simply to match applicants with the available openings.

(Neat Niche) **Executive Recruiter (Headhunter).** This is one of the few jobs that require no formal education yet can yield a six-figure income. What do executive recruiters have to do to earn the six figures? As a head-hunter, you work for a private agency engaged by corporations to lure top execs from other companies. What makes this a neat niche is that you get to work with highly accomplished people, and that you can earn big money if you can persuade enough HR departments to let you conduct their employee searches. You must also be able to sniff out top-flight execs, determine whether they're compatible with the client company's culture, and if so, convince them to take a job with that company. *Recruiters Online:* www.recruitersonline.com *(generally for lower-level execs). Association of Executive Search Consultants:* www.aesc.org *(for higher-level execs). Kennedy Information:* www.kennedyinfo.com.

Matchmaker. Today, few of us have the time, let alone the inclination, to hang out at *meet* markets on the off chance of finding Mr. or Ms. Right. Matchmakers who set up online, classified ad voice-mail dating services, or even provide an old-fashioned person-to-person service, can prosper in the small, growing cities whose markets are less likely to be saturated. These dating services not only save time, they offer an easy way to screen hundreds of prospects. Dating services come in all sorts of flavors. For example, one organization (See www.speeddating.com) sets up dinners at which you rotate having one-on-one seven-minute conversations with each of seven romantic prospects. *Links:* www.looksmart.com/eus1/eus317832/eus317889/eus271573/r?1&.

(Neat Niche) **Friend Finder.** If you're too busy to find a romantic partner, you're even less likely to take the time to find a friend. Many homebound seniors especially crave someone to keep them company. The biweekly nurse just doesn't do it. They want someone who has similar interests, time for schmoozing, and who won't stick them with needles. Enter the friend finder, the platonic version of the matchmaker. This is a virtually untapped market, and you may find success just by replicating the successful formula used by the romantic online, newspaper ad/phone dating services.

School-to-Work Coordinator. Schools are finally realizing that they graduate too many students ill equipped for real-world jobs. So high schools are hiring school-to-work coordinators. A coordinator may arrange for teachers to visit local workplaces. Some teachers, on seeing what it takes to succeed in today's workplace, change what they do in the classroom. School-to-work coordinators may also help students in career planning by bringing community members to schools to talk about their jobs, and arranging student job shadowing and internships. *National School-to-Work Learning and Information Center:* www.stw.ed.gov.

Casting Director. Would you find it fun to cast a sitcom? An epic motion picture? A feminine hygiene commercial? Casting director is one of those little-known but fun Hollywood careers. Here's how casting works: You write a breakdown (a list of all the needed characters) and e-mail them to agents and wait for submissions (photos and resumes). Then you pick people to audition. Casting Director Lisa Pirriolli says, "Casting is perfect for people who were unpopular in high school and this is their way of getting back at all the people who didn't ask them out." The bad news: You usually have to start as a volunteer. Check the *Casting Director's Directory* for firms that might need a slave like you. *Casting Society of America:* www.castingsociety.com. *Links:* www.aiastudios.com/links.htm.

Sales-oriented work

Salesperson. When you hear the word "salesperson," what's the first word that comes to mind? Pushy? While those types are around, many successful salespeople don't fit the stereotype. They are, however, self-starters who are pleasantly persistent and good at listening to the customer and explaining how a product can solve the customer's problems. They aren't reluctant to ask for the sale. A career in sales is one of the few routes to high income without college. Sales offers flexible hours and, if you're an outside sales rep, a chance to travel. Plus, it's nice to know that your income is directly related to your performance: The more you sell, the more you make. The problem with that is it's tough to know how much you'll sell. Even good salespeople will fail if the product, territory, or commission rate stinks. (Before accepting a job, ask one of the company's other salespeople about these.) Many salespeople are surprised to find that they actually spend less than half of their time selling. They answer technical questions, write proposals, take care of problems with product or delivery, and write reports to management. The Internet is eliminating many sales jobs — an intelligent Web site can do a better job of selling than many salespeople at a fraction of the cost — and is available 24/7, but at least until the next edition of this book is written, jobs for good salespeople should be available. *About.com's sales portal:* sales.about.com, Tom Hopkins' book: *Selling For Dummies*, 2nd Edition.

(Neat Niche) **Commercial Security Sales.** Employees and customers increasingly view employers as fat cats and are ever more willing to — let's be blunt — rob them. Of course, your basic off-the-shelf theft is popular, but creativity knows no bounds. Current ruses include selling the company's internal data to competitors and starting a company to sell a former employer's product that's been tweaked just enough to avoid getting caught. Corporations are eager to hear from salespeople with products and services that can stem the losses.

(Neat Niche) **Electrical Components Sales.** Electrical parts aren't sexy, but demand for these components is high, and few salespeople have the technical expertise to sell them effectively. An engineering background is a plus and sometimes a must.

(Neat Niche) **Sales of Instruments and Consumables to Biotech Companies.** The biotech industry is booming and its companies use a lot of expensive consumables.

(Neat Niche) **Internet Ad Sales.** Seemingly unlimited opportunity, especially as bandwidth increases. That will enable the use of full-motion commercials rather than those annoying and probably ineffective blinking banner ads.

(Neat Niche) **Big-Ticket Item Sales.** Like golf courses, airplanes, and custom software. The software that banks use to back up all their data costs each bank hundreds of thousands of dollars.

(Neat Niche) **Industrial sales.** I like this because it's under-the-radar — no one grows up thinking, "When I grow up, I want to sell conveyer belts." That means the competition is less and the pay is better. And, for the right person, it can be fun — getting to visit all sorts of manufacturing plants and helping them solve their problems. *Manufacturer's Agents National Association:* www.manaonline.org.

College Admissions Recruiter. The United States has almost 5,000 colleges and vocational-technical schools, 95-plus percent of which must recruit to fill their classrooms. Your title may be College Admissions Counselor, but a more accurate description is salesperson. You need to be able to soft-sell — sell without appearing to be selling. This is a great job for anyone who likes to travel and talk with teens and parents. A sense of humor and a repertoire of clean jokes go far. *National Association for College Admission Counseling:* www.nacac.com.

Don't confuse a College Admissions Recruiter with a College Admissions Counselor. The recruiter is hired by a college to recruit students to that college, whereas the college counselor's job is to help students find a college matching their needs from among the thousands available.

Fundraiser/Development Specialist. You may wonder, "Why the term 'development'?" Because a nonprofit organization *develops* prospective donors into actual donors — ideally, big donors. For example, your alma mater attempts to develop you in the beginning by sending you mailers and by staging events designed to make you feel closer to the college — to remind you of the good old days, even if, in fact, they weren't so good. Low-cost tickets to the football game, publications with stories designed to make you feel close to the college, and dinners with speeches by the best professors they can find are part of the cultivation process. Then, once you're feeling warm and fuzzy, the college starts with the solicitations — usually with direct mail campaigns and telemarketing banks. Plus, if according to the alumni questionnaire you filled out, you're a potential big donor, the college assigns an already-donating alumnus with similar interests to individually solicit you. A development office keeps precise records of how much you donate. The more you donate, the more they ask for the next time. A development officer's crowning achievement is convincing you to put the organization in your will or into a trust.

Development jobs tend to divide into *cultivators* and *harvesters*. *Cultivators* coordinate fundraising events, maintain donor databases, write pitch pieces and grant proposals. *Harvesters* are the direct pitchers. They must have the ability to get wealthy people to trust them quickly, to ask for large sums of money without blinking, and to endure rejection. Knowledge of wills and trusts is helpful. If you're older and polished, a career as harvester might work because many donors fit that description. *National Society of Fund Raising Executives:* www.nsfre.org. *Chronicle of Philanthropy:* www.philanthropy.com. Peter Edles' book: *Fundraising*.

(Neat Niche) **Fundraiser for Arts Organizations.** Fundraising for the theater or the symphony, and so on, lets you spend time around artistic types without having to fight the long odds against making a living on stage.

 Auctioneer. "$100 bid, now two, now two, will ya give me $200? $200 bid, now three, now three, will ya give me $300?" When we think of auctioneers, we think of one thing: fast talkers. But there's more. Auctioneers must enjoy selling and be masters at creating a sense of urgency while using a sense of humor. Acting skills can help. Side note: The auctioneer chants not just because it keeps the audience interested, but because it makes things go quickly. At an average household estate auction, the auctioneer's chant helps sell an average of 60 items per hour. Tobacco auctioneers may sell 500 to 600 lots per hour! Half of auction events are real estate and business liquidations. Auctions are used to sell everything from skyscrapers to amusement parks. With businesses going under, people going bankrupt, and homes, boats, RVs, and private planes going into foreclosure, good auctioneers are selling for high bids. And you don't need a lot of school to start chanting. Only 25 percent of auctioneers have a college degree. Many auctioneers learn on the job, and others attend short training programs. *National Auctioneers Association:* www.auctioneers.org.

(Neat Niche) **Fundraising Auctioneer.** Many nonprofit groups, from elementary school PTAs to United Way, have fundraisers. Auctions are among the most lucrative ways to raise money, but most are conducted by amateur auctioneers. That results in far lower bids than with a professional.

Other people-oriented careers

 Producer. Whether it's a TV news segment on legalizing prostitution, a local production of *Deathtrap*, or a DVD virtual trip to France, few things are more fun than coming up with an idea and putting the pieces together so it becomes a reality. That's what a producer does.

I'm not talking just about hiring the actors and behind-the-camera crew, I'm talking about solving countless problems like this: In the book, *Gig*, producer Jerry Bruckheimer tells the story of having spent a million dollars designing space suits in which the actors could breathe. In the middle of the shoot, Ben Affleck fell to the floor, suffocating in his space suit. The oxygen system had stopped working. Someone had to cut it open. No harm was done except that it stopped production, and for every lost minute, hundreds of people must be paid — an expensive meter always is running. Bruckheimer said, "So there's a little set story for you. And there are a million of those."

How to become a producer? David Wolper, producer of *Roots*, the 1984 Summer Olympics, and the Jacques Cousteau National Geographic specials, believes that if you're a go-getter, just find a cool idea you'd like to make happen, get a team of experts to agree to participate if funding is available, tap all the talented unemployed film production people you know (they're around), and then, pitch well-off people to fund it. *Producers Guild of America:* www.producersguild.com, www.producerlink.com. John Lee's book: *The Producer's Business Handbook*.

(Neat Niche) **Expo/Show Producer.** As an expo producer, you may put on a bridal show, a plastic manufacturer's convention, an art fair, or a conference on nanotechnology. Identify a need, get lots of exhibitors and enough attendees to keep them happy, and you may be able to make a year's income in a few months. *International Association for Exposition Management:* www.iaem.org. *International Festivals and Events Association:* www.ifea.com.

Event Planner. This career is the compulsive's dream — with endless details to get right, all by an unmovable deadline, plus a Nervous-Nelly client usually adding to the stress. To boot, you frequently have to give up your nights and weekends. To tell you the truth, I can't imagine why anyone likes this career, but many people do. Indeed, event planning is among the more aspired-to career choices among my female clients. That's the only reason it's included in this book. The good news is that this is a huge field. The meeting industry, predominantly conventions and expos, has a national market of more than $70 billion! Other niches: corporate parties and product rollouts, *Meeting Planners International:* www.mpiweb.com. *International Special Events Society:* www.ises.com. Judy Allen's book: *Event Planning*.

(Neat Niche) **Convention, Trade Show, or Expo Planner.** Planning these events offers big bucks in exchange for big headaches. *Professional Convention Management Association:* www.pcma.org.

(Neat Niche) **Reunion Planner.** "I can't believe it. Back when we were in school, he was skinny!" High school reunions are intriguing events but who has time to mail invitations, take reservations, hire bands, find food, arrange hotels, line up child care, plan activities, and more challenging — dig up all those missing class members? The reunion planner. Tracking down missing class members, mainly using online databases, adds a detective component to an already fun job. *National Association of Reunion Managers:* www.reunions.com. *Training course:* sweetday@tampabay.rr.com.

(Neat Niche) **Wedding Planner.** Twenty-five years ago, there were no wedding planners, but as couples marry later in life, many lives are too full to handle all the details of a wedding (like how to make the Elks Club look like the Ritz). *National Association of Wedding Planners:* www.nawp.com. *Susan Tatsui-D'Arcy's* Working Woman's Wedding Planner.

Trial Consultant. If OJ Simpson didn't have a trial consultant, who knows where he'd be living today? We think of trial consultants as helping to pick a jury, but they also coach witnesses and conduct mock trials and focus groups to try out different strategies. Beware if you're the defendant and the other attorney has retained a trial consultant. This is a cool career for lawyers who don't want to argue, psychologists who don't want to listen to patients' problems all day, and market researchers who'd rather deal with people than data. *American Society of Trial Consultants.* www.astcweb.org. *The University of Kansas offers a top training program:* www.ukans.edu/cwis/units/coms2/legalcom.html.

Temp Agency Owner. This is one of *Entrepreneur* magazine's "Hot Picks." Many full-time jobs are being replaced by temp positions. How can you capitalize? Start a temp agency. You can't compete with mega-agencies such as Manpower or Olsten, so pick a field where it's tough to find good employees — especially one you know a lot about. Examples include association executives, disabled employees, short-order cooks, medical secretaries, pharmacists, escrow personnel, and robotics engineers. If you're successful, you can consider franchising your operation. *American Staffing Association:* www.natss.org.

Relocation Consultant. You're moving to a new city. What's the best neighborhood to live in? Which are the best schools? Where should my husband look for a job? A relocation specialist living in that city can help you. Based on answers to a questionnaire about your wants and needs, the relocation consultant points you in the right direction. It's like having a wise, local relative. How do you get a job as a relocation consultant? Approach the local offices of national real estate chains. They're the most likely to be involved in long-distance relocations, and may offer relocation consultants to their customers. *Employee Relocation Council:* www.erc.org. *MonsterMoving:* www.monstermoving.com.

Personal Care Facility Owner. Many aging boomers can't stand their varicose veins, wrinkles, and fading eyesight. And because the surgeries have become easier, more people are lining up. Personal care surgery clinics are popping up, but the need, especially in small cities, may not be saturated. Don't worry, you needn't be a doctor. You can be the entrepreneur who opens the clinic, does the marketing, and hires the doctors to staff it.

Work with Data

Scientific data

Biologist. No field has done more to improve life. In the last decade alone, people working in biology/biotechnology have developed:

- Food crops that can grow in a previously infertile section of Latin America that covers 800,000 square miles — an area larger than the size of Mexico. Thousands of formerly starving people now can eat.

- Breakthrough drugs — like new proteins that lessen the effect of heart attacks, and protease inhibitors that greatly extend the life span of people with HIV.

- A method to identify a criminal (DNA analysis) that is thousands of times more accurate than conventional methods.

I had the good fortune to attend a presentation by five Nobel Prize winners. One of the few things they agreed on was that the field that will make the greatest impact on humankind in the coming decades is molecular biology/biotechnology. Many of us, when we think of biology, think of *macro*biology: studying different animals and plants. I recall, in high school, seeing cute pictures of endangered furry creatures. Indeed, many people choose to major in biology with such visions in mind. But the fact is, if you're considering a career in biology, know that most careers in biology today focus on molecules. From here forward, biology is mainly math. Actually, the name "biologist" is now misleading. Today, most biologists are part biologist, part chemist, part mathematician, and part programmer. They spend a majority of their time on the computer. Those with a whole-animal biology background will usually be limited to positions as low-level lab assistants or high school biology teachers.

A long-standing oversupply of biology Ph.D.s, makes competition fierce for Ph.D.-level jobs in biotech unless your background includes computer science, mathematics, or engineering. The good news is that ample bachelor's and master's level jobs are available at biotech and pharmaceutical firms. True, you aren't top banana, but you can have interesting opportunities, producing genetically engineered plants, animals, and drugs; running experiments, perhaps assisting in designing them and writing them up, and even co-presenting at conferences. In short, you can derive many of the benefits of a Ph.D. with less school and less difficulty landing a job. Choose your job carefully, though. In some labs, a bachelor's degree entitles you to clean rat cages. *Biotech Career Center:* www.biocareer.com, *About.com's biology portal:* biology.about.com. *BioSpace:* www.biospace.com.

(Neat Niche) **Genomics.** Now that the human genome has been sequenced, genomists are starting to discover what each gene does. Genes have been discovered that control everything from shyness to obesity.

These discoveries, of course, are key to using gene therapy to prevent and cure diseases and to enhance human potential. Progress has been amazing. Back in 1999, Princeton University researchers inserted a gene into a mouse. As a result, the smart mouse, nicknamed Doogie (for the precocious TV doctor, Doogie Howser) dramatically improved its memory and that of his offspring. This gives hope for curing Alzheimer's disease and mental retardation, and, if we decide it's ethical, to improve normal people's memory and that of their children. In the 1967 movie, *The Graduate*, Dustin Hoffman got a career tip: plastics. Today, if I were to give such a tip, it would be genomics. Celera: www.celera.com/genomics/genomics.cfm. *American Society of Gene Therapy:* www.asgt.org/.

(Neat Subniche) **Proteomics**. Genes work by expressing (generating) proteins. These proteins are the actual building blocks of human function and of disease. Learning how to fix defective proteins will result in many cures. For example, back in 2000, scientists at Zycos Corp. identified a protein that is expressed in nearly every major cancer but not in normal tissue. Major players in proteomics: Applied Biosystems, Amersham, Waters, Bio-Rad, Thermo Electron, Biocore, Agilent, and Roche Molecular.

(Neat Niche) **Bioinformatics**. Back in the 20th century, genes and the proteins they express were studied one at a time. Now, it's possible to study entire genomes at a time. Chemists used to study drug candidates one at a time. Now, they can assess a pharmacological characteristic of 500,000 compounds in a week or two. These studies generate an extraordinary amount of data that must be stored and available in a user-friendly format for interpretation. Who makes this happen? Bioinformatics specialists. They are a combination of molecular biologist and computer programmer. Biotech research companies are hiring a lot of them.

(Neat Niche) **Plant Geneticist/Botanist**. Plant geneticists have created high-protein grain that has saved many lives in developing nations. Less dramatic, orchids used to be affordable only by the wealthy. Now, thanks to plant cloning and tissue culture, anyone can afford a world-class orchid. (Now if they only figured out how to make them easy to grow.) Perhaps more important, plant geneticists play a key role in figuring out how humans develop from one cell into highly differentiated adults. This understanding is crucial to preventing and curing diseases. While some of this research can only be done on animals, much can be done ethically and inexpensively using plants. As a plant lover who likes intellectual challenges and wants to make a difference, if I were starting over, this is the career I would choose for myself. *Botanical Society of America:* www.botany.org/bsa/careers.

 Toxicologist. The Texas A&M toxicology home page begins, "Hardly a week goes by without hearing about a chemical that may threaten our health: pesticides in the food we eat, pollutants in the air we breathe, chemicals in the water we drink. Are these chemicals really dangerous? How much does it take to cause harm? Toxicologists answer these questions. *Society of Toxicology:* www.toxicology.org.

Biological Weapons Deterrence Specialist. Saddam Hussein makes us evermore aware that biological weapons can be as threatening as nuclear weapons, and much more portable. At a news conference, Al Gore held up a five-pound sack of sugar and warned that the same amount of anthrax released from a plane over the District of Columbia could kill 300,000 people. And creating that much anthrax is easy: For $10,000, and materials easily obtainable from scientific supply houses, a smart biochemistry major could produce five pounds of anthrax in a week. At the National Press Club, Ross Perot said, "If we can't keep drugs out of our prisons, which we highly control, how can we keep biological weapons out of our country?" The need for deterrence experts is obvious, the federal budget for it has grown, and the field is far from saturated. Hey, if you're intelligent, please get into this career. You could save our lives. *Links:* www.cns.miis.edu/webguide/chembio.htm. Robert Falkenrath's book: *America's Achilles Heel.*

Environmental Analyst. Typical project: In an area with higher-than-normal cancer rates, environmental analysts look for aberrations in the composition of the air, soil, and water, and then play detective and try to figure out what's causing the problem. Often in such a situation, the analysts find unexpected chemicals in the soil, air, or water. They then check to see if local companies are culprits. When a polluter is found, environmental analysts use subtle and not-so-subtle ways to get the company to clean up its act. Environmental analysts are hired by federal, state, and local environmental protection agencies such as EPA or OSHA or through consulting firms hired by governments, corporations, or citizen groups. *National Registry of Environmental Professionals:* www.nrep.org.

Hydrologist. Tom Stienstra, author of *Sunshine Careers*, reminds us that without water we have nothing. Hydrologists ensure that our water is as safe as possible. They gather data and then make water-saving proposals to corporations or government agencies. While some hydrologists work in labs, many have offices in the great outdoors. Hydrology is one of the few outdoors professions that pays a middle-class living and may require only a bachelor's degree. Can you picture yourself hiking into wilderness areas to take and analyze water samples, sneaking in reveries by a flowing stream? Just remember, many hydrologists spend a lot of time in front of a computer and at the water's source: frigid mountains and glaciers. *American Institute of Hydrology:* www.aihydro.org.

Meteorologist. Believe it or not, they're getting better at predicting the weather — not only tomorrow's weather but also next year's. This has profound implications. For example, imagine you are a farmer and know how wet and warm the next season will be. You can pick the perfect crop for that weather. You can be a meteorologist even if you're too shy to be on the nightly news. Meteorologists also work in agriculture, for cruise lines, ski resorts, the Department of Defense, and airlines. Meteorology is for the math and computer person who doesn't want to be a programmer. Of course, it helps if you're fascinated with the weather. Meteorology made it onto the list of cool careers because it's rewarding, but the job market is tight. Half of meteorologists are hired by the National Weather Service, which often requires a master's degree. Because predicting the weather requires integrating information from around the globe, a foreign language is a plus. *American Meteorological Society:* www.ametsoc.org/ams.

Geophysicists. Usually, the earth doesn't move. That is, unless you're in love or there's a volcano or earthquake. Geophysicists focus on the latter two in these neat niches.

(Neat Niche) **Volcanologist.** When will a volcano erupt? Volcanologists better not guess wrong. If they predict an imminent gusher and nothing happens, many people have been needlessly terrified and evacuated. If the volcanologist says, "No problem," and it blows, you've got fried community. According to *Time*, "Volcanology may be the most dangerous science since these vast laboratories can explode at any moment with a force equal to thousands of atom bombs." The United States has fewer than 200 volcanologists, and most have a Ph.D. I include very few careers with such poor prospects of landing a job and that require so much training, but *volkies* really love their career, so I couldn't resist. Volcanologists spend a lot of time in exotic places studying a fascinating phenomenon. Their work can save lives and property, and because children are so fascinated with volcanoes, they visit many schools, usually leaving an auditorium full of wide-eyed kids. *Links:* http://exodus.open.ac.uk/volcano/world/world_lists.html. Dick Thompson's book: *Volcano Cowboys*.

(Neat Niche) **Seismologist.** So you think seismologists predict earthquakes? Most don't. They actually create earth vibrations — much smaller than earthquake strength, of course. Why would they do that? Because it's a good way to determine where to drill for oil. Other seismologists figure out how to prevent mining disasters — and what to do when they guess wrong. Of course, some seismologists do get involved with earthquakes. They may help design a plan to make a building earthquake resistant, and try to predict when and where the next Big One will strike. Unfortunately, to date, despite all the Ph.D.s hacking away at it, dog barking still seems to predict as well. *Seismological Society of America:* www.seismosoc.org.

Agricultural Scientist. Are you a science type who doesn't want to be in a lab all day? An ag scientist's job is to find better ways to grow crops. You may work on a better way to control downy mildew on rose bushes or the glassy-winged sharpshooter on grapes or to keep oxalis weeds from taking over broccoli fields — all with minimal impact to the environment. Rather than work on control, you may work on prevention: developing plant varieties genetically engineered to be resistant to pests and disease. (A pox on those fear-mongering groups that exaggerate the danger of genetically enhanced seed — "Frankenfood," my eye. They're essentially the same as conventionally bred seed — except that they produce crops that are healthier and/or require less pesticide.) The largest employers are the government and university extension services. A master's degree is often required. *American Society of Agronomy:* www.agronomy.org.

(Neat Niche) **Entomologist.** Here or in remote jungles, you may gather and study data on the thousands of new insect species discovered each year. Which are threats? Allies? How to deal with them? Or you may visit a farm infested with some little terror and figure out how to nuke it without nuking the rest of us. *Entomology Society of America:* www.entsoc.org.

Food Scientist. How can we make a better tasting frozen pizza? Can we make a hot dog that tastes good without cancer-causing nitrites? How can chicken processors reduce the amount of pyelobacteria — which sickens thousands of people each year? Food scientists work for food processing companies to make better foods, and increasingly, for government agencies to ensure that the foods you eat don't make you puke. *Institute of Food Technologists:* www.ift.org.

(Neat Niche) **Flavorist.** The company says, "We need to make a packaged chicken soup mix that tastes like Grandma's. The flavorist's job is to create concoctions that simulate the real thing. He usually starts by combining items from existing products and/or a library of flavors. *Society of Flavors Chemists:* http://www.perfumflavor.com/organizations/organizations-sfc.html.

Statistician. Statisticians ensure that appearances aren't misleading. With half of the votes counted, Al Gore has a lead of 2,000 votes. Can CNN call Gore the winner? It was a statistician who guessed wrong. Yeah, mistakes can be made, you can lie with statistics, and everything can't be reduced to probabilities, but statistics do often lead to good decision-making. Not a bad payoff for one's career efforts. Florence Nightingale said that statistics is the most important science in the whole world: for upon it depends the practical application of every other science. *The American Statistical Association:* www.amstat.org.

(Neat Niche) **Biostatistician.** You answer questions such as "How effective is a new drug? How sure are we that a gene really expresses that protein? What are the chances of a side effect among pregnant women?" Among the many job openings for statisticians that I've looked at, by far the most are for biostatisticians.

(Neat Niche) **Sports Statistician.** Were you the kid who calculated the likelihood of this or that happening during the game? This may be your dream career. Sports statisticians are numeric journalists, creating interesting stats that enrich a journalist's article or broadcaster's reporting. Or your job might be to keep track of numbers that help a coach decide which players to play and which to bench. Can you make a living as a sports statistician? Gotta tell you — probably not. Most sports statisticians work for free or a pittance. Want to try to beat the odds? Hone your craft by being a high school or college team's statistician. Don't just record the basics. Be creative in coming up with cool statistics — for example, in the last minute, Biff Jones completes half the percentage of passes as he does in the rest of the game — Mr. Choke. If you've proved yourself at the high school or college level, send samples of your work — especially that creative stuff — to producers of pro sports TV shows (listed on the credits that roll down your screen at the end of the game). You might even send your material to the Elias Sports Bureau, which produces statistics for Major League Baseball, the NFL, and NBA. *American Statistical Association.* `www.amstat.org/sections/sis/career/index.html`.

Cryptanalyst. The government has just intercepted a secret message from a spy. Cryptanalysts decode it. A Web site contains thousands of customers' credit card numbers. Cryptanalysts encode it to deter hackers. In short, cryptoanalysts make and break secret codes. Most cryptographers have a Ph.D. in math. A secret decoder ring won't quite do. *Career stories of cryptanalysts:* `www.rit.edu/~pacsma/course210/cryptcar.htm`. *An outline of a self-study course in cryptanalysis:* `www.counterpane.com/self-study.html`. *Society for Industrial and Applied Mathematics:* `www.siam.org`.

Cancer Registrar. Because most cancers don't have a single foolproof cure, many treatment protocols are tried for each type of cancer. One way to figure out which methods work best for whom (for example, people in their 60s with leiomyosarcoma and diabetes) is to accumulate treatment records of every cancer case. Most hospitals and consortia do that, and the person in charge is the cancer registrar. This person doesn't just enter submitted information into the database; he often speaks with the physician, and even the patient for clarification. May you never get a call from a cancer registrar. *National Cancer Registrar's Association:* `www.ncra-usa.org`.

Computer data

Computer Programmer. Programmers start with a real-world problem, such as how to monitor how much electricity Minnesota uses per second. They figure out how that can be calculated and then use a programming language to "teach" the computer how to calculate it. That part, for really bright people, tends to be challenging, fun, and addictive. But after the basic program is written, major tedium usually follows. Debugging often means days of staring at screensful of numbers trying to divine which ones are wrong.

No surprise, programming will continue to be a career in great demand. C++ and Perl remain popular but Java is now king. Employers go especially wild for Java programmers with expertise in a content area such as chemistry, engineering, business, databases, or economics.

Remember though that today's hot programming language is tomorrow's dinosaur, so to be happy and successful as a programmer, you must relish the idea of continually reeducating yourself. A bachelor's degree helps but vendor-specific and vendor-neutral certifications (for example, those at `www.brainbench.com`) may enhance your employability more. Jobs abound in mundane areas such as intranet development (company computers communicating with vendors and customers), operating systems, and upgrading computers that run on old languages, but check out the neat niches below. *Association for Computing Machinery:* www.acm.org. *Independent Computer Consultants Association:* www.icca.org. *Forums:* www.itcareers.com. *Java links:* www.javaworld.com. *Jobs:* www.computerjobs.com.

(Neat Niche) **Wireless Device Programmer.** The Yankee Group predicts that 60 million people in the U.S. alone will have Internet access from their cell phones by 2005, up from 200,000 in 1999. And as cell phones, personal digital assistants, and pagers become even more ubiquitous, companies will undoubtedly pack even more features into these units. For example, cell phones now have digital cameras that can instantly, wirelessly, transmit your snapshots to your Web site. And as the baby boomers age, they'll demand chip-embedded appliances to help them in their dotage. Already, the Digital Angel, a tiny implantable device, monitors an outpatient's vital signs, and broadcasts anomalies and the patient's location to his physician. Know Java and VXML (which enables devices to respond to your voice), and you should have fun and make lots of money on this cutting edge.

(Neat Niche) **Virtual Reality Programmer.** You write software that is the ultimate training method: putting students in a virtual duplicate of the actual situation — military officers in war zones, doctors in surgery, and astronauts in spaceships. See www.creatures3.com for a state-of-the-art simulator. The current programming language of choice is VRML. For an intro, see http://vrml.sdsc.edu.

(Neat Niche) **Education Software Programmer.** Do you like the idea of creating software so kids actually learn something? Although teacher unions are unlikely to trumpet this, evidence is growing that students learn more from a good, simulation-centered computer program than from a live teacher. Corporations and parents are currently the biggest consumers of education software, but schools are increasingly being dragged along. *Links*: www.insead.fr/CALT/Encyclopedia/Education/Advances/Technologies. *Learning Circuits WebZine:* www.learningcircuits.org.

(Neat Niche) **Web Programmer.** Typically, you take the blueprint from a Web site designer and make it happen. Increasingly, Web programmers specialize in either the front- or back-end. Front-enders develop the site's interface. A sense of the artistic and what humans will like are key. Back-end specialists work on such matters as integrating a database into the site or ensuring that the site is compatible with multiple browsers. Whether front- or back-end, you must be technically current — that means way beyond HTML. That's being replaced by DHTML (allows for more interactivity) and XML, which is much more flexible than HTML, especially when dealing with data rather than text. Most important today is Java, the programming language that has replaced C++ especially for Web and other networked applications. Nice pluses: scripting languages (small tools such as JavaScript that provide goodies such as animation) Active Server Pages

(ASP), the older Perl that provides many e-commerce functions, and CGI scripts. If your site will need to access information from a database, and it probably will, you'll need to know SQL scripting. On the artistic side, common tools include Adobe Illustrator, Photoshop, GoLive, Dreamweaver, Flash, and 3D Studio Max. *The Web Guild:* www.webguild.org. *New York New Media Association:* www.nynma.org.

(Neat Niche) **Game Programmer.** Of course this sounds cool, and this field should grow as televisions start to incorporate high-powered game systems. The question is, how do you get hired? Most learn on their own, but if you're not a self-starter, the International Game Developers Association site (www.igda.org, then click on outreach) contains a list of schools offering courses in game design. When you've created a cool sample program, send it to game companies. Easy way to find them: read reviews of games on gamespot.com. They often include the name of the developers. Then use www.google.com to find their Web site and e-mail your creation.

(Neat Niche) **Computer Security Programmer.** From both inside and outside the organization, hackers steal information from company computers, or try to disrupt them just for the heck of it. This produces a strong demand for programmers called firewall developers, to foil the thieves. Also, corporations, the FBI, and the Department of Justice hire these cybersleuths to surf the Net to nab software pirates. The Business Software Alliance estimates that nearly one in two software applications is pirated. *See* www.ciao.gov *for info on the Federal government-sponsored "university" that trains hackerbusters. AntiOnline:* www.antionline.com. *Computer Security Resource Clearinghouse:* csrc.nist.gov. *High Technology Crime Investigation Association International,* www.htcia.org. *International Association of Computer Investigative Specialists,* www.cops.org.

 Newsletter Publisher. According to the Newsletter Publishing Association, 50 percent of new newsletters succeed, a higher percentage than other small businesses. And your chances are even better if you do things right:

- ✔ Choose a narrow niche. It's easier to sell 1,000 newsletters for home health nurses than 100 for nurses.

- ✔ Choose a topic that has an endless stream of new information that your target readers crave. Sample titles: *Power Plant Financing, Proteomics Update, Currency Options Insider, Bluetooth Quarterly, and Employment Law Digest.* Or focus on creating custom newsletters for nonprofits or clubs.

- ✔ Be sure an existing publication doesn't meet the need.

- ✔ Consider an online edition. If you have a large subscriber base, distribution costs will be lower.

- ✔ To market a newsletter successfully, you must buy the right mailing lists for solicitations and place ads at highly-targeted Web sites. *Newsletter Publishers Association:* www.newsletters.org, www.newsletter-clearinghse.com, *and* www.nlf.com.

Business data

Actuary. How much should an insurance company charge each employee of the Western Widget Company for health insurance? That's a typical question asked of an actuary. Actuary is a good career for someone who wants a prestigious career that applies math to practical decisions, and that offers salaries that can reach six figures. More good news: You can achieve the highest level of actuary (Fellow) without a graduate degree. You do have to pass ten arduous exams for which you can study at home or take classes at local actuary clubs or at universities. *Society of Actuaries:* www.beanactuary.org.

Economist. This is another career for the math-centric person who wants to do something that is at least potentially practical. Economists answer such questions as, "How will our company be affected if the minimum wage goes up?" "What are the economic costs and benefits of legalizing gambling in this county?" "What has happened to solar cell production and why?" In other words, economists predict and analyze production and consumption trends to help governments and companies make policy. Problem is, people's actual behavior often doesn't follow the predicted model. I'm always amused when I read a panel of blue-ribbon economists' predictions. They rarely agree. Nevertheless, a master's or doctoral degree is often required. *About.com's economics portal:* /economics.about.com.

> (Neat Niche) **Environmental Economist.** You figure out the economic impacts of activities such as building a theme park, restricting auto traffic in national parks, or creating a federally subsidized oil deal with Venezuela. *Jobs:* www.eco.org, www.environmentalcareer.com.

> (Neat Niche) **Forensic Economist.** You claim that your business partner ruined your business. How large were the damages? A forensic economist can tell you. Your spouse got run over by a car. How much should she get? An estimate will come from a forensic economist. Your spouse needn't die for you to need a forensic economist. You're divorcing her. How much alimony do you need to pay? A forensic economist would be happy to tell you — for a nice fee. *National Association of Forensic Economics:* www.nafe.net. *Links:* www.willyancey.com/forensic.htm.

Expense Reduction Consultant. A perfect career for a cheapskate. Your job is to review all a business's buying decisions: long-distance service, office supplies, printing, insurance — everything — making sure they're buying as wisely as possible.

Government Procurement Consultant. The nation's largest customer is the government — and it may be willing to pay $85 for a screw. That's the sort of customer that all businesses love, but most companies don't know how to get the government to buy from them. Your job is to teach them. Get an introduction at *About.com's government contracting portal:* `federalcontract.about.com`. `www.smallbusinessdepot.com` *matches small businesses with government contracts.* Matthew Lesko's book, *Government Giveaways for Entrepreneurs.*

Credit Risk Manager. This isn't a sexy job but it's high-paying and in-demand. Credit risk managers work for organizations that extend credit: credit card companies and other corporations, universities, even government agencies. Your job is to figure out who should get credit and how much. You must be computer-savvy and have at least a bachelor's degree in statistics, economics, computer science, math, or operations research. Six-figure salaries are common after just three to ten years of experience. *National Association of Credit Management:* `www.nacm.org`.

Securities Analyst. Would you find it fun to figure out if a company's stock or bond is a bargain? That's what securities analysts do. They're mathematical detectives who interview company employees and crunch a lot of numbers. One fringe benefit is that securities analysts may get fresh-off-the-press tips on stocks likely to go up. *Association for Investment Management and Research:* `www.aimr.org`.

UNCONVENTIONAL WISDOM

SEC rules prohibit trading based on information before it's released to the public, but how can government regulators keep insiders from buying the stock early — not in their own name, but in Aunt Sally's?

(Neat Niche) **Portfolio Manager.** After you've been an analyst for a while, the big step up is to portfolio manager. Pension funds, mutual funds, and large companies hire portfolio managers to decide which securities to buy and which to dump.

Want to play with other people's money but don't see yourself getting the MBA or CFA certification that's usually required in a portfolio manager? See the financial planner profile on page 65.

Web Store Owner. If you keep it simple, you should be able to earn at least a sideline income and have fun. Pick a niched product: fish tanks, Japanese crafts, whatever you love. Don't pick anything perishable, like African violets. A newbie won't be able to anticipate sales well enough — you'll likely have a house full of dead violets. Get a self-explanatory name for your site. So, if you want to sell Japanese crafts, the name better be something like Japanesecrafts.com. Not available? Try to buy it from its owner. Too expensive (more than $1,000 or so), it's probably worth picking another business. For most businesses, name is key. Next step: Create and host your site at `store.yahoo.com`. Not only is its site-creation software idiot-resistant, your site will be well-placed on Yahoo!'s heavily-trafficked search engine. Create the site yourself — you'll want to make too many changes to be dependent on a programmer. Keep your site simple: It must load quickly, enable you to find what you want quickly, and check out quickly. Forget cutesy graphics —

they slow things down. Speed sells. To maximize traffic to your site, try to make it the definitive one in your niche. For example, if you're selling window boxes, make sure your site has a great selection of fairly priced ones. Yes, you'll need a JPEG picture of each, but each should be small enough that the pages load quickly. To build traffic further, regularly e-mail your customers about your site's new features and products, and start a chat group on the site. *E-Commerce Times:* www.ecommercetimes.com, Sherry Szydlik's book: *E-trepreneur.*

Adventure Travel Organizer. More and more people are deciding that a week at a Hilton isn't the vacation they want. They want to go back to nature. Hiking, bird watching, backpacking, and other forms of recreation have seen double-digit growth since the early '80s according to the United States Forest Service. And in our search for the exotic, markets are building for the likes of dog sledding, hang gliding, sky diving, mountain climbing in the Himalayas, and exploring Antarctica and the Brazilian jungle. The market for general adventure travel is getting crowded, so nichecraft is particularly important here. *Adventure Travel Society:* www.adventuretravel.com. *Outside Magazine:* www.outsidemag.com. *Outdoor Network:* www.outdoornetwork.com/jobnetdb/. *Earthwatch:* www.earthwatch.org. *International Ecotourism Society:* www.ecotourism.org.

> (Neat Niche) **Student Travel Service.** Set up on or near a local college campus and focus on low-cost adventures. For example, set up mini Peace Corps-like experiences, in which groups of students assist villages in developing nations.

Exporter. In the movie, *Back to the Future*, Michael J. Fox went back in time and so had no trouble predicting the future. Exporters have it almost as easy. Many fads, for example blue jeans and e-commerce, move overseas a few years later. Think of a product in the U.S. that became hot in the last few years. Want to sell it in another country? By the time you set it up, that country's demand should start ramping up. Kenneth Weiss' book: *Building an Import/Export Business.*

Export Agent. Nearly any manufacturer wants to expand its market, but few small ones know the ins and outs of exporting: how to find the right foreign buyers, how to deal with them and with shippers, customs agents, and with all the regulations. The good news is that you can learn all this inexpensively. Use the U.S. Commerce Department's vast export resources (www.tradeinfo. doc.gov). Tyler Hicks, author of *199 Great Home Businesses You Can Start and Succeed in for Under $1,000,* suggests you find foreign companies seeking U.S. products from the Commerce Department's publication, *Trade Opportunities.* If you know a foreign language, concentrate on companies where that language is spoken. Locate U.S. companies selling what foreign buyers want by consulting the *Thomas Register of American Manufacturers (*www.thomasregister. com*)*. Tell the U.S. source that you have an overseas buyer for a specific number of items at such-and-such a price, and negotiate from there. A *Money* magazine report concluded that, among all home-based businesses, export agents are among the most likely to generate high income. *Manufacturers Agents National Association.* www.manaonline.org. *Alexandra Woznick's book:* Basic Guide to Exporting.

Appraiser. You're a professional treasure hunter, sifting through collections of coins, stamps, antiques, or art, and figuring out if there's treasure among the ordinary. As our population ages, the need for appraisers is increasing: in estate planning, or in divvying up the pie after the fact. And because big bucks are at stake, you may be well-paid. *American Society of Appraisers:* www.appraisers.org. *Appraiser's Net:* www.appraisers-net.com.

Work with Words

Writer. Self-expression — it's a powerful driver for many people, including me. My life gains meaning when I know that others will hear what I have to say. And written self-expression has particular power because there's time to be more reflective than when speaking. Although your odds of making a living as a novelist or poet are about as good as Firestone winning the Tiremaker of the Decade award, there are neat writing niches that may allow you to write without having to eat ramen three times a day. Whatever the niche, though, most writers must freelance. To succeed at that, you must pitch story ideas that are in sync with the publication, propose a compelling approach to the piece, and more important, explain why you're an ideal person to do it. *About.com's portal for freelance writers:* freelancewrite.about.com. *National Writers Union:* www.nwu.org. *Inkspot:* www.inkspot.com.

(Neat Niche) **Web Writer.** Your writing must be concise, generally laced with bullets, punchy anecdotes and statistics, and packed with fresh content — the Web operates at warp speed. Web writing is the ideal career for someone with a supermarket full of knowledge about one field, the ability to quickly track down additional tasty morsels, and then assemble it all into a quick but satisfying snack.

(Neat Niche) **Medical Writer.** Writing *Preparing for Your Hysterectomy* is a typical assignment for medical writers. Medical writers translate prevention practices and treatments into plain English. Who'll hire you? Medical Web sites such as HealthWatch or WebMD, HMOs and other health insurers, hospitals, clinics, and magazines that appeal to older readers. *American Medical Writers Association:* www.amwa.org.

(Neat Niche) **Politician's Writer.** Every politician needs one, from a city councilperson to the president. Political writers craft fundraising letters, speeches, and see-how-much-I'm-doing-for-you newsletters. One approach to landing a job is to write a fundraising letter for your favorite politician for free. Send it as a sample.

(Neat Niche) **Industry Publications Writer.** Ever thought of writing for *Pizza Today?* It's the glossy magazine for people in the pizza business. Thousands of such publications tend to pay writers well.

(Neat Niche) **Ghostwriter.** Here's a back-door route into ghostwriting, a cool gig. Contact celebrities, especially those who have been outside the headlines for a few months — last year's hero is usually afraid he's had his 15 minutes of fame. Ask if he'd like you to write a book about him. If he agrees, develop a proposal together and send it, probably through an agent, to publishing houses. When the book comes out, the star is listed as the author in huge type and your name is microscopic, if it appears at all. The name of Hilary Clinton's ghostwriter of *It Takes a Village*, Barbara Feinman, never appeared on the book. Celebrity ghostwriting may be the fastest route to a well-paying, if secret, book deal.

(Neat Niche) **Copywriter.** This offers one of the surer routes to a nonstarving writing career. Many copywriters think first about ad writing but also consider company annual reports, mail-order or Web catalog copy, telemarketing scripts, consumer information booklets, and restaurant menus. The key to being a good copywriter? Being able to put yourself in the readers' shoes: "What would make the reader act?" Robert Bly's book, *The Copywriter's Handbook. Editorial Freelancers Association.* www.the-efa.org.

(Neat Niche) **Technical Writer.** In this in-demand niche, you develop user manuals, articles about new products, instruction booklets, press releases, and online help files. It's often a high-pressure job because you're brought on after the product is completed and everyone's eager to get it on the market. *Society for Technical Communication:* www.stc.org; *About.com's technical writing portal:* http://techwriting.about.com.

Journalist. Like a career in acting or film directing, journalism is one of those job aspirations likely to result in poverty. I was on a top floor of the Time-Life Building talking with four editors from one of Time-Warner's major magazines, and everyone agreed how obscene it was that colleges continue to welcome more and more journalism majors even though only a small fraction will ever make a middle-class living in the field. So why is journalism on the list of cool careers? Because it's so rewarding and enjoyable that it's worth considering — if you love interviewing, digging up information, and cranking out clear prose rapid-fire. To increase your chances of landing a good job, specialize — science, technology, ethnic issues, and education journalists may have an edge. *American Society of Journalists and Authors:* www.asja.org. *Society of Professional Journalists:* www.spj.org. *Newslink:* http://ajr.newslink.org/newjoblink.html and www.journalismjobs.com and www.journalism.berkeley.edu/jobs/.

OOH

Many articles and TV news segments are slanted. Even in prestigious media outlets, too many journalists select stories so they can sell their viewpoint (for example, proaffirmative action). They fill each article with support for their position, carefully nuancing every word, adding just enough balance to make it look fair. Biased coverage is the main reason the media is distrusted. You may never completely control your biases but the public trust demands that you make your best effort.

(Neat Niche) **TV Newswriter.** You write the words that those public-idolized puppets called TV news anchors read, down to the transitions between one story and the next. You have to write concisely and with edge. Mervin Block's book: *Writing News for TV and Radio.*

Book/Magazine/Web Site Editor. The fun part of being an editor is finding great projects, convincing your editorial/publication board to say yes, and then helping the author to mold the project into something wonderful and salable without deflating the author into inaction. But getting into this field is tough, and your first jobs are usually low paying with long hours. If you insist on the book business, consider moving to the Big Apple, where 90 percent of the business is located. One rarely considered starting place is as an agent's assistant. You read unsolicited submissions (called the slush pile), and make connections with editors. Scan acknowledgments in recent books to find beloved agents. In magazines, try to get a first job as a fact checker or researcher. *American Society of Magazine Editors:* www.asme.magazine.org.

(Neat Niche) **Web Site Editor.** A Web site wants to be *sticky*, stimulating return visitors. Web editors are in charge of making that happen. One part writer, one part editor, one part businessperson, the Web editor comes up with content ideas for the site (a contest, a poll, a series of exposés, and so on), recruits writers, polishes submissions, and works with programmers to make them Web-ready. You needn't be a supergeek but you need to know your way around HTML, a Web design program such as *Dreamweaver*, and a graphics program such as *Flash 5. Association for Internet Professionals:* www.association.org.

(Neat Niche) **Copy Editor.** Everyone wants to write, but to get their writing into publishable form often takes some doing. That's why print and online publishers hire copy editors. Writers who want to maximize chances of publication also hire copy editors to polish their drafts into publishable shape. *American Copy Editors Society:* www.copydesk.org.

Resume Writer. Even many confident people find having to write their resume scary. "One page or two?" "How can I sound good without bragging?" "What about that employment gap when I was hitchhiking cross-country?" Enter the resume writer, a wordsmith who helps people present their best selves while resisting the temptation to overinflate. It's a good career for writers who enjoy interviewing people and can quickly convert that interview into a concise, logical resume. Linking yourself to an employment Web site, outplacement firm, or headhunter attracts more clients and work. So does conducting a resume seminar at job fairs and job-seeker support groups, sending postcards to seniors at local colleges (student directories are usually made public), and specializing in military personnel moving to civilian life, medical, legal, or technical professionals, or the physically handicapped (getting referrals from a local department of rehabilitation). *Professional Association of Resume Writers:* www.parw.com. *Resume software: ResumeMaker, downloadable from* www.resumemaker.com.

 Librarian. If you picture a mousy bookworm, update your stereotype. Today's librarian is a sociable cyberwhiz whose job increasingly focuses on helping patrons retrieve obscure information from mountains of electronic and print resources. Librarians who specialize in medicine, other sciences, law, or engineering, make more money. *American Library Association Library Resources:* www.ala.org.

(Neat Niche) **Private Librarian.** Hospitals, government agencies, prisons, magazines, TV and radio station news departments, and research departments of corporations and nonprofit organizations have libraries. Would you ever have thought Revlon had a library? The Brookings Institute? The United States Air Force? *Newsweek* magazine? Most large law firms? All hire librarians. *Special Libraries Association:* www.sla.org.

(Neat Niche) **Information Retriever/Independent Search Specialist.** We're already overwhelmed with information, and it's going to get worse. Our savior is the information retriever, who for a fee, goes beyond what a librarian has time to do. Retrievers surf the Net and databases such as Dialog and Nexis and phone interview the right people, providing you with a digest of the best information. The information glut is so overwhelming that information professionals specialize in aerospace engineering, mergers and acquisitions, politics, or medicine, for example. How do you get clients? Pick your specialty, give talks at its professional association, and write for its publications. *Association of Independent Information Professionals:* www.aiip.org. *American Society for Information Science:* www.asis.org. *Society of Competitive Intelligence Professionals:* www.scip.org.

(Neat Niche) **Internet Trainer.** The Three R's now have a fourth: *R*etrieving information from the Net and other sources. I imagine that many organizations and individuals would pay to have someone teach them effective Internet searching techniques.

 Web Content Finder. This job title subsumes many different types of positions. Karyn Marcus visits art galleries and openings to find art to post on artmecca.com. Diana Jacklich, after graduating with a degree in English literature, convinced management that she should join the wine buying team at wine.com. Eric Murken tastes ethnic foods, deciding which goes onto ethnicfoods.com. Web sites use people to dig up cool content. Online directory sites such as Yahoo.com need people to choose the best Web sites to list in their directories. Content aggregators such as www.about.com need people to assemble content for hundreds of channels. Bots (Web-surfing robots)

must constantly be refilled with on-target sites. *Tip:* Job titles for Web content finders vary. For example, Yahoo! calls its content finders, "catalog analysts." Whatever the job's called, for a bookish person who wants to be at the cutting edge, this can be a cool career.

 ***Information Abstractor.*** Would you enjoy synthesizing articles into a paragraph or two? Can you do it quickly? In an hour, an abstractor must abstract two to three articles. If you can do that, you'll be in demand because of the need to distill that relentless information explosion. Major hirers: Web sites, corporations needing to distill material for scientists and executives, and publishers of research abstracts. You'll be particularly in demand if you have content expertise, in law, medicine, engineering, chemistry, or real estate. To land a job, find the articles you'd like to abstract — see a directory such as the *Ebsco Index and Abstract Directory* — and submit sample abstracts. To get corporate work, send samples to corporate librarians and departments responsible for technical writing. *National Federation of Abstracting & Information Services:* www.fnais.org.

 ***Indexer.*** An index can make the difference between a book and a good book. Peter Farrell, author of *Make Money from Home*, calls a good index, "a minor work of art but also the product of clean thought and meticulous care." That work of art must usually be done quickly — publishers usually give indexers manuscripts just a few weeks before publication. Indexing is a self-employed occupation that requires a person with the odd combination of enjoying the solitary work of creating an index and the ability to go out, ask for business, and insist on reasonable compensation: $3 to $4 per manuscript page or $30 to $40 an hour. A degree may not be necessary. *American Society of Indexers:* www.asindexing.org.

Of all places, the United States Department of Agriculture offers two well-regarded online courses on indexing. Info on the basic one is at www.grad.usda.gov/programs_services/corres/syllabusedit3360.cfm. *See also, Susan Holbert's Indexing Service. She has indexed 100 books, including Rosalyn Carter's biography, and offers impressive-sounding training.* www.abbington.com/holbert.

(Neat Niche) **Internet Indexer.** Some search engines hire indexers. For a master list of search engines, see www.searchenginewatch.com.

 Social Science Analyst. Like to read? The federal government employs 15,000 social science analysts. Their main job is to read and research material about drug abuse, military effectiveness, and adult literacy and so on. Employment prospects are better with a graduate degree. State agencies, universities, think tanks, and corporations also hire such people, under differing job titles. *Association of Independent Information Professionals:* www.aiip.org. *Links to government jobs:* www.rileyguide.com/gov.html.

Ethicist. Dilemma: Robots can now create robots. Efficient yes, but could they eventually create a man-destroying army of robots. Probably not, but to avoid the risk, should research on robot-creating robots be illegal? If these practices are made illegal, will that simply transfer control of the technology to terrorist groups and rogue nations? Such dilemmas fill the ethicist's in-box. *American Society of Law, Medicine, and Ethics:* www.aslme.org.

Legal Transcript Digester. Here's an interesting legal career in which you don't have to be a lawyer. Preparation for complex trials can require hundreds of hours of depositions (interviews) and hundreds more hours of trial. The verbatim court reporter transcript is too cumbersome, so attorneys hire transcript digesters to condense the material. As usual, nichecraft helps: Nurses may contact medical malpractice law firms. Have a construction background? Contact a real estate attorney. A training course is available from Hillside Digesting Service: 800-660-3376.

Radio Guide Publisher. Why has no one done this yet? TV guides are ubiquitous yet no radio guides exist. When getting into your car, wouldn't you like to know what music is playing on which station? Who's debating whom on talk stations? Here's how you might make a living as publisher of a radio guide. Get local radio stations to e-mail you their program listings — they should be eager because you're offering them free publicity. Then sell the listings for newspapers to publish or local Web sites to post. For additional income, publish an advertising-funded radio guide to distribute free at supermarkets.

> (Neat Niche) **Celebrity Web Chat Listing Service.** Every day, dozens of august people chat online for an hour or two. But do you know who's chatting when and where? I don't. Why not publish a weekly guide that tells us?

Graphologist. Handwriting analysts are found not only at carnivals, police departments, attorneys, and employers also use graphologists to catch forgers or to verify that you wrote the ransom note. Your handwriting may also reveal your personality. In a job interview, you may say, "I'm hard-working," but your handwriting — something you can't control as well as your tongue — may say something different. Bonus: Graphologists can be the center of attention at a party. *The Handwriting Analysts Group:* www.handwriting.org.

Work with Things

Artistically done

Special Occasions Cake Baker. Most bakers are poorly paid production machines. Special-occasion cake bakers are the exception. You must be an artist, offering delicious masterpieces unavailable at your basic bakery. It should be the kind that when the bride and groom look at wedding pictures, they smile and say, "That was *some* cake!" If I wanted to become a cake baker, I'd look in my Yellow Pages under "wedding services" and visit wedding cake makers until I found a baker of superlative cakes who was willing to let me apprentice. Sandra Gurvis, in *Careers for Non Conformists* suggests that for cake bakers, a high metabolism and/or health club membership help counteract the inevitable taste tests.

Artist/Graphic Artist. Get real. If you have visions of hanging out in your loft, splattering paint on some enormous abstract canvas, congratulations — you have a cool hobby. *The Princeton Review* profile of artist careers reports that "as a purely self-expressing career, 90 percent of artists make under $1,000 per year on their art." If you expect to make a living as an artist, brand this into your brain: Seventy-five percent of the art available in the United States is produced by the advertising industry. Much of the rest appears on Web sites. And almost all is computer-generated art produced by people with excellent freehand drawing skills enhanced by the computer. You must make good friends with *Adobe Illustrator, Photoshop, Pagemaker,* and *QuarkXPress.* The good news is that demand for computer artists is growing. More good news: In production art, degrees don't count; your portfolio does. Send it to art directors at ad agencies or the new design/marketing agencies — and don't forget the small houses. Oh, one more sad truth: Only a third of people who start a career in graphic arts last five years. *About.com's graphic design portal:* graphicdesign.about.com. *American Institute of Graphic Arts:* http://www.aiga.org. *Graphic Artists Guild:* www.gag.org. *ACM SigGraph:* www.siggraph.org. *World Wide Web Artists' Consortium:* www.wwwac.org. *Long list of artist careers:* www.wallkill.k12.nj.us/finearts/ artcareers.html.

(Neat Niche) **Animator.** An architect develops a blueprint for a house, but the customer is nervous. Will it really be livable? So an animator develops a walk-through animation of the premises. Now the customer can do as many virtual walk-throughs as he likes before the first nail is hammered. This is just one of the new opportunities for animators. For the first time, computers can, at moderate cost, do animations sophisticated enough to appeal to adults that previously were impossible at any price. Science and industry, TV, films, Web sites, and computer games are jumping on the animation bandwagon. Downsides are low pay and highly structured work — this is not the career for freewheeling artists. The top animation schools are California Institute of the Arts and Toronto's Sheridan College. Wanna teach yourself? *3D Studio Max* and *Flash 5* are popular. *The International Animation Association:* www.swcp.com/~asifa. Animation World Network: www.awn.org. *About.com's animation portal:* animation.about.com. **Isaac Kerlow's book:** *The Art of 3D.*

(Neat Niche) **Special Effects Artist.** Create impossibilities that appear before our very eyes in movies or computer games. Have kinky black hair morph in seconds into straight blond, a 70-year-old's face transform into a teenager's, a lovely day degenerate into Armageddon. Top hirers of these digital magicians: Pixar and Industrial Light & Magic. *Key software:* Maya *and* SoftImage XSI.

(Neat Niche) **Textile Designer.** So many of my female clients wax rhapsodic about their love of fabric, color, and design. For them, textile design is a dream career. Computer-centric, yet still enabling you to touch, feel, and intuit what looks beautiful not only to you but also to users. *International Textile and Apparel Association:* `www.itaasite.org`. *Computer-Integrated Textile Design Association:* `www.citda.org`. *Textile Artists and Design Association.* `www.surfacing-tada.com`.

(Neat Niche) **Demonstrative Evidence Specialist.** Demonstrative evidence specialists create large computer-generated drawings, slides, and videos that attorneys use to present their cases to judges and juries. Because each situation is different, you're not a robot, and because the stakes are high, you make more than slave wages. *Article:* `www.sado.org/23cdn78.htm#b`.

(Neat Niche) **Muralist.** If you can't get a National Endowment for the Arts grant, convince city or local merchants to hire you to paint inspiring murals on graffitied buildings, in restaurants, apartment house or office building lobbies, on freeway underpass walls, even on billboard-sized signs.

(Neat Niche) **Commission Artist.** If you can create paintings that look good on the walls of rich people's living rooms, place an ad in an upscale magazine: "Create a gallery-quality painting to your specifications for a fraction of the cost."

Technical Illustrator. Three of the words I dread most are *some assembly required*. The "easy instructions," despite the drawings created by technical illustrators, usually don't help. Maybe you'll do a better job. Technical illustrators tackle projects more important than my patio furniture. They may, for example, create drawings of the inner workings of a rocket engine. *Society of Illustrators:* `www.societyillustrators.org`.

(Neat Niche) **Biomedical Visualization Specialist.** This field formerly known as medical illustration has come a long way. Thanks to software and imaging equipment, medical illustrators no longer are limited to what they can draw by hand. For example, they now can use computer-generated brain maps to demonstrate differences between a Nobel Prize winner and a retarded person or between the parts of the brain that are activated when thinking about math or about sex.

Conservator. A conservator's idea of bliss is restoring old paintings, furniture, autographs, books, and musical instruments to their former glory. A combination painter, refinisher, and chemist (Watch those fumes!), most conservators are hired by major museums. Government agencies sometimes hire them to restore historic properties. Alas, few jobs are available. *American Institute for Conservation of Historic and Artistic Works:* `http://aic.stanford.edu/`. *National Trust for Historic Preservation:* `www.nationaltrust.org`.

OOH

BHB

Cinematographer. It seems that everyone wants to be a film director, but what are the odds of making a living at it? Think lottery. How can you derive many of directing's benefits with fewer people competing for your jobs? Try cinematography. Cinematographers also direct on film sets. The major difference is that rather than directing people, they direct the cameras. *American Society of Cinematographers:* www.cinematography.com. Pauline Rogers' book: *Contemporary Cinematographers on their Art.*

Lighting Designer. Another backdoor into a film or theatrical career is lighting design. You train for this career in college-based stagecraft programs like the ones at UC Irvine and Cal Poly, Pomona. Lighting designers are hired not only in film and theater, but also for trade shows, and for lighting major buildings — hotels, corporate lobbies, museums, concerts, and theme parks. *International Association of Lighting Designers:* www.iald.org.

Foley Artist. Remember the sounds of the steamy sex scenes in the last movie you saw? They probably were created by a foley artist making dispassionate love to his own wrist. That crunching snow as the avalanche rescuers try to save the day? Walking on cornstarch in a burlap bag. Foley artists create sounds that are easier to record than those made during an actual shoot. The good foley artist must be an *audile*: able to look at an object and imagine what type of sound it produces. Take, for example, that vampire flick in which a character's guts get pulled out. It's raw chicken. *Motion Pictures Sound Editing:* www.mpse.org.

Exhibit Designer/Builder. Many artistic types who like to sling a hammer dream of becoming theater set designers, but that market is extraordinarily tight. But exhibit designing/building, a similar field, is less known and therefore easier to break into. You build the equivalent of theater sets for trade shows, expos, and museums. *Exhibit Designers and Producers Association:* www.edpa.com.

Neon Sign Maker. How'd you like a career of twisting colored glass into special shapes? Although this is a dying art, demand is high — a nice combination for you. Lee Champaign of the National Neon Institute (www.neon-school.com) says that after its 14-week training, you can get a job almost anywhere in the United States. Don't worry, you needn't be a Rembrandt. An artist creates the design. Your job is to bend the glass to match the design. *Other schools:* www.signweb.com/events/cont/schools.html *Links:* www.neonshop.com/neonweb. Wayne Strattman's book: *Neon Techniques.*

Holographer. Looking for a career that melds art and science? Wanna make something cool? Try holography. Holographs are no longer just '60s psychedelia, the field is growing. Holographs are used in new-product promotion, on ID and credit cards, in movie special effects, and even in medical diagnosis. Though some holographers learn on the job, others attend a special school, such as the one at The Museum of Holography in Chicago: 773-226-1007. *HoloWorld:* www.holoworld.com.

Die Maker. This is one metal artist who can expect to earn a living. Working from a blueprint or instructions, you develop the dies for metal or plastic products — from buttons to auto parts. Although you need artistic skills, you get lots of help from die designers. Die designing and cutting are computer-assisted. A shortage of die makers means job and salary prospects are good. No college is required. Most die makers learn as apprentices. *National Tooling and Machining Association* www.ntma.org.

Perfumer. What fun: playing around with different combinations of essences until you've come up with a fragrance that smells great and different. That's what perfumers do when new perfumes, soaps, laundry products, shampoos, lotions, or candles are created. Most perfumers learn their art in an extensive apprenticeship. Wanna try? *Perfumersworld.com* (www.perfumersworld.com) *offers an introductory training kit for $80. American Society of Perfumers* (www.perfumers.org). Kelly Reno's book: *Perfumes, Potions and Fanciful Formulas.*

Structured procedures

Computer Chip Layout Designer. This job essentially requires you to fit New York City onto a postage stamp. It sounds harder than it is. But like a chip, a potato chip, it's addictive. You can find yourself working 24 hours straight because, "I'm getting it. I'm getting it. It's almost done." You take engineer's specs for the 10,000-device chip, feed the info into a computer program that lays it out for you. Unfortunately, the computer layout invariably has errors that you have to fix by hand. That's where the art comes in. Your job is to cram those devices in as tight as possible and still get the chip to work. R. Jacob Baker's book: *CMOS Circuit Design, Layout, and Simulation.*

Tugboat Operator. This is a sailor's job that pays $50,000 or more and doesn't require long stints away from home. The job market is good. Fear of oil spills has resulted in regulations requiring most large ships to be towed into dock by a tug. Most tug operators get their experience by working on party or fishing boats or by attending a two-year maritime program. *International Organization of Master Mates and Pilots:* www.bridgedeck.org.

Heart-Lung Perfusionist. In open-heart surgery, the surgeon can't work on the heart if blood is squirting all over the place. So a machine is hooked up to an artery to receive the blood. The machine then, like a heart and lungs, pumps blood and air back into an artery on the other side of the heart and lungs, and circulation continues. Meanwhile, the heart is relatively bloodless so the surgeon can work. The surgeon hooks up the blood vessels and the perfusionist runs the machine. Sounds straightforward, but talk to any perfusionist and he'll mention one word: stress. One mistake can be one too many for a bypass patient. Calm people with a high tolerance for stress do well. There are upsides: You are intimately involved in saving people's lives, and salaries are excellent — generally starting above $60,000. Only a bachelor's degree is required. Perfusion is the smallest healthcare profession with only 3,500 practitioners in the United States. *American Society for Extracorporeal Technology:* www.amsect.com. *Heart Pumper:* www.heartpumper.com.

Prosthetist/Orthotist. An amputee walks in. You're going to make his or her artificial limb or brace. You must be able to work face-to-face with amputees and create limbs and braces with great precision. After all, you're preparing a device on which that person's ability to use hands or feet depends. Extensive training is required but many of the schools are public so it won't — pardon the expression — cost you an arm and a leg. *American Academy of Orthotists and Prosthetists:* www.oandp.org.

Pedorthist. A person needs special shoes — not because she has to match a dress, but rather because her feet are deformed from disease or injury. A podiatrist (foot doctor) sends her with a shoe prescription to a pedorthist, who examines and measures her feet and then designs or modifies shoes to fit. Demand for pedorthists exceeds supply and only 120 hours of training are required for certification. *Pedorthics Footwear Association:* http://pedorthics.org. *Board for Certification in Pedorthics* www.cpeds.org.

High-Security Driving Instructor. How'd you like to teach police officers how to conduct a high-speed chase? Show a diplomat what to do when a terrorist starts shooting at her car? Show an FBI agent how his car can intercept a moving vehicle? That's what security driving instructors do. Unless you want to take a vow of poverty, forget about being a regular ol' driving instructor — they often earn little more than minimum wage. That isn't enough for the privilege of having a terrified aspiring driver let go of the steering wheel at 30 miles an hour and head straight for a brick wall — yes it happens. *BSR Inc. (a well-regarded security driving school):* www.bsrinc.com.

Irrigation System Specialist. Nearly every homeowner, farmer, and golf course owner needs an irrigation system. And if you already have one, chances are it needs to be fixed or upgraded. Irrigation system design is a great career for someone who likes a combination of science and art, indoors and outdoors, business and environmentalism. Environmentalism? Yup, because modern irrigation systems save water, and fertilizing through the irrigation system allows less chemical fertilizer to be used. *The Irrigation Association:* www.irrigation.org. *offers training courses.*

Musical Instrument Repairperson. Kids are not known for their tender treatment of anything, let alone school musical instruments. That means plenty of repairs are needed. And, of course, even some older folks' instruments need work. Musical instrument repair is a great career for fix-it types who prefer to avoid things electrical. You should know how to play the instrument. Otherwise, how would you know if you fixed it? Noted training institutions include Badger State Repair in Wisconsin, Renton Technical College in Washington, and Red Wing Technical Institute in Minnesota. *National Association of Professional Band Instrument Repair Technicians:* www.napbirt.org.

(Neat Niche) **Piano Technician/Tuner.** This is a low-stress job. Working conditions are usually ideal, and you're nearly always assured of pleasing your customer. If you get bored, you can learn piano rebuilding. Despite the presence of electronic aids, piano tuners need a good ear. Unfortunately, the market for piano technicians is poor — synthesizers sound as good as most pianos, are much less expensive, can create many more sounds, are portable, and don't need to be tuned. *Piano Technicians Guild:* www.ptg.org.

Avionics Technician. In a $20 million airplane, $16 million is avionics (electronic equipment). It's been said that today's airplanes are flying computers. That means plenty of avionics to fix and plenty to upgrade. Electronics are always getting better, so many people are retrofitting — much cheaper than buying a new plane. Avionics technology is a career for tinkerers who read magazines like *Popular Mechanics,* and of course, who like airplanes. *The Mechanic:* www.the-mechanic.com, *Professional Aviation Maintenance Association:* www.pama.org.

Conference Taping Specialist. Tens of thousands of professional meetings take place each year in the U.S. alone, but only a fraction offer tape-recorded sessions for sale to those who missed sessions. This is a simple business. Equipment needs are modest: tape recorders, microphones, and a tape duplication machine. Marketing is straightforward — most of the world's associations are listed, along with their size and upcoming conferences in *Associations Unlimited*, which is available at many large libraries. Then just call the largest associations in your local area and make your pitch to the conference coordinator. You may be able to get a yes simply by touting the convenience to the organization's members, but your chances multiply if you offer the association a piece of the action. Neat niche: Posting recorded sessions on the Internet. *Web site of Audio-Visual Education Network, Inc., a company that has taped more than 2,000 conferences:* www.aven.com.

Computer Repairperson. As products become ever more electronic, ever more people are needed to repair them. It's a nice job with a pleasant work environment, the opportunity to use your brains to diagnose the problem, and high demand. And when you fix their mission-critical gizmo, they'll love you. *International Society of Certified Electronics Technicians:* www.iscet.org.

(Neat Niche) **Notebook Computer Repairperson.** Talk about a field with strong demand. More and more people use notebook computers, and because the notebooks are delicate and moved around so much, they break. Training doesn't require a Ph.D. A few months should do. Start with Ron Guilster's book: *A+ Certification For Dummies*. Then get certified by one or more notebook manufacturers, for example, Toshiba, Hewlett Packard, and Compaq.

(Neat Niche) **Music Synthesizer Repairperson.** Moving these delicate electronic orchestras from gig to gig means plenty of breakdowns and plenty of employment for you. With apparently no training schools, take a course in electronics repairs at a community college and then start tearing apart synthesizers and putting them back together. Get customers by asking synthesizer companies to certify you as an authorized service provider. Major players: Kurzweil, Yamaha, and Roland.

(Neat Niche) **Hard Disk Repairperson.** People are willing to pay through the nose to retrieve the data they should have been backing up.

(Neat Niche) **Robotics Technologist.** Does building and fixing robots sound like fun? Until recently, robots mainly welded cars and elevated highway beams. Today, they assist with hip replacement surgery, climbing and painting rusty utility towers, and installing space stations. One surprising job requirement: You have to be able to lift 50 pounds. Robots haven't yet been to WeightWatchers. *RoboticsOnline:* www.roboticsonline.com.

(Neat Niche) **Personal Digital Assistant Repairperson.** PDAs such as Palms have become ubiquitous and are expensive enough to justify repairing. Their portability increases their dropability and, in turn, your employability.

(Neat Niche) **Biomedical Equipment Repairperson.** This high-tech repair gig pays well because the machine must often be fixed now. A patient on a heart-lung machine can't wait long.

 Telecommunications Specialist. Today's corporate telecom system goes well beyond a switchboard. It likely includes cellular, intranet, Internet, perhaps satellite, videoconferencing, and yes, regular ol' phones. The telecom specialist helps a company figure out which combination of gizmos it needs and then supervises the installation. Listening and planning skills are key — a system is only good if it meets a company's current and anticipated needs. *National Association of Telecommunications Officers and Advisors:* www.natoa.org.

 Solar and Wind Energy Technologist/Installer. Few of the many technologist careers nurture the soul of the environmentally conscious like this one does. Not only are you keeping the environment clean, you're probably working for clients who are similarly minded. At least short-term, the real demand for solar and wind energy is in developing countries — they don't have the infrastructure to support conventional power plants. Most solar installers learn on the job, although some community colleges offer programs. *American Solar Energy Society:* www.ases.org. *Solar Energy Industries Association:* www.seia.org.

Millwright. Millwrights install and repair heavy industrial equipment. Few high school graduates picture themselves as crucial to the operation of a megacorporation, yet millwrights are. And it can be rewarding work. It can feel great to be called on to figure out what's wrong, and under the gun of time pressure, solve a problem that affects an entire plant's operation. You're also called on when a new piece of million-dollar heavy machinery is delivered. You're there to unload, inspect, and move it into position. That can mean deciding which ropes, cables, and hoists to use. It often means constructing special wood or metal foundations and using lasers to get the accuracy down to the millimeter. Fast-growing specialties include robotics, telecommunications, and medical diagnostic equipment. Most millwrights learn as apprentices or in community college programs. It's a largely unionized field, so the pay's good. *Apprenticeships:* www.doleta.gov/atels_bat.

Noise Control Specialist. Many owners of residences and workplaces near airports, freeways, schools, and factories willingly pay for some peace and quiet. This is a high-value specialty, yet the skills required are often modest. Often, all you're doing is insulating and double-glazing and weather-stripping windows and doors.

I do not understand why leaf blowers are legal. They are the noisiest things this side of an atom bomb, and the noise lasts longer. Plus their engines spew out carcinogens. And for what? To blow leaves around? What's wrong with a rake?

Electrician. I'm shocked that more people aren't becoming electricians. If you'd get a charge out of a career that requires working with your hands and your brain, this career could light up your life. And job prospects are spiking — the Department of Labor projects strong demand for electricians through 2008. While many electricians plug in via a four- or five-year apprenticeship, others get wired on the job, supplemented with classroom or correspondence courses. According to the federal government's *Occupational Outlook Handbook,* working as an electrician is among the best-paying of careers not requiring a college degree. And surprisingly, electricians are seriously injured by electricity at only half the rate of the general population. Just don't be color-blind: All electrical wires are color-coded! *National Electrical Contractors Association:* www.necanet.org. *International Brotherhood of Electrical Workers:* www.ibew.org.

Automotive Technician (Car Mechanic). Get that image of a grease-covered dude out of your mind. Today's automotive technician may spend almost as much time with a computer as with a wrench. Cars are heavily computer controlled, as is the equipment used to diagnose problems. If you have the ability to understand a complicated repair manual and a nose for diagnosing what's wrong, this is a better career than it used to be. More good news: Most automotive techs get their first professional job with no training other than having played around with their own car. Excellent opportunities are available for women because the work has become more automated, and physical strength is less important. *About.com's auto repair portal:* `autorepair.about.com`. *National Institute for Automotive Service Excellence:* `www.asecert.org`.

(Neat Niche) **Mobile Auto Repairperson.** Every car needs tuneups, oil changes, and brake jobs, and nearly every car owner finds it inconvenient to get them done: Drop off the car and somehow get to work in the morning, and then somehow get back to the shop after work. Enter the mobile auto repairperson. He does the work right where you park your car for work. What a business: huge demand, little competition, and ample markup. Ideal clients: large companies with a parking lot for employees. Explain to their human resources director that by allowing you to offer repairs in the company parking lot, their employees won't need to take time off work to get their car serviced.

Mobile Car Detailer. Many of us would like our car polished and cleaned inside and out but don't have the time to do it ourselves or to take it to a shop where we have to sit around waiting for it to be done. Enter the mobile car detailer. While the customer's car is parked at work or at home, the mobile car detailer does the job. This is another of those low-investment, no-brains, high-markup, easy-to-satisfy-the-customer businesses. One marketing approach is to get local new car dealers, especially luxury brands, to give a coupon for a half-price detailing to each new-car buyer. Luxury car buyers have just bought a new car and want it kept looking good, and you know they have disposable income. One bargain detailing may yield a customer who'll keep buying your service for years. A variation: Set-up shop in an airport, employee, or shopping mall parking lot.

OOH

Surveyor. Is that airport runway level? What are a park's legal boundaries? Where does your neighbor's land end? Surveyors figure these things out. They still use the old-fashioned theodolites on tripods, but increasingly use satellite-based Global Positioning Systems (GPS). Surveying is a fine career for someone who doesn't have a college degree but is comfortable around algebra and geometry, likes to learn as an apprentice, and wants an outdoor career with some status. The director of California's state apprenticeship programs told me that of the hundreds of apprenticeable careers, he'd say that surveying was the best. The job market is tight. *American Congress on Surveying and Mapping:* `www.survmap.org`. *Land Surveyors Reference Page:* `www.lsrp.com`.

OOH

Drafter. Can you picture it? Sitting at a drafting table with triangles and a T square drawing blueprints. Forget it. Although you still need free-hand drawing skills, most drafting today is done with a computer-aided design and drafting (CADD) program. The market is hottest for electronic drafters: those who draw circuit boards and schematic diagrams. *American Design Drafting Association:* `www.adda.org`.

Tile Setter. This strikes me as the perfect construction career. Progress is steady and readily apparent, and the results look pretty. Training is short, usually on-the-job, although apprenticeships are available. And here's the kicker — pay is higher than for most construction trades. Perhaps it's because of hours spent on your knees and the toll the chemicals take on your hands. But pay also is higher because half of tile setters are self-employed, which is double the rate in other construction trades and a sign that tile setters find it relatively easy to get work. *National Tile Contractors Association:* www.tile-assn.com.

 Locksmith. This is the only career in which you don't get arrested for picking locks. It's one of the better hands-on, physically undemanding occupations: strong need, short training, and many grateful customers. Just think of all those people locked out of their homes or cars, and companies and homeowners who need to keep the bad guys out.

> (Neat niche) **Electrical door-entry systems.** *Associated Locksmiths of America:* www.aloa.org. Bill Phillips' *The Complete Book of Locks and Locksmithing.*

 Farrier. Horses' hooves grow like our nails do, and when they're overgrown, a farrier must trim them and reshoe the horse. The saying goes: "No hoof, no horse." Pay is excellent — $50,000 to $125,000 a year is typical. Perhaps that's because few farriers can do it after age 45. It's said that every farrier has only so many shoeings in him. Other downsides: You must be careful to ensure you don't cripple the horse and that it doesn't give you a career-ending kick. But if you love the idea of doing physically demanding work with horses, are good with your hands, and don't mind having to face the likelihood of a career change in your 40s, horseshoeing can be a lucky career choice. *American Farriers Association:* www.amfarriers.com.

 Arborist. A career in which you start at the top — top of the tree, that is, pruning it, topping it, bracing it, and spraying it. When you climb down, you also advise on which tree to put where, and how to plant and care for it so that — unlike the feeble specimen in front of my house — it thrives. Do a good job and you'll have bolstered Joyce Kilmer's case: "I think that I shall never see a poem lovely as a tree." *National Arborist Association:* www.natlarb.com. *International Society of Arboriculture:* www2.champaign.isa-arbor.com.

 Gemologist. A gem of a career: looking at beautiful jewelry all day and deciding how much each piece is worth. Even better, after only a few months, you can become one of only 1,000 people to be certified by the Gemological Institute of America. Never again will anyone be able to pawn off a cubic zirconium as a diamond on you. If you can live with rhinestone pay, you may find this a sparkling career. *Gemological Institute of America:* www.gia.org.

Specialty Seamster. Rhonda Webb fits women who have had mastectomies with prosthetic breasts and special lingerie. She markets through surgeons and oncologists and meets clients in their own homes. She says, "People are very appreciative. It's so much more relaxed than walking into a cold department store with everyone hearing what your problem is." Under the radar niches: sewing or selling custom garments for paraplegics and quadriplegics, ultraorthodox Sikhs and Jews, corporate concierge sewers, and makers of theater curtains, wheelchair accessories, doll clothing, wedding gowns, company banners, and parachutes. *Professional Association of Custom Clothiers:* www.paccprofessionals.org. *SewStorm:* www.sewstorm.com and Karen Maslowski's book: *How to Start Making Money With Your Sewing.*

 Personal Chef. The United States Personal Chefs Association estimates that 25,000 personal chefs can find employment in the U.S., yet only 4,000 personal chefs are active in the entire world. This career is much better than restaurant cheffing because you cook smaller numbers of meals so you needn't spend long days, nights, and weekends, standing over a hot stove. And unlike when starting out in a restaurant, you design all the menus, a veritable executive chef. *American Personal Chef Association:* www.personalchef.com. *United States Personal Chefs Association:* www.uspca.com.

BHB

 Dog Trainer. Do you have the patience to teach Rover not to chew up the furniture or pee on the floor when Rover's owner can't? Do you like the challenge of convincing a dog to let you walk it rather than have it walk you? Do you think you can train a dog's owner to control its dog? Consider a career in dog training. Best way for *you* to train is to visit a few local training centers, watch a few pros work, and ask your favorite for an apprenticeship. Most states don't have licensure requirements. Anyone can claim to be a dog trainer, so choose your mentor carefully. *National Association of Dog Obedience Instructors:* www.nadoi.org.

(Neat Niche) **Service Dog Trainer.** We all know about guide dogs for the blind, but demand is increasing for dogs for the deaf. Your job is to train the dog to alert its master to specific sounds like a smoke alarm, a ringing phone, and a knock at the door. Because these dogs are generally large, and much of the training requires moving the dog, service dog trainers must be physically strong. *National Service Dog Center:* http://deltasociety.org/dsb000.htm.

(Neat Niche) **Working Dog Trainer.** What sort of work do working dogs do? Typical jobs are sniffing out drugs for the United States Customs Service and finding injured people in wreckage for local police departments. *Working Dogs Cyberzine:* www.workingdogs.com.

Pet Sitter. Americans are nuts about their pets. Forty-three percent of United States households have pets, more than the percentage of households with kids! Because pet owners travel just like other people, pet-sitting services are gaining customers. Pet sitting can be done three ways. You can open your home to Muffin, live in Muffin's home while its owners are gone, or make daily stops at Muffin's home. Don't think that pet sitting is the same as pet playing. Crises occur. Muffin can be sick or develop a case of separation anxiety when you show up. In such cases, you must instantly become a pet shrink or find yourself with a pooch that refuses to go for a walk or takes a bite out of your leg. More often, it's a matter of accommodating pet idiosyncrasies, like the cat who likes to roll around in the tub each morning after its owner showers. To keep the cat happy, the pet sitter moistens the tub and puts the cat in. The more likely way to make a middle-class income from pet sitting is to have a staff of sitters but that means you don't get to play with Muffin. *National Association of Professional Pet Sitters:* `www.petsitters.org`.

Pyrotechnician. Staging pyrospectaculars sounds like a blast, but it isn't easy to soar into this field. The problem is that it's dominated by a small number of private, mainly family-run businesses that like to keep their sky shows to themselves. But if this career sounds more exciting than a rocket's red glare, here are some good ways to start. Contact *American Fireworks News:* `www.fireworksnews.com`, *and Bob Weaver's Web site at* `www.fireworksland.com`. Your next step is to attend training offered during the spring by a local fireworks company or the two-day shooter's certification course offered each year by *Pyrotechnics Guild International* (`www.pgi.org`). Working as an assistant at a July 4th show or two also is worthwhile. It's seasonal work for most people in the field, but a small percentage keep busy year-round shooting fireworks for movies, TV, theater, concerts, and sporting events. *American Pyrotechnic Association:* `www.americanpyro.com`. *International Pyrotechnics Society:* `www.intlpyro.org`.

Product Tester. How'd you like to play with toys for a living? Be a toy tester for Mattel or Hasbro. Michael Ferraro tastes Godiva Chocolate for a living. Jack Brashears' job is tasting Jack Daniels whiskey. Product testers check out everything from software to cars. The field has limitations, though. A rather lazy person contacted the Simmons Mattress Company to ask if it uses mattress testers. They said no.

Diver. I wish I could tell you that the stereotype matches the reality, gliding through glistening tropical waters, harvesting abalone. Fact is, 90 percent of divers are construction workers for whom diving is just a mode of transportation to the job site. Except that you have the added challenge of doing it under the sea, so you can't run down to Home Depot for a part. That said, diving has pluses. Within a few years of deciding to become a diver — admittedly at low pay and with long hours — it proves to be one of the few outdoor careers that doesn't require a college education that can earn you $40,000 to $70,000 for a nine-month work year. Engineers can make more. You get to travel all over the world — often on a moment's notice. And there are prized neat niches: police divers who look for guys who have been fitted with cement shoes, research divers who assist marine biologists, and journalist divers who write articles and take pictures for magazines, books, and even screenplays. Before you take the plunge (I couldn't resist), remember that a typical job is working in the Gulf of Mexico, repairing oil rigs. *National Association of Commercial Divers:* www.naocd.org. *A no-holds-barred article:* www.naocd.org/schools.htm.

Work with People and Data

Optometrist. "Better with lens A or lens B?" After a while, I can never tell and feel like a dunce. In any case, optometrists examine, diagnose, and treat eye conditions, usually by prescribing glasses or contact lenses. In some states, they're even allowed to do some minor surgery. Optometry is among the most rewarding health careers because it identifies serious problems that usually have a ready cure. And because the population is aging, and because optometrists are a lower-cost alternative to ophthalmologists (medical eye doctors), the job market for optometrists is good. *American Optometric Association:* www.aoa.net.

Orthoptist. This is another option for people who'd like to be a doctor but don't have the grades or desire to spend that much time in school. Like an eye doctor (ophthalmologist), but under his general supervision, you check vision, perform tests from depth perception to color blindness, and do patient education. Orthoptists more often work with children. Any bachelor's degree plus a two-year program earns you a 35K salary to start and a career that some orthoptists say feels rather like being a physician. *Orthoptics Online:* www.orthoptics.org.

Pharmacist. Mushing medicines together with mortar and pestle? Forget about it. Today's pharmacist is often a front-line healthcare provider, teaching diabetics how to inject themselves with insulin, assisting with blood pressure monitoring, and ensuring that people know how to take their medications. The latter isn't as easy as it sounds. Many older people must take many medications, each of which must be taken at a different time, some of which must be taken on an empty stomach, others when not drowsy. Perhaps the most important thing a pharmacist does is ensure that drugs can be taken together. The TV show *Dateline* did a test in which an obviously pregnant woman walked into ten pharmacies asking whether two drugs could be taken together. Six of the ten pharmacists said yes. In fact, when a pregnant woman takes those two drugs together, it's lethal. Each year, thousands of people are hospitalized because they take prescription medications improperly. Pharmacists can be lifesavers. Some of the more interesting pharmacy jobs are in drug companies' research departments. Second choice: hospital pharmacies. In addition to filling prescriptions, you may conduct research, instruct interns, and assist surgeons in preparing infusions. *American Council on Pharmaceutical Education:* www.aacp.org/Students/students.html.

Genetic Counselor. We are becoming ever more aware that we are greatly affected by our genes. The upshot of recent *Time* and *Newsweek* cover stories is that our personalities and intelligence are significantly mediated by our biology. What do genetic counselors do? Typical example: A married couple both suffer from severe depression. They're thinking about having a child. A genetic counselor helps them understand the risk that their child will suffer from depression, facilitates their deciding whether to get pregnant, and helps them make peace with their decision. People enter this field from a wide range of disciplines including biology, psychology, nursing, public health, and social work. *National Society of Genetic Counselors:* www.nsgc.org.

OOH

Dietitian/Nutritionist. They're not just in the hospital basement any more. As we get more health conscious, corporations hire dietitians to plan healthy meals for their employee cafeterias and to promote sensible eating habits. (Frankly, I'd rather have a pizza.) Food manufacturers and supermarket chains use dietitians to evaluate prepared foods and put interesting low-calorie recipes such as endive salad with radicchio and sun-dried tomatoes into their ads.

UNCONVENTIONAL WISDOM

Endive, radicchio, and sun-dried tomatoes are undeniably trendy, but why? They are three of the world's worst-tasting edibles. How do such things become "in"? Health spas, weight-loss clinics and prisons use dietitians to make sure that visitors have a balanced diet. We don't want to lack any of the four basic food groups, now do we? My daughter says that our refrigerator seems to have a different four basic food groups: snack foods, jams, condiments, and science experiments.

UNCONVENTIONAL WISDOM

By the way, why do prisoners get dietitians to ensure that their diets carefully reflect the four basic food groups when your average teenager's diet is more out of balance than a unicyclist?

The previously mentioned dietitian careers are growing, but most dietitians still are kept busy with hypertension, diabetes, and obesity, in hospitals, clinics, and in their own private practices. I'm still hungering for that pizza, but I'll settle for some chow fun (fat, greasy, delicious Chinese noodles). *American Society for Nutritional Sciences:* www.faseb.org/asns. *American Dietetic Association:* www.eatright.org.

 Manager. Many people like to manage projects and other people. It's a good thing. Despite all the downsizing, the United States still has 36 million managers. What makes a management position good? The particular industry or government agency isn't so crucial. These things are

OOH

✔ An organization with enough money to do things right and pay you reasonably

✔ An organizational culture that values excellence *and* its people

✔ Compatible co-workers, supervisees, and supervisors

Assess those things before accepting a position.

That's what *you're* looking for, but what are employers craving? Kathryn and George Petras, in *Jobs,* describe today's employable manager: "Multilingual, a generalist with technical skills, computer literate, a doer, not a follower, a team player or team leader, a change agent."

You need to know about some downsides to a career in management. The workplace hierarchy is flatter, so opportunities for promotion are fewer. Indeed, a recent American Management Association survey of middle managers found that only 43 percent thought their job was secure, compared with 72 percent in 1991. And while on the job, managers certainly have their work cut out for them. Their bosses demand ever more productivity at the same time as new laws make it tougher to fire incompetents. And often, you're asked to supervise people who aren't even in the same city. For all that, companies should pay 100 grand, don't you think? Frankly, because of all the downsides, I believe that management can be considered a cool career only if you make the effort to see that the job you accept meets the requirements listed above. *About.com's management portal:* management.about.com. *For executive networking:* www.netshare.com. *Jobs:* www.careerjournal.com, www.execunet.com, www.futurestep.com.

(Neat Niche) **College Administrator.** A college campus is a great place to be a manager. Who can resist a beautiful environment, intelligent people, learning opportunities all around you, a prosocial mission, and work hours that tend to be more moderate than in the private sector — not to mention that things really lighten up between semesters and all summer? And few organizations have as many managers: often multiple layers of management for everything from governmental affairs to the physical plant. The downside is that office politics are particularly vicious on many college campuses. And political correctness is epidemic — how ironic that universities, traditionally the clarion callers for free speech are today among its greatest censors. Not surprisingly, colleges want their managers to have graduate degrees. It wouldn't look good if an organization selling degrees doesn't require them of its managers. *American Association of Higher Education:* www.aahe.org. *Jobs:* www.chronicle.com and www.hire-ed.org.

(Neat Niche) **College Student Affairs Administrator.** This career has nothing to do with steamy dorm room flings. College student affairs administrators coordinate the nonacademic part of student life, from student orientation to graduation. For example, they supervise the fraternities, coordinate residence hall activities and intramural sports, and sponsor antidrug programs. *National Association of Student Personnel Administrators:* www.naspa.org.

(Neat Niche) **Court Administrator.** One thing I've learned since writing the last edition of this book is that for many people, a job's setting can be as important as its tasks. Courts tend to be well funded, attractive, peaceful workplaces — unless of course, two lawyers are screaming at each other or a perpetrator decides to go nuts in the courtroom. (Oh, that was a TV show. Sorry.) Courts need administrators to do everything from coordinating judges' schedules, to figuring out how to get enough jurors, to developing more efficient systems for processing traffic tickets. And because these are government jobs, benefits are good, vacations long, and job security maximum. *National Association for Court Management:* http://nacm.ncsc.dni.us.

(Neat Niche) **Performing Arts Manager.** Many aspiring actors, singers, and dancers, who have realized why the word "starving" so often appears next to the word "artist," move to the back office as a way of staying around the field they love. Today's performing arts managers do more than supervise ticket sales. Indeed, their main job is usually to direct fundraising: coordinate galas, direct mail solicitations and the Web marketing effort, and schmooze with potential donors. The coolest such job may be the artistic director, who gets to choose what goes on stage and hire the director, crew, and perhaps on-stage staff. Performing arts manager salaries generally are low but survivable. Many people are willing to live modestly for a life that is even tangentially related to their creative love. *National Association of Performing Arts Managers and Agents:* www.napama.org. *Top training program for orchestra management:* www.symphony.org.

(Neat Niche) **Information Technology Manager.** This is where the jobs are. The term, "IT Manager" subsumes three kinds of jobs. You can manage an application, for example, the upgrading of an Oracle database. Or you can manage a desktop, for example, a company's UNIX network. Or you can manage an infrastructure, for example, an *application service provider* — a service that provides a Web site with complex software. No matter the specialty, information technology is among the world's fastest-changing fields. If you love life on the cutting edge yet have the communication skills to work with mere mortals, IT management gives you great opportunity for money, new learning, and for advancing the world's ability to communicate and conduct commerce. *Information Technology Association of America:* www.itaa.org. *IT Careers:* www.itcareers.com. (*See separate profiles in this chapter for Systems Analyst, Hardware Engineer, Software Engineer, Web Designer, Web Developer, Webmaster, Web Editor, and Database Administrator.*)

(Neat Niche) **Government Manager.** Aspiring managers shouldn't overlook government positions. Eighty percent of government jobs are managerial and professional compared with 25 percent in the private sector. In addition to quantity, government jobs often offer higher quality benefits, stability, and colleagues dedicated to the public interest. Plus, government agencies are encouraging a more customer-service orientation among their employees, so the stereotype of the semicomatose government worker is becoming less accurate. www.usajobs.opm.gov *lists all federal openings. For state and local government jobs, see* www.rileyguide.com/gov.html.

(Neat Niche) **Work-Family Manager.** According to *Self* magazine, this job title didn't even exist a decade ago. Yet today, thousands of companies have hired managers to develop and implement family friendly work policies such as flexible work scheduling, dependent care, and family leave. Most such managers have a human resource background. Average salary: $70,000. Work-family managers are overwhelmingly female. *Society for Human Resource Management:* www.shrm.org. *Jobs:* www.hrworld.com *and* www.hrimmall.com.

(Neat Niche) **Telecommuting Manager.** Already 12 million Americans work at home for at least part of the week, and this number will increase. Companies know they save money by not having to provide office space and by allowing their employees to avoid energy-draining commutes. Indeed virtual corporations — in which corporate headquarters doesn't even exist and all employees work out of their homes or briefcases — are on the rise. When meetings are necessary, a hotel conference room is rented. Telecommuting managers ensure that home-based employees don't spend the entire workday fooling around. Video surveillance (oops, I mean conferencing) will become more common. *Telecommuting management portal:* www.gilgordon.com/hub2.htm.

(Neat Niche) **Project Manager.** The project can be a new piece of software, an expansion into the Mexican market, or building a satellite. In any case, the project manager's job is to develop a design for the project and then coordinate its completion, usually using scheduling software. This job is good for someone who is second best in many things; for example, a software project manager needs to be good if not tops in programming, managing, art, interface design, and marketing. Project managers like their job because it has clearly defined milestones — lots of opportunities for clear wins. I just checked employment Web sites, and tons of job openings existed for project managers, usually but not always technology-related. James Lewis's book: *The Project Manager's Desk Reference.*

(Neat Niche) **Product Manager.** It's fun to be in charge of a product, even if it's toilet paper. You get to supervise decisions about everything: how thick it should be, should it be embossed with dots or doves, is it worth paying more to get extra soft paper, what picture goes on the packaging, how the sales force pitches the product, whether advertising dollars are weighted more heavily toward print, TV, or point-of-purchase? Linda Gorchels' book: *The Product Manager's Handbook.*

(Neat Niche) **Facilities Manager.** You run a corporation's facilities, from deciding where to lease to hiring the maintenance crew. My favorite subniche: stadium management. *International Facilities Management Association:* www.ifma.org. *Stadium Manager's Association:* www.stadianet.com.

(Neat Niche) **Association Manager.** Thousands of professional organizations exist, from professional associations to chambers of commerce. Each uses managers. One way to get a job created for you is to approach organizations that have been volunteer-run and are ready for a step up. Or start your own association. Surprisingly, many fields don't have one. What does an association manager do? Typically he ensures that new members are recruited, the membership list is maintained, dues are collected, the newsletter is sent out, the Web site is optimized, and meetings and conferences are planned and promoted. *American Society of Association Executives:* www.asaenet.org.

(Neat Niche) **City Manager.** You're involved in all aspects of running a city, from distributing the budget to overseeing park renovation to hiring key personnel. City managers are among the more powerful government officials who don't have to run for election. A master's in public administration is usually required. *International City/County Management Association:* www.icma.org.

(Neat Niche) **Environmental Manager.** Government agencies and corporations hire environmental managers to develop plans to minimize pollution to water, air, and soil, and to develop remediation plans when things go awry. Corporate environmental managers also draft environmental impact reports before expanding operations. *National Registry of Environmental Professionals:* www.nrep.org. *Jobs:* www.eco.org, www.environmentalcareer.com.

(Neat Niche) **Nonprofit Manager.** It's true that nonprofit management is especially difficult because staff is often largely volunteer and funds are limited, but The Cause is sometimes enough to make it all worthwhile. *About.com's nonprofit portal:* nonprofit.about.com. *Jobs:* www.idealist.org and www.nptimes.com.

(Neat Niche) **Community Affairs Manager.** For selfish and altruistic reasons, many companies, TV and radio stations, nonprofits, universities, and hospitals work hard at being good community citizens. Your job is to direct those efforts. You may set up a community blood pressure screening, a Christmas toy giveaway, or sponsor a neighborhood dispute resolution service. The usual point of entry is a college internship or volunteer position. *Public Affairs Council:* www.pac.org.

(Neat Niche) **Healthcare Administrator.** What's a healthcare system to do? Technology is advancing, healthcare laws are changing, HMOs are squeezing, population is aging, hospitals are closing, stand-alone clinics are opening, home healthcare is growing, and government regulations are increasing. The answer: Hire more healthcare administrators to make sense of the madness. But with increased pressure for cost-control, the number of administrators is stagnant. Yes, you can probably land a job with a master's in health administration from one of the 67 accredited programs, but who gets hired first? Physicians with MBAs. It's a good option for the doc who's had enough patient care and is tired of fighting with HMOs and Medicare to get reimbursed. Job prospects are best in home health agencies and group medical practices. *About.com's hospital administration portal:* hospital.about.com. *American College of Healthcare Administrators:* www.achca.org.

(Neat Niche) **Public Health Administrator.** Working for a government agency, you may coordinate healthcare programs for the poor, direct a safe-sex campaign, or administer vaccination programs. *Career Espresso:* www.sph.emory.edu/studentservice/Career.html.

(Neat Niche) **Human Resources Manager.** HR managers usually wear one of three hats. You can be a hiring specialist, for example, trying to recruit those tough-to-find programmers. You can be a benefits expert, for example, making sure that employees take maximum advantage of their benefits. Finally, you can be a problem preventer/solver. In that role, you may develop programs to prevent or deal with workplace violence, drugs, or racial enmity, and serve as mediator when problems arise. An ever larger part of an HR manager's work deals with issues of race, gender, and disabilities. The good news is that you generally get to be the nice guy. While other managers' main job is to make workers do more, better, and faster, your job is to keep things human. Yes, you're also trying to build the bottom line, but your efforts generally have a more compassionate quality — unless you're the designated terminator. *About.com's human resources portal:* humanresources.about.com. *Society for Human Resources Management:* www.shrm.org. (Also see Personnel Recruiter profile on page 21)

School Administrator. You may not think that turnover is high among school principals. It's a prestigious job with an important mission. Yet turnover *is* high, and here's why: Principals report that it typically takes two years of time-consuming, highly stressful, union-monitored effort to have even a chance of getting rid of an incompetent teacher. Thus, most principals feel forced to look the other way, and instead, must take the flak from complaining parents and students. Another source of principals' stress is that they often must take on more tasks than in the past. For example, they may be charged with establishing school-based drug/alcohol/crime prevention programs and developing partnerships with local businesses. Teachers' jobs are ever tougher, with more limited-English-proficient immigrant students, orders from on-high requiring teachers to serve ever more severely learning-disabled and emotionally disturbed students in the regular classroom. And not just serve them, but achieve the new mantra, "All students can learn to high standards." Principals must manage to keep teacher morale high under these trying circumstances. Yet another demoralizer is salary. The strong teachers' unions have gotten solid salary increases for teachers but administrators' salaries haven't kept pace. The result is that teacher salaries often approach those of the principals. The silver lining in all of this is that the job market for aspiring principals has never been better. And a principalship is a launchpad for often more-rewarding jobs as a district or county school administrator. *American Association of School Administrators:* www.aasa.org. Ronald Thorpe's book: *The First Year As Principal: Real World Stories from America's Principals.*

(Neat Niche) **Private School Founder.** The public schools, especially in mixed-socioeconomic areas, are increasingly prioritizing the needs of low-achieving children over those of other children. Parents of average and high achievers are becoming convinced that these schools are inhibiting their children from achieving their full potentials. Even liberal parents committed to the concept of public education are sending their children to private schools lest they sacrifice their children in the name of a political philosophy. Even the nation's leading public school cheerleaders, Al Gore and the Clintons, wouldn't send their children to the DC public schools. If you're willing to endure the headaches of starting and running a private school, you can find great demand. Your school needn't be expensive. Many parents don't care much about fancy facilities — better good teachers in wooden buildings than wooden teachers in good buildings. I know of a school that recently opened in Napa, California. It's starting out in a large tent, yet there's a waiting list for admission. Parents care that their schools have good teachers, good kids, and a fascinating curriculum. Provide those and you'll always have a waiting list, and you may even change the lives of children in ways that few other people do. *International Academy for Educational Entrepreneurship:* www.edentrepreneurs.org. Don Leisey's book: *The Educational Entrepreneur: Making a Difference.*

Labor Relations Specialist. Most of your work is done before you ever sit down at the negotiating table. Through the year, your job is to learn the needs of labor and management and to resolve disputes as they arise. If you work for a union, you may also try to unionize workplaces. Come contract time, the bulk of your work is still away from the negotiating table. At that point, your main job is to do the research needed to bolster your side's position. And then, of course, during negotiations, you get to play hardball, poker, or win-win. *Training opportunity: AFL-CIO Organizing Institute:* www.aflcio.org/orginst/index.htm.

Political Campaign Manager. Everyone who runs for office, from school board member in Lost Gulch, Wyoming, to president of the United States, needs a campaign manager. The campaign manager researches the opinions and voting patterns in the district, helps develop the candidate's themes, plans fundraisers, coordinates the direct mail and Web site, hires staff, trains phone bank workers, coordinates the door-to-door campaign, excites the media with a nonstop barrage of "news," and even helps design the campaign button. It's an exciting job: You're in charge of a winner-take-all contest that can make a difference in society. Start out by volunteering to assist in running the campaign for a local politician. www.politicalresources.com. *Links: National Political Index:* www.politicalindex.com.

In our crazy system, our leaders get elected largely on who presses the most flesh, buys the best database of expected voters, makes the speech with the most focus-group-approved soundbites, and more important, extracts the most dollars from special interest groups. If I had my way, elections would be just two weeks long and funded completely with a moderate amount of tax dollars. Each registered voter would receive a booklet with each candidate's voting record and personal statement. During those two weeks, the candidate could use the tax dollars to campaign as he or she saw fit and would be required to participate in at least one televised debate sponsored by the League of Women Voters. That's it. Substance, not fluff, and much less chance of our politicians landing in the hip pockets of special interest groups. Perhaps more important, because of the brief, honorable campaign, outstanding candidates, daunted or disgusted by what it currently takes to get elected, would be more likely to come forward.

Military Officer. This job title is a catchall for hundreds of occupations, from manager to doctor to engineer. A military career has many pluses: excellent free training, extensive benefits, a noble mission, and esprit de corps unmatched in most civilian jobs. Of course, you have to accept a life of uniforms, the bureaucracy to end all bureaucracies, and transfers to places you'd otherwise never choose. (Aberdeen, Texas, anyone?) And, oh yes, you can get your head blown off. Among the many routes in are ROTC, enlistment, Officers Candidate Schools, and the prestigious service academies such as West Point. Those service academies arguably offer the finest undergraduate experience anywhere. If you think you may like to "be all you can be," start by checking out the clearinghouse for military-related careers: www.militarycareers.com.

Succession Planning Consultant. A tough time for family businesses is when one generation realizes that it must allow the next generation to take over. Family members are often too emotionally involved to develop a wise succession plan on their own. Enter the consultant, a combination psychologist and businessperson. www.succession-planning.com. William Rothwell's book: *Effective Succession Planning*.

Fee-only Financial Planner. This is an especially good field for the older career-seeker. Most people with money are older and tend to trust people their own age. Especially as boomers age and worry about how in the world they're going to save the zillion dollars they say we'll need for retirement, the need for financial planners is accelerating. Social Security is unlikely to help. A survey found that more 20-somethings believe in UFOs than believe they'll ever see a penny of Social Security. And with an ever-wider range of investment and insurance options, many confused people want help. The good financial planner is as much a financial therapist as number cruncher or mutual fund picker. Unfortunately, the traditional financial planner has a conflict of interest: She makes more money if you buy high-commission investments and insurance, and makes even more if you buy and sell often. Enter the fee-only financial planner. These professionals get paid a flat fee, so their only motivation is to please the client. How to get clients? Develop relationships with estate-planning attorneys and make presentations at workplaces. Some say that the best financial planner training is the one you get if a brokerage house hires you. Others recommend the two-year, $2,000 self-study course offered by the *College for Financial Planning*: www.icfp.org. *National Association of Personal Financial Advisors (for fee-only financial planners)*: www.napfa.org.

Debt Collection Specialist. If you don't mind representing a business against a debtor, this is a good career. It's one-on-one problem solving — the sort of work many people like. And if the customer can't pay — the world doesn't end. There's always another debtor to call on. That's the key to success in this business — staying pleasant, solution-oriented, and nonconfrontational. It's a great home business. You can sit at home in your comfies with your feet up, with no overhead, and earn 25 percent to 50 percent of every dollar you retrieve for your client businesses. And there are plenty of dollars to retrieve. Consumer debt is $1.5 *trillion* dollars. *American Collectors' Association:* www.collector.com.

> (Neat Niche) **Commercial Debt Negotiator.** Many businesses accumulate too much debt. They hire you to negotiate with banks, collection agencies, and other creditors to accept a discount in exchange for immediate payment. You get clients by cold-calling businesses, or from bankers or collection agencies that refer customers with problems. Check to be sure that it's legal in your state to represent debtors in this way.

College Financial Aid Counselor. Guess how much it costs to send two kids to a brand-name private college for their bachelor's and master's degrees? $500,000! So, it's no surprise that frantic parents are flocking to financial aid counselors. These counselors function like tax accountants, helping you figure out how to plan and fill out the college and government forms to maximize your financial aid. *National Association of Student Financial Aid Administrators:* www.nasfaa.org. *College is Possible:* www.collegeispossible.com *and click on "Paying for College;"* Anna Leider's book: *Don't Miss Out.*

Corporate Intelligence Officer. An article in *Working Woman* reassures us, "No need for a cloak or dagger. Corporate intelligence staffers comb through perfectly legitimate sources of information — newspapers, competitors' sales materials, speeches, credit reports, databases, and interviews for the goods on competitors. "You really have to be good at getting information, which means getting people to trust you." *Society of Competitive Intelligence Professionals:* www.scip.org.

Work with People and Words

Public speaking

Radio/TV News Reporter. This is one of those long-shot glamour professions that may be worth the risk. You get to investigate fast-breaking stories, sometimes in dangerous environments, and report your findings live. Even in nonemergency situations, you usually have just an hour or two to gather your information before making your report. With the thousands of local news broadcasts, you may be able to land a job, at least if you're willing to start out in Podunk and work nights and weekends. Musts are writing skills, a good memory, and an authoritative on-air presence. News reporting is a launchpad for a news anchor position, which in addition to offering fame, pays awfully well for a job that mainly consists of reading aloud. *Investigative Reporters and Editors, Inc:* www.ire.org. *Center for Investigative Reporting:* www.muckraker. *Society for Professional Journalism:* www.spj.org. *About.com's broadcasting portal:* broadcasting.about.com. *RadioOnline:* www.radioonline.org. *Jobs:* www.tvjobs.com, http://www.journalism.berkeley.edu/jobs.

Sports Announcer. Sports continues to be a passion for millions of Americans. That's good news and bad news. The good news is there's plenty of demand for sports announcers: on radio, TV, before the game, during the game (play-by-play and color), and after the game. The bad news is that it half the sports fans would give their eyeteeth to make a living as a sports broadcaster. Who does make a living at it? People with the ability to analyze what's going on beneath the surface and who are a goldmine of interesting trivia to fill the large spaces of time in which nothing's going on in the game. Pluses are a commanding voice and a degree from a top broadcast journalism program like the one at Syracuse University. Even then, your first job will be likely to sound like this: "We're in the top of the 5th. Jasper High School's up 1-0."

Talk Show Host. I excluded this career from this book's first edition because the odds of making a living at it are small. But so many people see it as their dream career that I decided to include it and simply tell you how to maximize your chances of defying the odds. Start by thinking about what your unique style would be. Are you a particularly tough interviewer? Someone from the political far right or far left? With encyclopedic knowledge and palpable passion about something? An unusually self-revealing person? You'll probably increase your chances of success by incorporating your unusual characteristics into your talk show. For me, it's that I have the ability to answer practical questions quickly. So my show is heavily call-in and about a practical topic: work. I also like doing interviews in which I don't just ask the questions, I also participate in a conversation/debate — I often contribute almost as much content as the guest does. I'm also constitutionally fast. I talk fast; I interrupt. Rather than homogenizing myself into being just another mid-speed-talking host, I allow myself to be my regular, fast self. So, what are *your* unique attributes and interests? Make those the centerpiece of your radio persona and structure for your talk show. Then practice interviewing people and taking "call-ins," using that style. Do it at home and record the interviews. Critique yourself mercilessly. Have friends and family critique you too. When you've taped an interview you're proud of, edit it down to three to five minutes of great excerpts and hand-deliver it to the program director of every local radio or TV station. Any station that won't let you see the program director gets a mailed copy and a follow-up phone call two days later. That's how I got to host my first talk show, and now I'm in my 13th year as producer and host of "Work with Marty Nemko" on a National Public Radio affiliate in San Francisco. *Radio Online:* www.radioonline.org. *Talker's Magazine:* http://www.talkers.com.

Professional Speaker. This is another fantasy career with reasonable prospects. Despite the plethora of electronic alternatives, people want to hear live speakers. Quite a few people, including some no-names, make a living spreading their gospel at conventions, college campuses, corporate headquarters, and general public forums. Even cruise ships have added speakers to their menu of entertainment. Find an in-demand topic on which you are or could become an expert. Then read books such as *Speak and Grow Rich,* study tapes of great speakers, craft a solid outline of your speech, build in something experiential so they're not just listening to a talking head, and practice, practice, practice until you're able to convey something of real substance while making a powerful connection with your audience. Consider joining a local chapter of Toastmasters, where you learn public speaking principles and get to give talks to fellow members, a sympathetic audience. When you have a knock-your-socks-off sample videotape, send it to conference program chairs and lecture bureaus. The latter can help market you. *National Speakers Association:* www.nsaspeaker.org. *Toastmasters International:* www.toastmasters.org.

> (Neat Niche) **Speaking Coach.** Most of us are called on to "say a few words," whether at a staff meeting, a professional conference, a venture capitalist pitch session, or a toast at our child's wedding. If you're a good public speaker, why not teach others what you've learned? Acquire clients by giving talks on how to give a speech at professional conferences or at local corporations. Don't forget about law firms — many attorneys earn their living as smooth talkers.

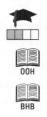

Employee Trainer. The need for training has never been greater. More students graduate from high school and even college without basic skills at the same time the modern workplace requires them to be communication whizzes and technomavens. Even those who graduated college with enough skills soon find they need to upgrade. Older workers feel they must stay up-to-the minute lest they be permanently put out to pasture. Trainers are needed in so many areas: from basic reading to advanced UNIX, peak performance to retirement planning, database management to diversity management. A current challenge for trainers is how to make people in welfare-to-work programs employable with today's ever more complex job requirements. *American Society for Training and Development:* www.astd.org. C. Leslie Charles' book: *The Instant Trainer.*

> (Neat Niche) **Software Trainer.** New software and new versions of old software continue to be released. Heaven forbid you should be saddled with Version 7.0 when Version 8.0 is available. As a trainer, it's a plus if you're certified by the software's manufacturer. Jobs are plentiful within large organizations, at training schools, at community colleges and adult schools.

> (Neat Niche) **Dream-Career Trainer.** Train clients for those difficult-to-get-into fields to which many people aspire: rock star, talk show host, athlete, comedian, artist, screen writer, voiceover artist, film director, or Web site developer, for example.

Health Educator. HMOs know that an ounce of prevention is not only better than a pound of cure, it costs less. HMOs' ounce of prevention is to hire health educators to teach people such things as how to lose weight, fit exercise into a busy day, or lower their cholesterol (as though people don't know that broccoli is good and cheeseburgers are bad). Nonetheless, a job conducting health seminars is, as jobs go, pretty salubrious. *Organization of Healthcare Educators:* www.o-h-e.org.

Golf Seminar Instructor. Suzanne Woo, a former lawyer, now makes her living teaching people the rules and etiquette of golf — equipment purchase, golf teacher selection, and the real draw: how to use golf for networking and to learn about co-players. Behavior on the course usually mirrors behavior in business. *A business golf Web site is* www.bizgolf.com. Gary McCord's book: *Golf For Dummies.*

Teacher. Here's how *The Princeton Review* Web site describes teaching: "Usually beginning at 8 a.m., teachers must begin the difficult task of generating interest in their often sleepy students. A good sense of humor and the ability to think like their students helps." Don't get seduced by 3 p.m. dismissal bells and summers off. Teaching today is no cushy gig. Schools now put everyone from the mentally challenged to the mentally gifted in the same class. It takes exceptional talent to develop no-snooze lessons for that wide a range of students, often including immigrant kids who may speak Spanish, Chinese, or Tagalog, but little English. Teachers also have far less power to remove children who chronically disrupt the class — and it only takes one. Students with severe behavior and emotional problems used to be placed in special classes. Now, except in the most extreme cases, they're mainstreamed. And new teachers, despite having the least experience, are often given the toughest classes. Now add the many hours after school preparing interesting yet valuable lessons for that wide range of students, correcting papers, and dealing with parents who complain that Johnny's individual needs aren't being met. Finally, remember that teachers are with kids all day, so they don't get much intellectual stimulation. You need a special mentality to do that for 25 years. I paint this stark picture because I believe that teaching is among the more important professions. That's the main reason it is on the list of cool careers. Because most public school teachers, after just two years, receive tenure for life, a bad teacher saddled by the golden handcuffs of job security, can be tempted to stay in the profession forever, damaging 30 kids at a time, year in and year out. So I want to encourage teachers to enter the profession with full knowledge of its realities. Too often, people decide to become teachers based on their own years as a student or on a rewarding experience as a one-to-one tutor. The experience of many of today's classroom teachers is quite different. *About.com's elementary education portal:* k-6educators.about.com. *American Federation of Teachers:* www.aft.org. *Jobs:* www.teacherjobs.com, www.privateschooljobs.com. *Teachers Planet:* www.teachersplanet.com. Pearl Rock Kane's book: *The First Year of Teaching.*

(Neat Niche) **Program Specialist.** Elementary schools often use specialists to visit classrooms to teach art, music, technology, or special education. This tends to be a rewarding job because you're the breath of fresh air in a student's humdrum day, and because you're able to focus on your specialty.

(Neat Niche) **English-as-a-Second-Language Teacher.** Immigration continues to jump. Bilingual education programs (teaching limited-English-proficient students in their native language) have not worked and, in California, been outlawed by voters. (See www.teachersplanet.com) These factors are increasing the need for teachers of English as a second language. ESL teachers are hired by K-12 schools, community colleges, adult schools, and by corporations for their immigrant employees. This career is often gratifying because most students are highly motivated to learn the subject — unlike some other school subjects. *National Clearinghouse for ESL Literacy Education:* www.cal.org/ncle. *Links:* www.ncbe.gwu.edu/links/biesl/esl.htm.

(Neat Niche) **Music or Art Teacher.** After years of decline, the schools are starting to hire more music and art teachers. A *New York Times* piece reported that education budgets throughout the country are showing restorations of money for art and music classes.

Something's wrong when the National Endowment for the Arts gives millions of dollars to a relative handful of artists who produce work that much of the public finds unappealing or even disgusting, while millions of schoolchildren receive little or no art instruction, something that can so enrich the lives even of nonartistic kids.

(Neat Niche) **Vocational/Technical Teacher.** Community colleges and post-secondary career colleges, and some high schools, hire specialists to teach in fields such as technology repair, business education, agriculture, plumbing, and protective services.

(Neat Niche) **Distance-Learning Teacher.** Busy adults are increasingly choosing to take courses online at home. Now the trend is spreading. At UC Berkeley, for example, traditional-age students can, 24/7, crank up any part of an interactive Intro to Chemistry course from their dorm room. And rural high schools can offer a wide array of Advanced Placement courses even if no local teacher is available to teach them. It takes special skills to teach via distance learning, so if you can make this your specialty, you should be in demand. *About.com's distance learning portal:* http://distancelearn.about.com. Karen Mantyla's book, *The 2000/2001 ASTD Distance Learning Yearbook.*

Athletic Coach. I coached an Oakland Boys Club basketball team. I went in with visions of using hoops to help kids triumph over their life circumstances but that proved overly ambitious. Just getting them to pay attention took everything I had. It was fun though, unearthing the neighborhood ringers and convincing them to play on my team. And the games were a rush, constantly figuring out what to do to give your team an edge, and trying to be the role model of calm intensity.

The usual starting job is a high school coaching position, but you only start to earn a decent income at the college level. There, you have additional responsibilities such as meeting with the media and big-time donors. And you must make recruiting trips to convince high school athletes that even though their SAT score is 750 (the verbal *plus* the math) and they have a C average at a weak high school, they can succeed in college classes. Because of Title IX regulations, the number of female sports teams is increasing, so job opportunities are good for women and not so good for men. If I were trying to break in, I'd write a letter to every top college coach in my field and see if I could get some sort of assistant job working for him or her. *Comprehensive Online Access to Coaching Help:* www.coachhelp.com. *Links:* http://careerideas-forkids.com/newpage15.htm.

Clergy. A clergyperson told me that the thing I thought was most important in a cleric turns out not to be a requirement at all: She said that many clergy have serious doubts about the existence of God. They are, however, strongly committed to helping people live richer lives using religion as a foundation. Sometimes this help is direct: sermons, religion classes, and ministering to people at high and low points of their lives, but clergypersons also spend a surprising amount of time in indirect service such as fundraising and administrative work. Except for the long hours and having to be on-call at all hours, the clergy is a wonderful profession with high status, reasonable pay, unmitigated do-gooding, and a good job market except for Protestant ministers (because their churches are merging). The situation is better for rabbis, and excellent for Catholic priests — lifetime celibacy is increasingly unpopular. Indeed, the Catholic Church has run full-page ads attempting to "collar" future priests. The first step toward investigating a career in the clergy: Speak with a clergyperson you respect, then contact the ordination organization for your denomination. *National Conference of Diocesan Vocation Directors:* www.catholic-forum.com/ncdvd. *Ministry Connect:* www.ministry.org. *Ask a Rabbi links:* http://judaism.about.com. Thomas Kunkel's book, *Enormous Prayers.*

Actor. The good news is that the job market may be improving a bit. With the proliferation of Internet video for entertainment and training, increased cable and satellite viewership, and more foreign demand for American productions, the need for actors is increasing. But there's plenty of bad news. For example, 80 percent of actors in the Screen Actors Guild (those who have already acted in a union job) earn less than $5,000 a year from their acting! Even the term *actor* is misleading. It implies you're acting, doing something. For the most part, actors wait. They wait to be hired. Once hired, on the set, they wait for their turn, for the weather to clear, for the technoids to set things up, for the producer, director, and minions to make up their minds. Casting Director Lisa Pirriolli, in *Gig,* says, "It's a horrible life . . . it's all about getting the job and about rejection. If you do get the job, it's all about doing it correctly and getting the next one, and the next one, just trying to become famous. And if you do become famous, it's all about being famous. And then it's about when your star is going to fall."

Okay. Despite it all, you've decided to try to make a living as an actor. Here are some keys to making it: First choose a niche. Are you the insecure villain type? A singing airhead? Be sure your headshot, sample reel, and resume capture your niche, and send the package to local acting agencies. It may be smarter to start in a large city other than Los Angeles or New York, perhaps Toronto ("Hollywood North") or Wilmington, North Carolina ("Hollywood East"). To get leads on gigs, contact each city's film commission. Or start out in *industrials* — training and promotional videos. It'll be much easier to obtain credits and develop a sample reel. To avoid starving in the meantime, rather than or in addition to waiting tables, consider interim jobs that help polish your craft: mock trial participant, mock patient (used in medical school training), role-player in employee training seminars or police crisis simulations, traffic school instructor, and Santa Claus. (Don't let your little kid read that.) *About.com's acting portal:* http://actors.about.com. *More links:* www.aftra.org/resources/links.html. *The Screen Actors Guild's tips for wannabe actors:* www.sag.org/wannabe.html. Robert Cohen's book, *Acting Professionally.*

Musician. Nothing inspires or heals like music. It can lift a depression, tame an angry soul, move one to gyrate with joy — even if you're alone in your kitchen. How terrific to have a career in which music is your main activity. But how do you fight the odds against making a living at it? First, you gotta find out if you really have enough talent. Don't count on your teachers to be candid. They have too much vested interest in encouraging you. Besides, it's hard for someone who knows you to tell you, "You're probably not good enough." How do you discover the truth about your talent? Play for (or send tapes to) people who *don't* know you but are in a position to pay you for your work: orchestra conductors, studio gig contractors, wedding band leaders, nightclub owners, and so on. If you audition 20 times and receive little encouragement, cut your losses. Make music your after-work passion. For example, join a community symphony orchestra. If you get sincere encouragement but not a full-time paying gig, you may have to be entrepreneurial to make a middle-class living. Find great musicians to join your musical group. Then seriously market it. For example, convince local government or corporate leaders to hire you to play at their events, play host to a party for wedding planners, or invite event planners via direct mail to visit your Web site, which contains audio clips of your music. *Musical Online:* www.musicalonline.com.

> (Neat Niche) **Soundtrack Sound Designer.** Increasingly, soundtracks, especially for computer games, are created as much by computer cut-and-pasters as by musical wizards. Instead of standing in the orchestra pit, this conductor sits at a computer with a library of sounds, special effects, music clips, and pastes together the mood of a computer game, commercial, or film trailer. *Cinema Audio Society:* www.ideabuzz.com/cas.

(Neat Niche) **Background Vocalist.** Ooh, ooh, wah, ooh, wah. Yeah, yeah. No this isn't the sound of sex. It's the sound of a background singer. This is an under-the-radar, sometimes well paying career for talented singers who can walk in, read the music, and crank out those "yeahs" and "oohs" so they give you goosebumps. Don't think you can be a second-rate singer. Unless the lead singer is a Celine Dion, background singers are usually better singers.

Incidental Music Composer. This career may provide a way into composing, a hard-to-make-a-living-at profession. Snippets of *incidental music* are everywhere, accompanying the action in a commercial or stage play, introducing a radio show, or welcoming you with those vapid jingles to "cool" Web sites. *American Society of Composers, Authors, and Publishers:* www.ascap.com.

Political Aide. Most politicians have paid aides. They research problems, draft legislation, and sub for the pol at rubber chicken dinners. This is a satisfying job. You actually have some power, and the work is varied and fast-paced. The usual route in is to start as an intern or campaign volunteer. Ask for more responsibility, and prove yourself.

Lobbyist. You're a lobbyist for the National Abortion Rights League. A law you'd like passed would allow teens to have an abortion without parental permission. You may actually have drafted the legislation, and you certainly dug up research that proves its benefits — for example, the legislation would result in fewer teen moms and avoid unsafe abortions. You play host to a cocktail party for key legislators and just enough other folks to make your goal less obvious. You write press releases and try to get on TV and radio to expound your position. That's the life of a *lobbyist*, a professional persuader of politicians. A law degree is a plus, but not essential. Lobbyist jobs are much like the sought-after jobs working for a senator or member of Congress and are easier to land. *American League of Lobbyists:* www.alldc.org.

If political campaigns were publicly funded, legislators would listen more to the public than they would to lobbyists who donate big bucks to campaigns to gain influence.

One-on-one

Speech-Language Therapist. Think of how you feel when you listen to a stutterer. Imagine how he feels. The speech-language therapist treats stuttering and other voice and speaking problems, from cleft palate to limited vocabulary to stroke victims trying to recover their speech. For many patients, progress is slow. Patience is a must. *American Speech-Language-Hearing Association:* www.asha.org. *Stuttering Science and Therapy Web site:* www.casafuturatech.com.

(Neat Niche) **Accent Reduction Specialist.** Many immigrants, especially those in professional jobs, are eager to improve their accents. You can help. To find clients, contact human resource departments at high-tech corporations. They often recruit from Asia to fill programmer, engineer, and scientist positions.

College Admission Consultant. "Which college should I go to?" "How do I get in?" "How do I find the money?" In high schools, college counselors typically help students answer these questions with individual counseling and group presentations. They may also get writer's cramp from cranking out all those student recommendations. In private practice, the work is one-on-one. As usual, specializing is wise, for example, in students with learning problems or those aiming for designer-label colleges. *National Association for College Admission Counseling:* www.nacac.com. *UCLA offers an online training program:* https://www.uclaextension.org/certificated/CF348.cfm?CertNum=CF348.

(Neat Niche) **College-Bound Athlete Consultant.** Many high school students are pulled kicking and screaming into doing their college applications. Not so with college athletes. They may not care any more than their peers about the joys of learning, but they do care about playing ball. These motivated clients make your job fun. You help Bruiser figure out which colleges will let him play a lot and satisfy him academically and socially. You're a bit like a junior Jerry McGuire: "Show me the scholarship!" Michael Koehler's book, *Advising Student Athletes Through the College Recruitment Process.*

Troubled Teen Consultant. Few things are more frustrating to parents than an out-of-control teen: School and parents are ignored, and sex, drugs, and rock-and-roll are extolled. What's a parent to do? They increasingly hire consultants to find after-school programs, tough-love camps, and therapeutic boarding schools, to help Junior — or at least, get the troubled teen out of Mom's and Dad's frazzled hair. *Independent Educational Consultants Association:* www.educationalconsulting.org.

Tutor. Many tutors love their jobs. They wax rhapsodic about the close one-on-one relationships, the visible progress, and the fact that you can earn money with minimal start-up costs and without endless training. How do you make a decent living as a tutor? Let local public school teachers know that, unlike chains such as Sylvan Learning, you make house calls. It also helps if you carve out a niche, for example, students with attention deficit disorder, or math for girls. I often give just one word of advice to people with patience and the ability to explain things clearly, motivate others, and self-promote: tutor.

(Neat Niche) **Computer Tutor.** Get referrals from employers, computer retailers, or local Internet Service Providers, or emulate the guerrilla marketer who got plenty of clients just by standing in front of a computer store and giving his pitch to everyone he saw walking out with a new computer. He often made an appointment on the spot.

Home Schooling Consultant. As disenchantment with public schooling rises, and story after story appears in the media about the high SAT scores and prestigious college admission rates of home-schooled kids, it isn't surprising that two million children are now home-schooled. But home schooling is no easy feat. As a consultant, you help parents and kids design learning programs and iron out problems. *American HomeSchool Association:* www.americanhomeschoolassociation.org. *California Homeschool Association:* www.hsc.org.

Working with People and Things

Polygraph Operator. Would you find it fun figuring out whether people are lying? That's what polygraph (lie detector) operators do. Hook up your subject to a machine that monitors heart rate and brain waves. If things start spiking when you ask, "Did you murder your husband?" your subject may be a step closer to Ol' Sparky. Most polygraph operators work for law enforcement agencies, but polygraph tests also are used by attorneys to prove that their clients are upstanding citizens and in pre-employment testing in sensitive industries such as day-care centers. You don't want a pedophile caring for your darling child. *American Polygraph Association:* www.polygraph.org.

I'd love it if someone developed a pocket-sized lie detector, and every time someone lied to you, it would beep. I'd pay a lot of money for one of those babies.

Occupational Therapist. You help a stroke patient relearn how to drive. You find an alternative for an arthritis patient who can no longer button a shirt. Using a combination of psychology, computers, braces, and a healthy dose of common sense, the occupational therapist is the practical soul who tries to put it all together. Bonus: Just a bachelor's degree in OT should do. The Department of Labor projects fast growth through 2008. *American Occupational Therapy Association:* www.aota.org. *Rehab Options:* www.rehaboptions.com.

OOH

Funeral Director. Many people cringe at this profession, but funeral directors are proud of their work. When a death occurs, a funeral director who helps family members make arrangements that feel right can be a real benefit in a time of need. Alas, too many funeral directors take that opportunity to push $5,000 caskets when a $500 one would do: "You wouldn't want to be cheap with your mother, now would you?" Training is moderate in length, rewards are considerable, and demand is growing thanks to aging boomers and because many funeral directors are about to retire. Not a bad combination. Do me a favor, though. Be sure to spend some time at a funeral home — other than when Granny Fern's lying in state — before deciding on this career.

OOH

Despite projected fast growth in this field, landing a job isn't easy. Because the career is desirable, many people keep this sort of business in the family. It may take a while to convince an employer that you're, pardon the expression, dying for the job. *National Funeral Director Association:* www.nfda.org. *American Board of Funeral Service Education:* www.abfse.org. *FuneralNet:* www.funeralnet.com. *Funeral Consumers Alliance:* www.funerals.org.

Electro-Neurodiagnostic (END) Technician (formerly EEG Technician).
END techs monitor brain waves. Why would you want to do that? In surgery, brain waves indicate how well the anesthesia is working. In a sleep clinic, brain waves help figure out what's causing a person's insomnia. Doctors use them to determine how well a medication is helping an epileptic. This is a cool career because, despite its important healthcare role, it can be learned on the job, and employment prospects are good. *American Society of Electroneurodiagnostic Technologists:* www.aset.org.

Diagnostic Medical Sonographer.
Commonly known as ultrasound techs, they perform sonograms, for example, to noninvasively determine how a pregnant mom and baby are doing, or evaluate a heart problem. *Society of Diagnostic Medical Sonographers:* www.sdms.org.

Low-Investment Food Operations Owner.
Simple, no-seating food operations can be relatively low-risk routes to high income.

(Neat Niche) **Pizza by the Slice Business Owner.** Pizza never goes out of style, has a large markup, and is a relatively simple business. One secret to success is to open your shop within smelling distance of a busy walk-in entrance to a college campus. Remember, the pizza has to be to-die-for. Find an ever-crowded pizzeria that serves delicious pizza and is located far enough from your proposed location that the owner won't fear your competition. Ask the head pizza maker to teach you how to make it. If necessary, pay for your lessons.

(Neat Niche) **Food Carts.** The most important thing about a food outlet is location. Subject to zoning restrictions, carts (a.k.a. roach coaches) enable you to vary location so you can be in front of a busy office building at lunch time, at the main exit of the local high school or college during the afternoon, in front of a busy movie theater in the evening, and near the stadium on game days. Carts not only make good locations possible, they also keep rent low, an unbeatable combination. Good candidates for cart-based businesses: sandwiches, soup, espresso, and pastries.

Espresso is my favorite cart business because the profit margin is so high — that $3 latte costs about a quarter to make. That sort of margin would impress even Joey the Loan Shark. Possible locations: in front of supermarkets, office buildings, hospital lobbies, malls, stadiums, or a combination thereof. As with all businesses, there are things to watch out for. For example, if the landlord sees you getting rich just by pouring coffee, he can toss you and install his intellectually challenged nephew. So get a long lease. Worried about status? Remember, you're not selling coffee, you're president of the Consolidated Cappuccino Company with operations throughout the region. *Links*: www.espressotop50.com. *Specialty Coffee Association of America:* www.scaa.org.

Parking Lot Oil Change Business Operator. Every car needs oil changes, and nearly every car owner finds getting them inconvenient. At best, you sit around at a while-you-wait oil-change service. Otherwise, it's drop off the car, somehow get to work, and somehow get back to the shop. Instead, imagine that when you pull into a parking lot at work, a shopping center, or the airport, you can request an oil change while your car is parked. Isn't that more convenient? What a business: big demand, large income potential, small investment, no extraordinary skills required, and little legitimate competition. Just find a large parking lot owner who'd like a new profit center. Shouldn't be too tough. *The Automotive Oil Change Association:* www.aoca.org.

Working with Words and People

Attorney. You're lousy at science and like to argue, so you go to law school, right? Catch this: Eighty percent of lawyers wish they were doing something else. Despite this statistic and a reputation for sleaze matched only by politicians, armies of college graduates run off to law school seeking money, status, an opportunity to change the world, and/or a *The Practice* wardrobe. It's a myth that law is an easy route to a six-figure income. Assuming you can land a lucrative gig, you'll probably work 60-plus-hour weeks — some law firms buy futons for their offices so the lawyers can sleep there. And many attorneys don't make big money. Indeed, many lawyers are forced to work as powerless paralegals who may make no more than garbage collectors.

Another myth is that lawyers spend most of their time in a courtroom. Even litigators spend only a small fraction of their time before a judge, and transactional attorneys, who draft agreements, may never see the inside of a courtroom. For most law jobs, the ability to make airtight arguments is key, but another essential is being detail-oriented. Law is about preparation, which often means reading through the sheaves of dry material you can't pawn off on your paralegal. Final myth: The law is a good option for people who want to cure social ills. Many students enter law school with that hope. The reality: Only a tiny percentage of lawyers end up with public interest jobs.

No profile of attorneys is complete without a lawyer joke. My current favorite: What do you call a lawyer gone bad? Senator. *About.com's law portal:* http://lawyers.about.com. *American Bar Association:* www.abanet.org. *Atticus Falcon's book,* Planet Law School.

There's money to be made in them thar hills. Most lawyers choose to live in or near big cities, but lawyers are also needed (well, desired) in rural areas.

(Neat Niche) **Computer Law.** My name is McDonald. I register my food business on the Web as www.McDonald#1.com (fictitious). Can the folks from the Golden Arches sue me? Following on the Napster.com lawsuit, I'm a writer, and I claim that anyone copying my articles on the Net without compensating me is infringing on my copyright. Am I right? My employer lends me a computer to use at home during the days I telecommute. One evening, on that computer, I write a love letter to my wife. The employer screens it and says it's unauthorized use of a company computer. Is the company right? Welcome to the world of computer law. *Computer Law Association:* www.cla.org.

(Neat Niche) **Sports Agent.** Ever since Cuba Gooding yelled, "Show me the money!" sports agents have gained a higher profile, not only among the public, but also among pro and even aspiring pro athletes. Most sports agents work for full-service sports management companies such as ProServ, which help with everything from product endorsements to estate planning. *About.com's sports law portal:* http://sportsbusiness. about.com. *Sports Lawyers Association:* www.sportslaw.org.

(Neat Niche) **Adoption Specialist.** How different this is from traditional adversarial lawyering — helping to match a child needing parents with parents wanting to adopt a child. It's a far cry from the other sort of family law: divorcing couples ready to kill each other over an armoire. *American Academy of Adoption Attorneys:* www.adoptionattorneys.org.

(Neat Niche) **Bankruptcy Lawyer.** Bankruptcies are at an all-time high. A lawyer told me that bankruptcy law is among the easiest types of law to practice — the procedures are straightforward and minimally adversarial. James Caher's book, *Debt-Free.*

(Neat Niche) **Employment Lawyer.** This is among the law's fastest-growing specialties. The Clinton-Gore administration extended legal employment remedies for minorities, the disabled, and people of alternative sexual orientations who believe they have been discriminated against in the workplace. Employers must be ever more careful to ensure that they comply with all laws and are prudently responsive to the ever-growing number of lawsuits. Employment lawyers are key. Of course, on the other side, claimants need lawyers to handle their cases. Bottom line: lots of work for lawyers. *National Employment Lawyers Association:* www.nela.org.

(Neat Niche) **Mediator/Arbitrator.** See the mediator profile on page 14.

(Neat Niche) **Education Lawyer.** Johnny has gone through 12 years of schooling and still can't read. Who's responsible? Many parents are claiming that the schools should be and they're hiring lawyers to file big-dollar lawsuits against school districts. Education lawyers, of course, also defend school districts against these and other claims. A typical case may involve a teacher who was fired for incompetence and claims that due process was violated or a child who falls off a schoolyard play structure whose parent claims inadequate supervision. *Education Law Association:* www.educationlaw.org.

(Neat Niche) **Patent Lawyer.** When we think of patents, contraptions may come to mind, but today, patents often are awarded for such things as genes, computer chips, and genetically engineered mice. The patent lawyer obtains that patent. He must understand both the science and the law to convince the United States Patent and Trademark Office that the new product truly is different from existing products. So it's no surprise that most patent lawyers have a science or engineering background in addition to a law degree. Robert Benson, a patent attorney for Human Genome Sciences, loves his job. "In the lab, you can only do so much research work, but as a patent attorney you get to experience literally hundreds of lifetimes of research work." *American Intellectual Property Law Association:* www.aipla.org.

(Neat Niche) **Space Lawyer.** As more and more satellites orbit Earth, disputes arise. Does a country have the right to launch a Star Wars satellite that circles the globe? Who owns which rights to the moon? They're already selling tickets for commercial space flights. What sorts of contracts are needed to protect the spacelines and their passengers? Space law is, as they used to say in the 1960s, a new frontier. *American Bar Association Forum on Space Law:* www.abanet.org/forums/airspace.

(Neat Niche) **Elder Lawyer.** Family members or nursing home staff, exhausted from caring for senile, incontinent patients, often commit elder abuse, leaving old people unturned so they develop bedsores or tied down with restraints for the staff's convenience. Lawyers specializing in elder law argue whether there's legal liability. *National Academy of Elder Law:* www.naela.org.

(Neat Niche) **Franchise Lawyer.** The public is attracted to franchises — paint-by-numbers businesses. Too often, however, the paint quickly fades. Franchisees complain that the promised extensive training turned out to be a quickie or that a foolproof method wasn't. Of course, for every plaintiff's attorney, there's a defense counterpart, so there's ample work to go around. *Franchising World:* www.franchise.org.

(Neat Niche) **Environmental Lawyer.** No one wants to despoil the earth, but companies and government regulators have different ideas of how much despoiling is avoidable. Even within the government, there's confusion as federal, state, and local regulations often contradict each other, providing plenty of fodder for environmental lawyers. *Environmental Law Institute:* www.eli.org. *Environmental Careers Organization*: www.eco.org.

(Neat Niche) **Tax Attorney.** Among law's highest-paid specialties, and it's easy to understand why. A corporation is structuring a deal — do it right and the company can save millions in taxes. Individuals, too, are willing to pay big bucks to a tax attorney — for example, when being audited for deducting that trip to Tahiti.

(Neat Niche) **Estate Attorney.** After a lifetime of work, you've accumulated quite a nest egg. Although you've already been taxed on that income, the government wants to tax it again when you die — nice way for the government to offer its condolences. The estate attorney's job is to write wills and trusts to minimize this double taxation. As baby boomers age, this specialty continues to grow.

Paralegal. To cut costs, paralegals are doing much of the work that lawyers used to do: researching cases, interviewing witnesses and clients, writing reports and legal documents . . . just about everything but appearing in court. You get to do that without needing a bachelor's degree plus three expensive years of law school. The most you'll have to complete is a four-year program, and many firms hire graduates of one- or two-year programs. Job-market dampener: An excess of lawyers is resulting in their being hired as paralegals. *Standing Committee on Legal Assistants, American Bar Association:* www.abanet.org/legalassts.

Administrative Law Judge. This is a *relatively* easy way to become a judge, but you still usually must be a well-connected attorney. The difference from the more familiar kind of judge is that administrative law judges rule on the laws and regulations of public agencies, and the process is more informal. Typical role: A school district offers a child with learning difficulties a special class, but the parents want the district to pay for a special private school. An administrative law judge decides. *Association of Administrative Law Judges:* www.aalj.org. Richard Hermann's book, *The Administrative Law Judge Handbook.*

Hearing Officer. A person denied a welfare claim has due process rights, one of which is the right to plead the case before a hearing officer. You may not need to be a lawyer.

Public Relations/Communications Specialist. I held the stereotypical view of public relations people — sleazebags — until I wrote my first book. In my heart, I believed it deserved to be read, but how was I to get it noticed among the 60,000 other books that were published *that year*? That made me realize that publicists can serve an honorable purpose. *Publicist* is actually only one specialization within the public relations field. Public relations types also develop corporate images consonant with community values, promote anyone from rock star to seminar leader, and of course, do damage control. I recall that when the Oakland Unified School District school board decided to mandate Ebonics for its students, a national firestorm erupted. Then the district hired a public relations firm, and its message was clarified (some say sanitized), and the storm blew over.

That's the bad part of PR. You're often a spin doctor, and you're perceived that way. If you want to be a self-employed PR person, specialize — for example, in environmental groups, biotech companies, or shareholder communications. Key skills include the ability to come up with clever ideas quickly and in quantity and pitch them compellingly to the media. Bonus: Many PR people get to go to cool parties attended by the media and glitterati. My vote for the most effective publicity stunt? When IBM pitted its Big Blue computer against chess superstar, Garry Kasparov. *About.com's public relations portal:* `http://publicrelations.about.com.` *Public Relations Society of America:* `www.prsa.org.` James Ogden's book, *Developing a Creative and Innovative Integrated Marketing Communications Plan.*

(Neat Niche) **Public Relations for the Travel Industry.** Paul Plawin, in *Careers for Travel Buffs,* writes, "In order to write about the delights of the Doral Beach Spa in Miami Beach, a Royal Caribbean Cruise, the beaches of the Bahamas, the fun and frivolity of Southern California, or the fjords of Alaska, public relations people must visit those destinations." Definitely a neat niche.

(Neat Niche) **Public Relations for High-Tech and Biotech Companies.** Companies with technical products include pharmaceutical makers, phone companies, and business-to-business software producers, which are often flush with cash and just starting to recognize the importance of public relations. *International Association of Business Communicators:* `www.iabc.com.`

(Neat Niche) **Investor Relations Specialist.** You may write a mutual fund sales brochure, a company's annual report, or articles for a corporation's shareholder magazine. The best-paying and highest-stakes jobs involve doing dog-and-pony shows to convince large investors, such as mutual fund managers, to invest in your company. *National Investor Relations Institute* `www.niri.org.`

Personal Historian/Biographer. So many parents ask their college student, "What in the world are you going to do with a degree in history?" Well, tell your parents about Ellie Kahn. Her firm, Living Legacies, produces custom-ordered histories of individuals, families, and historical buildings. She's compiled 80 histories in book, video, or audio format. I'm not surprised that she's successful. Most of us are egocentric. Deep down, we'd love to have a book written about us, but how do you turn that into a business? You can contact famous people who are in need of a boost. Offer to write their biography. When they agree, write a book proposal and find a literary agent to peddle it for you. Just plain folks may also want their stories recorded as personal legacies for future generations. Or someone may want a biography of his aging parent or a volume that tells his family history. Market through reunion planners or by placing ads in upscale community newspapers. *Association of Personal Historians:* `www.personalhistorians.org.`

Foreign Service Officer. Imagine working in the United States embassy or consulate in one of 250 foreign countries (the government's choice — Kosovo or Zimbabwe, perchance?). Your first job may include helping schnooks who lost their passports, but things usually get more interesting. Your job may include keeping abreast of political and economic conditions so that you can brief American policymakers. Or you may arrange cocktail parties for business and political leaders of your host country. A cool career but here's the rub: Eight thousand people apply for the 200 openings each year. Better be a good reader and writer, and have a knack for learning a foreign language in six months — and another language two years later. Urdu, anyone? *U.S. Dept. of State, Office of Recruitment:* www.state.gov/www/careers.index.html.

Foreign Language Interpreter or Translator. If you're fully bilingual, this is a pretty easy job: Just repeat what you heard or read. And the field is booming. Why? Asian companies are setting up shop in the U.S. Likewise, U.S. firms are importing Asian scientists, engineers, and computer programmers, and increased numbers of immigrants are entering the courts and medical systems. Most in-demand languages are Spanish, Russian, Japanese, Arabic, Chinese, French, and German. Good money is possible if you specialize. Medical, legal, and engineering interpreting are your best bets. No matter what your niche, it helps if you're not only bilingual but also bicultural. Understanding both cultures enables you to translate the nuances. The largest employer of interpreters and translators is the federal government. Other large employers are the United Nations and the Organization of American States. Perk: lots of all-expense-paid travel, but remember, it's often on a moment's notice. Downside: Instant translation software is already available — try it at www.lhsl.com. Within ten years, software may be good enough to put many human translators and interpreters out of a job. *American Translators Association:* www.atanet.org.

(Neat Niche) **Translation.** Instead of the spoken word, you translate written text. Translating written material is less stressful because you have time to think, or heaven forbid, look up a word in the dictionary. Plus, the work hours are more normal. Unlike translators, interpreters must attend events wherever or whenever they occur. Favorite subniches: translating film scripts, Web sites, and software.

Regulation Compliance Consultant. When a law or regulation changes, it usually means an opportunity for entrepreneurs. For example, a few years back, North Carolina decided to require all high school students to take an earth science course. Well, many of the state's teachers had never taught earth science, so an enterprising woman contacted the state's education department and got to provide earth science training workshops for teachers all across North Carolina. Every time you read a newspaper and hear of a new law or regulation, ask yourself, "Does that create an opportunity for me?"

Working with Data and People

Technical Support Specialist. I love these people. When I can't get my software to work, or worse, when I get an error message such as, "General Failure, Drive C," I reach for the phone and get a tech support person, who almost always straightens me out. Technical support can be a launchpad to other careers in high-tech because you get to understand products and their warts from the customer's perspective. Standout tech support people graduate not only to supervisor but also to sales, marketing, and even product development positions. But you may first have to pay your dues. Computers must run 24/7, and newbie help-deskers may have to work the graveyard shift. You also need the patience of a saint — people are often frantic when they call (or at least I am). *Help Desk Institute:* www.helpdeskinst.com. *Software Support Professionals Association:* www.sspa-online.com. *Association of Support Professionals:* www.asponline.com.

Software Architect/Engineer/Developer/Designer. This is what you do when you've been a programmer for a while and you're ready for a less coding-intensive job. You talk with your bosses, customers, and other stakeholders, figuring out what they want the software to do. You then design its architecture and supervise programmers who produce the actual software. When the problem's too tough for the programmers, you code it. The Department of Labor projects software engineering to be *the* fastest-growing job through at least 2008. Roger Pressman's book, *Software Engineering: A Beginner's Guide.*

Web Designer. Most organizations and millions of individuals want a Web site, and if they already have one, it's probably ready for an upgrade. Web designers sit down with the client to understand its needs and then create the blueprint and the look and feel, using an ever-cooler software toolkit. For simple sites, you may be able to use no-programming-required software such as *Dreamweaver.* For more complex sites, you'll probably need to know a fair amount about interface design and be able to work with such tools as Java and XML. You'll need to understand the technodetails that ensure the site works with multiple browsers and loads fast. Web designers often must also be bottom-line oriented, because the purpose of many sites is to sell something — the designer must figure out how to make the site not just interesting but also profitable. At the same time, he must have artistic sensibilities and facility with graphic design software. Web design is a fascinating job because it offers a little of everything: creativity, art, business, and top pay. Because of the enormous demand, a few months of training, some natural aptitude, and you may be hirable to create simple Web sites. *About.com's web design portal:* http://webdesign.about.com. *Internet Professional Publishers Association:* www.ippa.org. *Asssociation of Internet Professionals:* www.association. org. Jennifer Neiderst's book, *Web Design in a Nutshell.*

(Neat Niche) **Political Site Designer.** Mary wants to run for city council. A Web site is a good way to get her message out. Next, Mary's elected and wants to maximize her chances of running unopposed next time — she has to keep the site updated. Unfortunately, someone decides to run against her — time to upgrade the site again. Designing and upgrading politicians' Web sites is a great niche, not just because the work never runs out but also because you get to work for a cause you believe in — unless you decide to develop both sides' sites.

(Neat Niche) **Webmaster.** The Webmaster is an existing site's top banana. Unlike the Web designer, who focuses on creating a site, the Webmaster focuses primarily on its maintenance and upgrades. Like a Web designer, he supervises programmers and serves as liaison with the site's owners. If it's a small site, the Webmaster may do some or all the programming. (For key skills, see the Web programmer and Web designer profiles.) The gold-standard certification is the Certified Internet Webmaster. *International Webmasters Association:* www.iwanet.org. Steven Spainhour's book, *Webmaster in a Nutshell.*

Database Administrator. Among an e-commerce site's greatest treasures are its databases. A database enables customers to see if a product is in stock. Another database provides the site with information about its customers' preferences so that it can custom-market to them. So, no surprise, companies are dependent on database administrators, especially those with expertise in Oracle/SQL. The U.S. Department of Labor projects database administration to be among the fastest-growing occupations through 2008. *Database Central:* www.databasecentral.com. David Kreines' book, *Oracle Database Administration.*

Systems Analyst. What's the best way to enable a traveling salesperson to connect with his company's databases? How can a computer system enable all the employees, suppliers, and vendors to know the status of each order? How can three different computer systems talk with each other? The systems analyst, working with programmers and managers, develops the blueprint for creating computer-based solutions to problems like these. You may not need to be a hard-core programmer but you need some skills in programming, networking hardware, software, and data modeling to do what-if projections. Another key skill is the ability to translate between geek-speak and plain English. The more senior version of this position is systems architect. The Department of Labor projects systems analysis to be among the fastest-growing occupations through 2008. *SystemsAnalyst:* www.systemsanalyst.com.

Operations Research Analyst. One way that the U.S. manages to stay competitive in this global economy is its ability to create efficient production systems. The operations research analyst, a practically-oriented math whiz, is one of the brains behind it all. He may, for example, help the Green Giant figure out how much corn to plant and when to plant it. *Operations Research Society of America:* www.informs.org.

Purchasing Specialist/Supply Chain Manager. How'd you like to get paid for shopping? Well, it's not quite like at the mall. Purchasing specialists do the shopping for companies and government agencies. Of course, it doesn't hurt to have a good instinct for when it is and isn't worth going after a bargain, but this job has rapidly gone technological. Product sourcing is increasingly done on the Internet, and new supply-chain software helps ensure you get what you need when you need it instead of the old way, which meant lots of costly inventory sitting and doing nothing in a warehouse. Demand is great for people graduating from supply chain management programs such as the ones at Arizona State University or Western Michigan University, but any bachelor's plus enthusiastic interest in purchasing may be enough to get you in the door. *About.com's purchasing specialist portal:* http://purchasing.about.com. *National Association of Purchasing Management:* www.napm.org.

College Financial Aid Officer. At most colleges, more than half the students apply for financial aid. With only so much money available, your job is to distribute it equitably and to mollify or negotiate with students who got less than they had hoped for — and after filling out all that paperwork, some *are* unhappy. It's a nice job because it feels good to allocate money, breathing periods between crunch times are sizeable, you need only a bachelor's degree, and you get to work on a college campus — a pleasant work environment. *National Association of Student Financial Aid Administrators:* www.nasfaa.org. *SmartStudent Guide to Financial Aid:* www.finaid.org.

Accountant. You won't do well if you're the stereotypical accountant: a mumbling recluse. To get ahead, an accountant must be a good communicator, often imparting bad news: "No, you can't deduct that. No, you calculated that incorrectly. No, that is inadequate documentation." That naysayer role is one of the field's biggest downsides. But cheer up — for good accountants who are Certified Public Accountants (CPAs), there's light at the end of the bean-counting tunnel. Companies promote good accountants to positions such as comptroller and chief financial officer, where they function more like financial physicians than green-eye-shaded bookkeepers. They're involved in decisions about developing new products, how to use the Internet, how to best use existing capital and how to raise more, and even how to structure the company. Accountants and their closely related finance specialists, are a company's antidote to decision-making based on gut feelings. The Big Five firms (KPMG-Peat Marwick, PricewaterhouseCoopers, Arthur Andersen, Deloitte & Touche, and Ernst & Young) offer terrific training, great pay, and challenging assignments. Problem is, it's tough to get them to hire you. If they won't, most companies use in-house accountants, and the government — and not just the IRS — is full of them. If you want to move up, consider the Certified Management Accountant certificate, which is much easier to get than a CPA. And if you want to help people with their taxes or straighten out small business financial messes, you can simply hang out a shingle. *American Accounting Association:* www.rutgers.edu/accounting/raw/aaa. *Tax preparation franchise:* www.jacksonhewitt.com.

(Neat Niche) **Forensic Accountant.** This is a cross between an accountant and a detective. According to *U.S. News and World Report,* number crunchers are frequently called in by law firms, government agencies, and corporations to sniff out such indiscretions as phony insurance claims and improper securities trading and to testify in court. The Big Five firms alone hire hundreds of forensic accountants each year, and so does the FBI. Who knows? You may be asked to investigate the finances of Tommy the Blade's cement business. *Association of Certified Fraud Examiners:* www.acfe.org.

(Neat Niche) **Business Valuator.** Every day, companies merge or are acquired. Maybe someday, a grand total of one company will exist. Every one of those mergers and acquisitions requires someone to figure out the value of the company being merged or acquired. Those high stakes mean big bucks for you. Business valuators are also relied on when wealthy people divorce or die, determining the value of wifey's business or hubby's stock options. *Institute of Business Appraisers:* www.instbusapp.org. *American Institute of CPAs (*www.aicpa.org*) offers certification in business evaluation.*

(Neat Niche) **International Accountant.** Previously closed economies in Eastern Europe and Latin America are opening. The NAFTA and GATT trade agreements have reduced trade restrictions. As a result, companies are crying, "Find me an international accountant!" For example, an American company does business in Beijing. Which accounting and tax laws and principles apply? It sure helps if you speak the language.

(Neat Niche) **Healthcare Accountant.** When you have an operation, its cost depends on the answers to these questions: Are you on Medicare? Do you have private insurance? Which company? Are you a low-income patient? Are you paying your own way? (You pay more.) Not only is there rarely one set price, there usually isn't just one payer — a single surgery often gets paid for by the government, an insurance company, the patient, and sometimes after all that, the hospital eats some of the costs. A healthcare accountant keeps track of the entire mess.

(Neat Niche) **Environmental Accountant.** As environmentalism becomes religion, more government agencies are using environmental accountants to argue that the environmental damages caused by a company outweigh the benefits. And many companies — especially utilities, manufacturers, and chemical companies — hire other environmental accountants to prove the opposite, or simply to comply with the regulations. CPAs who also are engineers are in particularly great demand. *Jobs:* www.eco.org *and* www.environmental-jobs.com.

(Neat Niche) **Consulting Accountant.** CPAs are frequently called in on a consulting basis, perhaps to computerize a company's accounting function, facilitate a merger or acquisition, or provide advice on how to improve operating procedures. The Big Five accounting firms dominate the consulting field.

Commercial Banker. Banks no longer are limited to offering just checking and savings accounts. They can sell stocks, bonds, insurance, and toilet paper. (Just kidding about the toilet paper.) And all those new profit centers require managers. Other new sources of banking jobs are the new aggressive Web banks such as e*trade (www.etradebank.com) and Wingspan (www.wingspan.com). On the downside, the banking industry is consolidating — small banks are getting swallowed up by big ones, with layoffs coming soon after. But t's-crossed/i's-dotted types with a business degree, who crave prestige, may still find a banking career a wise investment. *American Banking Association:* www.aba.com.

Investment Banker. Business's growth hormone is money. A typical I-banker's assignment is to get money on the best terms. Are you willing to work into the wee hours and do lots of traveling to get a company the best deal on the money? You don't raise the dough by calling a few banks and saying, "Hi, will you lend us some dough?" Here's how investment bankers work: A growing private company needs more money. Should it go public? Issue bonds? Spin off a division? Get bought out? You do complex calculations to help the company come up with an answer. Let's say the company decides to go public and issue stock. You attempt to price it right. Then you hand off the project to a different kind of I-banker — the salesperson — who attempts to convince banks, mutual fund, and pension fund managers to buy your stock or bond offering. To sell requires more than a slick tongue, but that helps.

Most I-bankers are first hired with just a bachelor's degree (in any field, as long as it's from a designer-label college at which you got good grades). Your first job is as an analyst, a number cruncher. You usually need an MBA before making the big bucks. A couple of years as an I-banking analyst is usually a ticket to top-name MBA programs. But I'm talking full years. In *The Fast Track*, Mariam Naficy writes, "The amount you'll work in investment banking cannot be overstated. One analyst reported that he bought 50 pairs of underwear because he had no time to do laundry."

Many people, in part thanks to movies like *The Bonfire of the Vanities,* believe that investment bankers do absolutely nothing for the world. The reality is that their job is to help companies raise money so that they can bring a better product to market. Even media-reviled investment banker Michael Milken, by raising money for MCI as an investment banker, was key to making the telecommunications industry more competitive, and in turn, lowering all our phone bills. Before deregulation, you were paying 40 cents per long-distance minute. Now, you pay 5 to 10 cents. Thank an investment banker. The most sought-after jobs are at "bulge bracket" firms such as Goldman Sachs, but the fastest-growing segment is mid- to large-sized traditional banks, which are now allowed to participate in investment banking. *Careers in Finance:* www.careers-in-finance.com/ib.htm. *Ohio State U's finance portal:* http://www.cob.ohio-state.edu/~fin/overview.htm. **Mariam Naficy's book, *Fast Track.***

(Neat Niche) **Securities Trader.** One floor at an investment bank is called a trading floor. It's filled with rows of computers, and intense 20-somethings. Sales types are on the phones convincing institutional clients such as pension funds to invest in some stock or bond. Traders execute the buy or sell on the best terms — using quantitative analysis and plenty of guesswork. This is a career for people who are adrenaline-addicted, charismatic, and have thick skins. Not all traders have Ivy League degrees. This is the niche within investment banking in which street smarts, aggressiveness, a winning personality along with quantitative instincts can be enough to yield an obscene salary.

Business Loan Broker. This is a simpler version of an investment banker. Most businesses must borrow money. Your job is to find it for them. Tyler Hicks, author of *199 Great Home Businesses You Can Start (and Succeed in) for Under $1,000,* recommends finding borrowers through classified ads in the "business services" section of your local paper. Or you can phone companies, saying, "I have money available. $10,000 and up." Hicks claims that "Would-be borrowers will break down your door once word spreads." All businesses, but especially this one, must have business liability insurance. Every so often, one of your customers in need of money, may see you as a source and sue you if things don't go just right.

Venture Capitalist. A VC looks for budding businesses to invest in, usually in computers or biotech areas. Many proposals come in unsolicited, but some of the best investment ideas are discussed at a bar or on the golf course, so it doesn't hurt to be a schmoozer. After you find a prospect, you need MBA-level quantitative skills to assess the business's future value. Just as important, you need a nose for judging people because a business succeeds or fails as much on its people as on its product. Once you're convinced that a business is worth investing in, you need the ability to convince investors. VCs rarely work on their own. You either work for a venture capital firm or join one of the banks or corporations such as Cisco Systems and Sony, which have in-house venture capital shops. Because the salaries can be astronomical, most jobs at top VC firms (for example, Kleiner Perkins and Sequoia Partners) go to graduates of Harvard or Stanford MBA programs, which have specific tracks for aspiring venture capitalists. *National Venture Capital Association:* www.nvca.org. *Venture Capital Resource Library:* www.vfinance.com. Udayan Gupta's book, *Done Deals.*

Working with Data, People, and Words

Sports Information Director. The public is mad for information about its teams, and you're happy to give it to them. After all, it helps fill the seats. Your job is to create and distribute information to the media and to field their questions. You get great seats to the big game, your working environment is excellent, and you're closer to the team than anyone except the coaches. *College Sports Information Directors Association:* www.cosida.com.

Professor. A professorship has many upsides: the joy of creating knowledge and helping others acquire it through your classes, advising, writings, and professional presentations. You have intelligent, civilized (usually) colleagues, and after a few years, tenure for life. Plus, you get to work in one of the more appealing work environments: a college campus. The professoriate also has its downsides. More and more students are utterly unqualified to do college work and unwilling to work hard, yet routinely complain about too-tough grading if they get a C. (See the eye-opening book *Generation X Goes to College,* by Pulitzer Prize nominee Peter Sacks.) Despite students' virtual illiteracy, professors, except at two-year colleges, usually need a doctorate, which takes an average of 6 to 12 post-bachelor's degree years to complete, depending on the field. Does tenure sound good? Be aware that colleges increasingly hire part-timers and temp faculty. Prospects for permanent jobs are best in engineering, business, and computer science, and for Blacks, Hispanics, and Native Americans.

College classes stress the importance of treating labor fairly, yet colleges are notorious for hiring part-timers to avoid paying for benefits.

There's often pressure to publish journal articles when you'd rather be teaching. Ernest Boyer, former vice president of the Carnegie Foundation for the Advancement of Teaching wrote, "Winning the campus teaching award is often the kiss of death for promotion and tenure." A final minus: On many campuses there is pressure to be politically correct — to assign certain types of readings, express certain views, and even to pass students of certain races even though you believe the student's work does not justify a passing grade. American Association of University Professors: www.aaup.org. Hire-Ed: www.hire-ed.org.

Thesis Completion Consultant. Many graduate students get close to finishing their degrees but drop out because they have trouble doing their theses. You can help. You may help develop the questions to be addressed, plan the structure and analysis, and review a draft. *A useful newsletter is Thesis News:* www.asgs.org.

Proposal Writer. Every year, state and federal governments issue thousands of requests for proposals for every imaginable product and service. They may request proposals for 50,000 Navy uniforms, a state-of-the-art English-as-a-Second-Language program, or 300 desks for IRS offices. The 35,000 private and corporate foundations issue even more requests for proposals. Organizations that want to win these contracts often hire proposal writers to maximize their chances. Demand is strong for proposal writers who specialize in agriculture, communications, energy, business, education, or space exploration. To become a self-employed proposal writer, try reading the *Commerce Business Daily* and the *Foundation Directory Online* (www.foundationcenter.org) to find proposals you'd like to write, contact organizations that might want to bid on it, and offer to write the proposal. *The Grantsmanship Center:* www.tgci.com. Jim Burke's book and CD-ROM, *I'll Grant You That.*

Program Evaluator. "You're judgmental!" That's usually an epithet, but in this profession, you're paid to be judgmental. Typical scenario: You're hired to evaluate a school district's new reading program. You interview students and teachers, compare test scores with a control group, and write a report of your findings. It's fun being an evaluator because you get to check out lots of innovative programs, see what works and what doesn't, and make recommendations for improvement. The bad part is that many program sponsors don't really want your input; they've hired you mainly to meet a government requirement. After all, few people like to be evaluated. A master's or doctorate degree filled with statistics courses is usually the admission ticket to the profession, but program evaluators frequently use only the statistics they learned in their intro to stats class. *American Evaluation Association:* www.eval.org. John Boulmetis' book, *The ABC's of Evaluation.*

(Neat Niche) **Web Site Evaluator.** It seems like there are more Web sites than grains of sand. How do you know which sites are best in class? To help separate the wheat from the chaff, evaluation services such as www.lycos.com give awards to top sites.

Marketer. Your company wants to introduce a product — let's say a piece of edutainment software for teenagers. You review the competition to identify a gap in the market — for example, no good program exists to help high school chemistry students (fictitious). Then, with that general product in mind, you review demographic and psychographic data to find the market segments most likely to buy it. You conduct surveys and focus groups to see what features would attract your target market. You help select packaging and a marketing message, and last, figure out how best to use radio, TV, direct mail, and/or Internet ads. Demand is great for marketers with technical backgrounds — it's easier to develop a marketing plan for a circuit board if you're an engineer. If you want to be a self-employed marketing consultant, the key, as always, is to carve out a tiny but in-demand niche — for example, showing shopping malls how to set up promotions to bring customers to the mall. *About.com's marketing portal:* http://marketing.about.com. *American Marketing Association:* www.ama.org. Jay Levinson's book, *Guerrilla Marketing. Jobs:* www.marketing.com.

(Neat Niche) **Online Marketer.** Every Web site wants traffic. Your job is to get it there. Submit the site in the right way to search engines, conduct e-mail marketing campaigns, arrange link exchanges (I'll link to your site if you'll link to mine), make submissions to newsgroups, advertise on related sites and in traditional media. The job market for online marketers is strong. If you simply learn a lot from the sites below, you may be able to land a job. *Web Marketing Today:* www.webmarketingtoday.com, *Internet Marketing Center:* www.maretingtips.com, *Web Promote:* www.webpromote.com. *Promotion World:* www.promotionworld.com. Dan Janal's book, *Guide to Marketing on the Internet.*

(Neat Niche) **Trend Spotter.** Mervyn's department stores have a 30-person trend spotting division. Trend spotters visit clubs, cafes, flea markets, and malls to see what new and cool things kids are wearing. They develop the next "in" thing. In addition to retailers, trend spotters are hired by ad agencies, e-commerce sites, high-tech equipment manufacturers, even by the government. For example, when a city wants to see what's in store for it, it may send a trend spotter to Berkeley, California.

(Neat Niche) **Focus Group Leader.** A key step in developing a product is to ask a group of people about it. In today's jargon, that's called a focus group. Often, a focus group is simply a structured discussion, but it can be much more sophisticated. For example, before the president gives a speech, he reads a draft to a private audience of citizens carefully selected to be representative of the public audience. Each guinea pig has a dial that can be turned from 0 (I hate it) to 10 (I love it). They continually adjust the dial as the president speaks. He then need use only the material that gets a high rating. The focus group leader runs the proceedings and writes up the results. Richard A. Krueger's book, *Focus Groups*.

(Neat Niche) **Social Marketer.** The same techniques that Madison Avenue uses to convince you to buy a brand of cigarettes, social marketers use to get you to live more wisely. For example, the U.S. government now spends $200 million each year on prime-time commercials, mainly to spread antidrug or anticigarette messages. It's the flip side of product marketing: You're trying to build market share of *non*use. Alan Andreasen's book, *Marketing Social Change*.

How can the same government that sponsors antismoking campaigns subsidize tobacco growers?

(Neat Niche) **Film Marketer.** There's plenty to market: getting domestic movie houses to rent films and the filmgoers to see them. Then you have overseas, cable and network TV, and videocassette markets. Next are the airlines, so we don't get bored on those transcontinental flights. I'm not done yet. We can't forget about the T-shirts and baseball caps, now can we? *American Film Marketing Association:* www.afma.org.

(Neat Niche) **Marketing Researcher.** You design surveys to collect needed information. In addition to in-house corporate or nonprofit marketing departments, you can work for independent polling organizations. Biggies include Yankelovich, Gallup, Field, Harris, and Roper Starch. Pollsters have enormous power. A subtle change of wording can dramatically change a poll's results. The question "Would you eat corn that came from seeds specially bred to produce sweeter corn?" will yield a very different result than "Are you concerned about eating genetically engineered corn?" *Marketing Research Association:* www.mra-net.org.

Business Developer. Most businesses need someone to ask, "What alliances could I create that would build the business? Would it be to license our cool technology? Co-brand? Merge with someone?" *Business developer* is a new term for the old and crucial job of dealmaker. Surprisingly, for this key position, small companies often hire young, smart, silver tongues, not long out of college. Business Developer is one of the more responsible and heart-pumping jobs a young Turk can get. The e-Branded book, *Inside the Minds: Internet BizDev.*

 Idea Generator. So many of my clients love generating ideas but get bored when it comes time to implement them. Idea generator is a career for them. A small number of companies have a designated idea person. This person may function as a resource — when a company employee is looking for new ideas, she calls the idea generator. Or whenever a major new initiative is contemplated, the idea generator is part of the planning team. Most companies, however, have no such position. Take heart. If you think you'd be a great Minister of Brilliant Ideas, it may be worth trying to convince a company or nonprofit organization's president to create the position for you. See Chapters 14 and 15 for ideas on how to maximize your chances of making that happen.

 Management Consultant. Your job is to solve problems too difficult for an organization to solve by itself. Examples: A startup has a great idea but now what? A growing company needs a better system for managing the information flow. A firm wants to start selling in Asia. Yes, you need top analytical skills but must also be persuasive and tactful — even though you're a 20-something with no real work experience, you're telling a veteran what to do. You also must be willing to work long hours. The typical management consultant for a major firm works 50 to 80 hours a week and travels about 50 percent of the time. Management consulting is a great career for learning about the business world, to have major impact on a company while you're still in your 20s, and to hang around with really smart (and well-paid) people. However, for a decent shot at being hired by a top consulting firm such as Andersen or McKinsey, you must have good grades from a designer-label college and make a great impression in tough interviews. Small management consulting firms and self-employment are alternative possibilities. One self-marketing strategy is to write a proposal to the ten small organizations you think you can best help. *About.com's management consulting portal:* http://consulting.about.com. Mariam Naficy's book, *The Fast Track.*

 Corporate Identity Consultant. Large companies hire consultants to create the logos and slogans that capture their essence. This sells more product and encourages employees to feel good about the company. Although this may not be the most socially redeeming job, it pays well and sounds fun to me. *International Corporate Branding and Identity Center:* www.corporate-id.com.

 Organizational Developer. Today, organizations are as fluid as mercury. They reorganize, downsize, rightsize, anything to avoid capsize. Organizational developers help plan and implement changes by suggesting the wisest organizational structures, deciding who should fill job slots and how those jobs should be configured. They also try to motivate a downsized company's survivors. I can hear it now, "Don't worry. You won't be next. Let's give all for the dear old company. Remember the slogan, 'Our employees are our most important product.'" Organizational developers may also be involved in team building and diversity training. Some insiders, however, report that many ODs approach the latter two activities with trepidation because of past failures. When I recently suggested that a client, an organizational developer with 20 years of experience, might want to do more team building and diversity training, he grimaced, put his hands over his face and moaned, "Noooo! Anything but that!" *Organizational Development Network:* www.odnetwork.org.

Small Business Consultant. Many of the 600,000 people who start a business each year are scared of failing. Many small businesses can use help with marketing, accounting, finance, or technology. Alan Weiss's book, *Getting Starting in Consulting*.

(Neat Niche) **Business Plan Writer.** Many business owners know that they need a business plan but don't know how to create one. Inexpensive software packages such as *BizPlan Builder* or *Business Plan Pro* can help you make business plans look professional, but the key to being a good business plan writer is understanding what it takes to market, raise money for, and run a business. This sounds like a fun career, helping come up with the business idea and implementation plan but not incurring any financial risk or dealing with the mundane headaches of running the business. A way of finding clients: Teach a course at a local college's extension school on how to write a business plan.

(Neat Niche) **Client Prospecting Specialist.** Use databases and other tools for helping businesses find customers.

(Neat Niche) **Private-Practice Consultant.** Many doctors are running scared. So are many dentists, podiatrists, psychotherapists, orthodontists, veterinarians, chiropractors, lawyers, and CPAs. They're scared because they increasingly realize that being good practitioners doesn't make them good businesspersons. So they are turning to consultants to help recruit new customers, and develop better systems for billing and collections, payroll, records management, and personnel. Demand is great, and you work with educated people who have the money and motivation to pay you well. *Society of Medical-Dental Management Consultants:* www.smdmc.org.

Specialty Consultant. Consulting is a great career because your expenses are low and you get to keep all the profits. You must, however, be willing to market yourself hard. It helps if many people in your personal network can use your service. To get started, offer to do a consultation for free so you can quickly get a reference. Alan Weiss's book, *Getting Started in Consulting*.

(Neat Niche) **Security System Consultant.** Only one fourth of homes and businesses have alarm systems but many more people are thinking about installing one. The expertise required to become a consultant in this specialty is less than for most fields, but the stakes are high. Thus, customers may be willing to pay for a consultant. Find clients by distributing flyers at local small businesses and homes. Gain your expertise by working for an alarm company, and reading books such as John Traister's *Security/Fire Alarm Systems.*

Work with Data and Things

Archivist. What part of the National Park Service's enormous collection of information should be permanently maintained? Which of those items should be exhibited in national parks? How can the rest of the information be stored for easy access? Archivists answer such questions. Best background: a major in history and a master's in library science from a school that offers a specialty in archival management. *Society of American Archivists:* www.archivists.org.

Acoustician. We all know that acousticians ensure good sound in a concert hall, but they also keep our offices quiet so we can concentrate and our homes quiet so we can sleep. In addition, acoustics specialists help design loudspeakers and microphones, and recording and film studios. *Acousticians* also are the folks who created sonograms — safer alternatives to X-rays and invasive diagnostic tests. *Acoustical Society of America:* asa.aip.org.

Coroner/Medical Examiner. Did Professor Plum do it with the candlestick in the conservatory? Or did the victim die of natural causes? Medical examiners, who, in many jurisdictions, don't need to be M.D.s, answer such questions. It isn't the sort of medical career that makes a great first impression. You cure no one, and you spend your life mucking around with dead people. In fact, after a period of desensitization, playing around with corpses begins to feel normal. But it's rewarding work: One medical examiner described it as "the only career in which you enable dead people to save lives." *The National Association of Medical Examiners:* www.thename.org.

Microscopist. Imagine being able to look at something at 500,000 times magnification, in three dimensions. That's what today's microscopists can do. Why would you want to magnify something so greatly? To examine what happens to diseased cancer cells at the molecular level, to assess the quality of the ceramic coating on a rocket's heat shield, or to determine if the DNA of skin underneath a suspect's fingernails matches that of the person who was strangled. *Microscopy Society of America:* www.microscopy.com.

Cytotechnologist. You're the cancer detector. You examine biopsied cells using microscopes and chemical tests to see what's up. Obviously, this is a career for someone who is careful. A mistake can be devastating. *American Society for Cytopathology:* www.cytopathology.org.

Oceanographer. We've all seen them on TV. Diving off a spacious boat on a perfect day, exploring a coral reef in pursuit of new ways to preserve the ecosystem. Those types of oceanographers still are around, but increasingly they help restore shorelines and rehabilitate bridges. No matter the specialty, a career in oceanography has downsides that don't make it onto the *National Geographic* special. Many oceanographers spend months far from home, much of that time freezing in cramped quarters. Something else those TV specials don't highlight are the many hours oceanographers spend far from the sea: in their cubicles, crunching numbers. A master's or Ph.D. in marine science is standard, but people familiar with boats, electronics, or dive apparatus can get onto oceanographic expeditions without a college degree. *Oceanography Society:* www.tos.org.

Geographer. Michael Jordan was a geography major. Can't you just imagine him debating: "Hmm, should I be a geographer or a pro basketball player?" Well, assuming you don't have pro basketball potential, geography offers some pretty cool careers. Don't think that geographers mainly make maps. Only a small percentage do. (Mapmakers are covered under the separate "Cartographer" entry) Geographers are often experts on such matters as global warming, deforestation, and groundwater pollution. If you decide to become a geographer, you'll be in good company: Mother Teresa started out as a geography teacher. *About.com's geography portal:* http://geography.about.com.

(Neat Niche) **Location Expert.** Everyone knows that the three keys to a business's success are location, location, and location. Because geographers know about demographics, transportation, availability of labor, shopping patterns, and how cities expand, geographers are good candidates for helping companies figure out where to open up shop.

(Neat Niche) **Area Specialist.** The government or a corporation wants to understand a country so its plans are on target. Area specialists brief their bosses based on information from the media, government documents, aerial photos, and intelligence reports.

Geographic Information Specialist. How fast is a forest fire spreading? What's the best location for a highway? Worldwide, which crops will be bumper? (A favorite question of commodities traders.) Geographic information specialists use satellite photos, lasers, and computers to create maps that answer these questions. Sounds like you need a Ph.D., but only a bachelor's or master's is required. *About.com's portal on geographic information systems:* http://gis.about.com.

(Neat Niche) **Photogrammetry Technician.** You prepare maps of inaccessible regions using aerial photographs. This career requires just two years of education after high school.

(Neat Niche) **Precision Agriculture.** Instead of blanketing mammoth farms with pesticides and fungicides, precision agriculturists use computers and global positioning systems to enable farmers to apply chemicals on an as-needed basis.

Geologist. The career for people with and without rocks in their heads. Many geologists — petroleum geologists for example — don't even see the rocks they're studying because they're so far below the earth's surface. These geologists use computer data to answer one question: Where should we drill for oil? Guess wrong and the company loses millions. Guess right and you're a genius. You, of course, have lots of space-age tools — like gamma ray detectors — to help you guess right. Much of the work is outdoors and can be in remote locations for long periods, so it's a lousy choice if you value family life and a stable work environment. Most of the unexplored oil locations are abroad, so if you can speak a foreign language and are willing to relocate, job opportunities should be plentiful. The growth area in U.S. geology jobs is in cleaning up ground-based pollution. Our luck: the oil is far away and the pollution is right here. New employers of geologists are seismic data brokering companies, but the largest employers are oil companies and the U.S. Departments of Agriculture, the Interior, and Defense. *About.com's geology portal:* http://geology.about.com.

(Neat Niche) **Planetary Geologist.** Is there life on Mars? Can we introduce life onto Venus? The answers may lie on and beneath the planet's surface. Enter the planetary geologist. He may look at samples retrieved from space missions or simply look at photographs of planets, moons, and comets. Fewer than 1,000 planetary geologists are employed in the U.S. Most work for universities and NASA. A Ph.D. in planetary geology is a must. *American Astronomical Society,* www.aas.org.

Silviculturist. Silviculturists are forest builders. You create, restore, or maintain a forest or tree nursery. You're responsible for picking the right tree varieties, supervising planting, pruning, and harvesting, and conducting research on topics such as the best methods for ensuring rapid tree growth, or the effects of animal grazing on the forest. Though most silviculturists live in isolated locations, urban forestry is a possibility as cities look to provide islands of respite amid the maelstrom. *Society of American Foresters.* www.safnet.org.

Viticulturist. In plain English, this is a grape grower and often a vineyard manager. Typically, you work for a winery and direct the operations. You decide which grape varieties to use and how to grow them for best flavor. Because you're a manager, it helps if you know accounting. Although you aren't the farmer, you'll find yourself bending a lot unless you're in a research facility. But don't worry, there's free wine to dull any aches. *American Society for Enology and Viticulture:* www.asev.org. Jeff Cox's book, *From Vines to Wines.*

Pilot. This career has always struck me as boring. You're basically a bus driver whose bus has wings. Yet many people aspire to be pilots. It's the take-off, aerial views, and landing, the prestige and good pay, and perhaps, all those motel nights with flight attendants. Most pilots like their careers. But how to land a job? Those plum commercial airline jobs generally go to former military pilots and to others with thousands of air hours and certifications from an FAA-certified training school. The good news is that many under-the-radar pilot jobs exist. And many of them may be more interesting than long-distance commercial flights where you spend hours staring at instruments that are actually flying the plane, and as a reward for all that staring, you get jet lag. Neat niches: rescuing injured people, aerial advertising, fish spotting, flight instructor, tracking criminals, burial-at-sea, dropping aerodynamically packaged seedlings for reforestation, helicopter-based radio/TV traffic reports, emergency parts delivery, and patrol — oil and electric companies have pilots fly over pipelines and electrical lines to check for leaks. *Aviation Communication:* www.flightinfo.com. *Be a Pilot:* www.beapilot.com, *About.com's portal to aviation info:* http://aviation.about.com.

Work with Things and People

Hands-on health and beauty

Interior Designer. What fun! Helping people figure out how to make their homes or offices beautiful and functional. And you get to go on shopping sprees. Trouble is, if you expect to make a living, the job usually requires much more than shopping: reading blueprints, creating estimates for commercial and residential projects, developing mockups using computer-aided design (CAD) systems, and knowing whether you can knock down a wall without the building collapsing. In short, you're somewhere between a decorator and an architect. Interior *decorators* often practice without credentials, but interior *designers* must have a bachelor's degree, and to get the respected American Society of Interior Designers certification, must know building codes and space planning. The women.com site explains the latter: "If a person enters a building's lobby and can't easily figure out how to get to the bathroom or the elevator, then back to the lobby, you've got a problem." Side benefit: You have to have a cool-looking office. *American Society of Interior Designers:* www.asid.org. Jenny Gibb's *Handbook for Interior Designers.*

(Neat Niche) **Housing for the Elderly and Disabled.** To meet the needs of the elderly and disabled and to comply with the Americans with Disabilities Act, housing developers are turning to interior designers with special expertise in these areas.

(Neat Niche) **Elective Medical Care Clinics.** Fat thighs? Thinning hair? Varicose veins? Age-ravaged face? Impotence? Recent advances have made these treatable in nonhospital settings. So, free-standing clinics are popping up. These must have environments that inspire confidence. Enter the interior designer.

Home Stager. This is a well-paying career for artistic types without much talent. When a homeowner decides to sell, he's willing to invest a few bucks to make the house look its best. Stagers come to the house, recommend moving and removing furniture and decorations. ("That stuffed moose head must go.") They also suggest low-cost improvements, for example, painting one wall a dramatic color to enliven a nondescript room. Because the home seller stands to make big bucks, these one-day decorators can earn good money, and while it's an artistic career, staging doesn't require a Rembrandt. www.homestagers.com.

Landscape Architect. Preserving Yosemite Park, designing the U.S. Capitol grounds, creating Boston's "Emerald Necklace" of green spaces tying the city to the suburbs. Landscape architecture is a career for architect types who are interested in outdoor design. Projects can be mundane, like designing the spaces between buildings in an industrial park or building an artificial pond in a homeowner's backyard. Or they can be exotic like designing the landscapes of resorts, golf courses, zoos, urban plazas, colleges, cemeteries, landmark monuments, or scenic highways. *American Society of Landscape Architects:* www.asla.org.

Athletic Team Trainer. Suddenly a player goes down. You race out onto the field and must make an instant evaluation: How bad? Do we need the stretcher? A doctor? You don't want to overreact — the player, the team, the fans want to see her play again, or at least walk off the field, but of course, better safe than sorry. The athletic trainer's key skill is decision-making. He also has important decisions to make before and after the game. For example, injured athletes are usually dying to play again. The doctor has given the okay to play, but as you tape the player up, you notice him wincing. What should you do? Other interesting parts of the job are developing conditioning programs for the team and rehab regimens for injured athletes and motivating them to implement those programs. And there's more. Michael O'Shea, a trainer at the University of Louisville, explains, "The trainer is a 24-hour father confessor." Athletic coaching jobs on teams are tough to get, but there's growth at sports medicine clinics and corporate fitness centers. *National Athletic Trainers' Association:* www.nata.org.

Dentist. It's a myth that you have to be good with your hands to be a good dentist. Studies find that your average klutz can develop the hands-on skills. You do, however, need a good back. Many dentists develop back problems from constantly leaning over patients. Even more problematic, dentistry is stressful. It's no fun to see patients flinch (hopefully, not writhe) in response to your gentle touch. Despite the money and prestige, burnout leads more than a few dentists to stop practicing. The good news is that there are neat niches: *About.com's portal on dentistry:* http://dentistry.about.com.

(Neat Niche) **Veterinary Dentist.** You knock Fido out before starting, so there's no flinching (or biting) to stress you out. Also, it's a nonimpacted (pun intended) field.

(Neat Niche) **Cosmetic Dentist.** Help turn yellowed, cracked teeth into movie-star whites. Much more pleasant than having to tell unsuspecting patients, "I'm sorry, we'll have to do a root canal." Bonus: Only minimal extra training is required.

Dental Hygienist. More than just cleaning your teeth, a dental hygienist takes and develops X-rays, and administers anesthesia. In some states, hygienists even examine patients who are unable to come into the dentist's office. And, of course, part of their job description is to show you ugly pictures of diseased gums to guilt-trip you into flossing more. Dental hygienists must take precautions to avoid carpal tunnel syndrome and back pain. *American Dental Hygienists Association:* www.adha.org.

Surgical Technologist. Just a high school diploma plus a one-year program and you can play a role in the life-and-death drama of the operating room. The surgical technologist preps the patient (I remember having my chest shaved before my appendectomy. Not fun!), provides emotional support (I definitely needed that), and gets the surgical tools and machines ready in the operating room. During the operation, when the surgeon calls, "Sutures! Clamp! Retractor!" or any of those things they yell for on *ER,* the surgical technologist is one being yelled at. According to the Department of Labor, surgical technology is a fast-growing field. *Association of Surgical Technologists:* www.npginc.com/ast.

Cardiovascular Technologist. Heart disease is the number one cause of death in the U.S. and is the leading reason that men die eight years earlier than women. The cardiology technologist plays a key role in diagnosing the problem before it's too late. The range of tools for diagnosis has advanced well beyond the traditional electrocardiogram, using noninvasive ultrasound tests to measure blood flow to the extremities, for example. Cardiovascular techs have a stressful job, especially if they're assisting in heart catheterization — an invasive but accurate test for heart blockages. It helps to have a knack for calming people down. Entry-level jobs often require only on-the-job training, but a two-year degree in cardiology technology prepares you for top-level positions. *Alliance of Cardiovascular Professionals:* www.acp-online.org.

Dispensing Optician. This job is a nice blend: part-technical, part-people. You help people pick out the frames that make them look sexy, intellectual, whatever. You then take some measurements — for example, the distance between the patient's pupils so the lenses can be made the correct distance from each other. Then you make the actual glasses, grinding oversized lenses until they fit. In states where opticians are licensed, you can make a reasonable living. The growth is in the chains like Pearle and LensCrafters (owned by U.S. Shoe). Most opticians are trained on the job or by apprenticeship. *Opticians Association of America:* `www.opticians.org`.

Massage Therapist. This is one of the few careers in which nearly every customer is extremely satisfied. The best massage therapists are not only wonderful with their hands but demonstrate a sense of caring. Training is short, typically 500 hours, but be sure to enroll in a program accredited by the Commission on Massage Training. A downside is that you're on your feet all day doing physical work. Marketing tip: Develop relationships with concierges. Stressed-out traveling businesspeople often treat themselves to a massage at the end of the day. *American Massage Therapy Association:* `www.amtamassage.org`. Martin Ashley's Book: *Massage, A Career at Your Fingertips.*

> (Neat Niche) **Corporate Massage.** A corporate massage therapist is a stress buster who gives in-chair (or on a massage table in the conference room) massages to employees. Massage has been called the 21st century's coffee break. How do you convince tightwad employers to hire you? "No perk costs less and increases morale more. And your company is seen as benevolent, which can boost sales and make it easier to attract quality employees." Some corporations are going halfsies: they pay half, the employee pays half. Sounds like a deal to me, but at least one employer isn't at ease with on-site massage. The IRS office in San Jose offered on-site massage to its employees but there was a problem: the sound. The IRS's Morgan Banks explains, "You can't have taxpayers coming into an audit hearing 'oohs' and 'ahs.' Now we're looking for a room with thicker walls."

Cosmetologist/Makeup Artist. A fun job, making people look attractive while chatting with them. And training is short. Although most cosmetologists don't get rich, some, like my sister, do just fine. Sandy always loved putting makeup on others, so she learned everything she could about it, went to a manufacturer who put Sandy's brand name on ready-made cosmetics, and opened a store called *Let's Make Up.* There, Sandy did free makeovers and showed people how to do it themselves. When the women saw how good they looked, they usually bought fistsful of the stuff. Within two years, Sandy was making fistsful of money. *National Cosmetology Association:* `www.nca-now.com`. Kevyn Aucoin's book, *Making Faces* and Debbie Purvis's, *The Business of Beauty.*

> (Neat Niche) **Special Effects Makeup Artist.** How'd you like a career making up puppets and creature masks? According to the *Hollywood Reporter*, "Since 1992, membership in the Los Angeles Makeup Artists and Hairstylists Union has increased by more than 50 percent. There are 720 people working in this field and their handiwork is in demand like never before . . ." Michael Westmore, makeup supervisor at Paramount for the *Star Trek* series, says that he's never seen anything like the latest bull

market. "I've hired over 80 people myself." But not everyone's a bull. One insider warned that computer technology is replacing a lot of what special effects makeup artists do. *MakeUp Magazine:* www.makeupmag.com.

(Neat Niche) **Wedding Makeup Artist.** Many brides hire a pro to ensure that the bridal party looks luminous, not just for the ceremony, but for the zillion photographs that immortalize that one-of-a-kind (hopefully) day. The camera often requires that you wear special makeup to avoid looking washed out. To get clients, hold a mixer for wedding consultants and photographers. *Sally Van Swearingen's video:* How to be a Photogenic Bride (818-623-9309).

(Neat Niche) **FBI/CIA Theatrical Effects Specialist.** The CIA Web site says, "We are seeking candidates with three years in cosmetology, theatrical makeup, costuming, art/graphics." Antonio Mendez's book, *The Master of Disguise: My Secret Life in the CIA.*

Electrologist. Would you like to feel sort of like a doctor, make people look unquestionably better, yet get all your training in just four weeks? Those are the facts about electrology. Many women are self-conscious about having a moustache, beard, or hair outside the bikini line. Electrologists remove it hair by hair by inserting a fine needle into the follicle and then releasing a small amount of electric current using a foot pedal. They say it's painless, but I'll just take their word for it. New laser technology may make electrolysis obsolete, but it's too early to tell. Check out www.beautyworks.com/removal.htm.

Other Things/People Careers

Business Equipment Broker/Lessor. More people are starting businesses, and because new businesses often fail, more people will be ending their businesses. Business equipment brokers profit from both. They lease to new businesses and buy used equipment from companies going bust. And of course, they handle upgrades. As technology advances ever faster, rather than buy, many businesses prefer to take a two-year lease on the latest model, and in two years, lease the next-generation one. *Equipment Leasing Association:* www.elaonline.com.

Home Inspector. Buying a home can be love at first sight, but love is often blind. Enter the home inspector. Before consummating the deal, many buyers (or at least their less giddy Realtors) insist that the house be inspected. That can be your job. Of course, you'll need to know how to evaluate the soundness of a home's wiring, plumbing, heating, and building materials. Market your service to local Realtors, perhaps by giving lectures at local Board of Realtor meetings titled "How to Prevent an Inspection from Killing the Deal."

*American Society of Home Inspectors (*www.ashi.com*) offers an at-home training and certification program. Franchise:* www.pillartopost.com. *Certifications:* www.icbo.org/certification.

Home Remodeling Contractor. This may be the construction industry's most rewarding job. Typically, you help design the project, bid the job, hire the workers, and keep a nice percentage of what you charge, without ever getting your hands dirty. With the cost of buying a home continuing to rise, more and more people are choosing to remodel. The National Association of Home Builders estimates that by 2010, spending on remodeling will surpass spending on new homes. The same should be true for commercial jobs, which tend to be more lucrative. Neat niches: converting buildings for use by computer-intensive tenants such as dot-coms, upgrading biotech labs, home offices, greenhouses, and additions for elder relatives. *National Association of the Remodeling Industry:* www.nari.org. *Building Online:* www.buildingonline.com.

Golf Course Superintendent. Where do we put that new bunker? How do we schedule the groundskeepers? What's the best way to keep those greens perfect? To answer those questions, every golf course has a superintendent. This is another cool career that doesn't require a bachelor's degree: A two-year degree in turfgrass management will do. *Golf Course Superintendents Association of America:* www.gcsaa.org.

Garden Designer. Many of us allow our yards to decline into the too-natural look. Sure, we can hire a garden-variety gardener, but she doesn't have design skills. Landscape architects have design skills, but you may need a second mortgage to afford one. Enter what I call the Garden Doctor. He makes house calls and performs transplants. Armed with a laptop and software like *LandDesigner 3D* or *3D Garden Composer,* the Garden Doctor and client can design the perfect Eden right there on screen without lifting a shovel. When the design is just right, the homeowner can do the job or contract with the Garden Doctor. *Association of Professional Landscape Designers:* www.apld.com; *About.com's landscape portal:* http://landscaping.about.com. Cheryl Merser's book, *The Garden Design Book.*

> (Neat Niche) **Quick-Thumb Gardener.** She creates gardens that require minimal effort to stay looking good.

> (Neat Niche) **Interiorscaper.** Hotels, hospitals, restaurants, atriums, malls, universities, and corporate headquarters are potential clients. A cool company name: Plant Parenthood.

Park Ranger. People think this is the career for shy souls who spend their lives alone, peering out through binoculars for forest fires. Granted a few of those are around, but most park rangers spend lots of time with people — preaching the environmentalist gospel or pestering park patrons, "Do you have a fishing license?" "No dogs allowed," and "I'm going to have to ask you (drunken jerk) to leave the campground." A park ranger's first job is usually filled with physically demanding tasks such as shoring up eroding paths. Jobs, albeit low-paying ones to start, are available in national, and especially in state and regional, parks. Insider's secret: Job seekers overlook jobs on federal lands other than parks. Check out national forests, wilderness areas, wildlife refuges, and scenic rivers. (See www.usajobs.opm.gov.) Good paying administrative parks jobs are rare. For those cut out for this career, however, it doesn't really matter what the job is — nothing is better than a life in the wilderness. *Links:* www.indiana.edu/~naspd/related.html.

Fashion Designer. "Next year, I think our line of children's swimsuits should use more UV-resistant fabric in earth tones. Parents are tired of cutesy. For a change, we might also try a loose fit. Here's a sketch of a couple of designs. If you like any of them, I'll cut a few samples. Maybe we could try them out at our sales meeting or at a fashion show." That's the life of the fashion designer. This is another of those careers in which colleges admit many more students than there are jobs for. We often think of designers focusing on haute couture, but they may have a better chance of landing a job if they pick an under-the-radar niche such as children's swimwear. *International Association of Clothing Designers:* www.fashionexch.com.

> (Neat Niche) **Accessory Design.** Designs for shoes and handbags change almost as often as clothing designs, yet many aspiring clothing designers don't think of this niche, so it isn't quite as crowded.

Elder Mover. Many older folks want to trade their too-large home for a smaller place, but the project can be intimidating. In addition to the physical tasks, leaving one's home can be emotionally painful. Elder movers take care of everything from hiring the right movers to figuring out what will fit in the new home, from hooking up the VCR to setting their clients' slippers on the right side of the bed. *Tip:* Take pictures of each room in the old house and use them to help you decide where to put items in the new home. To get clients, develop relationship with the intake personnel at retirement homes, and bundle your brochure with their marketing materials.

Photographer. Taking pictures for a living sounds like fun, but can you actually make a living at it? Only if you're an aggressive marketer. Photographer Dennis Miller says, "Photography is 75 percent sales — *if* you're very talented; 95 percent if you're not." You also must be strategic. For example, most lucrative work is in large cities. Many people can take pictures but far fewer can take pictures with a digital camera and perform postproduction magic to create images that will dazzle and persuade — which is precisely what magazines and ad agencies want. *About.com's photography portal:* http://photography.about.com. *Professional Photographers of America:* www.ppa-world.org. Rohn Engh's books, *How to Sell & Resell Your Photos* and *SellPhotos.com.*

(Neat Niche) **Newborn Photographer.** It amazes me that life's most awe-inspiring event, childbirth and the day after, is rarely photographed professionally. Try to get a hospital director to grant you the exclusive right to offer photographic services to expectant parents who will be giving birth at the hospital.

(Neat Niche) **Government Photographer.** Government work can be an island of security in the photographer's sea infamous for low pay and irregular employment. The feds might hire you to take aerial photographs. Law enforcement agencies hire forensic photographers: "Did that piece of headlight come from a suspect's car?" Enhanced photographs of evidence can tell the tale.

(Neat Niche) **Industrial Photographer.** This is another photography job that's potentially stable. Plus, you get to work with top-of-the-line equipment. The downside is that the work is unlikely to quench your thirst for artistic expression. A typical project: taking photos of a prototype at each stage in its development.

(Neat Niche) **Photojournalist.** As newspapers try to stay competitive in ever-glitzier ways, they use more photos. The job market is still tight, but if you have expertise in digital photography and postproduction, this rewarding job may be a bit easier to land than in years past. *National Press Photographers Association:* www.sunsite.unc.edu/nppa.

(Neat Niche) **Lithograph Cameraperson.** You use computers and camera to lay out magazines and mail-order catalogs.

(Neat Niche) **School Photographer.** Taking headshots of 100 kids a day isn't the most creative work in the world, but plenty of customers are out there. At many schools, picture taking is an annual event. Another plus is that, unlike most photography niches, your evenings and weekends are free. *Professional School Photographers of America:* www.pmai.org/sections/pspa.htm.

(Neat Niche) **Photo Restorator.** That wonderful picture of great-grandpa has faded. A photo restorer can bring him back — alas just the picture, not him. Then there's that picture of you that came out wonderfully . . . except for that zit. A photo restorer can fix that. Remember how snapshots used to have squiggly edges? Photo restorers can even recreate those. Training: Read books on photographic history, hang out with photographers and airbrushers. *American Photographic Artisans Guild:* www.apag.net. *FocalPoint (*www.fpointinc.com*) offers an inexpensive kit for starting a photo restoration business.*

(Neat Niche) **Pet Photographer.** People love their pets, sometimes as much as their kids. I get great joy from looking at my amateurish shot of my dog's head lying in a teddy bear's lap. I'd guess — and I have no data to support this — that just as people pay to have photo portraits of their kids, they'd pay for a cute shot of their beloved pooch or puss. Here's how to find out, at minimal cost. Create an 8½-inch x 11-inch ad filled with your best pet photos. Mount the ad on a stand-up cardboard easel. To it, attach a pad of tear-off discount coupons. Place your easels near the cash register in vet's offices, pet supply stores, pet stores, and pet adoption facilities. Or rent a booth at dog shows. Owners of purebred show animals are especially proud of their pets.

(Neat Niche) **Real Estate Photographer.** As real estate sales move to the Web, soon, every listed property — from home to factory — will be in full view on the Net, with a 24/7 virtual open house, full of photographs. Someone's gotta take those pictures. Could it be you? See examples at www.ipix.com.

(Neat Niche) **Annual Report Photographer.** Every public company, every mutual fund, and every investment company is required to produce an annual report. The successful companies usually make theirs spartan, but the ones hungry for business make theirs a glitzy four-color magazine filled with, you guessed it, photographs. How to get gigs? Two-thirds of the work comes out of New York. Send your portfolio to each company's investor relations director.

Accident Reconstructor. "It was his fault. He ran right into me!" It's the job of the accident reconstructor to find out whether he's lying through his teeth. Using photographs of the crime scene, statements from drivers and witnesses, knowledge of the physics of what is and isn't possible, and computer simulations, accident reconstructors ascertain the truth. *Accident Reconstruction Communication Network:* www.accidentreconstruction.net.

Sports Referee/Umpire. I loved being an umpire. It was fun making a decision every few seconds that was respected — usually. Somehow, even getting booed wasn't so bad — when I was able to remind myself that in the larger scheme of things, it didn't matter whether it was a ball or a strike. And as a sports fan, umpiring was a way to be a part of the game even if I wasn't a great ballplayer. Don't count on making full-time money as an ump. Sure, top NFL refs make more than $250,000, but for most high school and college refs, officiating is a sideline, as much for the fun as for the money. There are perks, though. You get to travel, and it's a fun way to stay in shape, except in baseball, where umps mainly just stand there. The good news is that demand is high. You need the skills of a saint: competent decision-making under pressure and the ability to stay cool when coaches and fans yell in your face (or spit, as did pro baseball player Roberto Alomar). *Referee/Umpire HomePage:* www.gmcgriff.com/refonline. *Umpire Resource Center:* www.umpire.org. *Harry Wendelstedt School for Umpires:* www.umpireschool.com. *National Association of Sports Officials:* www.naso.org. Jerry Grunska's book, *Successful Sports Officiating.*

Stunt Person. Ready to dive from a cruise ship into a frigid ocean? How about getting set on fire? Leaping from a tall building? If so, maybe you'd like to be a stunt person. Be sure your health insurance is in place. Most of the "gags" that pay well don't just look dangerous, they are. The risk doesn't deter aspirants; competition is fierce for stunt jobs. You usually need to be quite an athlete and well trained. One training school, Stunts Are Us, is located in, of all places, Kenosha, Wisconsin (414-859-2379). Another school is the United Stuntsman's Association Stunt School: www.stuntschool.com. First step, though, for a career in which you swing from nooses and tumble down stairs is to read Jack Bucklin's *Stuntman* or the more widely available, *So You Want to Be a Stuntman*.

Work with Things and Data

Patent Agent. You get to do everything a patent lawyer does except appear in court. Sam invented a gadget that opens jars more easily and wants to patent it. Your job is first to assess if it's really new enough to justify a patent. If so, you draft a patent application to the U.S. Patent and Trademark Office. It describes, in words and pictures, how the new invention is different from anything that preceded it. People will always want to patent their innovations to protect their rights, and the position can't be automated, so there should always be a need for patent agents. A background in science or engineering is almost a requirement. *Patent and Trademark Office Society:* www.ptos.org.

OOH

Engineer. This is a career for math and science junkies who like to solve practical problems, usually by designing an object. Perhaps it's a hybrid gas/fuel cell car that can actually pass cars on the freeway, a snowboard that turns better, or a way for diabetics to take insulin that doesn't require injections. For the past ten years, engineering has been among the highest-paid, most in-demand, bachelor's level careers. And future prospects look great: The Department of Labor expects demand to stay hot at least through 2008, especially in electrical and software engineering. The bad news is that the admission ticket for the coolest engineering jobs is increasingly a master's degree. And because this field is so fast-changing, older engineers — often perceived as too many steps behind — face a tougher time in the job market. *National Society of Professional Engineering:* www.nspe.org. Celeste Baine's book, *Is There an Engineer Inside You?*

> (Neat Niche) **Biomedical Engineer.** Typical projects for these engineers include designing more functional artificial arms or legs, a computer simulation of brain function, and a monitor for hospital patients, astronauts, or deep-sea divers. *Institute of Electrical and Electronics Engineers:* www.ieee.org.

(Neat Niche) **Packaging Engineer.** How should a small toy be packaged so it's theft-resistant yet allows the shopper to play with it so he can plead, "Mommy, can I have it?" How should a drug be packaged so that it's child-proof yet accessible to an arthritic adult? What's the least expensive packaging that keeps frozen shrimp from smelling fishy after its journey from Thailand aquafarm to U.S. supermarket?

(Neat Niche) **Hardware Engineer.** Your job is to design and produce electronic devices. You might, for example, design the tone generator for an MP3 player, a computer chip for a robot that enables a world-class surgeon to do brain surgery on a patient halfway around the globe, or the procedure for mass producing that chip. No way around it, you have to be smart for this career, know a lot of science and math, and have the knack of solving hard problems thrown at you left and right. For example, when you're designing a new chip, a million unexpected problems come up — after all, you're charting new territory. Through it all, you have to communicate well, orally and in writing, to tease out what your bosses really want, fight with them if you think they're nuts, and coordinate with your teammates. After you've developed your widget, you help create documentation and training that ensures that users can actually use it. Hardware engineering changes constantly, so you better love learning new stuff. The Department of Labor projects hardware engineering to be among the fastest growing occupations through 2008. Job satisfaction is unusually high. More than 95 percent of hardware engineers stay in the field for life. However, according to a State University of New York at Stony Brook study, twice as many women as men leave the field. *Institute of Electrical and Electronics Engineers:* www.ieee.org.

(Neat Niche) **Telecommunications Engineer.** The Olympics are seen instantly around the world. A paralyzed person talks and a computer types his words as fast as he can speak. You check your e-mail with a palm-sized cellular device. The hero? Telecommunications engineers. What's next? Soon, your cell phone will respond to your voice commands to upload to your Web site photos you just took with your phone's built-in camera. When telecommunications engineers tire of working on the bench, they have limitless opportunities in sales, marketing, and management.

(Neat Niche) **Robotic Engineer.** Thousands of Cambodians lost limbs to land mines. Many such mines still remain. How can they be removed without more loss of life and limb? A robot. Robots are now used, not just for welding cars, but also for everything from battlefield surveillance to crop picking to long-distance surgery to nuclear plant maintenance. And soon, chances are that a robot will vacuum your house — but then again, they've been predicting that for 20 years and I'm still pushing my Hoover around. *Robotics Online:* www.roboticsonline.com. *American Association for Artificial Intelligence:* www.aaai.org.

(Neat Niche) **Sales Engineer.** It often takes an engineer to convince an engineer that his company needs to buy a high-tech widget. The engineer who can do that often commands a six-figure salary.

(Neat Niche) **Environmental Engineer.** Companies scared of tougher regulations and public demand for low pollution are spending big to prevent and cure environmental messes. The pollution prevention industry is already $1 billion a year and growing. Reports indicate, however, that because engineering graduates flocked to this field in recent years, environmental engineering is becoming saturated. Best job opportunities may be in Eastern Europe and Asia as they begin environmental cleanups. *American Academy of Environmental Engineers:* www.enviro-engrs.org. *Jobs:* www.eco.org.

(Neat Niche) **Spacecraft Engineer.** They're already booking seats on the first commercial space flight. More passenger spacecraft will come, but for the next decade, the real growth will be in designing and building unmanned vehicles. A typical application is monitoring pollution changes on Earth. Lockheed Martin has already built 875 spacecraft and clocked 1,100 years of on-orbit performance. Many people think that spacecraft engineering mainly involves designing the vehicle itself. Actually, the main work is designing the thousands of computer programs needed to drive the vehicle's many systems. Don't worry. You can still say you're a rocket scientist. *American Institute of Aeronautics and Astronautics:* www.aiaa.org. *About.com's portal to aerospace information:* http://aerospace.about.com. *Jobs:* www.spacejobs.com. Scott Sacknoff's book, *Space Careers*.

(Neat Niche) **Flying Car Developer.** It is absurd that the best idea transportation planners have for coping with gridlock is to simply stop building roads, thereby forcing people into mass transit that no matter how expanded, will greatly inhibit our freedom of movement. A solution: a flying car. Don't laugh. It vastly increases the amount of space in which people can drive — without spending a dime on freeway construction. Think it's science fiction? At least one flying car already exists (see www.moller.com/skycar). And it's radar-controlled to ensure that vehicles don't hit anything. *ABC News* did a feature on it.

(Neat Niche) **Nonpolluting Car Developer.** Gasoline engines are destroying the earth. Their pollutants are causing a rapid and irreversible decrease in the number of animal and plant species, which damages our ecosystem in ways we can't even imagine. And, of course, pollution may affect humans, too. For example, some cancers appear to be pollution-triggered. Whether or not you're a high-powered engineer, working to develop an environmentally clean car, probably using hydrogen fuel cells, may involve you in an effort that could save the planet. *EVWorld:* www.evworld.com.

Engineering Technician. Your job is to assist an engineer in designing and developing products. For example, you may test and troubleshoot electrical and computer systems or work on a survey party, calculating land areas, estimating costs, and inspecting construction projects. A two-year degree in engineering technology is the norm. In choosing to be an engineering technologist rather than a full-fledged engineer, you trade some prestige but need far less school and often end up with a quite interesting job. *American Society of Certified Engineering Technicians:* www.ascet.org.

(Neat Niche) **Laser Technician.** Lasers remove wrinkles, make welds, and yes, destroy oncoming missiles. While highly trained laser/optical engineers do most of the design work, you assist with the design and are in charge of building the lasers. *Laser Institute of America:* www.laserinstitute.org.

Inventor. Sixty thousand kids a year are treated in hospitals for trampoline-related injuries. So Mark Publicover invented JumpCourt, which provides 360-degree protection around standard-sized trampolines. JumpCourt is now sold in 7,000 outlets. How does an invention get invented? It starts by asking yourself: "What's annoying?" and "What could I invent that would solve the problem?" Inventors, mostly engineering types, usually develop their proto-types as an after-work spice to their corporate day jobs. How to do it successfully? You needn't build the prototype yourself. Find a model maker in the Yellow Pages. Then test out your prototype on potential customers and retailers. If it passes muster, find out what it would cost to manufacture — use the Thomas Manufacturing Register of 160,000 manufacturers to find one (www.thomasregister.com). Is it cheap enough to allow ample profit? Have them make a small run and you distribute it through trade shows, a Web site, direct mail, or wholesale it to retailers. Or try to get a corporation to buy (and not steal) your invention. Avoid services that promise to help market your invention. They usually cost you more than you earn. The Wal-Mart Innovation Network (www.walmartstores.com/win), however, provides a 13-page review of your invention for only $175. And if you score high enough, Wal-Mart may test market your invention in its stores. *Inventors Digest:* www.inventorsdigest.com. Maurice Kanbar's book, *Secrets from an Inventor's Notebook.*

Industrial Designer. What should an Internet access device that attaches to your eyeglasses look like? What's a cool design for a filling station gas dispenser? What should a new mountain bike look like? An industrial designer provides the answers. Good news: To be an industrial designer, you needn't be an engineer or an excellent artist. Industrial designers aren't the engineers; they work with engineers. And while it helps if you can draw, it is as important that you care deeply about how products are made, look, and feel. The rest can usually be taught. Top training institutions are Carnegie Mellon, Rhode Island School of Design, and Art Center College of Design (CA). *Industrial Designers Society of America:* www.idsa.org. *Interview with an industrial designer:* www.artschools.com/interviews/vogel.

(Neat Niche) **Packaging Designer.** Your company wants to introduce a new shampoo. Dozens of brands already are on supermarket shelves. Your job is to design the bottle so that shoppers are compelled to pick yours. Working with graphic artists, marketers, and accountants, you design the most compelling packaging possible within budget. www.packaginginfo.com.

(Neat Niche) **Toy Designer.** Sounds simple, but toy design, more than most careers, requires you to have expertise in many fields. You have to be enough of a developmental psychologist to know what sorts of activities will stimulate a 7-year-old. You must be enough of an artist to create something beautiful. You must be imaginative enough to think of all the ways a toy can break or be unsafe. You must be enough of an engineer to design a product that works. Next time you pick up a toy, have a little more respect for its designer. *Toy Manufacturers of America:* http://www.toy-tma.com/index.html. *New York's Fashion Institute of Technology offers a BFA in Toy Design:* http://www.fitnyc.suny.edu/academic/all_majo/2.11.02.html.

Cartographer. That's the fancy word for mapmaker. Though you still need some drawing skills, this is yet another field that's been revolutionized by the computer. New maps are often of remote areas, only now accurately mappable thanks to computer interpretation of aerial or satellite data. Cartographers may also map seascapes to identify coral reefs, or create drainage maps to help farmers plan irrigation. *American Congress of Surveying and Mapping:* www.survmap.org.

Enologist. Want to make wine for a living? A bachelor's degree and internships during crush time in wineries provide the preparation. Alas, only a few colleges offer a major in enology. The best-known program is at the University of California, Davis. *American Society of Enology and Viticulture:* www.asev.org. Jeff Cox's book, *From Vines to Wines*.

Brewer. Don't like wine? How about beer? Although I'm not sure the craft brewing fad will last, beer drinking will. Don't think the job is mainly tasting. It's part chemistry, part management, and okay, part tasting. *About.com's portal to information on beer:* http://beer.about.com. *Master Brewers Association:* www.mbaa.com.

Broadcast Technician/Broadcast Engineer. This is a back door into a field whose front entrance is mobbed. And you don't even need performing talent. Broadcast technologists operate and maintain the cameras and other recording equipment in Webcasting, radio, and TV studios and on remotes. An utterly nonrandom example is going to Hawaii to cover the Aloha Bowl. The bad news is that you must often work nights and weekends, and the pay can stink. Training is less than a year at a private technical school or a bit longer at a community college. But there's an alternative. The broadcast engineer at my radio station told me that in decades past, techie teens would, like groupies, hang out at radio stations to learn broadcast engineering. Now, few do, perhaps because most teens view radio as passé. That leaves an opportunity for you. *National Association of Broadcasters Employment Clearinghouse:* www.nab.org. *About.com's radio portal:* http://radio.about.com. *Radio Online:* www.radioonline.com. *TV Jobs:* www.tvjobs.com.

(Neat Niche) **Webcasting Technician.** It's already happening. Hundreds of radio stations make their shows available live or archived on the Net. This cool career will undoubtedly expand, and by the time you're reading this, video-compression technology and fatter-piped Internet access should mean that you'll be able to watch your favorite TV shows, movies, even that rare footage of Albert Einstein holding forth in his lab, whenever you want. There should be great demand for technicians who know how to make it all happen. *International Webcasters Association:* www.webcasters.org. *Streaming Media World:* www.streamingmediaworld.com.

Criminalist. He is lying dead. Near the corpse lies a tiny white hair. The criminalist picks it up. Under the microscope, it's clear that it's a pet hair. A visit to three suspects' homes finds that one of them has a pet whose hair matches exactly. Criminalists use physical evidence — a weapon, a clothing fiber, blood, drugs, even vapors — to prove a link between the suspect and the victim. It's safer than a detective job because you usually show up after the danger is over. Criminalists need only a bachelor's degree, ideally in forensics/criminalistics, but biology or chemistry is often okay. When you get bored with picking up stuff at crime scenes, get a master's degree and you may get to do more interesting work like analyzing crime patterns to help the cops plan their strategy. *American Society of Criminology:* www.asc41.com.

(Neat Niches): **Ballistics, Fingerprint Analyst, Arson Investigator, Forensic Chemist, DNA Analyst, Forgery Analyst** (See graphologist profile.)

Historic Preservationist. America has hundreds of thousands of buildings under protection of the Landmarks Preservation Commission — 21,000 in New York City alone. In many of these buildings, continuing efforts are made to restore the property to its original state. That means hiring people who can do research to find out what the building looked like way back when, and who have the management skills and/or artistic ability to recreate it. Much of this work is done on a volunteer basis, but a few jobs are available for the eager and well trained. *National Trust for Historic Preservation:* www.nationaltrust.org.

Work with Things, People, and Words

Filmmaker/Director. What could sound cooler: "Hi, I'm a feature film-maker"? Beyond sounding cool, directing feature films *is* cool. You get to orchestrate the telling of a story that you put in front of millions of viewers. And the process — the ultimate in creativity and camaraderie, with you leading your film crew that's working intensely for months, and then it's done — you can sit back and watch your masterpiece and see the money roll in. What a dream! Unfortunately, for 99.99 percent of aspiring filmmakers, it is only a dream. Even many graduates of the top film schools (UCLA, USC, and NYU) end up never earning enough even to pay back their student loans, let alone to make a subsistence living as a filmmaker. Nevertheless, if my daughter said, "Dad I want to be a filmmaker," I would not discourage it — the prospect is just too exciting. I'd rationalize that if she couldn't make it as a filmmaker in Hollywood, she could somehow make a living directing training videos. Worst case, in a few years, she'd have to read the next edition of this book. *American Film Institute:* www.afionline.org, *Association of Independent Video and Filmmakers:* www.aivf.org. Steven Ascher's book, *The Filmmaker's Handbook.*

Restaurant Menu Creator. There are countless restaurants, and each of them needs a menu, many of which need to be changed periodically. Because the menu is what the customer reads at the moment of truth — when deciding how much to spend — an appealing menu design can mean big bucks to the owner. So if you become an expert in menu design, you may be able to charge amply for your services. Start by studying restaurant menus. Compendia are available at hotel concierge desks, in the *Entertainment Guide*, and online. *MenuPro software (*www.menupro.com.*)* and David Pavesic's book, *Menu Design.*

Work with Data, People, and Things

Nurse. Today, whether the patient gets well depends as much on the nurse as on the doctor. As cost-cutting pressures increase, registered nurses are doing more and more substantive medical care. Bedpan cleaning is now mainly handled by medical assistants. To get the best nursing jobs, though, a two-year degree no longer cuts it. A bachelor's is fine, and if you have a master's, the floodgates open. According to the Health Resources Services Administration, 400,000 nurses with master's degrees are needed for such positions as nursing supervisor, nurse practitioner, nurse educator, midwife, and anesthetist. Yet, only 140,000 nurses have a master's. Here is a field in which a master's makes sense.

I keep hearing stories of nurses who often ignore patients' call bells, and more important, who make life-threatening errors. Please, only consider nursing if you are, even when stressed, a caring, detail-oriented person. *About.com's nursing portal:* `http://nursing.about.com`. *National League for Nursing:* `www.nln.org`; Suzanne Gordon's book, *Life Support; Three Nurses on the Front Lines*.

(Neat Niche) **Nurse Practitioner.** You get most of the benefits of being a physician with few of the liabilities. You get to do the fun parts of doctoring: exams, health education, and treating treatable conditions like that sore throat. And if things get too tough, you refer your patient to a physician. And you needn't subject yourself to four expensive, exhausting years of medical school, an even more exhausting year of internship, and two to four years of residency. A two-year training program following your bachelor's in nursing, and you're in. Typical salary: $50,000 to $80,000. *American College of Nurse Practitioners:* `www.nurse.org/acnp`.

(Neat Niche) **Nurse Anesthetist.** Anesthesiologists earn more than $200,000 a year, and HMOs don't like that one little bit. So HMOs increasingly prefer nurse anesthetists because they can pay them $75,000 — good money for a nurse — and still save a bundle. Some general nursing experience plus a two- or three-year program after the bachelor's degree opens the door to this prestigious, important, but stressful position. *American Association of Nurse Anesthetists:* `www.aana`. *About.com's portal to info on anesthesiology:* `http://anesthesiology.about.com`.

(Neat Niche) **Nurse Midwife.** More and more moms-to-be and healthcare bean counters are attracted to midwifery's combination of lower costs and more human touch. And midwifery can be a gratifying career. Not only do you deliver babies, you provide pre- and postnatal care such as teaching moms to breast-feed. Registered nurses must complete a year of additional training for nurse-midwife certification. *American College of Nurse Midwives:* `www.acnm.org`. Juliana Van Olphen-Fehr's book, *Diary of a Midwife*.

(Neat Niche) **Obstetric-Gynecological Nurse.** Experience the miracle of childbirth on a daily basis. This can be a stressful job, and not just in a problem birth. A writhing mom in labor can raise the stress level of a stone. OB-GYN nurses need a calm demeanor.

(Neat Niche) **Transplant Coordinator.** You've drunk yourself into a stupor once too often, so your liver is kaput. Doc says you need a transplant. The transplant coordinator decides where you belong on the waiting list. (Too far back, in your soused opinion.) When someone dies whose liver is the right size and blood type, the transplant coordinator schedules the team for surgery, and gives you your pre- and postsurgery education. *Center for Organ Recovery and Education:* `www.core.org`.

(Neat Niche) **Wellness Coordinator.** Large employers hire wellness coordinators to arrange health fairs, conduct blood pressure and cholesterol screenings, coordinate noon aerobics and stop-smoking classes, and, of course, encourage employees to eat more Brussels sprouts and less Häagen-Daz.

(Neat Niche) **Patient Discharge Planner.** As hospitals release patients more quickly, discharge planners help patients transition to in-home care. A planner decides if Mrs. McGillicuddy needs a home-health aide, trains her or her family how to administer injections and other treatments, and helps the family solve problems as they arise. The work is generally less stressful than direct patient care.

(Neat Niche) **Case Manager.** A 90-year-old woman has been battling cancer for five years. Her cancer has now spread to her liver, and she is in pain. Should she receive another operation? How about painful physical therapy for her atrophying leg? Should she be in the hospital? At home? In a hospice? What should and shouldn't the HMO pay for? The case manager is the coordinator of this decision-making process and has one of the more interesting roles in the managed care system. After reviewing the record, speaking with the patient, family, healthcare providers, and insurance company, and leading rounds, the case manager makes recommendations that balance the interests of everyone involved: the payer, the hospital, the family, and, of course, the patient. Toni Cesta's book, *The Case Manager's Survival Guide.*

(Neat Niche) **Clinical Trials Coordinator.** A pharmaceutical company develops a new treatment that works on the computer and with rats, so it's time for human subjects. Nurses are hired to examine potential patients, administer the treatment, ensure that patients are complying, and write reports. This is a neat niche because it's little known, in demand, and a different experience for the nurse burned out on patient care who would enjoy being part of a research team. *Clinical Trials Listing Service:* www.centerwatch.com.

(Neat Niche) **Menopause Counselor.** Menopause has come out of the closet, if the number of T-shirts proclaiming, "I'm out of estrogen and I have a gun," are any indication. As they enter the "change of life," some women seek support beyond what their gynecologist can provide during the 12-minute annual exams that HMOs usually pay for.

(Neat Niche) **Nurse Informatician.** Nurses need to access lots of data: patient records, drug contraindications, disease ins-and-outs, and insurance gobbledygook. Someone has to work with the computer programmer to develop systems that are nurse-friendly and to be on call to help nurses having trouble extracting information. The pay's good, the job's rewarding, and there's no blood and gore. *American Nursing Informatics Association:* www.ania.org.

(Neat Niche) **Nurse Legal Consultant.** Law firms are inundated with people who want to sue their doctors or hospitals for medical malpractice. To evaluate those claims' legitimacy, lawyers hire nurse legal consultants to review the medical records, and if the case seems meritorious and involves nursing malpractice, to research the nursing literature to develop the case's foundation. Nurse legal consultants also testify in trials as expert witnesses. *American Association of Legal Nurses:* www.mnrs.org. *Online training program:* www.kaplancollege.com.

Exercise Physiologist. Athletes are learning to perform better, not just with a coach's help, but with that of an exercise physiologist. The latter may, for example, show an athlete how to improve by using slow motion, computer-analyzed tape of exactly what his muscles are doing. In addition to consulting with teams, exercise physiologists get jobs in sports medicine clinics and corporate fitness centers. *Exercise Sciences Association:* www.exercisesciences.com. William McArdle's book, *Essentials of Exercise Physiology.*

Respiratory Therapist. We can live for days without food or water, but without air, we're dead in nine minutes. Respiratory therapists' job is to keep patients breathing — often not just the very old, but also the very young. Newborns must often be placed on sophisticated ventilators. Your job is to monitor the ventilators to ensure proper oxygen, CO_2 and pH levels. You also administer aerosol medications and perform chest therapy to drain mucus from the lungs. Respiratory therapists are among the first persons called to work with doctors to treat acute asthma attacks, head injuries, and drug poisonings. *American Association for Respiratory Care:* www.aarc.org.

System/Network Administrator. "The network is down. What the heck happened?" "Oh my gosh, I lost my data!" System administrators install and repair those oh-so-complicated contraptions. You're a combination mega-Tinkertoys assembler, electrician, Unix or Windows 2000 programmer, and fix-it person. The job's tough but it's fun because you get to see how all the pieces fit together, and there's variety, including needs assessment with actual human beings, hands-on computer diagnostic brainwork, plus you're crucial to everyone who uses the system. You receive heartfelt thank-yous when you get people back up and running. This is no 9-to-5 job. You work until it's fixed. You are well paid, though. The Department of Labor projects great demand through at least 2008. The entry-level job to this field is the network installer. *Network Professional Association:* www.npa.org. *About.com's portal to networking info:* http://compnetworking.about.com.

(Neat Niche) **Computer Security Administrator.** Your job is to configure and run an organization's firewall, authorization system, and antivirus program. You may also develop and administer policy. This is a complicated field and specialists are raking it in. To get started, take courses and certifications in security (see www.sans.org/giactc.gtm) and monitor the Computer Emergency Response Team site (www.cert.org) to learn about the latest threats.

Quality Assurance Specialist. If you'd get a kick out of checking out products to see if they're up to snuff, this job's for you. And actually, you often get to do more than try to make the software crash or sniff around the production line. QA people are often brought into meetings with higher-ups and taken on sales calls — you, more than anyone, can describe all the steps you've taken to ensure that the product works as advertised. The downside: You're the person who's telling everyone to improve — not likely to make you popular at work. The upside: The boom in Web sites and Web-based software creates a huge need for software testers. With the rush to get products to market before a competitor does, it isn't surprising that software testers don't catch everything. Syndicated columnist Bob Weinstein reports that Microsoft employs 3,000 testers, yet upon release, MSWord reportedly had 60,000 bugs. *American Society for Quality:* www.asq.org. Ed Kit's book: *Software Testing in the Real World.*

Pre-employment Tester. To avoid costly hiring mistakes and charges of discrimination in hiring, employers increasingly are supplementing interviews with formal testing. Consultants select off-the-shelf instruments and develop customized tests to predict which candidate is likely to do the job best. *Society for Industrial & Organizational Psychology:* www.siop.org. Richard Jeanneret's book, *Individual Psychological Assessment.*

School Computer Coordinator. Schools are filling with computers, but after planting, many groves of Apples are gathering dust. The main problem is teachers who don't know how to use them effectively. Enter the school computer coordinator — combination network administrator, teacher trainer, and hardware troubleshooter with a knack for figuring out how to help Johnny with whatever seems not to be working. *International Society for Technology in Education:* www.iste.org. *George Lucas Educational Foundation:* www.glef.org.

Planner. Should Wal-Mart be allowed to open a store in your city? What's the wisest plan for revitalizing downtown? How can we make the county environmentally sustainable without destroying the economy or greatly impeding people's quality of life? To address such questions, you, the planner, review copious data, conduct studies and public hearings, and before making a recommendation, probably wear many hats, including that of an engineer, economist, architect, sociologist, and politician. A silver tongue is essential if you expect even vestiges of your plan to survive irate community groups. Many planners specialize in urban or rural land use, transportation, housing, air quality, water quality, health and human services, historic preservation, or hazardous materials. Increasingly, you need a master's degree except in small agencies or those away from metropolitan areas. To land a good job, have skills in environmental sciences and know geographic information systems software. Then volunteer/intern for planning committees and commissions. *American Planning Association:* www.planning.org.

FBI Special Agent. Are you an aspiring James or Jane Bond? The reality is usually less exotic, investigating such mundane dalliances as your basic fraudulent bankruptcy, but FBI special agents do search out kidnappers, finger mobsters, catch bank robbers, and foil biological weapons terrorists. Downsides are that you travel a lot and are alone most of the time. The FBI employs more than 10,000 special agents, and they prefer a graduate degree in law or accounting or fluency in a foreign language. (Doesn't sound much like the requirements I'd list if I was recruiting for FBI agents, but what do I know?) Entry-level job title: clandestine service trainee. *Federal Bureau of Investigation:* www.fbi.gov. John Douglas' book, *Guide to Careers in the FBI.*

Are you 37 or older? Forget it; the FBI wants to hire young. So do most employers, but age discrimination laws prevent it. The FBI is above all that.

Private Investigator. You're worried that your husband is fooling around. Or that one of your employees is collecting disability but is, in fact, on the golf course. Or that your nanny is abusing your darling daughter. Who you gonna call? Your friendly private investigator. He'll hang out in the neighborhood, talk with some folks, hopefully without arousing suspicions, dig through online public information, and use that time-honored P.I. technique: dumpster diving. PIs must be able to read people and persuade them to give you information. Remember Colombo?

BHB

Some danger exists here. For example, a wife has a husband followed, but hubby catches you, the private investigator, and wants to redecorate your face. The good news is that such mishaps are rare, especially nowadays, when many more cases are solved by a computer search than by stakeout. This is a cool career if you're clever and have a knack for not getting caught. Best training: apprentice with a pro. *National Association of Legal Investigators:* www.nali.com. Robert Scott's book, *The Investigator's Little Black Book 2.*

(Neat Niche) **Employee Background Checker.** When one of San Francisco Mayor Willie Brown's key employees was caught lying on his resume, His Honor shrugged, "Everyone lies on their resume." As job and tenant applicants seem ever more likely to stretch the truth, and government regulations tighten about what can and can't be asked, companies increasingly turn to pre-employment checkers to verify information on resumes and to contact former employers. Edward Andler found that one-third of all resumes contain "some level of creative writing." His book, *The Complete Reference Checking Handbook. IMI DataSearch:* www.imidatasearch.com.

Risk Management Specialist. The insurance industry is an attractive employer because of good salaries, but for many people, it's a turnoff because of the nature of the work. One of the more rewarding insurance careers is in loss prevention, or as it's increasingly called, risk management. Rather than, for example, being an adjuster, whose job is to give loss victims as little as possible, the risk manager has the more pleasant role of helping a business develop a strategy to prevent losses. *American Risk and Insurance Association:* www.aria.org. *About.com's insurance portal:* http://insurance.about.com.

Video Yearbook Publisher. Most high school yearbooks are still done the old-fashioned way: a printed book. A video yearbook can be a compelling alternative. How to get customers? Contact high school principals and PTA presidents. Get permission to videotape the senior class in action, and then sell video yearbooks. A franchise is available: *International Multimedia Yearbooks:* www.multimediayearbook.com.

Work with Data, Things, and People

Physician. I include this career partly because you'd think I was nuts if I omitted such a prestigious, well-paying profession; but listen to this: There is an oversupply of doctors, especially specialists, in most urban and suburban areas. Many experts believe that demand for doctors, especially specialists, will decrease as HMOs increasingly use nurse practitioners and physician's assistants to lower costs. Even if a doc can find a job, HMOs severely constrain how physicians can practice medicine: Visits are shorter, and more and more treatments are subject to external scrutiny. Meanwhile, malpractice suits climb. Perhaps the biggest minus is that a physician's life is extraordinarily stressful. Consider the typically six to eight years after college that it takes to prepare to be a physician, the enormous cost of medical school, the fraternity-like hazing called internship, the strain of high-stakes decision-making, having to inform unsuspecting patients of severe illnesses, and the now prohibitive costs of starting your own practice. And there's more. Medicine is changing so rapidly that it's impossible to keep up, so many physicians practice while feeling guilty that because of their own lack of knowledge and HMO constraints, they may not be giving their patients the best possible treatment. Because physicians have ready access to mind-altering drugs, many docs turn to them for stress relief. *American Medical Association:* www.ama-assn.org. *DoctorLink:* www.doctorlink.com. *Jobs:* www.practicelink.com, wwwMddirect.com, *and* www.mdrsearch.com. Marita Danek's book, *Becoming a Physician*, Robert Marion's book, *Learning to Play God: The Coming of Age of a Young Doctor.*

For many aspiring physicians, physician's assistant and nurse practitioner (see profiles) may be a smarter career choice even though it obviously has less prestige and lower income potential. If, however, you want to consider the M.D. route, there are neat niches:

(Neat Niche) **University Student Health Service Physician.** College student health problems are usually curable, you have no overhead, and you work in a beautiful, stimulating setting.

(Neat Niche): **Infectious Diseases.** As you're reading this, terrorist groups and governments are refining their ability to create one-of-a-kind mutated viruses to use as bioweapons. Natural selection is creating superbacteria that are resistant to even the most powerful antibacterials. The likelihood of contracting infectious diseases is growing because of easier worldwide travel, more crowded public transit, and increasing sexual promiscuity. I'm not just talking about rare, newly discovered pathogens such as the dreaded West Nile or Hanta viruses. Cases of the formerly thought-of-as-cured tuberculosis are increasing, even here in the U.S. And then there's AIDS: the virus itself, and the myriad opportunistic infections that its victims contract. Infectious disease researchers and practitioners do some of our most important and challenging work. *Infectious Diseases Society of America:* `www.idsociety.org`.

(Neat Niche) **Occupational Medicine.** This niche offers many advantages. **Need:** On-the-job accidents and job-related illnesses are frequent, with a relative shortage of occupational medicine docs. **Compensation:** Employers and insurers know that your efforts to prevent on-the-job illnesses and accidents will save them lots of money, so compensation is good. **Variety:** Internal medicine, psychiatry, surgery, epidemiology, toxicology, forensic medicine, administration, preventive medicine — occupational medicine encompasses them all. **Success rate:** You help a high percentage of your patients. *Occupational medicine portal:* `http://gilligan.mc.duke.edu/oem`.

(Neat Niche) **Hospital Research Director.** Many hospitals, even those unaffiliated with universities, conduct research. Research director is a great job for a burned-out doc who'd like to improve the quality of medical care rather than just implementing the status quo. Grant proposal writing skills are key.

(Neat Niche) **Cosmetic Surgeon.** Newly available techniques are making it ever more likely that you'll delight your patients. Society tends to denigrate cosmetic surgery as a narcissistic luxury, one that objectifies the body rather than focusing on a person's substance. I used to think that way myself. But I've seen so many people's lives improve as a result of the surgery — they feel much better about themselves every minute of every day and are even more productive at work. So, I've become a fan. I wonder if cosmetic surgery has done more to improve people's sense of well-being than psychotherapy. *About.com's plastic surgery portal:* `http://plasticsurgery.about.com`.

(Neat Niche) **Sports Medicine.** As the fitness fad continues, the number of weekend warriors grows, and in turn, so does the number of injuries. Most of these are fixable, so sports medicine is rewarding. *American College of Sports Medicine:* `www.acsm.org`.

The evidence for the benefits of exercise is flimsy. Of course, people who exercise more live healthier and longer, but which causes which? Does a strong constitution make one more likely to have the energy to exercise, or does the exercise create a strong constitution? Before the doctors guilt-trip us into taking hours from our already crowded weeks to sweat our fannies off, we deserve better evidence that it's worth our while.

(Neat Niche) **Infertility Specialist.** Women working outside the home are deferring parenthood, sometimes until getting pregnant isn't so easy. Enter the infertility doctor, with an ever-growing array of fixes including in-vitro fertilization, now with egg screening to help ensure normalcy. What's next? Probably sooner rather than later, to maximize chances of a normal baby, cloning one of the parents. *American Society for Reproductive Medicine:* www.asrm.com.

Physician's Assistant. This career is very similar to nurse practitioner. See that profile on page 113. To enter this field, you need a bachelor's degree in a science/health field and a few years of experience as a nurse, EMT, or paramedic. *American Academy of Physician Assistants:* www.aapa.org. Terence Sacks' book, *Opportunities in Physician's Assistant Careers.*

Audiologist. A master's-level job with doctor-level prestige. Plus, the field's terrific new tools make you look like a miracle worker. For example, new hearing aids enable the user to amplify only those frequencies with a hearing loss. For the self-conscious, some new hearing aids are so tiny that everything fits into your ear canal except the gizmo you pull it out with. The nation's most famous user is Bill Clinton. Many audiologists get out of the office, and spend part of each week in hospitals, rehab centers, and special schools. Oh, there's one part of audiology that isn't prestigious: You spend a fair amount of time removing earwax. *American Academy of Audiology:* www.audiology.com.

Veterinarian. A vet is like a doctor except you have to know a half-dozen species, none of which can describe their symptoms to you. About.com's veterinary portal: http://vetmedicine.about.com.

(Neat Niche) **Laboratory Animals Vet.** It's the easiest vet residency: Working hours are 9 to 5, no weekends, and you get to work in a medical school or drug company setting. There are ample jobs because most animal research must be supervised by a laboratory animal vet.

(Neat Niche) **Veterinary Cardiologist.** Demand is growing, treatments are improving, and earnings are excellent for these heart specialists.

Veterinary Technologist. Much shorter training than for veterinarians, yet veterinary techs get to do much of what vets do. Let's say poor Fifi isn't feeling well. You, the vet tech, might take her medical history (if you can speak dog), give her an exam, and take her blood (poor Fifi). The vet diagnoses the problem as a bladder infection and prescribes an injection that you administer. Next, even poorer Bowser comes in — he was run over by a car. The vet decides to operate. You administer the anesthetic and assist in surgery. You're even allowed to stitch Bowser up. Bowser also has a broken leg. You take the X-rays, the vet sets it, and you apply the cast. Finally, you educate Bowser's mommy or daddy about how to take care of Bowser during his recovery. You needn't be dogged to land a job since there are four job openings for every vet tech graduate in the United States. The problem is that salaries are in the doghouse. *North American Veterinary Technologists Association:* www.avma.org/navta.

Paramedic. A person is having a heart attack. Or three teens are down after a gang war. Or there's a bad car accident and bleeding passengers are tangled in the wreckage. The paramedic is first on the scene to try to save the day. If you thrive on adrenaline but can stay calm, be gratified by your saves but not burned out by your losses, this can be a rewarding career. Training is short. Initial certification as an emergency medical technician (EMT) is frighteningly short (just 100 to 120 hours!). Full paramedic status requires 750 to 2,000 hours and certifies you to do the stuff they do on *ER.* This is a burnout profession, so after a few years, figure on going for an RN or physician's assistant degree. *National Association of Emergency Medical Technicians:* www.naemt.org.

Physical Therapist. A construction worker with an injured back, an older person recovering from a stroke, an infant with a birth defect. All of these are typical physical therapy patients. The therapist's job is to develop programs to relieve pain and restore function. Many of us think of a physical therapist as the person who coaches the patient through exercises, but in many cases, that's done mainly by less expensive physical therapy assistants. The physical therapist is the patient's plan maker and instructor. Over the past decade, PT had been one of the fastest growing occupations, but now, supply is meeting demand, and admission to PT school (a master's program) has become difficult, only a notch easier than medical school. *American Physical Therapy Association:* www.apta.org. *Rehab Options:* www.rehaboptions.com. *Jobs:* www.rehabjobs.com.

> (Neat Niche) **Sports Physical Therapy.** As the fitness craze spreads through the formerly sedentary, newbies to the exercise world are stubbing their toes and worse. Sports physical therapy tends to be a more rewarding, less burnout-prone niche than traditional physical therapy, which more often deals with cases in which progress is slow.

Acupuncturist. Insert needles, manipulate carefully, restore balance in energy fields, and possibly help everything from weight loss to pain control, arthritis to upper respiratory infections. Not only is the public willing to try, the insurance companies are starting to pay. Even biggies such as Cigna, Aetna, and Blue Shield are now covering some acupuncture expenses. However, since the last edition of this book, a literature review on the award-winning Web site Quackwatch.com casts new doubt on acupuncture's efficacy: www.quackwatch.com/01QuackeryRelatedTopics/acu.html. A pro-acupuncture site: www.acupuncture.com.

Work with Things, People, and Words

Curator. A museum exhibition begins with your idea. You then choose the objects that best convey the idea and create an innovative way to install the exhibit. Then you work to publicize it. In between exhibitions, you try to acquire interesting stuff, all in one of the more peaceful work environments imaginable. Most curators major in an academic field such as art, history, archeology, or computer science, and then join a museum, zoo, or college or government library in that field. To advance, you usually need a master's in museum studies. Museums are expensive to maintain, so to land a good museum job, you usually must have business expertise (translation: an MBA). *American Association of Museums:* www.aam-us.org. *Jobs: The Museum Employment Resource Center:* www.museum-employment.com.

Architect. When a filmmaker wants to create a character worthy of respect, he often makes the person an architect. After all, architecture is an ideal blend of art and science, creativity and logic, big picture and microdetail, like ensuring that the wiring meets the requirements of Section 3.02.05 of the Springfield County Building Code. Alas, for the first few years, architects spend a lot of time on the latter and far less on design. A good architect must be an excellent communicator; someone who can tease out what the client really wants and convince the Springfield County Building Department that the wiring deserves a variance to Section 3.02.05. He must also be a good project manager — a building is comprised of a thousand headaches. Patience is beyond a virtue; it's a necessity — the client or the city is always changing something. One thing you needn't be good at is drawing, thanks to CAD programs such as Architectural Desktop, which are now dominant in architecture. *About.com's portal to info on architecture:* http://architecture.about.com. Roger Lewis's book, *Architect?*

> (Neat Niche) **Green Architect.** Some evidence suggests that inhabitants are healthier in green buildings. Because these buildings make extensive use of natural light, people in them feel better, and with careful material choices for carpets and drapes, and good ventilation, people don't cough or scratch their eyes because of poor air quality. People feel better in green buildings, not only because the materials are safer, but also because they're largely recyclable and energy-efficient so you feel like you're doing your part for the environment. http://architecture.about.com. James Wines's book, *Green Architecture.*

> (Neat Niche) **Senior Housing.** Aging boomers will require housing to meet their physical needs.

> (Neat Niche) **Entertainment Architect.** Design movie sets, theme parks, resorts, venues, and museums.

Corporate Security Consultant. Corporations have always had a problem with security, and not just with customers. Employee theft is an even greater problem — for example, stealing client lists or proprietary technology. Now with corporate property ever shrinking (genes, microcircuits, formulas) and surveillance technology ever more sophisticated (such as software that cracks encryption codes), the field of corporate security is, well, exploding. To succeed, specialize — in museums, hotels, or e-commerce sites, for example. *American Society for Industrial Security:* www.asisonline.org. *International Association of Professional Security Consultants:* www.iapsc.org.

(Neat Niche) **Violence Prevention/Resolution.** Workplace violence is epidemic. More than 500,000 incidents of workplace violence occur each year. Courts increasingly find that the lack of a thorough violence prevention/ intervention plan is evidence of liability if a worker assaults another worker. This creates a job market for you.

Business Home Economist. For years, women have been ridiculed for going into home economics, so few do anymore. Finally, the need has exceeded demand. Business home economists are used by manufacturers of large appliances to do demonstrations and by large department stores to suggest what to buy and how to display it. Supermarket chains, food manufacturers, and trade boards employ business home economists to prepare and present information to consumers. The Egg Board, for example, may ask a business home economist to develop a booklet showing how to prepare eggs without unduly clogging your arteries. *American Association of Family and Consumer Sciences:* www.aafcs.org.

Ahead-of-the-Curve Fields

Would you like to get in on the ground floor? Imagine, for example, if you had gotten into television or computers when they first came out. But what will be the blockbuster fields of this decade? If the leading edge calls to you even though it sometimes turns out to be the bleeding edge, keep your eyes open for developments in these areas.

Viral Defense. The most devastating weapon in the next war will be one of two viruses: a biovirus, mutated to ensure that no vaccine is available. Or it will be a computer virus designed to stop the stock exchanges, banks, or Internet. The president has admitted that we don't know how to stem these threats. Career implications: Toxicologists and computer security specialists will be treated like royalty. Jonathan Tucker's book, *Toxic Terror.*

Biometrics. "What's my password for my Schwab account? For that Web site? For my calling card? Passwords and PINs are multiplying, easy to forget and easy to steal. And they'll soon be obsolete. Your iris or your fingerprint will prove your identity. Biometrics is changing the way we identify ourselves. www.biometricgroup.com.

Web Commercials. The likely way that Web sites will start to make money? Commercials. As the Internet begins to support full-motion video, Web sites will require users to watch commercials every ten minutes, just as when we watch TV. And just as television stations charge big bucks to advertisers, so will Web sites. People who specialize in producing Web-optimized commercials may be on the ground floor of an enormous industry.

Gene Therapy/New Reproductive Choices. Back in 1999, Princeton scientists demonstrated that they can increase mouse intelligence and that of its progeny by adding a gene. This suggests that we soon will be capable of using gene therapy not only to cure disease but also to enhance humans, physically and mentally. When the science advances and the ethical concerns have been carefully addressed, I am convinced that gene therapy will be *the* field of the 21st century. First, gene therapists will be allowed to alter genes only to prevent or cure diseases. For example, a gene therapy treatment for Parkinson's appears to control and even reverse this devastating disease. But I predict that human' temptation to enhance themselves and their children will be irresistible. Imagine that you were thinking about having a baby but a test revealed that you'd have a 50/50 chance of passing on a gene cluster for low intelligence, but that if you elected to replace that cluster, your child would likely have above-average intelligence. Don't you think that some parents would desperately want that option? Career implications: Get a research lab job at a university or biotech company that is developing any of these technologies:

✔ **Genomics and proteomics.** Thousands of companies are working on figuring out what each gene does and which proteins they express.

✔ **Cloning.** (See below.)

✔ **Egg selection** will be one of the earliest "gene therapies," enabling a woman, when she's young and her eggs maximally healthy, to freeze thousands of her eggs so she can better control when she gets pregnant. That way, her baby will be conceived with a young, healthy egg, even if she's in her 40s. Perhaps of greatest benefit, right before getting pregnant, she will likely be able to have hundreds of her eggs tested to pick one that has no defective genes.

Cloning. A one-in-a-million hybrid produces a cow that has less fat. Cloning will enable us to reproduce the cow. Thousands of people each year die waiting for an organ transplant — cloning can save their lives. Even more heartening, cloned organs are likely to be young. A study found that six cloned cows show signs of being younger than their chronological ages. So your cloned heart, for example, will be like the one you had when you were young.

Ethical concerns about full human cloning should dissipate as people realize that cloned babies will not be identical — environment plays a large role in determining who we are. People also will come to see cloning for what it is — giving birth to a delayed identical twin. Also, like current versions of assisted reproduction, such as in-vitro fertilization or even the birth control pill, as the concept of cloning becomes more familiar, fear will diminish. Human cloning will probably first occur in other countries, with America soon adopting it in response to the demand. Would anyone prefer that only rogue nations' scientists be permitted to clone humans and their organs?

Career implications: Soon, jobs for researchers developing less expensive, more reliable ways to clone stem cells into organs will become available. People with a bachelor's degree in molecular biology may soon be able to land positions as "organ engineers" — the people who will use stem cells to actually create the organs, and later, complete humans.

Anti-Aging Research and Practice. Certain substances appear to slow the aging process — antioxidants, for example. Even more exciting, scientists have begun to unlock what actually causes aging, including certain enzymes and shortened telomeres, the appendages to DNA molecules. More recently, scientists at LifeSpan Biosciences have identified four genes whose expression is highly correlated with aging. They're now asking, "Would turning off those genes inhibit aging?" As the public begins to understand that major life extension may be possible, public demand for such research will grow, and in turn, so will the research opportunities. Of course as the evidence gets stronger, the demand will become greater for physicians and other health-care providers who specialize in anti-aging.

Nanotechnology. Nanotechnology is the ability to manipulate, molecule by molecule. This will enable the creation of molecule-sized machines. Why would anyone want such a small machine? Well obviously, you'll be able to wear a heckuva powerful computer on your wrist. But more intriguing applications may include cleansers that can remove any stain, insulation that can keep homes at a constant temperature, and true medical miracles. In 2000, *Time* magazine reported, "A diagnosis of pancreatic cancer would be devastating to any of us, bringing with it the horrors of debilitating chemotherapy and a slim chance of surviving the next five years. Fifteen years from now, however, you might not even bat an eye at the news. Your doctor will simply hand you a capsule packed with millions of nanosensors, each programmed to seek out and kill the cancer cells in your body . . . And that's not all. One day, autonomous "Nanobots" far smaller than motes of dust will patrol the body, repairing aging organs and fixing genetic damage before it can turn into disease." The U.S. government just funded a $500 million nanotechnology initiative — see www.nano.gov. That site also contains links to other nanotechnology information.

Cryonic Suspension. Thanks to nanotechnology, in 50 to 150 years, we will likely be able to repair age-damaged cells — for example, by lengthening the aforementioned telomeres. More and more people are deciding to be frozen in liquid nitrogen upon their deaths, hoping to be revived when science has advanced enough that this molecule-by-molecule repair can be done. Though the odds of all this working out are small, the alternative is absolute certainty of being eaten by worms, and an eternity of death.

Artificial Intelligence. Scientists have touted artificial intelligence for decades, but slow computing power and crude programming languages have inhibited progress. Things are starting to change: We already have $40 software programs to diagnose medical problems, almost do your taxes for you, and design a landscape that looks great year-round in your microclimate. Artificial intelligence programs help mutual fund managers decide whether to buy a stock, corporations to decide how to market a new widget, and the FBI to determine the best response to a terrorist threat. TradeTrek (www.tradetrek.com) claims that its artificial intelligence program enables anyone to "trade stocks like a pro, and consistently beat the stock market." The future? In routine situations, virtual lawyers may be able to tell you what law and regulations apply, far more accurately and less expensively than your live shark. And a few years later, according to Ray Kurzweil, holder of nine honorary doctorates and author of the *Age of Spiritual Machines*, the thinking robot of sci-films will become a reality. *American Association of Artificial Intelligence:* www.aaai.org. Movie: Spielberg/Scorsese's *A.I.*

Virtual Reality. One of education's few unassailable truths is that we learn by doing. Computer simulations enable students to do things that are normally impossible to do, or at least do safely, such as perform surgeries or fly airplanes. The next level of simulation is to virtually *be* in the environment — virtual reality. Virtually land on the surface of Mars and decide what to explore and how. Be virtually transplanted to Argentina and fend for yourself in Spanish. Be virtually teleported into the Battle of Gettysburg, in the role of General Grant, deciding what to do next. The options are limitless, and all represent a monumental improvement over traditional lecture, textbook, and conventional computer-based instruction. Of course, applications of virtual reality extend far beyond education and entertainment. For example, already, virtual reality goggles enable architects to give clients a real sense of what their building will be like, down to whether there will be glare from their desk. If anything's wrong with the building, it can be easily fixed before the first nail is hammered.

Online Education and Training. For the past 20 years, technophiles have been predicting that computer-based instruction would start supplanting live instruction. It hasn't even come close to happening. I predict that this time it will be different, because online courses will soon amalgamate three powerful features: full-motion video on-demand, interactivity with artificial-intelligence-powered simulations, and human interactions via e-mail and chats. Combine all three and online education becomes vastly superior to in-person instruction, especially compared with the lecture class. Instead of having to commute and find a parking spot to listen to some instructor, good, bad or indifferent, drone on, you'll get a hand-picked, world-class lecturer, augmented by simulations and discussions that any student (even a home-bound elder) can access on demand, 24/7. Additional pressure to move to online education will come from the ever-faster pace at which knowledge grows — impossible for the average instructor to keep up with. Perhaps the most compelling use for online education will be K-12 education. Political exigencies (which I think are absurd, but that's another book) are forcing students of all abilities — from developmentally disabled to gifted — to be placed in the same teacher's class. Without computers, it's virtually impossible to provide all the students with appropriate-leveled instruction. Simulation-based, individualized modules will revolutionize instruction. Teachers' roles will be primarily to get kids unstuck and to preside over socialization activities. *Association for the Advancement of Computing in Education:* www.aace.org. *WebNet Journal:* www.webnetjrl.com.

Convergence. All media — TV, Internet, stereo, VCR, computer — will soon reduce to one box, enabling you to interact with galaxies of information and entertainment material. *Time* magazine predicted: "All content — movies, music, shows, books, data, magazines, recipes, and home videos — will be instantly available anywhere on demand."

Convergence will allow for such goodies as contextual shopping. You'll watch a Madonna concert (which of course, would begin whenever you want). You want to see what she looks like from behind. No problem, one click. Then you decide you like her shoes. One click and you've ordered it, so-called T-commerce. Before turning off your box, you'll be alerted to upcoming attractions based on your past selections.

I believe *the* killer app will be immersion. Combine the convergence and virtual reality trends, and I predict that millions of people will spend their evenings, not watching sitcoms, but *experiencing* amazing things in 3D: You'll virtually be flying the Mars Explorer, performing open-heart surgery, exploring the Amazon jungle, batting against Roger Clemens, climbing Mount Everest.

Career implications: Work for an artificial intelligence firm, one of the six broadly diversified content companies (Disney, News Corp, Seagram, Sony, Time Warner, and Viacom) or a broadband Internet infrastructure company such as Inktomi (www.inktomi.com). Also pipe owners (for example, AT&T, which has covered both the phone- and cable-based delivery systems) should be big beneficiaries of the convergence movement. See About.com's portal to info on broadband: http://broadband.about.com, NYU offers a program in interactive telecommunications: http://itp.nyu.edu/html/inf_index.html. More of a hands-on type? Design and build those all-in-one media boxes or the new Internet backbones that will be required to handle the increased bandwidth.

Wireless Telecommunication. Third-world countries can't afford the cost of wired radio/TV/internet/phone infrastructures. Wireless is their dream come true. In advanced nations such as the U.S., more and more businesses are networked. Not only is the massive tangle of cables usually just one mishap away from a problem, cables tether workers to their office. Wireless telecommunication, for example, using infrared BlueTooth technology, will offer answers. We all love freedom. Imagine that embedded in a watch-sized device you'll wear on your wrist, you'll be able to access the Internet, shop, phone, take pictures, and watch video-on demand. That's what wireless telecommunication companies are developing.

E-Commerce. Yes, some people will always love the idea of touching and feeling items before buying them, but ever more people and businesses will gladly trade that away for the pleasure of not having to traipse around hoping to find what they need. People appreciate the greater selection and price comparison available on the Net. Many people also don't like dealing with salespeople. With a bricks-and-mortar vendor, the salesperson you happen to get can be good, bad, or indifferent, whereas on a company's Web site, you always get the best information available.

Many vendors also prefer selling on the Web. There's no cost of a store, no shoplifting, it's easy to track and market to customers, and the e-store can be open 24/7 at no additional cost.

The things that have heretofore inhibited e-commerce are rapidly being fixed — slow-loading catalog pages, an inadequate site search function, weak presale advice, cumbersome checkout procedure, dicey customer service. With these weaknesses mitigated, the percentage of transactions on the Net will skyrocket.

Career implications: E-commerce will put many salespeople, distributors, and bricks-and-mortar businesses out of business. Work for a category-leading company with a serious commitment to e-commerce, for example, the leading broker of elder housing. The Internet also will affect the priests of professional expertise: lawyers, librarians, and doctors, as people expect instant information with the click on a link. No matter what your field, to maximize chances of survival, one of your first questions should be: "How should I use the Internet?"

Market Rationalization. Yes, if a customer needs a high level of service, it may make sense to patronize a small vendor, but in most cases, shopping at a small vendor is irrational. Large ones, such as Home Depot, provide better selection at better prices. Buyers who do most of their shopping with the little guy essentially are providing him with an act of charity. And as charitable as Americans are, they have a limit. So, the number of little guys should continue to decline. *Career implication: In general, go with the big boys.*

Home Schooling. Public schools are ever more focused on the needs of the poor and low-achieving. So, middle-income parents, especially in mixed socioeconomic areas, and especially if their children are bright, are deciding that their children's needs are unlikely to be well met in the public schools. One parent told me, "I thought that one of the main benefits of paying taxes was public education. Well, I can't get that benefit without risking my child's future." So parents in droves are home-schooling their children. In just 20 years, the number of American home-schooled has gone from 300,000 to 2 million (!), and growing. It's tough to beat the combination of one-on-one instruction aimed at a child's personal interests, from someone who loves him. And home schooling's growth rate will accelerate even faster as more compelling online courses and edutainment come available (for example, see StarPeace at www.montecristogames.com). But home schooling is a daunting task. How can you capitalize careerwise? Train parents to home school better. Or provide one-on-one small-group tutoring in math and science, which are generally poorly taught by home schooling parents. Offer that tutoring in-person, by phone, or via Internet instant messaging. Or create activities that bring homeschoolers together — physical education, field trips, sports and music activities. *About.com's homeschooling portal:* http://homeschooling.about.com.

Mass Customization. Warp-speed advances in computer technology are enabling companies to create customized products in mass quantities. Dell and Gateway computer companies ushered in this revolution by building computers-to-suit. Greeting cards (bluemountain.com), custom music CDs, one-of-a-kind Barbie dolls, and customized college textbooks followed suit. I predict that modularized homes will be next — a way for the masses to own a custom-designed home. But my vote for the coming killer app for mass customization is clothing. Go to the clothier's Web site, pick a style, fabric, and color, enter your body measurements, and UPS will deliver your custom-tailored garment to your front door. No more endless shopping mall treks in hopes of finding something that looks great not just on the mannequin, but on our very unmannequin-like bodies. (See www.tc2.com/Home/HomeMass.htm.) Land's End is already working on this. Other likely candidates for mass customization: upholstered furniture, window treatments, and, within a decade, drugs.

Non-Polluting Vehicles. Cars give people freedom that mass transit can never touch, even if we tripled the mass transit budget. But cars, trucks, and buses pollute. The answer: non-polluting cars. It's unclear what combination of fuel cell, electric, solar, and gas-powered engines will emerge as optimal, but it is clear that soon, government will require vehicles to be much easier on the environment. *Institute of Transportation Studies:* www.its.ucdavis.edu.

Aging Parents. Boomers don't want to send their aging parents to a nursing home. Besides, they can't afford it — they haven't saved enough for their own retirements. And with people living longer than ever, the issue will be unavoidable. Businesses that can make life easier for boomers to care for their aging parents will thrive. Ideas include build in-law units, "Coping with Alzheimer's" coaching for family members, and geriatric care management to handle the details of an aging person's life when the children reside in another city.

Finally, two non-technotrends that I believe will offer tremendous career opportunities:

- ✔ **Eastern Europe and China.** A decade after opening Eastern Europe to capitalism, some of the kinks have been worked out. Now may be the time to jump in. Entrepreneurs, do what you know over there. One American set up a medical journal publishing company in Poland. Another conducts corporate training in Hungary. Both of those fields are fairly full in the United States but wide open in Eastern Europe. Both Americans are now millionaires. And now that China has permanent trading status in the World Trade Organization, its 1.2 billion (!) people represent a hugely untapped, if Wild West-like market.

- ✔ **Haves versus the Have-Nots.** The decades-long trend of ever-growing differences between society's haves and have-nots must be addressed. Well-paying jobs require ever-higher-level skills that seem unreachable by growing numbers of people. Their inability to compete renders them economically vulnerable, which reduces their chances of ever rising from poverty and increases the likelihood of social unrest. Issues such as healthcare will not have easy solutions. The "have-nots" use health-care resources at a far greater rate than others. Should they, even though they don't pay into the system, and may even be illegal aliens, be allowed to use more healthcare resources than U.S. citizens who do contribute? Even if it decreases the quality of health care available to the contributors? Especially in the area of health, where we're often literally talking life or death, there will be strong feelings on both sides of this issue. Researchers and policymakers are sorely needed to figure out solutions to the haves/have-nots problem that don't require confiscatory taxation policies that would generate a revolt from the haves.

Not-So-Cool Careers

All of the following are popular careers, and no doubt, there are happy people in them, but, for most folks, I think the 500-plus cool careers profiled in these Cool Career Yellow Pages are a cut above. Lest you think I forgot about your favorite career, or wanted to know why it didn't make it into the hallowed halls of the Cool Careers Yellow Pages, here are my excuses.

Of course, if, despite my reservations, you're excited about pursuing one of these so-called "not-so-cool careers," don't let me or anyone else stop you from pursuing it. Each person must listen to his or her own heart. I've met many people whose parents, teachers, and friends told them not to pursue a particular career and who surprised everyone by becoming happy and successful in it.

Advertising Executive. This is a tough field to break into. It requires long hours, and it has high turnover in the first few years. Even if you survive, only a small percentage of ad execs make serious money. Besides, do you really want to devote your work life to convincing people to buy Tide versus Fab?

Chef. Despite the glamorous image, in the end, being a chef means lots of hours over a hot stove where tempers flare and stress is high. Kitchen help tends to be variable, and because you're usually working nights and weekends, your social life tends to revolve around getting drunk with them. Creativity is rare; repetition of the same few recipes is common. Only a tiny fraction of chefs get the fame and big bucks. See chef Anthony Bourdaine's acclaimed tell-all book, *Kitchen Confidential*. Personal chefs, however, have it better. See the profile on page 55. Also, a few supermarkets are starting to hire chefs to provide gourmet meals to time-starved customers. If that trend grows, supermarket chef could be a cool career. See this book's next edition.

Chemist. Most of the job growth in chemistry is in biochemistry. That field is covered in the "Biology" profile.

Chiropractor. Some people swear by chiropractic, and some studies show that it is sometimes more effective than medical approaches for lower back pain. So chiropractic can be a rewarding profession when practiced well. But for the amount and expense of the training involved, I decided that there were enough minuses to keep chiropractic out of the august group of cool careers. Chiropractic requires a two-, and increasingly, a four-year science-intensive college education followed by four years of chiropractic doctoral education (all 17 accredited institutions are private and therefore expensive) plus demanding national and state board exams. After all that training and cost, there is serious controversy over the effectiveness of chiropractic beyond treatment of lower back pain and similar ailments. Many chiropractors, egged on by practice-building consultants, claim that spinal manipulation — chiropractors' main technique — can address a wide variety of ills. But according to QuackWatch, a member of the Consumer Federation of America that focuses on health-related fraud and winner of more than 40 awards as a top health Web site, "Very few health problems can be influenced by spinal manipulation. There is no logical reason to believe that regular spinal 'checkups' and 'adjustments' provide any general health benefit." For the complete report, see www.quackwatch.com/01QuackeryRelatedTopics/chirosell.html. To get the chiropractic profession's side, visit the *American Chiropractic Association's Web site at* www.amerchiro.org.

Court Reporter. In the first edition of this book, I included court reporting in the Cool Careers Yellow Pages. I'm excluding it this time. Yes, the pay is still good, yes, the work environment is still pleasant, and the job market is still growing because of the increasingly clogged courts and government requirements that TV shows be captioned. In the end, though, I decided to exclude court reporting because of technology. By the time you finish the two- to four-year training, there's a reasonable chance that voice-recognition software will have started to render you obsolete. With so many less risky career options, why choose this?

Fiction Writer. Lottery odds against making even a subsistence living at this. Good hobby, though.

Firefighter. Too boring for days at a time, and when it's not boring, you're often in danger. Plus, you have to live in a firehouse with a bunch of other firefighters.

Hotel Manager. It's a long road to obtain this position, one that often requires much menial work along the way.

Middlemen. Insurance, real estate, or stockbrokers, wholesalers, and so on. Sooner rather than later, the Internet will eliminate many of these jobs. There's even an impressive term for the trend: disintermediation — it means eliminate the middleman.

Overseas careers. Worker permits are tough to get, especially for better-paying jobs. Also, many Americans find that living abroad is less rewarding than vacationing there.

Performance Artist (singer, comedian, dancer, and so on). Long odds against making a middle-class living doing this. Good hobby.

Physicist. This is a field that requires an especially challenging Ph.D. to qualify for a substantive position, and the Department of Labor predicts a poor job market for physicists. People with physics backgrounds are more likely to find employment in engineering, especially hardware engineering and geology, both of which are profiled in the Cool Careers Yellow Pages.

Police Officer. Too dangerous, plus your job is basically to keep a lid on an enormous problem. You never get to deal with the core causes. Besides, there's a surprising amount of paperwork.

Politician. Although a half-million people make a living as politicians, I can't call it a cool career. The main reason is that the process of getting elected is so absurd. Your private life is made public. The process consists mainly of telemarketing, nonstop door-to-door flesh-pressing, and rubber chicken dinners, none of which reveals anything about your competence to do the job. And then there's the fundraising: taking money from special interests that will expect something in return; and no matter how much money you raise, you usually must contribute a lot of your own money to fund the absurdity. If the campaigning were just a few months every four years, it might be tolerable, but most successful politicians find themselves running continual campaigns, spending as much time campaigning and fundraising as they do governing.

Real Estate Salesperson. Only 20 percent of real estate salespeople make a middle-class living. And those who make big money usually work big hours, including many nights and weekends. Real estate sales jobs are commission-only, and it takes months for a deal to close, so you usually need at months of savings to support your start-up. Finally, I believe that long-term prospects for real estate salespeople are poor. In coming years, online househunting will eliminate much of the work that Realtors currently do. One bright spot: senior housing. The many baby boomers seeking elder housing for their parents (and soon for themselves!) will require more handholding than a computer can provide. And older people generally are more distrustful of computers anyway. If I were to become a Realtor today, I'd focus on senior housing.

Retail Buyer. The excess of American stores portends more consolidations. If a chain store can't put a little guy out of business, it usually buys it — the chainification of America — resulting in less hiring of buyers and additional pressure on existing ones. Most buyers work long hours. In addition, computerized ordering has eliminated many buyer jobs.

Retail Manager. Long hours, low pay, high burnout. America is over-stored.

Travel Agent. The low pay and relentless telephone work with clients endlessly changing their minds are too small compensation for the travel benefits. Besides, travel Web sites are eliminating much of the need for travel agents.

job good.
life good.

Monster.com is your link to a successful career.
Just visit our Career Center for the latest advice and
television listings from author Marty Nemko.
Then post your resume and start fielding the offers.

Chapter 3
The 25 Most Revealing Questions

In This Chapter
▶ Assessing values
▶ Assessing abilities
▶ Assessing passions
▶ The big picture

*Y*ou meet. Your heart starts pounding. You fall madly in lust. You don't stop to think that he's married to his work. Or that her earning potential is worse than an aspiring artist's. Or that, actually, he's pretty boring. A lifetime of listening to him? Get serious.

Or the opposite, you meet the logical choice: intelligent, employed, no vices. The facts are all there, but the chemistry's not.

As in finding a mate, finding a career should involve both your head and your heart.

You've already used your heart: you picked out the careers from the Cool Careers Yellow Pages that make your heart beat faster. Now it's time to use your head. Which of those careers (or perhaps another career) logically makes sense? The problem is that if you're like most career searchers, you're not sure.

That's where the 25 questions in this chapter come in. Over the years, with my clients and callers to my career radio show, I've tried every approach imaginable to tease out people's *career musts:* the things people really want and need in a career. I've found these 25 questions to be the most helpful to most people.

Making the Process Easier

When a doctor takes your medical history, she knows that only a few of your answers to her many questions will reveal anything significant. She still asks all of them because she can't know in advance which questions are significant for you.

The same is true of these 25 questions. Only a few will reveal one of your true *career musts*. Questions that yield one usually elicit an immediate "Aha!" So if you have even a hint of trouble answering a question, skip it and go on — that question is unlikely to be significant for you.

Mark your answers directly on the questionnaire. Be sure to focus on your career *musts*. Don't pick career characteristics that would be nice but aren't *musts*. People who include all the "that-would-be-nice" characteristics end up with a mile-long list, which leaves them not much better off than when they started. So record only the things you'd really love your career to offer.

Try, too, to answer the questions with a fresh mind — don't automatically give answers that conform to your current job, to the career you're contemplating, or to your parents', spouse's, or society's expectations.

After you've answered these 25 questions, I'll tell you how to make use of your career musts.

Your Values

1. **Are any of the following *crucial* in your next career? If not, leave this item blank.**

   A minimum salary of (specify):_____

   A prestigious job title

   The opportunity for self-expression/creativity

   A specific location (specify) — examples: at home, a particular city, near water):_____

   A particular work environment (specify) — examples: at home, in the wilderness, on a college campus, well-funded nonprofit, the military, in a big city, in the country, in a luxurious office building: _____

   A fast- (or slow-) paced job

   Short training time

   Being self-employed

Working on a team

Working by yourself

Working for a small (or large) organization

Working for a nonprofit

Working for the government

Working for a particular cause (specify): _____

2. **Write your worklife mission statement**:

   In one sentence, describe what you'd most like to accomplish. If that suggests a career or a career must, write it here:

   _____

   _____

   _____

3. **What are you inauthentic about?**

   Most people don't act in accordance to their own values. They're inauthentic, perhaps about money, work, pleasure, or their relationships. Does this suggest a career must?

   _____

   _____

   _____

Your Abilities and Skills

4. **To be successful and satisfied at work, should you spend the bulk of your workday on one or two of these? (As usual, if none pop out at you, leave it blank.)**

   Speaking one-on-one

   Speaking to groups

   Reading

   Writing

   Working with data, numbers, or computer code

   Supervising people

   Being entrepreneurial

Helping people

Doing office work

Working by yourself

Convincing people

Making something artistic with your hands

Making or fixing something

Perhaps most important, other? _____

5. **Do you have *specific* expertise that you know you want to use in your career? Write it here**.

   For example, a degree in molecular biology, ability to program in Java, three years of import-export experience.

   _____

   _____

   _____

5a. **Do you have a *more generic* skill or ability you know you want to use in your career?**

   Especially consider attributes that people compliment you on or which few people have. For example, Edgar had a knack for calming people down, and easily landed a job as a crisis counselor. Another client had a knack for developing tests and surveys. He found a job with a polling organization.

   _____

   _____

   _____

6. **What do you find easy that many other people find hard or stressful?**

   Many people aren't sure what their best skills are. It's no panacea, but you may want to consider taking the aptitude test battery in James Barrett's book, *Test Your Own Job Aptitude or the Campbell Interests and Skills Survey,* available for $17.95 at www.usnews.com/usnews/edu/careers/ccciss.htm.

   _____

   _____

   _____

Your Passions

7. If you were to write a book or movie screenplay what would it be about? Does that topic suggest a possible career for you?

_____

_____

_____

8. What articles are you most likely to read carefully?

_____

_____

_____

9. Is there a type of organization you'd love to work for?

Here are some that my clients picked: TV news show, shopping Web site, filmmaking company, guitar manufacturer, educational software company, snowboard factory, American Association of Retired Persons, biotech company, cosmetics firm, Environmental Protection Agency.

You'll have much less competition for good jobs and for advancement in fields that few people aspire to work in; for example, the scrap metal industry, database administration, heavy equipment manufacturing.

_____

_____

_____

10. Have you or someone you love faced an adversity that suggests a career that excites you?

Having undergone a mastectomy, Rhonda now fits other women who have had mastectomies with prosthetic breasts and special lingerie. Rhonda meets clients in their own homes and says, "People are very appreciative. It's so much more relaxed than walking into a cold department store with everyone hearing what your problem is."

_____

_____

_____

11. **What are you angry about? Do you want a career that addresses that anger?**

    For example, a client was angry about affirmative action hurting white males. He became a career counselor specializing in white males.

12. **If you see a passion or two on this list that you'd *love* to be part of your next career, circle it/them.**

Research	Creating beauty	Getting a good deal
Music	Plants	Mathematics
Dance	Sports	Accounting/taxes
Selling	Construction	Books, magazines
Public speaking	Newspapers	Educating/training
Web sites	Architecture	Travel
Machines	Mass transportation	Biotechnology/Genetics
Telecommunications	Artificial intelligence	Photography
Television/radio	Environmental issues	Religion/spirituality
Information systems	Science	Counseling
Human rights	Sewing	Health planning
Consumer advocacy	Law	Healthcare
Landscaping	International affairs	Fitness
Aviation	Labor-employee relations	Drug abuse
Aerospace	Insects	Foreign languages
Real estate	Electronic equipment	Management
Criminal justice	Outdoor recreation	Urban/regional planning
Computer hardware	Film	Animals
Computer software	Theater	Cars
Cooking	Energy	Investments
Writing	History	Politics
Food	Sex	Relationships
Law	And perhaps most important, something else: (specify)	

13. Is there a certain type of person you definitely want to work with? If so, circle the type in this list; otherwise, leave this item blank:

Children

Teens

Adults

Older adults

The physically sick

The mentally troubled

The highly intelligent

Those of average intelligence

Those of low intelligence

Arty people

Entrepreneurs

Nerds

People who build or fix things

Happy people

People with a problem (Feel free to be more specific):

People of a particular race, gender or sexual orientation (specify):

Alone

Perhaps most important, other (specify):

14. Do any of these self-employment categories excite you?

Be self-employed in a high profit margin, niche field that has little competition. Perhaps used parts for 18-wheel trucks?

Pay $10,000-$100,000-plus to have a business's how-tos laid out for you (buying an existing business or franchise).

Something that people complain about that suggests a business you can start.

A hobby or personal interest that can be turned into a business.

A product or service you'd like to sell.

Replicating a successful business in a different geographic area; for example, opening a New York-style pizza place in the South, or selling previously best-selling computer equipment in third-world countries.

Creating a template for a difficult-to-stage event and replicating it for different customers, for example, fundraising auctions for nonprofit organizations.

A grungy business, which means there are few competitors. Examples: commercial bathroom maintenance, hazardous waste disposal, high-voltage electrical work.

Distributing the work of creative people. Examples: agent for performers or artists, film distributor, owner of an online art gallery.

Big-Picture Questions

15. What are your peak accomplishments?

These are achievements that you had plenty of drive to complete and which gave you a strong sense of accomplishment. If you can't think of at least two from adulthood, go back to your younger days. Does looking at your peak accomplishments suggest a *career must* or even a career?

_____

_____

16. Describe your dream workday, from the moment you get up until the moment you go to sleep. Does that suggest a career must or even a career?

_____

_____

17. What career do your parents, partner, or close friends think you should pursue?

If you don't know, ask them. But don't too quickly accept or reject their advice because of the source. Make an open-minded choice.

_____

_____

17a. If you didn't care what your family and friends thought, what career would you pursue?

_____

_____

18. What would your twin tell you to do?

_____

_____

19. Do you know of a wealthy, well-connected, eminent, or highly skilled person who can help you get hired for a better job than you can get on the open market? If not, leave this item blank. If so, what kind of work would you want to do for that person?

It bugs everyone. You wonder, how in the world that person got that great job? Well, she may have known someone. Especially if you're short on technical expertise, knowing someone can often help you get a better job than you can get on the open market.

_____

_____

20. If you acted like a true grownup, what would you do?

_____

_____

21. What would you like your life to look like 10 years from now? Any implications of that for your career choice?

_____

_____

21a. Imagine that years from now, an article announcing your retirement appeared in the newspaper, What would you love it to say about your career?

_____

_____

22. Sometimes, what you need more than anything else is a change. What career appeals to you that would represent a dramatic change from what you're currently doing?

_____

_____

23. **If you're thinking about a career change, what makes you think that it's wiser to seek a new career, rather than a new job in your same career or doing more to make the most of your current job? (Seek out new assignments, a new boss, or work on your personal demons.)**

   _____

   _____

24. **Take the College Board's Career Questionnaire (**http://cbweb9p. collegeboard.org/career/html/searchQues.html**) or Princeton Review Career Quiz. (Go to** www.review.com/career **and click on "TPR Career Quiz.") Write any results that you believe are crucial to your career.**

   _____

   _____

25. **Deep down, some people know what they want to do. They simply need to be asked point-blank. Richard Bolles asks, "What job would you love to do more than any other in the world?"**

   _____

   _____

Now, what to do with all your answers? Turn the page.

Chapter 4

Integrating Head and Heart

. . . .

In This Chapter

▶ Distilling what you discovered from the 25 Most Revealing Questions

▶ Identifying careers that fit your *career musts*

▶ A virtual career counselor

▶ Deciding on the final career(s) to check out

. . . .

Great! You've used your heart to pick out careers that feel good from the Cool Careers Yellow Pages. You've used your head to answer the *25 Most Revealing Questions*. Now, I show you how to integrate head and heart so that you end up choosing a career that satisfies you both rationally and emotionally.

Julie Finds a Career

For the past 20 years, Julie has been a biologist for one of the nation's largest cosmetics manufacturers. She used to like her job, but now hates it. Much of her work is now automated, so she spends half her time monitoring a machine and the other half feeling useless. Trouble is, her biology training was 20 years ago, so she's no longer marketable as a biologist. She browsed the Cool Careers Yellow Pages and, on gut feeling, picked out restaurant menu designer, neon sign maker, personal assistant, optician, and speech therapist. Julie's answers to the 25 Most Revealing Questions revealed that her logical *career musts* came down to just three things: a job that requires a detail-oriented person, an opportunity to work with her hands, and a chance to be her own boss. In light of those career musts, she eliminated personal assistant. She tried to come up with other careers that satisfy her career musts that sounded even more interesting but could not. Even though it wouldn't involve working with her hands, Julie decided to look first into speech therapy. Join us in the next chapter for the poignant conclusion of *Julie Finds a Career*.

That's a real-life example. Now here's that career-finding process, step-by-step.

Discovering Your Top-Choice Career(s)

I'm going to be straight with you. Despite my best efforts, the rest of this chapter requires concentration and can be, frankly . . . well . . . let me just say it . . . boring. However, it's also important. Otherwise, I would have simply pressed the delete key. Stay with me. Most of you will find this chapter worth the effort. The good news is that it's short.

Step 1: List your career musts

Look back at your answers to the 25 Most Revealing Questions and copy here the answers you consider most significant. These are your *career musts*.

_____

_____

_____

If you listed more than five *career musts,* see if you can whittle down to the five most important without feeling like you're cutting off your right arm. *Hint:* You can often "cheat" by combining two *musts* into one.

Step 2: Do the careers you picked satisfy your career musts?

Look at how well each career you picked from the Cool Careers Yellow Pages satisfies your career musts. Does that make you want to eliminate any of those careers?

Step 3: Do your career musts suggest other careers?

Look at your career musts. Do any other careers come to mind that are at least as interesting as those you picked from the Cool Careers Yellow Pages?

If you can't come up with any other careers, see the virtual career counselor later in this chapter.

Or ask your friends to brainstorm with you — a decent party game. Here are some examples:

- When Jacque saw "sales," "romance," and "aesthetic" among her career musts, she added wedding planner to her list of possible careers.

- When Luther saw "writing," "travel," "high-income," and "fluent in Spanish," he added "marketing communications writer for a fast-growing company that does business with Central America" to his list of possible careers.

Many people's career musts are quite general — for example, "I like managing and communicating with adults." To avoid a difficult job search, you need to narrow your focus. Here's a solution: Decide *where* you might want to use those general career musts. For example, maybe you'd like managing and communicating with adults in a hospital, or in the financial services industry, or on a cruise ship to Bora-Bora. Or decide *who* you want to work with? Artsy types? Business people? Techies? Gifted children?

A wise client named Eric said, "Managing is managing, so why not pick an uncrowded industry, one that most people wouldn't think of?" He looked through the index of the Yellow Pages and stopped at "acid manufacturers." He read up on the acid industry, e-mailed all the local firms, and soon got a management job with a minimum of competition.

A virtual career counselor

Stuck? Can't come up with careers that incorporate your *career musts?* Try these steps. This process simulates what I actually do to come up with career ideas for clients. It's easier than it looks. Give it a shot.

1. **Come up with one career that incorporates three of your career musts.**

2. **Ask yourself what feels wrong about that career.**

3. **Come up with another career that fixes what's wrong.**

4. **Repeat Steps 2 and 3 until you make the career as desirable as you can.**

5. **Now, see if you can incorporate one or more of your remaining career musts into the career you identified in Step 4.**

To create more career options, repeat the process with the same or different three career musts.

Here's an example:

Terry's career musts include the following:

- Systems analysis in Windows 2000 environment
- Work with smart people
- Explain complicated things in plain English
- Work at home
- International opportunities

Here's how Terry played virtual career counselor:

1. **Come up with one career that incorporates three of your career musts.**

   Terry comes up with "train people in systems analysis." (That fit his first three *career musts*.)

2. **Ask yourself what feels wrong about that career.**

   "I'm afraid that training would get boring," Terry realizes.

3. **Come up with another career that fixes what's wrong.**

   Terry thinks, "Okay, what if I do systems analysis training in another country?" (one of his other career musts). His reaction: "No, still feels boring. Besides, the toilet paper will be worse. Okay, what if, instead of training on systems analysis, I do systems analysis *consulting.* That would give me a new challenge with each new client. Hmm."

4. **Keep repeating Steps 2 and 3 until you make the career as desirable as you can.**

   "Okay, systems analysis consulting. Not bad. What feels wrong? I'm not a good marketer. Okay. I'll hire a marketing whiz. Okay, what still feels wrong? I'm afraid it would be lonely. Okay, I'll take a part-time job so that I'll see people on a regular basis. That would also give me some income while I'm cranking up my consulting business. Okay, that feels pretty good."

5. **Now see if you can incorporate one or more of your remaining career musts into the career you identified in Step 4.**

   "Well, the international thing is the only career must I haven't incorporated. And as I look at the career I created for myself, I don't mind giving that up. I think I'll be able to satisfy my travel urges on vacations."

Additional help

Do you want more options than you have been able to come up with on your own? It may be time for a bit of professional help. Consider seeing a career counselor in private practice or at a college or community career counseling center. You can request a list of local nationally certified career counselors at www.nbcc.org. Here's another alternative: I offer career counseling, by-phone and in person: 510-655-2777.

Step 4: Remember what careers excite you

One or more of the 25 Most Revealing Questions may elicit not just a career must, but an actual career that excites you. If so, do you like it at least as well as those you picked from the Cool Careers Yellow Pages? If so, add it (or them) to your list of possible careers.

Step 5: Pick one or more careers that might actually work

Look at all your possible careers:

- ✔ Careers you identified in Steps 3 and 4
- ✔ Careers you picked from the Cool Careers Yellow Pages
- ✔ Other careers you're considering — like going into your uncle's widget business

And now, ta-dah, the moment of truth: Is there at least one career that feels like a real possibility? If yes, go to Step 6. If not, see Chapter 21.

Step 6: Find out more

Before making your final career choice, you'll probably want to learn more about that top-choice career(s) of yours. Chapter 5 shows you how to do just that.

Chapter 5

What's That Career Really Like?

. . . .

In This Chapter

▶ Reviewing printed information

▶ Using the Internet

▶ Getting the scoop from people in the field

▶ Visiting a workplace

▶ Trying out a career

. . . .

You've found a career (or three) that sounds good. But what if you picked wrong? What if you fail in that career? Or you succeed but are totally miserable?

This chapter boosts your chances of picking well. It shows how to find out what a career is really like — before taking the plunge. And it's not complicated. Reading, contacting, and visiting are the three approaches. Read about the career, and if it still sounds good, contact a few people in the field, and if it still feels right, visit a few people at their workplace. This chapter shows you how to make the most of all three approaches.

A side benefit of all that digging around is that you have insider information about the career, which should make you *molto impresivo* in job interviews.

The Busy Person's Way to Check Out a Career

Despite all the benefits, I find that many career seekers, especially those with full-time jobs, won't take the time to thoroughly investigate a career. So, here's the much-better-than-most-people-use approach:

1. **Read about your target career at the Web site(s) listed in the Cool Careers Yellow Pages.**

2. **If the career still sounds interesting, find out more about it by visiting one of the Web's major career information portals,** `www.rileyguide.com`, `www.acinet.org`, **or** `www.careersonline.com.au` **and drill your way down until you find information on your target career.**

3. **If the career still sounds interesting, go to** `Amazon.com` **and use the career as the search term.**

   At least skim the book that seems most interesting.

4. **If the career still sounds interesting, that's your career.**

   Don't worry about whether it's the perfect career — few off-the-shelf careers ever are. Rather than sitting on the sidelines waiting for perfection, you'll more likely approach nirvana by simply picking a career that feels pretty good, getting well-trained in it (the topic of Part II of this book) landing a good job with a good boss in that career (the subject of Part III) and then molding that job to fit you (the topic of Chapter 19).

For those of you who find that *McSearch* approach too quick and dirty, read on.

Julie Finds a Career: The Final Episode

In the previous episode of *Julie Finds a Career* (in Chapter 4), after browsing the Cool Careers Yellow Pages and answering the 25 Most Revealing Questions, Julie decided to look into speech therapy. She never dreamt what she would find, right on her computer. In the online *Occupational Outlook Handbook,* Julie discovered a specialty within speech therapy that she had personal experience with: swallowing problems. Her grandmother, after a stroke, was unable to swallow, and had to be fed with a feeding tube until her death. It is one of Julie's most vivid memories. Julie got chills at the thought that perhaps her career could focus on helping people avoid the feeding tube.

And as she continued to read, Julie found out that speech therapy was even a practical career choice. Because of the aging population, demand for speech therapists is expected to increase greatly. Even better for Julie, who wanted to be self-employed, the OOH says that demand for speech therapists in private practice is expected to grow dramatically due to the use of contract services by healthcare providers. And although she would have to go back to school, the OOH indicates that much of the course work is basic sciences and math, all of which she had taken.

For the first time in 20 years, Julie was excited about her career prospects. Eagerly, she visited the American Speech-Language-Hearing Association Web site. There, she found dozens of articles about swallowing disorders, many of which listed authors and contact information. She phoned those contacts to ask about the more personal aspects of the job. Among other things, she learned about the field's dark side. Swallowing specialists frequently face a particularly painful situation: when a stroke patient is in an irreversible coma and has lost all ability to swallow. At this point, the speech therapist must discuss whether to insert a feeding tube. That would prolong the comatose person's life but it also usually means that the family must continue to pay enormous medical bills just to keep him in a coma.

Shaken but still stirred, Julie asked two local swallowing specialists if she could visit them at work. The visits clinched the decision for Julie. She saw her grandmother in the patients and could picture herself as the speech therapist helping them. Now, it somehow didn't matter that this career didn't have one of Julie's career musts: working with her hands. Now, it somehow didn't matter that she had to go back to school, or that she'd have less income for a while — the two things that had so scared Julie that she stayed for 20 years in a job in which she was unhappy. Now, somehow, all the fears and the obstacles seemed conquerable. Julie had found her perfect work.

Researching a career may sound boring in the abstract, but for Julie, and perhaps for you, it can change your life.

Reading about a Career

Books and articles are among the most underrated products. (And a college education may be the most overrated, but that's another book.) If you're willing to do only one thing to check out a career, read. A good book or article constitutes access to the best, most thorough, and most carefully organized ideas. And they're available to you at any time, day or night, for the cost of a large pizza — or free at the library.

By reading an article or skimming a book, you learn what took an expert years to figure out. Consider the *Occupational Outlook Handbook*. It includes authoritative profiles of 253 of the most popular careers, based on interviews with many people in those fields. What a treasure! Reading the OOH is like hearing what thousands of people have to say about their careers. Plus, the information is distilled for you and available whenever or wherever you want it. To me, that's cool.

Why read before phoning or visiting?

Okay, so why would you read about a career before you contact someone in that field? Simple: You don't want to sound like a dodo. Read about the career and you're more likely to impress your contacts as being worth their time. Who knows? One of them may then be willing to take you under wing, reveal inside secrets, and maybe even help you get hired.

Also, boning up in advance means that you'll make the most of your contact — you'll only need to ask about the things you couldn't discover on your own.

Best stuff to read

"All right, so you've guilt-tripped me into reading stuff. What should I read? And please don't tell me to read something boring." I'll do my best.

Try this elegantly simple approach recommended by Mary-Ellen Mort, career librarian and founder of jobstar.org, a leading career site.

1. **Call your area's central library and ask which branch (or local college or high school) has the best career collection. If no career collection is available, ask for the business collection.**

2. **Visit or call the librarian in charge of that collection, and describe the career you want to learn more about.**

   That's all you need to do. The librarian is likely to help you find the right information. It's that simple.

I'll let you in on a librarian's secret: In addition to books and periodicals, today's libraries have powerful online and CD-ROM services — too expensive for home users — that can search enormous databases for information about your target career.

But what if you live hours from a decent library? Or what if you're a do-it-yourselfer who'd rather I hand you some cool references? No need to consult them all. Just pick one or two that jump out at you.

- ✔ *The Occupational Outlook Handbook* **($19 or free online at** `www.bls.gov/ocohome.htm`**).** Its strength is its authoritativeness. Its weakness is that it avoids any subjectivity. So it's great on the facts, lousy on the feel. For the latter, use the next two books.

- ✔ *The Princeton Review Guide to Your Career (4th edition).* This book provides insider profiles of 175 popular careers. Each profile includes sections on "a day in the life," "paying your dues," "associated careers," "past and future," and "quality of life" in the profession two, five, and ten years after entry in that field.

- ✔ **Professional association publications**. A professional association's Web site often contains a gold mine of information about the field. It often uses the collective wisdom of many people in the profession to select the best, most accurate information available. I provide Web addresses of associations for most of the 500-plus careers in the Cool Careers Yellow Pages. *Best Home Businesses for the 21st Century,* by Paul and Sarah Edwards, provides comprehensive profiles of 100 top home businesses.

Using the Internet

The Internet, of course, provides a wealth of information. For example, WetFeet.com's "Careers and Industries" section is filled with insider information on popular fields. Similar: www.vault.com's forums. Others:

- ✔ **O*NET, the Occupational Information Network** (//online.onetcenter. org/) is a comprehensive database of information on thousands of careers, including skill requirements, salaries, and so forth.

- ✔ **The Riley Guide** (www.rileyguide.com): This site links to other sites for hundreds of specific occupations.

- ✔ **America's CareerInfoNet** (www.acinet.org) is a service of the U.S. Department of Labor, and offers links to some of the Net's best career information sites.

- ✔ **Industry Link** (www.industrylink.com): Does what it says: links you to information on many industries.

- ✔ **Your favorite search engine** (Mine are google.com and ixquick.com): Use the profession as the search term.

  Search engines are amazing tools. Imagine a librarian who can search the world's largest library (google.com searches 1.3 billion Web pages) to find each reference that includes the word or phrase you're interested in. Then this wonder-librarian stacks the items in order of how frequently your word or phrase is used. That's a search engine. And it's free. Plus, you have access to this "librarian" 24/7 in the comfort of your home. I love search engines!

- ✔ **The search feature at Amazon.com** (www.amazon.com): Simply enter your career and out pops book titles with your career in the title. The listings often include descriptions and even reviews of the books.

- ✔ **Myjobsearch.com.** (www.myjobsearch.com) Click on the career planning button and then the career exploration button and you'll find links to career information on hundreds of fields.

- ✔ **The postings on your field's online discussion groups.** There's a comprehensive list of these groups at www.liszt.com and www.topica.com.

Contacting People in the Field

You can't find out everything by reading. Talking to people lets you ask the questions that your reading didn't answer. It's also a way to start building your professional network.

Many career seekers are reluctant to call people in the field. The two main reasons are "I don't want to impose" and "I'm afraid I'll sound stupid." Remember that most people like to talk about their careers. And if they don't, they're adults — they can say no. Even if you are imposing, in the larger order of things, that's okay. The time will probably come when you're in a position to help someone. If you do, you'll have settled your karmic account. And if you do sound stupid, so what? How important is that in the larger scheme of things?

Need more prodding to pick up the phone or send that e-mail? Chapter 22 offers cures for *procrastitis.*

"Okay, okay, but whom do I contact?"

This list should yield you more contacts than you can stomach:

- If you have a friend or relative in your target career, you can start there. At the end of the conversation, ask for the names of colleagues you might speak with.

- Attend a local meeting of your professional association or an on-campus professional club.

- Get the phone numbers of members of the professional association by checking its Web site or by phoning its national or regional office.

- Talk with the editor of the professional association's magazine or newsletter. Editors often have a finger on the field's pulse, and may be willing to share some nuggets.

- Your college's Web site or career center may maintain a list of alumni who are willing to tell their career tales.

  Go to www.topica.com, find an online discussion group of people in your target career and post a query such as, "I'm thinking about a career in XXXX. What should I know about it that might not appear in print?"

- If you have chutzpah, just open your Yellow Pages and start dialing. Use your printed Yellow Pages for locals, anywho.com for out-of-towners. Out-of-towners may be more willing to talk with you because they're not as afraid you'll become a competitor.

Each person's viewpoint is idiosyncratic. One dentist may gush that business is booming while the next dentist moans that attracting new patients is like pulling teeth. (I couldn't resist.) So don't get too swayed by one person's opinion.

What to say

Count on getting turned down a lot in your quest for information, but the following approach works often enough, and, unlike oft recommended ruses, it's honest.

When you phone, you'll rarely get your target person. The key to getting through a gatekeeper or voice-mail jail is to briefly tell your true human story. Here's a gatekeeper example:

Hello, my name is (*Insert your name*). This may be one of the weirder (*Trust me, that word works*) calls you've gotten today, but I really need your help. I'm still trying to figure out what I want to be when I grow up. I think I may want to be a (*insert career*), but I'm not sure yet. I've read about the career but feel I should talk with someone in the field. Can I ask you to see if your boss might be willing to answer just a few questions about what it's like to be a (*insert career*)?

If the gatekeeper can't or won't put you through, ask for your target's e-mail address. But for now, assume that you have your target person on the phone. This approach works well:

Hello, I'm (*insert your name*). I'd really appreciate your help. I'm considering becoming a (*insert career*). I've read a lot about the field but would like to talk with someone who's actually in that career. I wonder if I could ask you a few questions about your experience as a (*insert career*).

If the person says that now isn't a good time, ask when you can call back or whether you can meet in person.

Next, ask your questions. You may have your own, but these questions are likely to elicit useful information: There are more here than you need. Pick your favorites.

- How'd you get into this career?

- Can you walk me through a typical day?

- What do you find to be the best and worst things about your career?

- What have you found to be the skills most important to succeeding in your career?

- Can you think of anything you know now that you wish you'd known when you were deciding to enter this field?

- Can you think of anything I should know about this field that is unlikely to find its way into print? (My favorite question.)

- Describe your background and interests. Then ask, "Do you think I should consider this field? Any other fields I should consider?"

- Any advice about the smartest way to prepare for this career?

- Are there jobs in this field that provide particularly good learning experiences?

- In this field, where are good job openings listed?

- What kind of salary can I expect?

- Are there any particularly interesting specialties within your field?

✔ How is the field changing?

✔ Why might someone leave this field?

✔ Do you know someone else you think I should talk with or something else I should read before deciding whether to pursue this career? Any event I should attend? Any organization I should join?

✔ Any other advice you'd give someone entering this field?

If the conversation went well, ask if you could spend an hour watching that person at work.

Visiting a Workplace

Why visit? Because, like sex, some things you just have to experience to fully appreciate. Watching someone at work is the next best thing to trying it yourself.

Craig, for example, thought he might want to be an arborist (tree surgeon), but after spending an hour on-site with a professional, realized that having to spend that much time on high branches, often in bad weather, outweighed the joy of artfully shaping trees.

 If you won't visit at least three people in your target career, I recommend you visit none. That may seem like odd advice, but remember that a single person's version of a career is idiosyncratic. Say you're contemplating becoming a career counselor. Your visit to a chain career counseling service will likely take you to a downtown office building, where the counselors dress in suits and use a counseling style that emphasizes asking questions to draw out the client's own ideas. But if you visit me, you see a career counselor dressed in a sweater and chinos in a home office who generates many career ideas, asks the client to react to each, and refines the next idea based on that feedback. You may love one of those career counseling modes but not the other, and if you visit only one career counselor, you'd get a limited sense of your options.

What to do during a visit?

Okay, so you're on-site. What now? Simple. Just ask the person to show you around and to let you watch him do tasks that are central to the job. If possible, get introduced to others in that career at the worksite.

Use your head and your heart. Rationally, can you see yourself doing this work, day in and day out? Emotionally, do you sense that you'd feel good in such a career?

A virtual visit

If you live on an isolated farm, it may not be easy to visit an urban planner. That's why videotapes can be valuable. In some ways, career videos are better than in-person visits because they usually round up a variety of people in the profession, ask good questions, and give you the full tour. And a virtual visit is perfect for those shy souls who simply can't make themselves set up an in-person visit, let alone ask lots of good questions during the visit. Large libraries, especially those in a high school or college career center, should have a collection of career videos. Marginal videos on 200 careers can be viewed at `www.acinet.org/acinet/resource/videos.htm`.

After the phone call or visit

Even if it feels like a technique, write a thank-you letter — and not just because it's polite. Yes, recipients recognize thank-you letters as formalities, but those notes still tend to impress and, at minimum, keep you in the recipient's mind. That little note can motivate the recipient to offer you more counsel, or even help you land a job.

But there are thank-you notes and there are thank-you notes. Here's an approach that has worked for my clients. It's more informal and open than traditional versions.

Dear Sam,

I so appreciate your allowing me to watch you make artificial limbs. I'd never have realized how psychologically demanding working so closely with an amputee can be. Helping a person to replace his arm is such a personal thing!

I'm now sure I want to be a prosthetist. It balances art, science, and the need to be a real human being. If I work hard at it, I can do this.

I'll follow up on your suggestion to check out Cal State University, Dominguez Hills' program. If you have any other advice, I'd love it if you'd call me. And if I have a question, I hope you won't mind if I call you. Thank you so much.

Sincerely,

Jane Eager

Getting Serious

Here are a few time-consuming but potentially worthwhile activities for checking out your top-choice career. Time-consuming, yes, but much less so than making bad career choices.

- ✔ **A seminar or short course in your chosen field.** The professional association for that career may offer live, taped, or on-line versions. You'll find thousands of such courses cataloged at www.alx.org and www.astd.org/virtual_community/seminar_agent. Also check your local college's extension catalog. Taking a short course will help you assess both your aptitude for and interest in the field.

- ✔ **Conferences and trade shows.** These are excellent places to learn about a career. You have hundreds of practitioners plus their suppliers and customers all in one place. Exhibit areas sell tools of the trade, and ongoing workshops teach you the field's basics and cutting edges. Plus, the many meals, breaks, and parties are specifically designed to facilitate chatting.

- ✔ **Volunteering, interning, or project work.** Nothing takes the place of an actual tryout. A brief one is often enough to show you what you need to know about a career. Before deciding to become a high school teacher, Derrick volunteered as a classroom aide. After a week, he began to feel the draining effect of trying to keep 30 students — a different 30 every 50 minutes — motivated, let alone educated. He also quickly tired of the conversations in the teachers' lounge. Teaching wasn't right for him. Two weeks of volunteering saved him two years of training plus many more years of unhappiness in a career he did not like.

  A short-term volunteer or low-pay stint can be well worth your time — think of it as a tuition-free education. Working for little or nothing gives you power — the power to ensure that you get to do meaningful work. So, before signing on, negotiate your role. Licking envelopes for an oceanographer won't give you a good idea of what the job is like. Accompanying the oceanographer on a weeklong stay in a bathyscaph will.

Good internships can often be created simply by asking a desired mentor if you could be her slave in exchange for some mentorship. The advantage of that approach is that you get to pick your supervisor. Or find existing internships: See www.rileyguide.com/intern.html.

Okay. After all this digging around, your top-choice career should be getting clearer.

Rick, LaTonya, David, Tim & Jennifer

Rick was totally bored selling lease financing. He considered alternatives from handwriting analyst to driving range manager. In the end, however, he decided to become a massage therapist "because that was the easiest path: the training is short, there was a good massage school nearby, and I heard that the job market was good. It's been three years now, and I'm still happy as a massage therapist although I don't make much money. I'm glad my wife is an accountant."

LaTonya had seen women treated poorly in the military and, when she left, considered starting a small business as a gender-equity consultant to the military. But entrepreneurship seemed too scary so she took a job as an operations manager for a nearby company. That job taught her a little about all aspects of a business, from sales to marketing to accounting. With the confidence those newfound skills have given her, she's thinking about starting that gender-equity auditing business.

David. For seven years, David was running a record shop, but the Internet was killing his business. Not only can music lovers now order online, they can download their favorite cuts, usually without paying a penny. So, David began thinking of an Internet career. He went to school for Webmaster certification and registered with temp agencies. He landed a few short-term, entry-level freelance gigs, which added crucial experience to his resume. He was no longer sounding like an outsider trying to get in. After that, within just two weeks of looking for a full-time job, he got eight interviews and landed a job with a Web development firm. *(Reported in* The 5 O'Clock News.*)*

Tim. "I quit my well-paying but meaningless career as a typesetter and took a bad-paying job working with AIDS patients. It's 17 years later and it has been a wonderful experience, but now I'm starting to worry. I'm 50 and not prepared for retirement. No nest egg. Do I bail out from work that I love and find some good-paying but less meaningful job? Do I have to cut my expenses by taking in roommates? I don't know."

Jennifer described herself as a "fru-fru type." Her job was selling skin care products, a multi-level marketing scheme. One day, her friend turned down a job — financing specialist at a car dealer — because she didn't want to work weekends. Jennifer's friend urged her to apply for it even though there was nothing "fru-fru" about car financing. The opportunity fell in Jennifer's lap. She was making a pittance selling face cream, so she applied and ended up getting the job. A few promotions later, Jennifer was making $200,000. "I don't mind at all that it's not fru-fru."

Chapter 6

Finding the Courage to Commit

· ·

In This Chapter

▶ When no career is attractive enough

▶ When you're afraid of failing

▶ When you're fighting inertia

▶ A final check

· ·

*N*o matter how much analysis you do, it can be hard to make that final decision and say: "Yes, this is the career I want!" This chapter helps you make that decision.

People hesitate to act on a career choice for four reasons:

✔ Not enough information about your prospective career

✔ No career is clearly superior

✔ Fear of failure

✔ General inertia

These courage builders address all four.

When You Don't Know Enough about a Prospective Career

What's making you nervous about your proposed career? Sometimes, getting more information can give you courage. Examples:

✔ **"Am I good enough in math to be an economist?"** Possible solution: Ask economists how much math they use and whether niches exist that require less. Can you do that much math?

> ✔ **"Does a market really exist for the product I'm thinking of selling?"** Possible solution: Ask potential customers.
>
> ✔ **The cost and time of training.** Possible solution: Keep asking around. Often, there's shortcut training or, at least, ways to fund it.

Could reading something, talking to someone, or observing a workplace help you decide whether your prospective career is a wise choice?

When No Career Seems Attractive Enough

Sure, maybe you just need more options. If so, Chapter 21 offers 11 more sources of cool careers. But sometimes, you can look through every career collection in the world and still have a hard time committing. Often, that's because you're holding out for a career that is clearly superior to your other options.

True, some people know, early on, that they were meant to be a doctor, ballet dancer, or whatever, but those folks rarely use career guides. If that uniquely perfect career were going to hit you like a lightning bolt, it probably would've done so long before now.

If I filled a room with 100 people who love their careers, most of them would say that before entering the career, they weren't sure they'd love it. Most of them could easily have chosen another career. What brought them to career contentment was getting started, choosing something. That enabled them to turn their attention toward the things that make a career wonderful: getting good training, finding a good job or self-employment opportunity, and then tailoring it to fit their strengths, weaknesses, and preferences. As a result, only after they started to experience success could they say, "I love my career."

So, pick your favorite careers from The Cool Careers Yellow Pages and from the 25 Most Revealing Questions. Then distill that input using the virtual career counselor in Chapter 4. Next, take a moderate amount of time to check out a prospective career(s) using the approach in Chapter 5. Finally, select your top-choice career, even if it doesn't generate career ecstasy. *As long as a career seems clearly better than the status quo, choose it.* Until you've gotten into the career, you can't really know for sure that it'll make you happy. But taking steps down one career path is more likely to help you figure that out than additional thinking at the trailhead.

Be passionate in pursuing the career, even if you're ambivalent. That's key to ensuring your success. Focus on:

✔ **Getting the best training possible.** Good training makes you feel and be competent. The best training often is found at a student-oriented college rather than at a prestigious, research-oriented one. Even more practical training options include mentors, workshops, tapes, and articles.

✔ **Doing a thorough job search:** If you can get multiple job offers, you maximize your chances of finding a job with good co-workers, learning opportunities, and an organization you feel good about.

✔ **Molding the job you get to fit your strengths.** Revise your job description to make use of your assets. Propose projects you'd find fun. You may even be able to incorporate some advantages of other careers you considered. For example, if you choose interior design over photography, make before-and-after photos a part of your service.

✔ **Recognizing that your career contentment depends not just on a well-suited career and job, but on other factors as well:**

• **Accepting that work is work.** Even those who have worklives that many people envy usually think that work is still work. Work isn't often as pleasurable as going out to eat, watching TV, walking in nature, or being with someone you love. I can gratefully accept that work is work, mainly because I value being productive, feeling needed, having structure, and earning a living, even when it isn't fun. If you make this mindset permeate your workday, you can feel good about your worklife, even if you don't have a dream career.

• **Maintaining an accepting attitude.** It's easy to resent work's many moments that are too hard, too easy, too stressful, or too boring. Or you can view those moments with a Zen-like acceptance and a commitment to handle each moment with grace. For me, this is the key to happiness, not just in a career, but in life: handling each moment with grace.

At minimum, starting down a career path helps you learn that you made a wrong choice. Millions of people change careers. Indeed, the average person has four careers and a dozen jobs in his lifetime. If your next career choice bombs, you'll find out a great deal about yourself and make a better choice next time. You'll certainly make a better choice than if you had attempted to divine the perfect career while sitting on the sidelines.

When You're Afraid You'll Fail

Fear of failure is sometimes legitimate — in your gut, you know your chances of success are small. It's reasonable to be scared when applying for a job as computer engineer when your highest-level previous job was computer assembler. But sometimes, even if your rational mind believes you have a reasonable chance of success, your fear of failure makes you too scared to give it a try. These courage builders may help.

Recognize that it's usually worth risking failure

Many successful people have failed a lot. In high school, I was an office clerk — I got fired for making too many careless errors. My first professional job was as a school psychologist. Another person and I split the full-time job. After one year, they offered the entire job to the other guy — I was too impatient with the teachers. My first book was rejected by 18 publishers before one publisher offered me the grand sum of $5,000 for it. Yet if you look at my bio in the front of the book, I daresay you'd call me a success. To maximize your chances of success, try difficult, exciting things, and when you fail, ask what you can learn from it.

Failing usually is better than not trying at all. Not trying is the one sure way to absolutely guarantee that you fail. You'd be surprised how often trying something hard works out. Your adrenaline is pumping, you scramble a while, and eventually do okay. And that feels great.

Yeah I know, your fear of risk-taking stems from your childhood: Your mother taught you not to take risks, or your father yelled at you too often when you made a mistake. And I also know that kindly shrinks inadvertently support your inertia. "I know how difficult it must be when your parents were so tough on you." Bottom line, you gotta make yourself get over it. Rationally, if the benefits of trying something exceed the risks, feel the fear and do it anyway. Force yourself to stay focused on taking small steps and getting help when you're stuck.

All your ducks needn't be in a row

Many people think that before starting their career, they must have a crystal clear idea of their ultimate career goal and *know* they have the potential to succeed. It rarely works that way.

Many successful people get their first jobs with only a general idea of their career direction. Many are unsure whether they have the potential to succeed in that career. They simply sally forth. Kumar, a new college graduate, had the sense that he wanted to work in high-tech but couldn't be any more precise than that. He got a quickie entry-level certification in Java and Oracle and stuck those on his resume to see what the bait yielded. He got a job as a junior programmer for an e-commerce site. Who knows whether he'll end up happy in his career, but I'd sooner bet on him than on someone who waited for crystal clarity before acting.

The chief resident at a New York medical school greets each year's interns by saying, "Each of you is entitled to one clean kill. It is impossible to become a good doctor without lots of practice, and inevitably that means you're going to kill someone. Accept it. Over your lifetime, your worth as a doctor will be determined not by your early errors but by the sum total of what you do." If that's true for doctors, it's probably even truer for you — I suspect that your early errors will be less likely to kill someone. Remember, every newbie scrambles. Key to success then is to stop stewing and start acting.

General Inertia

Humans are not exempt from the laws of physics: An object at rest tends to stay at rest. Few of us leap at the thought of making radical changes. Yet, of course, you're reading this book because you want a better career. The courage builders in the following sections may help you choose to have one.

Compare your options against the status quo

Instead of comparing your candidate career(s) to some abstract ideal, compare it to the status quo. After all, that is your other option.

On a sheet of paper, make a column for each option you're considering, including the status quo. Write the advantages of each option. To get you started, here are some common advantages of the status quo and of changing careers.

Some advantages of the status quo

- You remain comfortable. Change is difficult.
- You avoid the time, cost, and difficulty of landing a new job, the stress of the learning curve, and having to prove yourself to a new boss and co-workers.
- You keep your friends on your current job.
- You avoid failure. If you fail in your new career, you may lose income and status, plus you probably won't get your old job back again.
- You avoid success. If you're successful, your time may not be your own anymore. That gardening you used to enjoy? No time. Those romantic weekends? No time.

Some advantages of changing careers

- ✔ More job satisfaction.
- ✔ More money and the things it can buy.
- ✔ More prestige.
- ✔ You get to learn new things.
- ✔ New friends.

The Judge Judy technique

Pretend you're a lawyer and give all the reasons why Career A is better. Then pretend you're the opposing lawyer and give all the reasons why Career B is better. Finally, be Judge Judy and render a decision.

Try out your new career as a sideline

Unsure whether your new career will work? Charlie was a customer support rep for a cable TV provider but liked the idea of producing videos of playful interviews with company employees for showing at company parties. Charlie started his video business as a sideline, not wanting to quit his job until he was sure he could make money at his new pursuit.

How Marty Nemko made a career decision

I was teaching graduate students at Berkeley when I realized I'd never be happy as a professor. I am practical at heart. I wouldn't be content in a career in which my primary task was to publish esoteric articles in the *Journal of Educational Psychology,* but I couldn't think of a career that really excited me. The best I could come up with was career counseling, but that felt just okay.

I nevertheless took the plunge. In the beginning I was unhappy and asked myself why. The job was too passive; sitting and listening most of the time. So I adopted a more active style, but the job still needed more spice, so I volunteered to host a weekly radio show on careers and education. That opened the door to the other cool things I now get to do.

Molding my career to fit me converted a so-so career into a happy one. I truly am eager to get up each weekday morning — well, most weekday mornings. If I had remained as a professor until I found a career that excited me right off the bat, I might still be waiting.

Give yourself a trial period

Can you make it as a singer? Will that pizza-by-the-slice business be worthwhile? Reduce your risk by giving your new venture a fixed amount of time. On your calendar, circle a date perhaps a year from now. If, by then, you don't see signs that you'll succeed in your new endeavor, drop it. Limiting your risk can give you the courage to give it a shot.

Take an assistant position

If you're scared about going for a professional position, try to find a job as an assistant to a professional in your chosen field. Yes, you may have to make coffee and copies and even pick up dry cleaning, but working at the elbow of a pro is a great way to launch your career. Often, these jobs aren't advertised because they don't require previous experience — even the employer's cousin Rufus can do it. So, cold-call dream employers, explain that you're looking for your first job in the field and ask if they might need a motivated assistant, If not, offer to volunteer for a day whenever they're facing crunch time. A hard-to-refuse offer.

Choose more than one career

Can't decide? Choose them all. Having more than one career at a time can be exciting but you'd better be a quick study and enjoy long hours. For some people, this doesn't work. It's hard enough to succeed in one career.

How Sarah Edwards created a cool career

My job at the federal regional office of Head Start was exciting, filled with lots of travel and responsibility. But I had a family. The stress of juggling it all put me in the hospital. Working from home as my own boss seemed like the perfect solution, but doing what?

Looking through my high school yearbook, I was struck that many people had valued talking to me about personal challenges. A counseling practice seemed like the perfect career. I'd be my own boss and I could work from home. I completed a graduate program, got my license, and opened a psychotherapy practice. At first, I enjoyed helping people, but after a time, working with unhappy people all day became depressing. I missed traveling and working to change the world. And I wanted to work with Paul.

We decided to write a book about working from home. It added the excitement I was missing. I was still helping people, but I help them create better career and lifestyle opportunities. We write at home. We even broadcast from home. We do travel to speak and do media appearances. This combination works for me.

How Paul Edwards found his perfect work

From the time I was 4 years old, my mother programmed me to become a lawyer. After 20 years of schooling and the ordeal of passing the bar exam, I achieved her dream. I was a lawyer, but I didn't like practicing law. It focuses on details and fault-finding. I only tolerate details and I love working cooperatively.

But having accepted what I was going to be when I grew up, I didn't know where to start. I tried several management jobs, but that wasn't for me either. I wanted the freedom of being my own boss doing work that would enable me to grow. So, in going out on my own, I tried different things — first political consulting, then corporate training.

What I really wanted was to work with Sarah and do something original. So I asked her to join me in writing a book about working from home. Twelve books later, I've found that developing books uses the problem-solving and strategizing I liked about law and politics while speaking and doing media calls on my communication skills and challenges me to grow.

Choose a less radical option

If you're not sure it's worth tackling a totally new career, choose a less radical option. Maybe one of these can work for you:

- **Tweak your current job.** (See Chapter 19.) Many people who think they need a new career can solve their problem by changing bosses, renegotiating their responsibilities, or improving their skills.

- **Find a new job in your current career.** Maybe a different organization's culture can cure your workplace woes.

- **Find a different niche within your current career.** Sick of being a biologist in a lab? Try field-based biology. The Cool Careers Yellow Pages lists neat niches in many careers.

- **Stay in the same industry but change job titles.** Or change industries but keep the same job title. www.acinet.org and http://online.onetcenter.org list industries that employ people in particular occupations.

- **Find more meaning outside of work.** Pursue a hobby that allows for self-expression; do volunteer work; fall in love.

A Final Check

It's time. You've reviewed lots of careers and picked the one that feels best. Now it's time for a final check: Does your career have all five signs of being right for you?

1. **Can you, within an acceptable amount of time, acquire the knowledge and skills to succeed in this career?**

   If you're unsure, ask someone in the field to review your previous efforts. Or try to understand an introductory textbook, or find someone to teach you a bit of the field's essentials. Are you getting it? If you're unsure what knowledge or skills the career requires, find out by reading more about the career or by visiting members of the profession.

2. **Can you get the time and money to train for this career?**

   Before rejecting a career on this basis, read Chapters 7 and 8, which describe cost- and time-effective ways to get the training you need. And if you're thinking of starting a business, Chapter 20 shows ways to get the cash flowing quickly.

3. **Will this career likely sustain your interest?**

4. **Are you likely to enjoy working in this career's environment?**

   For example, at home? Outdoors? In an office?

5. **Are you likely to enjoy the typical people interactions in this career?**

   If so, congratulations. Sounds like you've found a cool career!

Part II
Getting Smart

The 5th Wave   By Rich Tennant

"So what if you have a Ph.D. in physics?
I used to have my own circus act."

In this part . . .

Competence: It's one of life's great feelings. Getting up in the morning, knowing that you're a pro, confident that when you get into work you'll be able to handle most of what comes your way. This part shows you better ways to be competent.

Chapter 7

Degree-Free Career Preparation

- -

In This Chapter

▶ Should you go back for a degree?

▶ How to learn more than you would in a degree program

▶ Getting an employer to hire you over someone with more degrees

- -

Everyone may tell you the rule is "In order to do this work, you have to have a master's degree . . ." But you want to find out about the exceptions.

— Richard Bolles, *What Color Is Your Parachute?*

*I*magine how you'd feel knowing that you are an expert, someone who can be counted on to do the job wonderfully. Nothing is more central to career satisfaction than feeling competent.

Of course, one key to competence is good training. Chapter 8 shows you how to make the most of a degree program. This chapter helps you figure out whether you need a degree at all. More often than you might suspect, there are wiser ways to prepare for your career. This chapter even shows you how to convince an employer to hire you rather than someone with more degrees.

Lousy Reasons to Go Back for a Degree

If you have a good reason, going back for a degree can be a fine idea. Alas, many people don't. Here are the classic lousy reasons:

✔ **To help decide what career to pursue.** Mistake. Most degree programs expose you to only a fraction of the career options. Far better to choose your career using the methods in the previous chapters.

✔ **To postpone looking for a job.** This book helps you find a fine career and land a rewarding job without undue pain. No need to spend years and megabucks to postpone that.

✔ **To impress friends and family.** Aren't there less costly and time-consuming ways to do that? How about landing a good job years sooner than if you had gone for a degree?

✔ **To feel legitimate.** As I explain in this chapter, in many fields, you can more legitimately prepare for your career outside a university, at what I call *You U.:* a self- and mentor-selected combination of articles, seminars, professional conferences, the Internet, and on-the-job training. Don't commit years of your life and lots of money just to create the illusion of legitimacy — sometimes what a degree mainly provides.

✔ **To dazzle employers.** In many fields, your boss is likely to be more impressed with a well designed You U. education than with a diploma that both of you know doesn't mean that you're career competent. In this chapter, I show you how to dazzle employers more legitimately.

Good Reasons to Go Back for a Degree

Of course, there are good reasons for a back-for-a-degree stint:

✔ **For your enlightenment.** A degree program can help you become an informed citizen and to experience life more richly.

✔ **Some fields absolutely, positively require a degree.** For example, if you want to be a physician, the state isn't going to let you treat patients just because you had a mentor. In fields like engineering, management consulting, investment banking, and at top corporate law firms, employers generally ignore applicants who aren't waving a prestigious diploma.

✔ **If major efforts to effect a career change without going back to school have failed.** You hate your current career, so you've taken seminars and networked in your target field's professional association, sought out mentorships, read key trade publications and books, redone your resume to emphasize your transferable skills, and cold-contacted dozens of potential employers in your target career, and everyone's saying you need a degree.

✔ **You need the structure of school.** To design and follow through on a You U. education, you must be a self-starter, even if you have a mentor. (This chapter shows you how to find one.) Many people need the structure of school: Be there from 7 to 9 p.m., Tuesdays and Thursdays; read pages 246 through 384 by next Monday; write a term paper as follows; be tested from 2 to 4 p.m. December 20.

✔ **You want the consistent social contact that comes from meeting from 7 to 9 every Tuesday and Thursday night.**

Will the Piece of Paper Be Worth the Time and Money?

Many people recognize the drawbacks of getting a degree, yet they insist it's worth the time and money because of what the piece of paper, the diploma, can do for them. Will that be true for you?

Paul and Sarah think it's generally a good bet. They have seen many people try to pursue a career without a degree and struggle harder as a result, not just because employers insist on the degree but also because of the psychological barrier of not having a degree. Many such people feel inferior because they acquired their learning outside of school.

I am far less enthusiastic about the value of a degree. When I think back on all my degree-holding clients, despite their spending all that time and money on degrees, many feel like imposters in their careers, having a diploma but not feeling competent to do their jobs. That's far more psychologically damaging than having acquired competence while lacking only a piece of paper that attests to it. Higher education may be a reasonable way to become a more sophisticated connoisseur of life, but if your goal is to advance your career, in many fields, I have become convinced that higher education is among the most overrated, overpriced products of all.

Yes, people with degrees earn more over their lifetimes than people who don't, but that doesn't mean that the degree is the main reason. They earn more mainly because degree seekers, on average, are more able and motivated to begin with. If you locked a group of degree seekers in a closet for four years, that group would likely earn more over their lifetimes than a group of people who don't pursue degrees.

In her book *Success Without College, New York Times* editor Linda Lee cites a recent *Newsweek* article by Robert Samuelson: "Going to Harvard or Duke won't automatically produce a better job and higher pay. Graduates of these schools generally do well. But they do well because they are talented." The article was titled, "The Worthless Ivy League."

What do you think the following people have in common? Malcolm X, Barbra Streisand, PBS *NewsHour*'s Nina Totenberg, Maya Angelou, Ted Turner, Governor Jesse Ventura, IBM founder Thomas Watson, architect Frank Lloyd Wright, former Israeli president David Ben Gurion, Dell Computer founder Michael Dell, Woody Allen, Warren Beatty, Domino's pizza chain founder Tom Monaghan, folksinger Joan Baez, Bill Gates, *Pulp Fiction* director Quentin Tarantino, ABC-TV's Peter Jennings, Wendy's founder Dave Thomas, Thomas

Edison, Blockbuster Video founder and owner of the Miami Dolphins Wayne Huizenga, William Faulkner, Jane Austen, McDonald's founder Ray Kroc, Henry Ford, cosmetics magnate Helena Rubenstein, Ben Franklin, Alexander Graham Bell, Coco Chanel, Walter Cronkite, Walt Disney, Bob Dylan, seven U.S. presidents from Washington to Truman, Leonardo DiCaprio, cookie maker Debbie Fields, Sally Field, Jane Fonda, Buckminster Fuller, Dreamworks co-founder David Geffen, astronaut and senator John Glenn, Roots author Alex Haley, Ernest Hemingway, Dustin Hoffman, famed anthropologist Richard Leakey, airplane inventors Wilbur and Orville Wright, Madonna, satirist H.L. Mencken, Martina Navritalova, Rosie O'Donnell, Nathan Pritikin (Pritikin diet), chef Wolfgang Puck, Robert Redford, oil billionaire John D. Rockefeller, Eleanor Roosevelt, NBC mogul David Sarnoff, Apple Computer founder Steve Jobs, and thousands of computer whizzes?

Not one of them has a college degree.

Of course, these people are exceptions, and it can be argued that only the exceptionally brilliant or demonstrably unintelligent can afford to forgo that diploma.

The fact is that most people — average or superstar — learn more by doing rather than by sitting in university classes. Later in this chapter, I show you how, in many fields, you can prepare for a career better from outside a university than inside one. And I demonstrate how to convince an employer to hire you over applicants who got their career preparation at a university.

But first, you need to know one of higher education's dirty secrets. College catalogs usually talk about the careers possible with this major or the careers possible with that major. This misleads the reader into thinking that if he spends the years and the money, he'll land a professional job in a field related to that major. Here's the truth: In many fields, as you will now see, nowhere near enough professional jobs exist for the number of degree holders.

For example, I was sitting in one of the executive suites in the Time-Life Building, meeting with four editors of one of Time-Warner's major magazines. In the course of conversation, someone said, "It's obscene what these schools of journalism are doing. They're accepting millions of students into their journalism programs knowing full well that 90 percent of them will never make more than McWages from journalism." Everyone nodded.

Some bad news

The October 1997 issue of *Phi Delta Kappan*, a prestigious education periodical, provided this discouraging information:

> A Rand Corporation report concluded that new doctoral degrees in science and engineering average 25 percent *above* appropriate employment opportunities. A National Science Foundation study found a 41 percent oversupply of Ph.D.s in the supposedly in-demand electrical engineering field and a 33 percent oversupply in civil engineering. Rand charged that universities are oblivious to the job market. . . .

> Thousands from other professions face the same situation. Even graduates from America's most prestigious business schools are finding no guarantee of a job. An amazing 16 percent of newly minted MBA graduates of Stanford University were unable to find jobs. Less prestigious business schools fared even worse: 40 percent of the graduates of Ohio State's business school could not find jobs; the figure for the University of Georgia was 30 percent; for the University of Texas at Austin 24 percent; and for Tulane University 24 percent. Experts project that of the millions of university graduates, only a mere 20 percent will find the well-paying, challenging jobs for which they were trained.

That data was collected in 1996. Now, graduate schools admit even more students.

You U. — Often a Better Way

In more fields than you may think, motivated adults can use an approach to career preparation that offers greater payoff than going back for a degree. I call it "You University."

At You U., you, perhaps with the help a mentor you select, decide what you want to learn and then design a plan to learn it. One of my clients, Phillip, wanted to learn how to create partnerships between corporations and schools. Instead of going back for a largely misfitting master's in education or business, he did a You U. "master's."

First, Phillip searched the Internet for articles on business-education partnerships. Then he interviewed, by phone, people at corporations who were involved in those partnerships. One of those people suggested materials he should read and mentioned an upcoming conference on business-education partnerships. At the conference, our hero attended sessions, spoke with other experts, and found out about an on-target newsletter and an Internet discussion group. He also visited corporations with model school programs.

Now, imagine that you are a corporate employer looking for someone to develop a program with local schools. Would you rather hire someone with a master's in education, or someone like Phillip, who attended You U.? Good choice. Phillip got hired as a school liaison by one of the Baby Bells.

When prominent nature recording artist Jonathon Storm decided to switch from pursuing an architecture degree to becoming a recordist, instead of changing majors, he left school to learn directly from a master. He contacted the nation's leading nature recordist and asked to study personally with him. Today, Jonathon is a master.

Just look at the differences (summarized in Table 7-1) between degree programs and You U.

Starting with the basics, in a degree program, you must show up at specified times at that not-so-nearby university — assuming you can get a babysitter and afford the tuition.

In a degree program, you're taught by Ph.D. types, theoreticians who often are often out of touch with the practical knowledge that students, especially those people whose goal is career preparation, need most. Worse, you're stuck with whichever professors happen to be at that college.

In contrast, if you attend You U., you're taught by precisely the right sort of people. Whether you're looking to become a graphic designer, a systems analyst, an engineer, or whatever, you can probably find a master practitioner willing to mentor you for a fraction of the cost of college tuition. (See below for ways to find one.) You can take seminars or certification programs taught by some of your field's leading practitioners. As you'll see, easily searchable, online databases offer plenty of these learning opportunities in every imaginable field.

And if you *are* looking for theoretical knowledge to round out your education, books, audiotapes, and videotapes allow you unlimited access, 24/7, to the world's best theorists. For example, The Teaching Company (`www.teachco.com`, 1-800-teach12) sells audiotapes and videotapes of hundreds of liberal arts courses taught by some of the best professors at the most prestigious colleges.

And if you want or need the contact of on-campus college courses, at You U., you're not bound to only one campus. You can find the best professor in your locale for each course. In major cities, you have a number of universities to choose from. (There are many ways to find the good professors. For example, most colleges publish a list of their teaching award winners.)

You U. is beyond comparison with regular degree programs, but I do it anyway in Table 7-1.

Table 7-1	Degree Program versus You University
A Degree Program	**You U.**
A massive amount of information all at one time, when you don't have the opportunity to apply it.	Especially if you learn on the job, you learn what you need when you need it.
Many required courses. Sometimes a course is required mainly because a professor likes to teach it.	Study only what you need and want. Often, get what you need in a fraction of the time it takes to earn a degree.
Get a degree, only to find that you don't remember, let alone use, much of what you were taught. Own a sometimes-valuable piece of paper.	Because you learn what you want, how you want, at the pace you want, often when you have the chance to apply it, you remember much more.
Learn when it's convenient for the professor, like Mondays and Wednesdays from 7 to 10 p.m.	Learn when it's convenient for you.
You are passive. You focus on learning what the professor wants to teach, fearing a low grade if you don't. Many students leave school with poor self-esteem. This is often because of professors who teach material that is of little value outside the classroom yet is difficult, so students feel dumb.	You are empowered. You study what you want; to the level you believe necessary. You U. builds self-reliance and self-confidence. A key part of what makes a career feel good is the sense that you're an expert in your field. In many careers, you're more likely to feel like — and be — an expert with a "degree" from You U.
The material, especially in science or technology, is often obsolete. As long as professors keep cranking out articles in their microniches, many universities care little that they don't update their course material.	You can get up-to-the-minute information: on the Internet, from periodicals, by talking with people in your field, and from seminars offered by the leading practitioners in your profession.
Costs range from $10,000 to more than $100,000, not to mention the loss of what you could have earned had you not been in a degree program.	Costs are 50% to 90% less than in a degree program.

Convincing Employers to Hire You Without That Degree

Imagine that you are an employer. Will you consider this candidate?

Dear Ms. Hirer,

I know that when you're inundated with applications, it's tempting to weed out those without a prestigious MBA, but I believe I'm worth a look precisely because I don't have an MBA at all.

I seriously considered going back for an MBA, but after carefully examining the courses I would have to take and their relevance (or, too often, lack of relevance) to becoming an outstanding software marketing manager, I concluded that the two full-time years could be more profitably spent.

I contacted directors of marketing at leading Silicon Valley software companies and offered to work for them for no pay in exchange for their mentoring. I figured that was cheap tuition for the on-target learning I would receive. A marketing manager at Hewlett-Packard took me on. After three months, I felt I had learned about as much from him as I could, whereupon I made a similar arrangement with a director of marketing at Cisco Systems.

In these apprenticeships, I was deeply involved in a number of projects similar to those mentioned in your ad, specifically Internet marketing and managing a national consumer branding campaign. In addition, I attend American Marketing Association conferences, read the best articles and books recommended by the AMA, and spend much of my commute time listening to relevant books on tape. To get the bigger picture, I even read a couple of books by leading academics.

But now comes the moment of truth. In choosing a self-directed education over a traditional one, I believe I prioritized substance over form. Now the question is: Will you consider interviewing me?

I hope that you will appreciate my having developed a beyond-the-box learning plan, that I was assertive enough to make it happen, and persistent enough to see it through to completion, even though I didn't have a professor and deadlines forcing me to do so. Perhaps more important, in working at the elbow of top hardware marketing executives, I learned a tremendous amount about how to do the job well. I recently discussed my approach with an MBA holder from Stanford, and he said that I probably learned more of real-world value than he did.

I'm hoping you will call me for an interview, but as any good employee, I won't just passively wait. If I haven't heard from you in a week, I will take the liberty of following up.

I enclose samples of the deliverables I produced during my work at Hewlett-Packard and Cisco.

Thank you for your consideration.

Sincerely,

Christopher Wah

Again, imagine that you're the person in charge of hiring. Would you interview Christopher? Even if other applicants had Ivy League degrees? During a recent speech, I asked the 300-person audience that question. Almost everyone raised his or her hand. On my radio show, I asked the same question of the associate dean of UC Berkeley's Haas School of Business, and even he agreed that he would interview Christopher.

So, before heading back for a degree at State U. — let alone Big Bucks Private U. — ask yourself whether the smart choice might not be You U.

A cool compromise

A certificate program is often a good compromise between You U. and a degree program. You can find a directory of certificate programs at America's Learning Exchange (www.alx.org/cert_search.asp) or the Alternative Careers forum within Gonyea Online Career Center on America Online (keyword Gonyea). Or check the Web site of your professional organization. Looking for a high-tech job? Experts say that a winning combination is a vendor-specific (for example, Microsoft) certification and a vendor-neutral one (for example, those available on brainbench.com.)

Apprenticeships represent another enticing option. Lots of supervised hands-on, punctuated by some practical, low-cost community college classes — and you earn while you learn. Interested? Check out the federal government's clearinghouse of apprenticeship information: www.doleta.gov/atels_bat/.

Planning Your You U. Education

It's simpler than you may think.

Finding a mentor

Start by finding a mentor who is an expert in your field, someone who can suggest resources, ensure that you're covering enough of the bases, and answer your questions. Expect to compensate your mentor either with money or by volunteering as her assistant. The latter can be instructive in itself. Sometimes though, people, especially older people, are willing to mentor you for free. Many people 50 and older feel a strong desire to pass on their wisdom to the next generation.

Where to find a mentor:

- ✔ Someone in your field whom you already know, like, and respect.
- ✔ At a meeting of your field's professional association. Some such associations have formal mentoring programs.
- ✔ Posting a request for a paid mentor on your field's Internet discussion group.
- ✔ Calling SCORE, the Service Corps of Retired Executives (listed in the Federal Government section of big-city White Pages).
- ✔ The Yellow Pages. Some people find mentors simply by opening the Yellow Pages to the appropriate category and dialing until they find the right person.
- ✔ Someone who supervises interns. Don't know of anyone? www.rileyguide.com/intern.html is a portal to databases of internships.
- ✔ Perhaps that unusual professor with enough practical knowledge may be willing to coach you.
- ✔ Post a flyer at the local senior center, or an ad in its newsletter.

Instant Ivy-Leaguer

How'd you like to be able to put a prestigious college's name on your resume without undergoing a rigorous admissions process, and after attending class for just a few days? Most designer-label colleges allow the public to take in-person or online seminars, workshops, and often full courses. It's the easiest, fastest way to get Harvard onto your resume.

You don't have to limit yourself to one mentor.

Figuring out what to learn

When talking with a potential mentor, ask this question: "I'm trying to learn X, Y, and Z, using books, articles, the Internet, tapes, and seminars. Any titles you'd particularly recommend?" In addition to asking your mentor(s), you can pose this question to other professionals in the field. Additional ideas can come from:

- ✔ A respected member of your professional association.
- ✔ Your association's Web site.
- ✔ Public, college, or corporate libraries and their librarians.

Sources of courses

Consider local colleges' extension programs and regular colleges that focus more on students than on research.

Some people are more satisfied with home-based classes: online, video, audio, and/or text. As long as you're a self-starter (and not tempted to cheat), they're fast, at-home convenient, and less expensive. They also offer other advantages:

- ✔ With tens of thousands of choices from one-hour quickies to semester-long comprehensives, you can pick an e-class on the right topic and in the right length for you. With e-classes, you choose what you want instead of what your local university happens to be selling that semester.

- ✔ Before signing up, you can check out an e-class's quality more easily than with a live course — most online courses offer a demo. You can check out five courses in an hour without leaving home. The quality of on-line classes is especially variable. Do check out a course carefully before paying your money.
- ✔ E-classes usually allow you to set your own pace.
- ✔ Increasingly, e-classes are more interactive, sometimes including simulations, demonstrations, and e-mail discussion groups.
- ✔ When a question is asked, *you* get to answer it, without embarrassment, unlike in a live class where only the called-upon student does.
- ✔ You can replay (and fast forward!) as often as you like. Try fast-forwarding a live instructor.
- ✔ You can attend class in your slippers.

I'll bet the house on this

I'm convinced that the bricks-and-mortar college's heyday for adult students is over. Increasingly, online learning — getting your knowledge on a just-in-time basis with at-home convenience — puts that 7 to 9 p.m. Tuesday and Thursday, campus-based class to shame. And just wait until we get our Internet access through cable: Less jerky, faster-loading video will bring to your home computer top teachers bolstered by cool simulations for you to participate in.

I'm even more certain that online learning will largely replace that backbone of traditional college education: the large lecture class. I'll bet the house that the large lecture will soon be as obsolete as a 286 computer.

These resources offer a treasure trove of distance- and in-person learning opportunities:

- **America's Learning Exchange** (`www.alx.org`). Although sponsored by the federal government, this database of training and education resources includes many thousands of public and private-sector learning opportunities, online and live.

- **The American Society for Training & Development's Seminar Agent** (`www.astd.org/virtual_community/seminar_agent`). This database has 450,000 training seminars and similar events offered by 1,200 university and private sector-sponsored training providers such as American Management Association, IBM, New Horizons, DigitalThink, Dun & Bradstreet, ExecuTrain, and Oracle.

- **Seminar Information Service** (`www.seminarinformation.com`) offers a database of 360,000 live seminars and trade shows.

- *Peterson's Guide to Distance Learning* (**revised annually**) **and online at** `www.lifelonglearning.com`. This massive database focuses on credit-bearing distance learning courses offered through universities.

- **Learn2** (`www.learn2.com`). This site won *PC Magazine*'s award for *the* most useful how-to Web site. *Yahoo! Internet Life* magazine recently named it one of the Internet's "50 Most Incredibly Useful Sites." Lycos picked it as its "#1 Distance Learning Site." It offers 1,200 designed-for-the-Web courses that emphasize interactivity, and often animation. For learning in shorter bursts, it offers quickies on thousands of topics, from how to varnish a wood surface to how to make phone calls from your PC.

- **About.com**. A portal on distance learning. Advice plus lots of links. `http://distancelearn.about.com/education/distancelearn/mbody.htm`.

- ✔ **Hungry Minds** (www.hungrymindsuniversity.com). Hungry Minds catalogs 17,000 online courses by such Web heavyweights as UC Berkeley Extension, UCLA Extension, and business specialist University of Phoenix, plus courses from private vendors, and one-on-one advice available from experts on hundreds of topics.

- ✔ **Globewide Network Academy** (www.gnacademy.org). A searchable database of 24,000 primarily college-sponsored distance learning courses and 2,200 programs.

- ✔ **Mindedge.com** (www.Mindedge.com). 20,000 distance courses and seminars — plus 6,000 textbooks and 3,000 videos.

- ✔ **The Small Business Administration** (www.sba.gov). This U.S. government agency offers many courses for current and aspiring businesspeople.

The book and the article are among the most underrated learning tools. You can often find on-target ones by visiting your professional association's Web site. Or visit a college bookstore that offers a training program in your target field. Or recruit electronic slaves called *bots* to search the entire Internet 24/7 for material that includes the key words you select and deliver the articles right into your e-mail automatically. MegaCool! Find top bots at www.botspot.com.

Another time-effective learning method is the tutor. For example, rather than taking a course in Macromedia Flash, get a study manual, and have a tutor (try www.tutor.com to find one) start you off. Then keep a list of questions and problems, and use that as the basis for the next session.

As good as You U. can be, it's certainly not right for everyone. Ready for a back-for-a-degree stint? Chapter 8 can help.

Learning by franchise

Another practical approach to career training is to buy it as part of a franchise. Look for companies that have a proven system, have been in business at least five years before franchising, have been franchising for at least five years, and have at least 10 franchisees. For *Entrepreneur* magazine's top 500 franchises, visit www.entrepreneurmag.com/Home/HM_Static/1,1845,dbapp_fran500index,00.html.

Lifelong Learning

Lifelong learning has become a cliché, and it can sound exhausting — forever upgrading yourself until you retire or drop. But there is an upside. In past generations, after years on the job, many people felt bored — like they had been there, done that. There always have been new things you *can* learn, but now to survive, there always are new things you *must* learn. Consider staying permanently enrolled in You U. — that self-designed approach to learning what you need when you need it, conveniently. That can mean one or more of the following:

- Join or form a group of your peers that connects live or electronically, to discuss problems and solutions.

- Don't let the monthly issues of the magazine from your professional association stack up.

- Attend at least one professional conference a year.

- Find one or more mentors. Times have changed. A mentor/protégé relationship used to be a one-at-a-time, time-intensive deal. Today, such a relationship is likely to be more fluid. You call with a question, exchange e-mails on a new development, and occasionally commiserate over a cup of coffee. Ideally, you'll have a few mentor relationships, some in which you're the mentor, others in which you're the protégé.

Chapter 8

Degree-Based Career Prep

. . . .

In This Chapter

▶ Finding the right college or grad school

▶ Getting into a hard-to-get-into college or grad school

▶ Paying for your education

▶ Making the most of your back-to-school stint

. . . .

A t its best, a back-for-a-degree stint in school can be a blast: Taking a few years away from the real world, learning stuff you're really interested in; meeting lots of interesting fellow students, and mentoring with a wise professor who takes you under wing and lines up a cool job for you after graduation. That ideal is too rarely realized, but this chapter shows you how to maximize your chances.

Choosing the Right Program

When going back to school, finding the right program is usually more important than finding the right college. This section helps you, step-by-step, to do just that.

Be sure you've identified your career niche

Trust me: Don't make the mistake of thinking to yourself, "I'll figure it out while I'm in school." One of two bad things too often happen:

> ✔ You never find out about a specialty you could love. Let's say you're interested in psychology and simply choose a school with a psychology program. There is, however, a niche — organizational psychology — that you would have loved to specialize in if you had only known it existed. Alas, your college's psychology program doesn't offer that specialization. Moral of the story: Choose your niche first and then find a program that prepares you for it.

✔ You take a course from a charismatic professor who loves her specialization — let's say geriatric recreation. Her enthusiasm is infectious. Now you get excited about geriatric recreation. Maybe the professor even shows an interest in you: "That was an outstanding term paper, Jim." You find yourself deciding to specialize in geriatric recreation. It's understandable — no more anxiety about not having a career goal. And a professor's flattery can be intoxicating, precluding you from taking a hard look at the realities of a career in this field — for example, that a geriatric recreation leader usually makes less money than a welfare recipient.

So please choose a career niche before deciding to which colleges you'll apply. If you need help finding a specialty, read, and talk with people in your field.

Identify programs that train you in your niche

Here are some ways to find the right program for you:

✔ Massive searchable databases of degree programs are offered through Web sites like `Petersons.com`, `gradschools.com`, and `www.usnews.com/usnews/edu/home.htm`. The latter has a separate database of all the nation's community colleges. A community college can often be a smart choice for career preparation — even if you already have a bachelor's or graduate degree.

✔ The *Directory of Private Career Schools and Colleges of Technology* catalogs the thousands of colleges whose purpose is first and foremost, preparing you for a particular career.

✔ Comparing offerings at your local colleges by visiting their Web sites or reviewing their catalogs.

✔ Seeing if your field's professional association has descriptions of relevant programs.

✔ The military offers world-class training for a surprisingly wide range of careers. And not only is it tuition-free, you get paid to learn. See `www.militarycareers.com`.

Assess the program's quality

Talk with students close to finishing the program or recent graduates. Probably no more valid way exists to assess a program's quality than talking with its customers.

How can you do this? If the college is far away, you may be able to e-mail students through the college's Web site. If it's nearby, sit in on an advanced class that includes students who have almost finished the program. At the end of class, go up to a group of students and ask, "Do you like the program?" and "What are the best and worst things about it?"

How do you get to sit in on a class? Just phone the college and ask to be transferred to the department secretary who can tell you when and where an advanced class meets. Ask for the instructor's phone number and office hours so you can request permission in advance.

While you're on the phone with the instructor, ask a few questions such as, "What should I know about the program that might not be in the official program description?" or "What's this program's actual average time to completion?" Some programs report the "expected" time to completion, but not the time it takes the average student, which can be years longer. In my Ph.D. program, the "expected" time to completion was four years. The actual average time? Seven years!

You might also ask the secretary to persuade a few recent graduates to phone you. They're in a wonderful position to assess how valuable their degree program was.

Read through the official materials

Although a college's Web site is the electronic equivalent of a sales brochure, you can usually find much of value there.

- Find out whether a program's emphasis matches your interests. You don't want a psychology master's program that focuses on Freudian theory when you think it's a bunch of hooey.

- How many full-time professors teach in the program? A small department can mean too few choices.

- Do the required courses sound interesting? How about the assignments? Will the workload allow time in your schedule for respiration? To find out, check the syllabi. They're often available on the college's Web site or through the department secretary.

Assess the program's true cost

The listed tuition and fees are irrelevant. As on an airplane, passengers pay different amounts and few pay the full fare. To find out approximately how much you'll pay, *before applying,* describe your situation to a financial aid officer at the college, and get a written estimate of how much financial aid you're likely to get that is cash, not a loan. If you don't get a satisfactory answer, contact the head of the program you're applying to.

Finding the Right College or Grad School

Many people choose their cars more carefully than their college. Would you buy a car without a good test drive? Colleges seem so difficult to judge that many college shoppers often fall back on the institution's reputation: "Harvard has a great name, so it must be good, or at least the Harvard name on my diploma will get me a good job."

Not necessarily.

The problem is that most prestigious colleges hire and promote faculty based on how much research they can publish (usually in a tiny arcane area) — not the best instructors for those of you interested in preparing for your career . . . unless, of course, you're planning to become a professor.

I can hear you now — "but the brand name on my diploma will open career doors!" Yes, a designer label on a diploma is a plus in the job market. But top students may get an at least equal advantage if they attend a less prestigious college because there they are more likely to get practical rather than theoretical instruction, top grades, personal attention, leadership opportunities, and superb letters of recommendation. My own daughter, who was admitted to Williams College, one of the nation's hardest-to-get-into colleges, instead opted for a less selective one, largely to save me $70,000 over her four years. Because she was able to excel at that less selective college, she got noticed by her professors, one of whom gave her a tip on a job in the White House. She ended up working for almost a year in Hillary Clinton's research office. (We have cool pictures of her with Hillary on our living room wall.) Lest you think my daughter is an exception, 40 percent of the nation's CEOs got college degrees at public universities. Bonus: Less selective colleges will often give a large scholarship to top students. Although it's easier to make career connections at a prestigious college, as you'll see below, many, many students, having mortgaged their financial security and that of their parents by attending expensive private colleges or graduate schools, graduate feeling disillusioned, even ripped off. You may protest: "But look at the most successful people! So many came from places like Harvard and Yale." Yes, Ivy graduates are disproportionately represented in top positions, but that doesn't mean the institution caused that. On average, Ivy-caliber students are smarter, come from better schools, and have brighter, better-connected parents. You probably could lock top students in a closet for those college or grad-school years, and on average, they'd end up with better careers than other students. And locked in a closet, they wouldn't have to endure the unrelenting pressure of having to compete in every class with the world's top academic superstars. A study reported in the *American Economic Review* concluded that *even in terms of earnings,* "What matters most is not which college you attend, but what you did while you were there. (That means choosing a major such as engineering or computer science, choosing professors carefully, getting to know them, making the most of classes and assignments, and finding leadership opportunities. More on that later in the chapter.) Measured college effects are small, explaining just 1 to 2 percent of the variance in earnings." (James, et. al., 1989). Loren Pope, in *Colleges That Change Lives* (Penguin, 2000) wrote that in 1994, "The *New York Times* reported that a quarter of Harvard's class of 1958 had lost their jobs, were looking for work, or on welfare, just when their careers should have been cresting . . . Many in the class of '58 thought their degrees ensured career success. They were wrong. 'The autobiographical sketches written for the 35th reunion did not radiate with expressions of success and optimism' said author and Yale professor Erich Segal. 'Quite the contrary, they seemed like a litany of loss and disillusion.' And Harvard was not alone. Alumni groups at other Ivy League schools, the author added, 'are reporting that their members in growing numbers are suffering from the upheavals in corporate America.' If there is a lesson in all this it is that a degree from a college like Harvard is no longer the lifetime guarantee of success in careers that it used to be."

Despite all that, many people simply choose the most renowned college they can get into. It's understandable. Designer-label colleges attract lots of smart students, so chances are, something will rub off. And some employers — investment banking firms, for instance — tend to round-file resumes from applicants without a "Top 25" diploma. Even with other employers, you may ask, "If I go to Who Knows U., how will I compete in the job market against graduates of Brand Name U.?" Fact is, the job search strategies in Part III, which most people don't use, can fully compensate for the advantage of a brand-name diploma.

Getting in

Sure, medical schools, many law schools, Ph.D. programs, a relative handful of MBA programs, 5 percent of undergraduate schools, and a few other degree programs, are difficult to get into. But those constitute only a tiny fraction of the offerings at the nation's 3,500 colleges and universities.

An easier way into an Ivy League degree program?

Many prestigious colleges offer a program that makes it far easier for people with nontraditional backgrounds (working adults, child geniuses, and so on) to gain admission to a bachelor's degree program. These special programs are not well-publicized so it helps to know their specific names. Harvard: Extension School. Yale: the Special Studies Program. Penn and Columbia: School of General Studies. Georgetown: Liberal Studies Program.

Fact is, most undergraduate colleges are 98.6 schools — all you need to get in is normal body temperature. (I'm exaggerating only slightly.)

And as I've been stressing, just because a college is difficult to get into, doesn't imply that the school is better. I liken designer-label schools to a Jaguar car. It has a prestigious name and costs a fortune, but ironically, it is more of a hassle (requires more maintenance and has more frequent breakdowns) than inexpensive cars with less exotic names. I must admit to feeling a certain pleasure driving along in my Toyota and seeing some fussmobile broken down along the side of the road.

The hassles with selective colleges start with the challenges of getting in but don't stop there. Professors at selective colleges are more likely to care about their research than about their students. The high concentration of academic stars also instills fear in many students — inhibiting them from speaking up in class and/or turning them into studyholics. The student health center at Harvard reported that the second most common student complaint is stress and burnout.

When you were a teenager, you may have been more likely to fall in love with someone because he or she played hard to get. By now, you realize that's foolish. Please apply that mature thinking when choosing a college or grad school. Many people aspire to be accepted to hard-to-get-into colleges mainly because they're hard to get into. Far better to fall in love with a college because of what it is, not how hard-to-get it plays.

It's a buyer's market. Because college selection is so name-driven rather than quality-driven, many colleges and graduate schools, including high-quality ones, can't fill their classrooms — largely because their diplomas don't bear a brand name. The message to you is: Be picky. Most colleges — perhaps even those that will do you the most good — may want you as much, or more, than you want them.

My favorite place for adults to earn a legitimate bachelor's degree quickly

Thomas Edison State College (609-984-1150; www.tesc.edu): Called "one of the brighter stars in higher education" by *The New York Times,* TESC offers a wide range of associate and bachelor's degrees plus a master's in business, to its 9,000 students. It grants extensive credit for prior learning, including learning acquired through life experience. You can complete your additional units through any combination of exams, live, or distance courses offered anywhere in the United States, including TESC's many self-study courses. A TESC degree is well regarded. For example, 90 percent of its bachelor's graduates gain admission to their first choice graduate school. The kicker is that TESC is a public college, so the price is right.

TIP

Some test-prep advice

A note about preparing for The Test (SAT, GRE, GMAT, LSAT, or MCAT). If you're self-motivated, rather than taking a course, use a CD-ROM such as Inside the GRE. Not only is it $25 versus $1,000, but you don't waste time getting to and from the test center, and you can have a lesson whenever you want, 24/7. The CD-ROM provides a completely individualized approach so you don't waste time going over stuff that's too easy or too hard. In a course, you're particularly likely to get inappropriate-level instruction if you're a nonaverage scorer: below the 40th percentile or above the 90th percentile on a practice exam.

Getting into killer colleges

Despite all my warnings, say you do want to get into one of the most selective colleges. Okay, here are the keys to gaining admission to places like Harvard and Princeton.

For starters, of course, you need top numbers. An A-average or better and a score above the 90th percentile on The Test (GRE, SAT, MCAT, LSAT, or so on) puts you in the running. But most applicants to designer-label institutions have numbers in that range, yet only some get admitted. It usually comes down to a single factor: Compared with another student with similar qualifications, will you *benefit* the institution more? "Who me?" you say. "Me, benefit a college?" Yes, you. Benefits fall into the following categories:

✔ **The student has potential to do big things**. Remember, these colleges can afford to select only the nation's top applicants. Do your past accomplishments suggest that you have the potential to do truly big things like invent something, become a CEO, or be elected to high office? Does your admission essay convey ambitious yet realistic future plans? Are you so well connected (your father is on the House Ways and Means committee, for instance) that you're likely to be in a position to have real impact? Your application, especially your essay, must make a convincing case that you're likely to do big things.

✔ **The student is likely to particularly enrich the campus community.**

- A true intellectual can invigorate classroom discussions as well as her professors.

- A person of color may lend a different perspective to discussions in and outside the classroom. Some sorts of diversity, however, count less: An Appalachian, a Vietnamese boat person, the child of a brilliant scientist, or an Israeli war veteran usually receives less of an advantage in the admissions process.

- A person with the ability to play on varsity sports teams, or to perform in campus music and drama offerings, improves the quality of the college's offerings. (These talents typically give a significant admission edge only to undergraduate applicants.)

- An iconoclastic thinker is likely to spout unconventional but intelligent ideas in and outside of class. But be careful: Political correctness is rampant on college campuses. Writing an application essay advocating conservative ideas is risky.

✔ **A professor views a student as particularly desirable.** This is a perception that the applicant usually must bring about. A typical approach: You find a professor who specializes in a subject in which you're interested. You phone her, have a good conversation, at the end of which you both agree it would be great if you were the professor's advisee and research slave. That professor — usually in response to your request — writes a note about you to the admissions committee. No surprise, that boosts your chances of admission.

✔ **Students whose family members have given a bunch of money to the college.** These students usually receive an edge in admissions proportional to the size of the bunch.

✔ **Students who are a uniquely good fit for the program to which they're applying.** How do those students benefit the college? If you choose a particular program because its unusual aspects are just right for you, you're likely to be satisfied, and more likely to donate money to the college. So if you're applying to Duke's Ph.D. program in biomedical engineering, explain the specific reasons why you prefer it over its major competitor, Johns Hopkins.

Finding the Money

Adults, particularly those applying to graduate schools, have a tough time finding aid because government financial aid formulas penalize working adults. It's worth applying because you'll probably get a government-guaranteed loan, and you may use a lifelong learning tax credit, but don't hold your breath waiting for cash aid.

Get the financial aid applications early. Some colleges' deadlines are almost a year before the enrollment date. These deadlines are firm. Meet them.

Harvard's money-making machine

$9 billion: Harvard's endowment in 1996.

$14.5 billion: Harvard's endowment in 1999.

11.1 percent: The percentage increase in Harvard's tuition from 1996-1999.

$2.5 million: The *profit* Harvard makes each year from MBA application fees alone.

(Adapted from *Harper's* magazine.)

It may be worth applying for a private scholarship — you know, like the David Letterman Scholarship, which is reserved for students just like Dave: C students at Ball State University. To find private scholarships you may qualify for, use one or more online search programs. College is Possible (www. collegeispossible.org/paying/scams.htm) links you to five massive databases of scholarships that you can search for free. Those searches will likely generate dozens of good fits, but it's usually only worth applying for perhaps your five to ten best shots. The odds of winning are tiny, so it's a waste of time to apply for too many. If, however, you're Black, Hispanic, or Native American, or are an academic superstar, it's worth applying to 10 or 20.

Reference Service Press publishes a large database of scholarships set aside for minorities, the disabled, and women: Currently, it's available at America Online (keyword RSP) and by time you read this, it should also be at www. silverplatter.com or at your library.

You can often wangle some bucks with a letter, or by pleading your case in person, to your local chapter of a fraternal organization such as the Kiwanis or Rotary club.

Money is often available for veterans. Speak to your military branch's benefits office.

If you're applying to a graduate program, don't just contact the institution's financial aid office; contact your specific department's office also. Often, it has special funds.

A great source of info and links on financial aid: www.finaid.org.

Why is college so darn expensive anyway?

Colleges keep raising tuition. Four years at a brand-name private college costs $150,000. The government's response: urging us to start saving when Junior is in the 6th grade. Plus offering tons of new federal aid to students — which simply allows colleges to raise tuition even higher — at taxpayers' expense.

Why is no one asking colleges to be more efficient? For example, should professors really be earning a full-time salary for teaching two or three classes a semester and working on research that's useless in the real world? Why aren't interactive video-based online courses, taught by the nation's best professors, used instead of large lecture classes? That would raise quality while lowering cost.

Comparing the Deals

If you apply to more than one college, before saying yes to one, carefully compare financial aid offers:

- ✔ How much cash will you have to come up with?

- ✔ How big a loan will you have to pay back?

- ✔ As long as your income stays the same, will your *cash* award be renewed each year, or once they have you, how likely is it that they'll pull the plug?

If your award from your top-choice college seems too low, try to negotiate a better deal with the financial aid office. The key is to provide new information that can justify a new decision. For example, you can explain that other colleges have offered you better deals. Or point out that your financial picture isn't as rosy as the financial aid form makes it appear — you have big medical expenses, or your home badly needs major repairs. Sometimes, sending an itemized budget to the financial aid officer can make your situation clearer.

Making the Most of the School You Choose

A pair of identical twins could enroll in the same program at the same college, yet one twin could benefit much more than the other. This section shows how to make the most of your back-to-school experience.

Make the effort to find good teachers

You know as well as I do that a good instructor can make medieval linguistics come alive, while a bad instructor can turn Rock'n'Roll 101 into a snore. Be a savvy consumer when you enroll:

- ✔ **Pick the campus's teaching award winners.** The list is usually in the college's catalog or available through its office of academic affairs.

- ✔ **Get picks from students or TAs who've been around awhile.**

- ✔ **Check student ratings of professors.** At some colleges, students have access to the results. Check with the student government office.

- ✔ **Ask the department secretary.** They see all the faculty evaluations and some might even give you an answer other than, "All the professors are good."

- ✔ **Check out syllabi.** Often they're on the Web, or the department secretary has them.

- ✔ **Look at the required books in the bookstore.** A great way to avoid spending $200 on textbooks you won't read anyway.

- ✔ **Over-enroll.** If you plan to take three courses, sign up for four, attend the first session of each, and drop the worst one. No need to put up with a professor so monotonic that he sounds like a high school student reciting the Pledge of Allegiance.

- ✔ **Choose courses that help prepare you for your profession.**

- ✔ **When in doubt, choose the teacher rather than the course title.** European Epistemology taught by a great teacher is usually better than Human Sexuality taught by a dud.

Read first

If you do the assigned reading, you're more likely to stay awake in class. You're also more likely to participate, which also helps you stay awake. Do I sound like your mother or what?

In class, stay active

Classes may or may not be interesting, but if you just sit there, your chances of remembering much of what the professor and other students said after the course is over are about as good as of swatting a fly with a hammer. You're much more likely to remember when you're actually involved, so ask a question, make a comment. Of course, you'll be hated if you talk all the time, so the next best way to be active is to ask *yourself* a question every minute or so. Questions such as, "What's the real-world relevance of this?" or "How might I use this in my career?" (This is one of those ideas that makes sense to me, but to be honest, is utterly untested. If you think it's a stupid idea, no problem.)

Choose your advisor well

A bad advisor is someone whose office you want to escape from as soon as she's signed your paperwork. A good advisor can help you find good professors, sign you on as a research or teaching assistant, become your career coach, line up job leads, ponder the meaning of life with you, and make sure you don't find out three days before you expect to graduate that you're missing Statistics 101. Before settling on an advisor, chat with a couple of candidates whose specialization sounds interesting to you.

One-on-one

We learn best in one-on-one situations. Beyond your advisor, look for opportunities for one-on-ones — even on a one-time basis. See a prof during an office hour, a peer advisor when you have a problem, a student who said something that aroused your interest.

Adapt assignments to fit you

Want an easy way to personalize your education and ensure that your education prepares you for your specialty? Make your assignments meet your needs. Term papers and fieldwork assignments can tie into your career plans. If an assignment doesn't turn you on, propose an alternative. You'll be surprised how often the prof says yes.

Don't take crap

A member of the orientation committee at Harvard gives the following advice to incoming students. She advises, "Fix it. If you can't, ask. If someone says no, ask someone else." If you think of this every time a problem arises, you're on the path to college happiness.

Rachel, Sal, Jim & Lori

Rachel. After Rachel had finished her bachelor's degree in English, a friend told her, "Get a skill that will always pay the bills." So Rachel became a licensed vocational nurse, but quickly became bored. A creative lover of words, Rachel's job mainly consisted of passing out pills, giving shots, and cleaning bedpans. She thought about switching to librarianship, but after looking at the library school curriculum, she thought, "Too dry." Then, Rachel heard that a volunteer position was open at a nearby kindergarten. She took it and immediately knew she had found her career. "I feel alive here." In her first teaching job, however, she felt far from alive. "So many of the children came from tough homes — crack dealers and such. I'm not the best person to cope with that." So after just five weeks, she left. Rachel's next job was at a school in a more affluent area. "Now I'm in teaching heaven. I put in long hours but I don't mind because I love my job."

Sal was earning $1,000,000 a year as a mortgage broker, yet he came to see me! "I don't want to go to my grave thinking that my greatest achievement was to save someone an eighth of a percent on his mortgage." Through college, Sal had been fascinated by physics and math, and had always loved hiking and backpacking. So, it wasn't surprising that the career idea that made Sal light up was hydrologist. Sal quit his million-dollar-a-year job, went back to school to learn hydrology, and last I heard, was collecting water samples somewhere in North Dakota.

Jim was a new-media communications manager at a Fortune-500 company. He hated his boss and, besides, was ready for something more exotic. In his spare time, he wrote screenplays and looked for a way out of the company. Years earlier, he had taken the Foreign Service exam, not even sure he wanted to become an embassy official, yet when he was notified that he passed, there was his escape. After six months of intensive language instruction, he's now at an embassy halfway around the world. He's still unsure he wants a permanent career in the Foreign Service. He misses the greater efficiency of the private sector.

Lori was a city government administrator but never liked it. Her heart was in art. Yet she had a heavily mortgaged home that she loved and didn't want to take the risk of trying to make a living as an artist. Instead, she decided to try to land a job that combined her love of art with her administrative skills — for example, museum administrator — but couldn't find one that paid well enough for her to keep her beloved home. So Lori decided to stay at her job for four more years until she can take early retirement. At that point, she plans to fill her life with all the things she loves, including art and philosophy classes, travel, and redecorating her home.

Part III

A Better Way to Land the Job

The 5th Wave   By Rich Tennant

RESUME
Robert Cosgrove
17 State St
Borgin Il 71661

SWM seeks successful
corporation for long
term relationship.

"My sense is you're personalizing your
resume too much."

In this part . . .

"Most of us hate to look for work. Period. We want the great job to knock on our front door and say, 'I'm here.' . . . It's the Job Charming fantasy. . . . Most of us also hate to market ourselves. . . . It feels sleazy."

— Cheryl Gilman, *Doing Work You Love*

Good! You've picked out a career. Now you need to find someone good to hire you. This part shows you a proven, better way to do just that. It's generally easier and faster than traditional methods, and doesn't require sleaze.

Plus, how to successfully negotiate salary — even if you're negotiating with Ebenezer Scrooge.

Chapter 9

What Really Works

In This Chapter

▶ A more pleasant way to land a job

▶ A little realism

▶ Eight faster (really) ways to land a job

Conventional wisdom says that the following is the right way to land a job. Can you picture yourself doing this?

Sally is ready to start phoning prospective employers and networking contacts at 8 a.m. because that's when they are most likely to be at their desks without gatekeepers. She checks her list of contacts, which she maintains using contact-tracking software, and begins:

> "Hello, this is Sally Jones. May I speak with Harry Hirer?"

> "Hello, this is Sally Jones. May I speak with Margie? We were roommates back in college."

> "Hello, this is Sally Jones. May I speak with the person in charge of marketing?"

> "Hello, this is Sally Jones. I'd like to find out more about your industry. Can we get together?"

Sally cajoles and prods gatekeepers; she leaves tantalizing voice mail messages, and diligently follows up on unreturned phone calls. Day and night, Sally is networking: "I'm looking to use my skills in planning, management, and communication. Do you know anyone in a position to hire someone with my background?"

I ask again. Can you picture yourself doing that? Although many career guides ask you to follow that regimen, I find that many people don't stay with it long enough to succeed, no matter how much they are coached and prodded.

A Better Way to Land a Job

This entire part of the book is devoted to showing you my not-too-difficult, not-pushy-person's custom-tailored approach to landing a job. Here's an overview.

- ✔ **Create a good-enough resume.** After the first few hours, tweaking a resume rarely makes enough difference to justify the effort. Job seekers put only so much effort into a job search. I want you to put your effort where it counts.

    Next, from the following approaches, simply pick the ones likely to work best for you — I show you how to predict which ones will. And after you see which approaches are working best for you, de-emphasize the others. It sounds obvious, but you'd be surprised.

- ✔ **Find on-target want ads.** Yes, check the Sunday newspaper, but also search the Internet. One of the Internet's tools is automated job scouts that screen literally millions of jobs on the Net 24/7 to find openings on-target for you and deliver them right to your e-mailbox. The Net offers a lazy person's approach to landing a job. If it doesn't work for you, forget about it — on to other methods. You haven't wasted much time.

- ✔ **Identify a handful of dream employers.** I show how to find your dream employers in Chapter 12. Write to them honestly, humanly, and without overselling yourself. Gently follow up with a phone call. If they don't return the call, the heck with them.

- ✔ **Identify a small number of people in your personal network who may know someone who could hire you for the sort of job you're looking for.** If these people don't have any leads, ask them to keep their antennae out and call you if they hear of anything — you just recruited a scout. If you don't hear from your scouts, call them back once. If they don't return the call, the heck with them.

- ✔ **E-network.** No personal network? Too shy to use it? Try e-networking. The Net offers low-stress ways to make connections in your target field — and no one ever has to see that you're in your sweatpants.

- ✔ **Write to a few search firms that specialize in your field.** If you don't hear back, the heck with them.

- ✔ **Attend one or more job fairs.** You'll find dozens of employers in one place, all of whom are eager to talk with job seekers.

- ✔ **Convert your job interviews from interrogations to first dates.** I show you how in Chapter 16.

Many people search for jobs more effectively if they have the support of others. Perhaps it's just a daily check-in with a friend. If you prefer group support, the well-regarded 5 O'Clock Club groups (www.fiveoclockclub.com) have branches in major cities. Your local unemployment office can tell you about other options.

That's it. No one-size-fits-all regimen, no excessive pushiness, no massive networking, no sleaze required. And with moderate effort, it works, even if you're not an aggressive person. In the following chapters, I show you the best and simplest approach to each of those steps. I understand that you have things you'd rather be doing than looking for a job.

When you're self-employed, you don't have to land a job, but you do have to land customers or clients. For advice aimed specifically at the self-employed, see Chapter 20.

Be Real

Many likeable people suddenly become too formal when they become job seekers. Imagine that you're an employer and an applicant says, "I believe I'm well-suited to the position." Or "I'm seeking an opportunity with a dynamic company." Ugh. Instead of donning this phony, job-seeker persona, talk and write humanly, honestly, even playfully in every step of your job search. Consider this excerpt from a letter to a headhunter:

> I knew I shouldn't have left New York for Knoxville. I love big-city life, from Scribners to Chinatown, but it was so tempting: sales manager for the Home & Garden Network in its crucial start-up phase. I figured that I could be happy anywhere, so I moved myself and my dog to Knoxville. But culture in Knoxville is the *Star Spangled Banner* at the University of Tennessee football game. After two years in the old South, it would be great to come home. Do you know anyone in New York who might throw a life preserver to an overboard sales manager?

Mightn't you consider helping this person if you could? The standard "I-believe-I-am-well-qualified-for-the-position" approach usually creates resistance; the human approach encourages connection.

Please don't oversell yourself. If you're just a basic good hard worker, describe yourself as just that. It is a mistake to try to pass yourself off as a star. The thought of having to do all that B.S.ing will stress you out and make you more likely to procrastinate in your search for work. You'll probably sound unnatural and therefore won't be successful. And if, against all odds, you manage to bamboozle someone into thinking you're stronger than you're likely to be, you risk failing on that job, and making you and your boss or customer miserable. So don't make a false impression. Sell who you really are. You'll enjoy your search for work more and be more likely to end up with work you'll do well. Besides — although increasingly this quality is seen to be unimportant — it's honest.

The Keys to a Fast Job Search

Even though I've tried to make the job-search process as fast as possible, to keep your expectations realistic, you need to know that fast is relative. Many people fail in their job searches because they give up too quickly. Yes, you may luck out and find your dream job in two weeks, but realistically, you can figure on spending a few hundred hours. Actually, that's not a lot of time — only a few months to end up in a position that should keep you contented for years.

Here's the key to getting a job quickly. Successful job seekers spend only a modest amount of time on preparation. They don't need to clean their desks before beginning. They spend just a bit of time preparing for phone calls. They don't spend much time primping their resume or fussing over the design of their business cards. They spend almost all their job-hunting time directly contacting target employers by e-mail and phone, responding to ads on the Internet, and asking well-connected people for job leads. Kate Wendleton, president of the 5 O'Clock Club, a national small-group career counseling service, wisely says, "You know your job search is on track when you have six to ten warm leads at any one time."

A Computer is a Virtual Must

Access to the Internet is key. If you don't have a computer or Web access, most libraries do, and librarians can help you get started. Commercial firms like Kinko's also rent computer time. But think about buying a PC — you'll need it in every aspect of your job search (and the games are cool). Prices have dropped like a stone. Name-brand Compaq or Hewlett-Packard base-model computers, plenty fast enough, complete with printer and monitor, can now be had for $600 and companies such as NetZero.com offer free Web access and e-mail.

A Special Note

A number of the ideas in this part may be different from what you've heard or read before about how to land a job or get business on your own — for example, I believe the want ads are an underrated job-search tool and that networking is overrated. I ask only that you read with an open mind. If you remain unconvinced, go back to the standard advice. But I have found that, especially with the sorts of people who use career guides, the approach you are about to read should yield you better work faster.

Eight faster (really) ways to land a job

The one-sentence solution

Richard Bolles, author of *What Color is Your Parachute?*, reports that 69 percent of job hunters land jobs simply by opening their local Yellow Pages, calling employers in their favorite category, and asking if those companies are hiring for the position the seeker desires.

You can be fast and even playful: Susan called all the museums and aquariums in her Yellow Pages (sometimes she just dropped in!) and said, "Hi, I'm an experienced manager who loves museums. My company just downsized, so I'm looking for a job. I figured I'd go direct. Is there a nice person I could talk with who might need someone like me?"

It can also work if you're self-employed and looking for clients. Whenever public relations consultant Michael Cahlin needs business, he simply gets out the phone book and starts calling companies he would like to work with. He asks them if they're happy with their PR. Usually they aren't, and soon he has several new clients.

This simple, direct strategy works, but when dealing with a larger organization, it's usually smarter to visit their Web site and e-mail a senior person from there.

When you're still not sure what you want to be when you grow up

Sometimes, despite oodles of career exploration, you still remain open to lots of options. Not one of the career goals you've explored feels so good that you're ready to focus just on it. Standard career counseling advice tells you to go back and explore some more. But I've found that rarely works. A better approach is picking out some employers that seem desirable (close to home, having a good reputation, selling a product that sounds cool), and phoning or writing the CEO. Leave a voice mail if necessary: "My name is XXXX. I'm 25 and I'm still not sure what I want to be when I grow up. I've done a few things I'm proud of (insert two or three, each in just a phrase). Can you see a place for a person like me working for you? (*Insert reason you chose that company — for example, I live three blocks away.*) My phone number is (*insert number*). Thanks."

The old-fashioned job search (with a new twist)

The traditional job search meant poring over the want ads in Sunday's newspaper. Today's version includes one tiny difference — You can sift through literally millions of want ads in seconds using the Internet. Visit major job search sites such as `monster.com`, `jobsearch.org`, `hotjobs.com`, `nationjobs.com`, and `careerbuilder.com`, enter your favorite search terms or geographic locations or browse various categories of jobs — you'll likely encounter plenty of interesting jobs you never would have thought about. While you're there, sign up for their job scouts. That way, whenever an on-target job opening hits their site, you'll be notified by e-mail. See a job you like? Don't make a federal case out of it — just paste a plain-text version of your resume into an e-mail preceded by a cover letter, explaining, item by item, how you meet the job requirements listed in the ad.

The biggest steak in Texas approach

Dan Kennedy, author of the *No BS Marketing Newsletter*, insists this is a sure-fire way to land a job. Target ten successful entrepreneurs or CEOs of small- to mid-sized growing companies in the field you want to work in. Research their lives and companies, perhaps by reviewing the Who's Who database (available online from many libraries) or with your favorite search

(continued)

(continued)

engine, using the CEO's name as the keyword. Prepare individual letters to each of your targets, selling yourself — adding, "Someone must have given you your first chance . . . " and offering to work for free. FedEx those letters. If you don't hear from them quickly, pursue them with phone calls, e-mails, ideas, anything you can think of to secure interviews. Kennedy says, "I'll bet you the biggest steak in Texas that within 30 days, you'll be working for one of those 10 leaders."

The one-employer strategy

Sometimes, you have a dream employer. Perhaps it's a world-famous expert you idolize, the organization whose cause you most believe in, or the company that makes the coolest product, or simply the well-regarded company that happens to be headquartered within walking distance of home. In these situations, it's worth launching a full-scale assault on that employer. Learn everything you can about the employer. Yes, look at the company's or person's Web site but also — if it's a public company — check it out at the Wall Street Research Net (www.wsrn.com). In addition, tell Company Sleuth (www.companysleuth.com), what company you're tracking and it e-mails you every new news story about the company. If your target company is private, simply ask a salesperson to send you the packet of material that goes to prospective customers. Identify at least a few people in the organization with the power to hire you or recommend that you be hired and start a relationship with them — use "the biggest steak in Texas approach." You may soon find yourself working for your dream employer.

The get-in-the-door solution

If you're pursuing a first job in a new field, the key is to get in the door. Don't worry so much if the first job is as an assistant or even as a receptionist. The key is making it known, early

on, that you're smart, eager, and nice. Read what comes across your desk, ask questions, gently propose ideas, volunteer for projects that go beyond your entry-level duties. Tried-and-true career launchpads are:

- **Customer support.**

- **Assistant to a professional whose job you aspire to.** Yes, you may have to get coffee, make copies, even pick up his dry cleaning, but being at the elbow of a pro, especially if you work hard to learn what he's doing and why, is a great way to propel your career.

  Often these jobs are not advertised for because they don't require previous experience — the hirer usually knows someone who can do that job. So, don't be afraid to cold-call dream employers, explaining that you're looking for your first job in this field and asking if they need a motivated assistant or customer support person or even a volunteer to work for a day to help with an urgency or to do some task other employees hate. If you're really gutsy, walk in to your target employer. If there's a receptionist, explain that this is your dream employer and ask if she'd be nice enough to let you talk with a kind potential hirer. It works more often than you may think.

- **Temping.** Even if your assignment is just a one-day clerical assignment, make the most of that one day and you may find yourself with a job. Tell people at the water cooler you're looking. Look at internal job postings. Impress your boss with your intelligence, energy, and good cheer. Offer to do more and higher-level things than you were hired for. Tell her you're looking for a permanent job.

- **Substantive volunteer positions.** Volunteering to serve on the board of a small nonprofit can be a great career move. Door-to-door fundraising less so.

✔ **Make 'em an offer they can't refuse.** Target a dream employer. Learn about how you can help them. Then, if no job is forthcoming, offer to work for a few days or a week at no risk. At the end of the week, they can pay you whatever they want, including nothing. Even if you get zilch, and they don't go on to hire you, you can legitimately say you did a project for a respected employer.

Have someone sell you

One of the best ways to get a job is to have a respected third party call a headhunter or hirer on your behalf: "I've just heard that *(insert your name)* may be open to the possibility of leaving *(insert your employer)*. He's terrific. You should get your hands on him while you can."

Walking in

If someone phoned you asking if you wanted to adopt a baby, chances are you'd say "No." But if that same baby was dropped on your doorstep, you'd probably give it quite a bit of attention, and at least see if you could help get it cared for. The same holds true with walking in to an employer. Turning down a phone call is easy, but turning down a flesh-and-blood human being is much harder. So, if you have the guts, walk in, explain that this is a dream employer and you'd love to talk with someone who might be able to help you figure out how you could get hired.

You may want to try one of the above job-search methods first, and if it doesn't work, come back and read the rest of this part of the book.

Chapter 10

Creating Your Mind-Set

In This Chapter
▶ Staying upbeat
▶ Shrugging off fear of failure
▶ Getting that chip off your shoulder
▶ Making time for your search

A good mind-set will make your job search more successful, maybe even borderline fun.

Staying Up

Sometimes it happens fast. Because you're brilliant, lucky, or both, you land a cool job in just a few weeks. Alas, it doesn't always work that way. So it helps if you have staying power. The good news is that staying power is at least a partially acquired trait. Here are some mind-sets that have helped my clients stay the course.

You're going to the mall

People who enjoy shopping 'til they drop say that what makes shopping fun is that it doesn't require a lot of preparation, and that it's a cross between a treasure hunt and a costume party. You walk around the mall searching for treasures, asking salespeople to point you in the direction of items that you're likely to consider treasures. You try stuff on, most of which looks worse on you than it does on the rack, but it's still fun, like a costume party.

A job search is the same thing. With only a modest amount of preparation, you're exploring a "mall": your target career's milieu. You look around (by reading, searching the Net, phoning people in likely workplaces, and visiting work sites), ask people for directions to the areas within the "mall" most likely to have what you're looking for, and sooner or later, you find something good.

If you think of your job search as a visit to the mall, it helps create the right mind-set: only a moderate amount of preparation, plenty of exploration, trying stuff on, and enjoying the process, even if you don't end up buying anything for a while.

Playful yet persistent

Some of my most successful clients treat their work search like a game. Their motto: "Playful yet persistent." To acquire that mind-set, it may help to think of looking for work as a treasure hunt in an enchanted forest. Along the way, you meet obnoxious trolls, helpful munchkins, and maybe a fairy godmother or two. If you can laugh off the trolls, and take pleasure in the game itself so that you don't get frustrated even if it takes a while to find the treasure, you'll eventually find it (although it may not be the treasure you started out looking for). It's particularly important that you adopt this mind-set if you are desperate for a job — desperation can show, and few employers want to hire someone who's desperate.

Here's what I mean by "take pleasure in the game itself." Each phone call, each interview, each cover letter, can be tense or enjoyable. It's largely a matter of your mind-set. Every task in a job search, becoming self-employed, indeed in life, can either drain your energy or enhance it. Some experiences, such as a killer rejection, are unavoidable drains, but most experiences are, at least partly, under your control. For example, trying to make a cold call interesting, even playful, can build your energy, even if the call leads nowhere.

Even a rejection can be taken playfully. Margaret interviewed for a job at a major Boston university. The interviewer was rude and snide. When she got the rejection letter, she fed it to her guinea pig. He loved it. And so did she.

The truth option

If, during your search for work, you try to be someone you're not, you'll necessarily be nervous. But if you let yourself be your real self — yes, your best self, but yourself — you'll be more relaxed, and when you get hired, you'll be hired for who you really are. That, of course, means that you're more likely to succeed in your new work. Some people can fake it well enough to land a job, but they can't and wouldn't want to fake it forever. Better to show them the real you.

Fake it 'til you make it

This approach seems to contradict "The truth option," but keep reading. Sometimes, the key to feeling more upbeat is to act the way you would if you were *not* ready to pull your hair out. You may actually start to feel better. In psychologist's lingo, "Often, behavior change precedes and causes attitude change." In plain English: Fake it 'til you make it. To do so while still being honest, pretend that you are your best self. Think of the hour in your recent past when you were most confident, most together. Especially at key moments in your job search, pretend you are that best self.

Breathe

Whenever you feel stress, take a deep breath. Nothing so simple is so potent. The breath increases oxygenation to your brain, thereby improving your thinking power. A breath relaxes your neck and torso muscles. A breath gives you a break. Breathe. Do it now.

Three balls in the air

When you have a hot job lead, it's easy to stop looking for others. Fact is, the odds of a hot lead turning into a job are much less than 50/50. Here's a useful goal: Have three balls in the air at all times. If one falls, find another. Keep three balls in the air for a while and you'll soon be able to stop juggling.

Be in the moment

I believe that the following phrase is the key to enjoying every moment, even of your job search, which is not at the top of most people's fun lists. The phrase: Be in the moment. Stop thinking ahead so much. Instead, try to get into every little task — whether it's the puzzle of deciding what to say in your resume, or the challenge of convincing a gatekeeper to let you talk with a prospective client. I am trying to enjoy the challenge I'm facing right now: how to phrase this paragraph so that it's helpful but not preachy. (I'm not sure I solved the preachy problem.) One moment at a time — at least in my opinion, that is the key to a successful career and a happy life.

Get support

Sometimes, all the strategies in the world can't generate enough fire in your belly. Often, the answer is to gain energy from the support of others, ideally fellow job seekers. Find job-search support groups through churches, unemployment offices, and chambers of commerce. A number of large cities have branches of the 5 O'Clock Club (`fiveoclockclub.com`) and 40 Plus (`www.fp.org/chapters.htm`). Both offer weekly group sessions for job seekers.

Finding the Time

Many people who want to start a new career claim that their biggest impediment is lack of time. Sometimes, their problem has little to do with time. It reflects their mixed feelings about finding new work. Many people are scared of change, even if their current life is unhappy.

Of course, lack of time can be an impediment. The solution comes down to one word — *priorities*. "Where among my priorities is looking for new work? Am I willing to cut some corners at work so I can pursue this? Am I willing to tell my family that I have to spend parts of my evenings and weekends on launching my new career? Am I willing to give up TV until I land a job?" Assuming that you really do want to land a new job, and you're not finding enough time to spend on your quest, it can mean only one thing. You're consciously or unconsciously choosing to do other things.

Throughout the week, when you have a choice of what to do, make it a point to ask yourself, "Am I going to work on lining up my new work or not?" If you truly want a new career, you will find enough time.

Put blocks of job search time on your calendar. Treat them as you would any other appointment. Although you'd love to, you wouldn't miss an appointment with the dentist. Isn't your career as important?

Don't dismiss the value of two-minute snippets of time. The week is filled with them, and they are relatively painless ways to get rolling again.

Job searching, of course, is tougher for people with full-time jobs, but it's usually doable. Phone calls to contacts are best made at the beginning and end of a standard work day and during lunch hours because that's when hirers are likely to be at their desks without gatekeepers screening their calls. You can schedule interviews at the beginning or end of the workday or even on weekends — many employers recognize that they can't expect candidates to be available for interviews during the workweek. At night and on weekends, you can search the want ads, the Web, or libraries for job openings and information on prospective employers. You can work on your resume, cover letters, thank-you letters, brochure, and mock interviews or presentations. You can read this book. So even if you're working full-time, there's plenty of hope.

Shrugging Off Fear of Rejection

Do you dread making contacts because you fear rejection? See if adopting any of these mind-sets helps.

You say you have no real skills?

Sure, the want ads make it seem like every job requires you to be a technogeek, but fact is most jobs, especially nontechnical ones, aren't advertised. Many, many good jobs require mainly those generic skills we take for granted: intelligence, people skills, organization, communication, and reliability. David Wolper who was the producer of *Roots,* the *1984 LA Summer Olympic Games, LA Confidential,* and who brought Jacques Cousteau to TV, said that his main skill was talking to people on the phone. My wife is Napa county's superintendent of schools and she insists that the key job requirement of her job is common sense. These are not exceptions. For example, 37,000,000 managerial positions exist in the U.S., and most of them don't require that you be able to program in Java, perform chemical assays, or create a blueprint using *AutoCAD.* They mainly require some combination of people skills, organization, communication, reliability, and the ability to learn quickly. Don't you have at least some of those skills? So, go forth and tell prospective employers that you do.

It's all in how you think of it

Are you afraid you'll seem like a loser if you ask people for job leads? The key is how you think of it: You're not desperate; you're simply exploring to see if there might be a more satisfying work life for you. People can respect you for that. Many of them wish they had the guts to do the same.

What would God think?

Even if you're an atheist, this mind-set can help: Ask yourself, would God think you should make that call?

The library book mind-set

When you're at the library looking for information, you pick a book off the shelf, glance through it, and if it isn't helpful, simply move on to the next book. Try to think of each person you contact in your job search like a book in the library. If one person isn't helpful, simply go on to the next one with no more emotion spent than if that person was an unhelpful library book.

The only game in which batting .050 is good enough

The good news about a job search is that you only need to find one good job. It's not like in baseball where you need a good batting average. I like Tom Jackson's description of a job search in *Guerrilla Tactics in the Job Market:*

NO. NO. NO. NO. NO. NO. NO. NO. NO. NO. NO. NO. NO. NO. NO. NO. NO. NO. NO. NO. NO. NO. NO. NO. NO. NO. NO. NO. NO. NO. NO. NO. NO. NO. NO. NO. NO. NO. NO. NO. NO. NO. NO. NO. NO. NO. NO. NO. NO. NO. **YES**.

The two gold miners

Imagine two gold miners. Each time the first miner tries a vein that turns out to contain nothing but rock, he gets frustrated. The other miner, knowing that he only needs to strike gold once every 50 times to make enough money, stays cool. Is there any question as to which miner ends up making more money? Any question as to whom is a happier person?

Rejection as a blessing?

Look at a rejection as a blessing in disguise. It may keep you from a job that is wrong for you. At least think that way.

What's the worst that could happen?

Picture the worst cases: embarrassing yourself in an interview for a cool job, sending out a bunch of job applications and never hearing from any of the employers, plugging away for six months and still not getting a job. Ask yourself, in the larger scheme of things, would your life really be that terrible? Couldn't you do something to compensate?

A tool for curing more deep-rooted fear of rejection

How you handle stressful situations, such as those that come up in a job search, is affected by your childhood. For example, as a child, were you considered stupid? Made to feel guilty for speaking up? Expected to live with scarcity? Disliked by your parents? Were your role models inadequate: For example, did you have a lazy or short-tempered parent? Solution: Every time you feel uncomfortable during your job search, in a memo pad, write the event, your internal response to it, a childhood-rooted explanation for your internal response (if there is one), your external response, and what, if anything, you want to do differently next time.

Getting That Chip Off Your Shoulder

Upon probing, a number of my clients admit they resent having to look for a job.

Some think that with their qualifications, a job should practically fall into their laps. Or they've had jobs fall in their laps before and somehow expect it to happen again. Yes, jobs do fall into people's laps, but that can take months or even longer, and the new job is unlikely to be like the one you worked so hard to select for yourself in Part I of this book. Placing your hopes on a great job descending on you like manna from heaven is risky.

Other people resent looking for a job because they're frustrated that it's taking so long. Fact: It takes the average person a few months to land a good job. A job hunt, even when done well, is rarely a sprint; it's a medium-to-long-distance run. Knowing that up front is better than starting to sprint and finding yourself fading in a few weeks.

Still others are bitter that they were let go from a previous job.

No matter what reason and no matter how legitimate that reason, a chip on your shoulder decimates your chances of landing a job. Even if you don't actually say, "I'm angry!" people know. It may sound unsympathetic, but the best advice I can give is: If you want to land a job quickly, get over it!

If you can't make yourself get over it, try this approach before spending a dime on a shrink. Every time you become aware of a chip-on-your-shoulder thought, in that *instant,* force yourself to replace it with a constructive one. Ask yourself, "What's the next one-second task I need to do to line up the work I'm seeking?" Sounds simplistic, but it works for many of my clients. Frankly, I used this system when I felt overwhelmed with the task of writing this book.

Chapter 11

The Right Resume in Much Less Time

In This Chapter

▶ Resume-writing as a few-hour, not few-week activity

▶ A just-right resume in ten easy steps and one hard one

▶ Chronological, attributes, or hybrid resume?

▶ Honorable tricks

▶ Solutions for an imperfect work history

▶ Creating your electronic resume

Creating a resume is a great first step in your job search. It usually helps you realize that you've accomplished more than you think. Plus, it distills your accomplishments into impressive sound bites that you can use in interviews and networking.

Here, I show you how to create a good-enough resume. "Good enough?" you protest, "Good enough isn't good enough. It's hard enough to get a good job with a fabulous resume. Hey, Nemko, I thought you said that you were going to show us the best way to land a job, and right off the bat you're compromising — a *good-enough* resume?"

No compromise. Here's why it's smarter to create a good-enough resume rather than a perfect one. Many job seekers nitpick their resumes for weeks before going on with their job search, thereby delaying their hiring, which means lots of lost income.

Worse, spending too much time on a resume can mean you don't get a job. Here's why: I've found that job seekers have only so much energy to give to a job search before burning out. Too often, they use up too much of that energy in crafting the perfect resume, leaving too little for the far more important task of contacting employers. It's like an athlete who spent so much effort in pre-race warm-up that he was too tired to run well in the race.

A resume is a few-hour activity, not a few-week one. Jobs are rarely won because of the tweaking done beyond those first few hours. Use the following proven time-effective approach: Knock out a draft of your resume, get feedback on it from a couple of trusted friends, prospective employers, or headhunters, and then move on to activities more likely to benefit you than extra resume primping.

Yes, your resume should demonstrate competence and create chemistry. Yes, it should be formatted for easy reading. Yes, it shouldn't have errors in speling (just kidding). But no, it's not worth taking the time to craft your resume as carefully as a prenuptial agreement.

Remember, many of today's employers usually use resumes only for a quick screen — average inspection time is 15 seconds (or one millisecond if it's autoscanned). Why? In part because employers know they can't trust resumes: More than one-third of resumes contain inflated credentials, and even the honest ones can't be trusted. Thanks to rev-up-your-resume books, software, and resume ghostwriters, a resume may better indicate whether a candidate got help on her resume than whether she can do the job.

So put your job search time where it counts — in putting your letter, work sample, and maybe your resume in the right people's hands.

Notice that in the previous sentence I said, "*maybe* your resume." Why? Because unless your work history is likely to be superior to that of most other candidates for your target job, you're better off hitching your prospects on your letter, work sample, and perhaps a bio (a brief listing or narrative of your highlights). And remember, if you're looking for work as a self-employed individual or small business, never use a resume. Use a bio, portfolio, or presentation kit.

A Just-Right Resume in Ten Easy Steps and One Hard One

Purists may sniff, but here's my client-tested, not-too-fussy, not-too-lazy, just-right guide to creating a plenty-good-enough resume. Everything you need to know in a dozen pages.

Step 1: Write your name and contact information

This information includes your home address, phone number(s), e-mail address, and, if you have one, your personal Web site address. The latter is a good place to display your work samples.

Don't use your employer's e-mail address. It suggests that you're job hunting on company time. (You wouldn't do that, now would you?) Instead, sign up for a free e-mail account at a service such as Yahoo.com or Hotmail.com.

Step 2: (Optional) Write your job target

If you'd consider a wide range of jobs and you'd rather have your first impression stand or fall on your highlights section (see Step 9), then you don't need a job target. Include a job target only if you have a specific job target and would turn down anything else, or if you're writing a job target tailored to a specific job opening. A job target can follow this form: "A position requiring abilities A and perhaps B plus personal attribute Z." For example:

- ✔ Management position requiring the ability to make good decisions quickly, solid understanding of office computer systems, and unquestionable integrity.

- ✔ Psychologist position requiring successful experience with drug abusers and with diverse populations, and the ability to remain calm under stress.

- ✔ Petroleum geologist position requiring extensive knowledge of computer-based drill site analysis and Alaska field experience, and the ability to work well in isolation.

- ✔ High school English teacher position requiring successful experience in teaching advanced-placement classes and the willingness to take on extensive after-school responsibilities.

- ✔ Cushy job requiring a laid-back personality, the desire for a six-figure income, and the willingness to accept it without feeling guilty that it wasn't earned.

Step 3: Choose a format: chronological, attributes-based or hybrid

The main headings in an attributes resume are — no surprise — your attributes (skills, expertise, abilities). Figure 11-1 shows an example.

In contrast, a chronological resume's main headings are the jobs you've held, listed in — again, no surprise — chronological order, with your most recent job listed first. (See Figure 11-2.)

If your best job was not your most recent, rearrange the order so that it's listed first.

Attributes Resume

Maynard G. Krebs
9 Dobie Dr.
Gillis, MN 66696
e-mail: whatmework?@whitehouse.gov

Job Target and/or Summary

Attribute that would most impress the target employer:

Evidence of that attribute #1
Evidence of that attribute #2
Evidence of that attribute #3 (optional)

2nd most impressive attribute:

Evidence of that attribute #1
Evidence of that attribute #2
Evidence of that attribute #3 (optional)

3rd most impressive attribute:

Evidence of that attribute #1
Evidence of that attribute #2
Evidence of that attribute #3 (optional)

Education

Personal Interests

Figure 11-1:
An
attributes
resume.

If you're concerned about your boss finding out that you're looking to leave, your resume might indicate that you're working for a major consumer products company rather than for Procter & Gamble, and that the period of employment is 1997–present rather than June 1997–present.

Almost all employers prefer a chronological format, so consider an attributes or hybrid format only if you've never held a job related to your desired position; for example, you've always been a supermarket bagger and are now seeking a job as a physics teacher.

If your work history is weak but you'd rather show it to an employer than create the impression that you've been a slacker all your life, use a hybrid resume. This tacks an unannotated work history onto an attributes resume. That way, after you've impressed the employer with an attribute set that says you can do the job, a briefly-stated wimpy work history may matter less.

Step 4: Pick out a specific resume to use as a model

A large collection of model resumes can be found at Rebecca Smith's e-resume site: www.eresumes.com/gallery_rezcat.html. Pick one that

- ✔ Uses your chosen structure — chronological or attributes.
- ✔ Has content relevant to your target job.
- ✔ Uses language and has a feel that you like.

Use that resume as a template. In addition, you might keep handy one or two more of your favorite model resumes as sources of phrasing or inspiration.

This next step is the hard one. I'll do my best to make it as easy as possible.

Step 5: Draft a resume that follows the structure, language, and feel of your model resume

List just your best two or three accomplishments. Staying that focused ensures that the employer actually reads your best selling points in the few seconds that most resumes get on first screening. It also makes the reader curious to know more. To find out more, he or she has to do precisely what you want — interview you. Plan on keeping your resume to one or maybe two pages.

If you have many accomplishments and want to weed some out, put yourself in your target employer's shoes. Ask yourself: Which few accomplishments are most likely to impress your target employer. What skills and attributes would I most want if I were hiring someone for this position? What have I done, in and out of work, that proves I have those skills and attributes?

Chronological Resume

Maynard G. Krebs
9 Dobie Dr.
Gillis, MN 66696
e-mail: whatmework?@whitehouse.gov

Summary

Professional History

1998-present Title, employer

Accomplishment that would most impress the target employer
2nd most impressive accomplishment
3rd most impressive accomplishment (optional)

1996-1997 Title, employer

Accomplishment that would most impress the target employer
2nd most impressive accomplishment
3rd most impressive accomplishment (optional)

1993-1996 Title, employer

Accomplishment that would most impress the target employer
2nd most impressive accomplishment
3rd most impressive accomplishment (optional)

Education

Personal Interests

Figure 11-2:
A chronological resume.

What accomplishments?

Quantitative achievements are powerful and easy to cite. For example:

- ✔ Developed proposal that received $25,000 foundation grant.

- ✔ Only one accident in two years as operations supervisor.

- ✔ Conducted study that resulted in a 20 percent decrease in my employer's phone bills and earned me a cash bonus (which only partly compensated for the personal phone calls you made to your girlfriend in Shanghai).

- Especially impressive are achievements that compare your performance to a benchmark. For example: Ranked second of 15 salespeople in net profit generated. Of course, you don't have to mention that the other 13 were part of the state prison's early-release program.

Less quantifiable accomplishments are also fine:

- A quote from your performance evaluation or letter of recommendation: "Tawanda is one of our brightest and most easy-to-get-along-with employees."
- Successful projects: "I developed a new procedure for assaying immunosuppressants."
- Increased responsibility: "Within three months, was given sole responsibility for the agency's largest graphic design projects."
- Compliments you've received from co-workers or satisfied customers. (Do not mention the time you were complimented for finally getting something right.)

Get letters of reference early in your job search. Not only will they be useful for your resume, they're great for sending along to prospective employers.

Some accomplishments can be particularly powerfully stated as PAR stories. In a *PAR story,* you describe the *p*roblem you were faced with, how you *a*pproached it, and how it was *r*esolved. Take the accomplishment, "Only one accident in two years as operations supervisor." By itself, it's okay, but here's what it reads like as a PAR story:

> When I was hired, three serious accidents had occurred during the previous year. (Note that this will benchmark the achievement about to be mentioned.) One man lost part of a finger. I observed and interviewed all the assembly line workers and the former supervisor, and we developed a new plan for reducing accidents. In my two years as supervisor, the company experienced only one accident, a slightly twisted ankle.

Remember, to get a job offer, you must prove three things:

- You can do the job.
- You will do the job.
- Your personality fits the organization.

So don't forget about "soft" accomplishments such as people skills and Boy/Girl Scout attributes like reliability and hard work. If true, include such accomplishments as:

- Voluntarily worked, on average, a 55-hour workweek. Took only four sick days in three years.

> ✔ Well-liked by co-workers. If they gave an award for employee most likely to be asked out to lunch, it would be me.

"I still can't think of enough accomplishments!"

Try these:

Think of all the people who benefited from your efforts. What would they say about you? Any statistics you can cite?

Sometimes, you can jog your memory by looking at a list of action phrases and verbs. A long list can be found at

content.monster.com/resume/resources/phrases_verbs/

Don't forget about unpaid work or school activities if necessary.

"But I have no previous experience in that line of work!"

If you're trying to land your first job in a particular field, your previous experience, by definition, will be less applicable to your target job. The good news is that nearly everyone has accomplishments that use *transferable* attributes — those used in a different context that would be helpful in your target job.

For example, if you're a new college graduate seeking a job as a TV news reporter, an accomplishment using transferable attributes would be "interviewed 50 students to identify new strategies for an anti–alcohol abuse campaign. Findings were heavily used in the final project design."

Or, say you're tired of being a starving artist and decide you want to become a content manager for a dot-com. You would highlight accomplishments as an artist that might be relevant as a content manager, for example, "Curated an art exhibit, including design, text, and marketing. The event attracted 285 people. A review in the *New Orleans Times-Picayune* called it, 'Bold and fascinating.'"

My favorite example of a transferable skill: A prostitute decided to give it up. What transferable skill did she put on her resume? Excellent customer service. True story.

Honorable tricks

Thanks to your computer, you can adapt each resume you send out so it focuses on the parts of your background most impressive to that employer. That isn't sleazy. If you were a prospective career-counseling client, wouldn't you want a counselor to describe how he helps people in your specific situation?

If your employers are more impressive than your titles, list those first, and vice versa. Perhaps boldface the impressive part.

> **IBM,** clerk.

> **Product manager,** Dewey, Cheatham & Howe.

Some more tips and tricks include:

- ✔ If your firm is impressive, describe it. If not, just list it.
- ✔ If your employment chronology isn't perfect, put the dates on the right side where they'll draw less attention.
- ✔ Throughout the resume, boldface phrases that are particularly impressive. Remember that your resume may get only 15 seconds. It would be a shame if your best accomplishment would have been read in the 16th second.

Solutions for an imperfect work history

Here's how to present flaws honestly without killing your chances of landing a job.

Problem: You're unemployed.

Solution: Consider getting a volunteer or temp job for a prestigious employer in your desired field. Or set yourself up as a consultant. Before putting consultant on your resume, do have at least one consulting assignment (even if unpaid), so you have an answer when the interviewer asks, "Well, Binky, tell me about one of your consulting assignments."

Problem: You've job-hopped.

Solution: Give reasons why you left; for example, it was a temp position, or you had to move because your spouse got a job offer she couldn't refuse. If you left because of an incompatibility with the company, be sure your job target states what sort of employer you want to work for — for example, a small company seeking a self-starter who can wear many hats.

Problem: Your have little or no work history.

Solution: You haven't been catatonic all this time (I hope). Even most party-hearty, kickback, down-a-brew types have done enough constructive things to fill a resume, at least a one-pager with lots of white space and wide margins. So make a list of your accomplishments: classes you've taken, projects you completed, volunteer work, and so on.

Your accomplishments still look skimpy? Create them. For example, volunteer to do a project for a friend, or even better, for a prominent employer.

If you include volunteer work, call the work section of your resume "Experience."

Don't use vague language to hide what you were doing, like the homemaker who wrote: "Operations manager for multi-dimensional enterprise." Such creativity appears deceptive, which is the last thing you want an employer to think.

The late Yana Parker suggested that parents who stopped working to raise their kids be honest, and be sure to include any out-of-home paid or volunteer work. For example:

> 1991–present, Full-time parent. Handled intricate logistics for 2- to 3-year-olds involved in 27 activities with 14 other toddlers. Plus community work involving fund-raising, voter registration, and community service committee work.

Problem: A gap in your work history.

Solutions: List your resume in years rather than months. Fill in the gaps with any education or volunteer work.

That solution, however, doesn't solve David's problem. He worked for a firm that took on too much work with a too small budget, so David burned out and took a yearlong vacation.

My recommendation: Tell the truth. In addition to being honest, the truth often works wonderfully. For example:

> April 2000–March 2001, Personal Sabbatical.

> I have never had a break, and figured while I was still plenty young enough to enjoy it, I would spend a year on pure pleasure: traveling in Europe for two months, helping my brother remodel his kitchen, taking golf lessons, even cleaning out my basement! And lest you think I was a

total slug, I attended a landscape architecture conference, and during a drive through California, I visited a half-dozen award-winning landscape architecture projects.

Are you surprised? A narrative in a resume? And so informally written? Yes and yes. If there's one key to landing a job that you'll be happy and successful in, it is to tell your true, human story throughout the process: in resumes, cover letters, cold calls, and interviews. In today's era of the oh-so-packaged job applicant, a candidate who tells his or her true story often stands out as the sort of person the employer wants in her organization. And if the employer thinks not, it's a sign you don't want to work there.

You may ask, "Shouldn't a story like that go in the cover letter, not the resume?" Answer: It should go in both. It's wise to repeat crucial material that explains away problems and creates positive feelings about you. Besides, resumes and cover letters have a habit of separating from each other, as when the recipient of your resume and cover letter forwards only your resume to his boss.

Problem: You're older.

Solution: Ignore the conventional advice to hide your age by listing only your ten most recent years of work history. During an interview, your age will be apparent. Better they should know sooner than later. If they have their heart set on a young sprout, they're not going to hire you anyway. Better to get screened now than to get your hopes up, do a great job in the interview, and still not get the job.

Step 6: Write the education section

Normally, the education section follows the employment section, but list your education first if it's more impressive than your work achievements. This is true of most job seekers just starting out.

Include your grade-point average if it's at least 3.0 in your major or overall. Also include any honors, like Dean's List or cum laude. (No, second prize in your fraternity's belching contest doesn't count.)

If you started but never finished college, simply list the years of attendance and your major. For example:

1999–2000, Kegger College, major in sociology.

If you're still working on your degree, write your expected graduation date.

If not obvious from your major, list courses that are particularly relevant to your career goal. Include education outside of school, such as seminars.

For example, David wrote:

2001 Continuing Education:

Geohydrology issues in shoreline foundations. University of California, Santa Barbara Extension.

TrackIt: advanced methods. HungryMinds.com (www.hungryminds.com) training program.

2000 B.S. in Landscape Architecture, California State Polytechnic University, San Luis Obispo. 3.3 overall grade-point average, 3.5 land-scape architecture grade-point average.

Special career-applicable courses:

Three years of college-level Spanish. (moderate fluency)

Business courses in project management and finance.

See Chapters 7 and 8 for an easy way to legitimately put an Ivy League college onto your resume.

If most of your career-relevant learning occurred outside of school, describe it. Figure 11-3 shows the education section of an aspiring curator with a career-irrelevant major and lots of out-of-school education.

If you learned things that may impress an employer, you might add ". . . which taught me XXXXXX." For example: "BA in political science, which taught me survey methodology, database management, and statistical analysis."

Step 7: Optional sections

List awards, community involvement, professional affiliations. Only include these if they're likely to impress your target employers. Fellow of the American Academy of Sciences, yes. Member, Hell's Angels, no.

Step 8: The personal section

Here, you list volunteer activities, personal interests, hobbies, and so on. This section can sometimes be a door opener. Seeing a resume from a fellow backpacker can move an employer to pick up the phone.

Education

Academic Education

1998, Williams College, BA in political science

Curating-Related Education

1996-1998 Apprenticing/coaching by:

   Miriam Weinstein, curator Williamstown Art Museum

   Dave Murphy, curator, Kansas City Museum of Art

   Sharon Presley, curator, Chicago Museum of Science and Industry

Professional conferences

American Association of Museums, each annual conference from 1995 to the present

Seminars

The Business Side of Curating: three-day pre-conference workshop, American Association of Museums, 1996

Exhibit Traffic Planning: Williamstown Museum symposium

1994-present Independent reading: 7 books, 50+ articles (titles on request)

Figure 11-3:
The education section of a resume for a person with plenty of out-of-school education.

Step 9: List your highlights at the top of your resume

This is the most important part of your resume. Here, spend time. In the few seconds your resume may get from its recipient, this is the only part you can be sure will get read.

You have three options: Most people will choose just one, but if two are more impressive in your case, include them both.

Option 1

In one line each, list the few accomplishments that will most impress your target employer. Call it a summary.

> **SUMMARY:** Received A.S.L.A. Award as landscape architect on U.S. Highway 1 shoreline restoration project.
>
> Top evaluations from supervisor: "Gets the job done right, plus he's fun to be around!"
>
> Seventeen completed projects. Excellent customer satisfaction (many references available).
>
> Solid knowledge of AutoCAD 2000, and TrackIt project management software.
>
> Led 12 friends on a trip down the Amazon.

Writing a summary of qualifications is easy if you have lots of successful experience in the field you're targeting, but what if you have no such experience? For example, if you've just graduated college and you're seeking a management training position, but your only paid job experience is as a waitress at Hooters. Your summary of qualifications might look like this:

- ✔ Selected for and completed my university's student leadership program.
- ✔ Vice president of sorority — planned budget, and led many events.
- ✔ Extensive coursework in oral and written communications.
- ✔ Elected as dorm representative to housing council.

Or, let's say you're a career changer. You've been a stockbroker for 10 years, came to the conclusion that capitalism is the root of all evil, and want to become a fundraiser for a nonprofit. Your summary of qualifications might be:

- ✔ Demonstrated ability to cold-call, develop relationships with, and secure funding from prospects.
- ✔ Expertise in adapting and using customer database management systems.
- ✔ Long-standing commitment to nonprofits. Currently member, board of trustees, Manhattan chapter of Sierra Club.
- ✔ Excellent financial management and budget skills.
- ✔ Extensive investment expertise — useful in soliciting planned gifts.

Option 2

A short paragraph describing the things about yourself most likely to impress your target employer. This is a good option if you're a good employee who can't point to specific achievements. The key here is to imagine yourself as the employer. What attributes would he most want that you honestly can claim? Let's say it's a nursing position.

SUMMARY: Four years as general medical-surgical nurse, known for exceptional concern for patients and absolute accuracy in treatment and in providing emotional support. Supervisor wrote, "Jan is thorough and remarkably helpful not just to patients, but to all of us."

Option 3

A short paragraph that quickly tells your human story — what brings you to wanting this job. Weave in the best thing(s) you bring to the table. This is the preferred option if your best shot at the job is making a human connection rather than selling your previous experience.

SUMMARY: I was able to work with a number of patent examiners as an engineer at Loral. As time went on, I became fascinated with what they do. After a year of intensive preparation, I now am eagerly seeking a position as assistant patent examiner.

Often, the most qualified person doesn't get the job. One reason: Another candidate created chemistry. A resume summary and cover letter are excellent ways to give you an edge when you know your actual qualifications are unlikely to be top-of-the-heap.

Step 10: Get feedback

Show your resume to a respected friend and then a potential employer or personnel recruiter. Make any recommended changes.

John Sullivan, professor of human resources at San Francisco State University, suggests that you have your reviewers circle all the items in the resume that impress them, put an X through all items they don't like, including typos, and a question mark next to all items that confuse them or slow them down.

Step 11: Stop obsessing and start celebrating

You're done!

Your Electronic Resume

Today, most job seekers need an electronic version of their resume. Even newspaper want ads may request one. And an e-resume is often required for posting online or responding to an online ad. Your computer skills would look rather thin if, to respond to an online ad, you had to print out your resume and fax it rather than just click and send. Here's how to convert your resume into an electronic version:

✔ Most large employers electronically scan resumes to find words that match keywords in the job description. So, review your resume to ensure that, if appropriate, they include industry buzzwords. Don't know what those buzzwords are? Pick them out of intriguing job ads. If some of those buzzwords don't fit naturally into the body of your resume, list them in a section at the end of your resume entitled, "Additional keywords."

✔ Describe your job using nouns rather than verbs: manager rather than managed, programmer rather than programmed.

✔ After developing your resume, you need to create a version you can send directly in an e-mail. You ask, "Can't I just send it as a Microsoft Word attachment? Everyone has MS Word?" First, not everyone has MS Word. And many employers don't like attachments because they can have viruses and because they take time to open. Don't worry. It's easy to make your resume e-mail friendly.

✔ In your e-mail cover letter to a prospective employer, write, "To ensure my resume's readability on your system, I enclose it two ways: An unformatted version is in this e-mail and a fully formatted version is attached as an MS Word file."

✔ To create that unformatted version using MS Word:

> To make it more readable, Margaret Riley Dikel, coauthor of *The Guide to Internet Job Searching,* recommends that you put your section headings in caps and use a plus sign to bullet items on a list. Surround italicized words with asterisks. Use the space bar instead of indents. Alter the margins so that they're 65 characters wide. To do this, you'll, alas, have to count the number of characters in each line. And when you get as near as possible to the 65th character, hit the Enter key to wrap the line.

> When you're done, e-mail your e-resume to yourself first, so you can see how it looks.

> Save the final version among your saved e-mails.

> When you want to e-mail your resume to someone or post it on your site, select (shade) the entire resume and press Control-C. Then move your cursor to the place in your e-mail (or resume-posting site) at the exact place you want to insert your resume. Press Control-V to insert it.

> *Note:* Increasingly, employment Web sites don't allow you to insert your resume. They ask you to create, at their site, a mini-version of your resume, using their format. In those cases, you can do it quickly by keeping a printed copy of your resume in front of you and copying the requested information.

Want an Electronic Handholder?

Want an electronic handholder as you develop your resume?

Consider ResumeMaker (www.resumemaker.com), a free online resume builder. It has 25 professionally designed formats to choose from and it walks you through all the steps. It also has an index of thousands of resume-enhancing words. More important, it is remarkably easy to use — I was using it successfully from the moment I cranked it up. The basic version is available free at the site. The full version with a larger database of suggested phrases is downloadable for $40.

Want a Human Handholder?

Okay, okay. I know that despite all my efforts to make do-it-yourself resume-making straightforward, some people want a human handholder. Some nationally regarded resume writing services include Susan Whitcomb (www.careerwriter.com) and Kathryn Troutman at www.resume-place.com, who is especially good for developing resumes for government jobs. By the time you read this, they may be so big that they need to hire underlings to do the work. Try to get the big enchilada, but if you get referred to an "excellent associate," be sure to ask that person for three sample resumes of people who actually got hired. Then call those clients and ask how they liked the resume writer.

Chapter 12

Finding Your Dream Employer

. . . .

In this chapter

▶ Why you should work for a large company

▶ Why you should work for a small company

▶ The upside and downside of start-ups

▶ The upside and downside of nonprofits

▶ Why government jobs are underrated

▶ Self-employment?

▶ Finding your specific dream employers

. . . .

*Y*ou've come a long way. You've picked out a career. You've trained for it. The next step? Finding a great employer. But who would be a great employer for *you*? Would you be happier in a large company? A small one? A start-up? A nonprofit? The government? At home with just you and Bow Wow? And once you've decided what type of organization you want to work for, how do you find a wonderful specific employer? This chapter offers some answers.

Just What Sort of Organization Should You Work For?

Of course, deciding whether to work for a large or a small organization, a for-profit or a nonprofit, is like asking whether it's better to eat at a restaurant or to eat at home — it depends on who's doing the cooking. But some generalizations can be made.

Top six reasons to work for a large company

Larger companies have plenty going for them:

- ✔ **More stable employment.** Despite relentless mergers and downsizing, large employers remain more likely to retain employees than small ones. Small businesses have a nasty habit of going out of business — so long job, so long stock options. For every employee who got in on the ground floor of Yahoo!, thousands of yahoos hold sexy-sounding but worthless pieces of paper.

- ✔ **More advanced technology.** It's expensive to keep up with the latest and greatest. That's a luxury that mainly large companies can afford.

- ✔ **More likely to provide sophisticated training.** If a company has 100 employees who need the same training, it can justify the cost of developing a first-class program.

- ✔ **Stronger legal protections.** Most large companies work hard to ensure their workers harassment- and discrimination-free workplaces. And if you have a problem, the company has a human resources department that's trained to pounce immediately.

- ✔ **Better benefits.** Health, dental, and retirement plans tend to be more generous.

- ✔ **Status.** It feels better and looks better on your resume to say you work for Hewlett-Packard than for the Western Widget Waxing Company.

Top six reasons to work for a small company

Small companies also have their pluses:

- ✔ **More control.** It's been said that at a large company, you need approval to blow your nose. In a small company, you're more likely to have the authority to blow some cash on a project that excites you.

- ✔ **More job opportunities.** Small companies create most of the jobs.

- ✔ **Variety.** You get to wear many hats. For example, a scientist at a small company may be part lab rat, manager, marketer, and even salesperson.

- ✔ **Easier to get hired without formal credentials.** Many small companies are less insistent that you have that piece of parchment. They just want to know you can hit the ground running.

> ✔ **You're more likely to see your impact.** Fewer employees means that your impact is greater. That feels good — unless, of course, you're screwing up.

What about start-ups?

Of course, any newborn business can be called a start-up, but today, the term mainly refers to fledgling Internet or biotech firms.

WARNING!

If you're the one doing the starting up, it's exciting. You get to conceive of your own brainchild and try to see it through to fabulous riches. But if you're just another employee at a start-up, especially a *dot-com,* I gotta warn you. Not only may the excitement be less, for every start-up millionaire, dozens of start-up employees are working 65-hour weeks for 40K a year, with stock options no more valuable than toilet paper. And talk about quality of life? Sure, at dot-coms you may be allowed to throw a Frisbee, but don't let that fool you — many start-ups are modern-day sweatshops. One new college graduate working at a Multimedia Gulch start-up complains, "Every week feels like finals week." Another groused, "Sure they feed you good lunches and let you bring your dog to work, but that's just to ensure you never have an excuse to leave the office." Finally, there's the job security issue. Dot-coms are dropping like flies. Today's dot-com is likely to be tomorrow's dot-bomb.

That said, many people love working for start-ups. They love the informal, crazed atmosphere. They like discovering something new every day — happy dot-comers are learning junkies. They crave the adrenaline rush of everyone cranking 15-hours-a-day to get a cool product to market before the competitor does, with a chance to score serious dollars as a reward. And because of the warp-speed pace, you can be an entry-level employee in January, and by March, you're director of operations for 18 countries (without the slightest idea of what to do). Think that can happen at Procter & Gamble?

No-nonsense about nonprofits

People romanticize about working in the nonprofit sector. And true, it *is* wonderful to work for a cause you believe in alongside people willing to volunteer or work for peanuts because they too believe in the cause. Yet turnover in the nonprofit sector is high. Why?

> ✔ It's easy to lose sight of the clean air you're trying to protect amid your day-to-day routines. Most tasks within nonprofit organizations are the same as those in the private sector: managing employees, administering budgets, writing reports, and so on.

> ✔ Budgets are often too tight, which can mean spartan surroundings. It can also mean that you may have to do without things that private sector employees take for granted — like a computer that gets repaired before the next generation of computers comes out.
>
> ✔ Nonprofits are run largely by volunteers, the quality of whose work is variable.

Working for the government

When you think of a government job, what do you think of? A postal worker? A pencil-pusher? The government employs millions of professionals: doctors, lawyers, economists, engineers, scientists, accountants, planners, and managers.

Indeed, the U.S. government is America's largest employer, with 17 million employees. One in seven Americans works for federal, state, or local governments. And despite the much-reported streamlining, the federal government alone hires 1,500 new workers *every day*.

Some people shun government jobs because they hear that government is shrinking. This is a mistake. I believe that government employment will increase greatly as Democrats gain power. Democrats, of course, believe in bigger government. To convince you to consider government employment, I'd better explain why I'm so certain that the Democrats will gain power:

> ✔ We haven't yet seen the full impact of motor-voter registration. People yet unregistered are more likely to be low-income, a group that votes heavily Democrat.
>
> ✔ Birthrates in the past 20 years have been much higher among minorities (who overwhelmingly vote Democrat).
>
> ✔ The 2000 census increased the number of counted minorities, the demographic group that votes more heavily Democrat.
>
> ✔ Increased immigration means new voters who vote heavily Democrat.
>
> ✔ The schools, media, and colleges, which are the major influences on our thinking, are more liberal and activist than ever.

Not only does the government employ millions of people, it pays them well. Except at top levels, government pay averages about the same as private sector pay. And unlike the temp-happy private sector, a high percentage of government employees hold full-time positions with full benefits and exceptional legal protections.

The stereotype that government employees are apathetic because the government lacks profit-making incentive is not valid. In fact, a different, sometimes equally powerful motivator exists in many government offices: The recognition that government's purpose is to serve all the people, not just the company's owners.

Self-employment

Self-employment is a wonderful option and a terrible one. It depends who you are. You don't need a lot of money to stake your business. You don't need an MBA. You don't even need a new idea — many people succeed with copycat businesses. In fact, it's often easier to succeed when you can learn from the mistakes of pioneers. To be successfully self-employed, you must have practical smarts and the attitude of a self-starter. If you have those two qualities, here's why I'm high on self-employment despite the long hours and the worries that come with being your own boss:

- ✔ **Control.** Many of us enjoy control. When you're self-employed, you're president. Want to try selling a new product? You can, anytime you want. Want to hire someone? You won't have a six-month approval process. Want to reduce your record-keeping? You won't have a boss warning you about accountability standards.

- ✔ **Perfect for the uncredentialed.** Try convincing a company to let you be the president without a decades-long climb up the organizational chart. If you're self-employed, you can instantly go from gofer to CEO.

- ✔ **Reasonable job security.** Sure, most new businesses fail during the first five years, but you can cut your risk in half by operating your business from home. And among smart self-starters who follow the advice in Chapter 20, the odds of staying in business are about as good as those of keeping a job. You can't lose your job because of a personality conflict, a change in management philosophy, a boss who decides he needs someone with a different skill set, a merger, an acquisition, or a downsizing.

- ✔ **You get to keep all the profits.** So many employees save their employers sheaves of money and get nothing for it. Many employees are grateful for an attaboy and a cost-of-living raise.

- ✔ **The pride of creating a business.**

- ✔ **Flexibility.** Yes, you'll probably have to work your butt off, especially in the early years, but on your own terms. Want to work 'til midnight on Tuesday and play golf on Wednesday? It's your call. Want to be home for your children after school? You're the boss. Want to work at home, in your pajamas, with hard rock blasting? Yes, ma'am!

Finding Your Dream Employer

Okay. You've figured out what type of organization you want to work for. Next step: finding your dream employers within that category of organization.

Creating your list of dream employers

The standard advice is to develop a long list. Bad idea. Are you really going to take the time to do the research necessary to convince 50 employers that each one is the ideal one for you? Besides, why not put your effort into the few that are really more likely to make you happy? Aim for between 2 and 25 employers. Sometimes, a continual, multi-front assault on just your few dream employers can pay off.

Are there employers you know you'd die to work for? If so, skip ahead to Chapter 14. Chances are, though, you need suggestions. The simplest and perhaps best way to find your dream employers is to find a library with a great business section and tell the librarian that you want a list of employers that meet your specifications — for example, well-regarded environmental nonprofit organizations in Westchester County.

Or if you'd rather find dream employers by yourself, the following information can help you find small telecommunications firms in San Diego, large fashion houses in New York, or fish farms in Dubuque. Well, you may have trouble finding the fish farms.

Sources of local dream employers

There are many ways to find your best bets:

- ✔ If you're still in college, attend a meeting of your field's professional club; for example, the biology club. Club members often know of cool employers. Even if you never attended that college, you'd probably be allowed to attend a meeting of a local college's club.

- ✔ Ask friends, colleagues, competitors, suppliers, customers, headhunters, and counselors at a local college's career center.

- ✔ Ask attendees at a local chapter meeting of your field's professional association.

- ✔ Check out the "best" lists: Big-city general newspapers (find links to them at www.newslink.org) and business newspapers such as *Business Times* (www.bizjournals.com) regularly list the "best," fastest-growing, and largest organizations. A portal to such local publications is at www.myjobsearch.com/employers/emerging.html.

✔ Consult the *Adams Job Bank* series of books, available for 33 individual metropolitan areas. Each profiles thousands of local employers listed by category and company size and includes contact information.

✔ Try the chamber of commerce. To avoid the party line, "All our members are good companies," ask a specific question such as, "I'm looking for a job as an economist. Do you know of any good, fast-growing small companies that might be good places to work?"

✔ Check out features in local magazines and newspapers about fast-growing companies, new product introductions, and profiles of notable employees.

✔ Call your favorite government agencies (find them in the blue-trimmed pages in the front of your White Pages) and ask the purchasing department for the names of outside contractors who employ people in your target job. Many government agencies outsource much of their work to contractors.

✔ Check out your field's category in your local Yellow Pages. Sometimes an employer's ad calls out to you.

✔ Check the "associations" listing in your Yellow Pages for a list of local nonprofit organizations.

✔ Fast-growing companies are often fun to work for. Find them by seeing who places large multi-job advertisements in local newspapers or many local listings at an employment Web site, who has a booth at a job fair, or who is recruiting on a local college campus. To find the latter, just call a local college's career center and ask for a list of the employers that are recruiting on-campus.

✔ Look for interesting company T-shirts. I'm only half-joking. I suspect that it's a good sign if an employer creates cool T-shirts for its employees.

✔ Don't ignore your current employer. Tweaking your present job to fit or getting a transfer is usually easier than convincing some stranger to give you the perfect job. If you trust your boss, have a heart-to-heart chat and describe your dream job. If you're skittish, try the human resources department; it may guarantee confidentiality. Be sure to verify that before spilling your guts.

Sources of dream employers farther away

It's even easy to find great employers thousands of miles away:

✔ See the "Business and Employer Rankings" at www.rileyguide.com/busrank.html. It links to dozens of "best company lists," from *Fortune* magazine's list of "Cool Companies" to the *Industry Standard's* "100 Most Important Companies in the Internet Economy". Another large compendium of "Best Businesses" lists is at www.hoovers.com/company/lists_best.

- Check out WetFeet (www.wetfeet.com). For each of 60 leading and emerging fields, there's a dossier that includes the industry's leading players and a "Real People Profile" of one or two industry insiders. Also see The Vault (www.vault.com), which contains inside information such as strategic direction and corporate culture on more than 3,000 of America's largest employers.

- Ask on Internet discussion groups. To find on-target ones, visit www.topica.com and www.liszt.com. Once you find an appropriate group, just post this question: "I'm looking for a job as a *(insert desired job)*. Can anyone recommend good places to work that might be hiring?"

- Browse through an on-target industry directory. A portal to hundreds of them is at www.myjobsearch.com/cgi-bin/mjs.cgi/employers/directories.html.

- Browse www.thomasregister.com. It contains product and contact information on 157,000 companies. You can search by company name, brand name, or type of product.

- Consult the *U.S. Government Manual* (www.access.gpo.gov/nara/nara001.html) and *The Budget of the United States Government* (//w3.access.gpo.gov/usbudget/index.html) for indications of which federal agencies will be growing. Kathryn Petras, coauthor of the book, *Jobs*, explains, "This is a clever way to get a real head start on everyone else. Every year, *The Manual* . . . tells the policies and priorities of each federal agency or department. *The Budget* goes one better; it tells where the money is going. Often agencies with increased allocations will be hiring."

- Check Dan Lauber's *Job Finder* books for lists of field-specific directories.

Want to find a cool start-up?

Here are some places to find cool start-ups:

- About.com's portal to start-up sites: http://jobsearchtech.about.com/careers/jobsearchtech/msub32.htm.

- Top Startups (www.topstartups.com): Contact info, press releases, and web addresses of 200 mainly venture-capital-funded start-ups.

- Startup Zone (www.startupzone.com): Hundreds of start-ups to cold call, their job listings to apply for, plus discussion groups and a collection of current news articles on start-ups so you can sound knowledgeable.

- PriceWaterhouseCoopers Money Tree (www.pwcmoneytree.com): This site lists hundreds of companies that recently received venture financing plus links to their Web sites.

- Startup Network (www.startupnetwork.com): A database of 3,000 job listings at high-tech start-ups.

- ✔ CMGI (www.cmgi.com.): 60 emerging Internet companies that have been funded by this Nasdaq-1000 venture firm.

- ✔ Venture Wire (www.venturewire.com): an e-mail newsletter profiling new companies that have just received venture capital.

- ✔ 216.156.244.236: A foul-mouthed-titled Web site where insiders predict which start-up will bite the dust next. (Why do I suspect that you're going to check out this Web site before the others?)

- ✔ My favorite technique: Search megajob sites such as careerbuilder.com and careers.yahoo.com, using only your nearest town as the search term. That identifies short-commute companies in growth modes, including start-ups in stealth mode — those working in secrecy.

Want to work for a nonprofit?

My favorite portal into the nonprofit world is *Idealist* (www.idealist.org). It links to 20,000 nonprofits, posts hundreds of job and internship listings, thousands of volunteer opportunities in the U.S. and around the world, plus a collection of nonprofit news Web sites. See also www.opportunitynocs.org and www.volunteermatch.org.

Finding the right people to talk with in each organization

Don't even think about starting your letter, "To Whom it May Concern." You immediately come off as lazy. You need a name, ideally someone with the power to hire you:

- ✔ The big enchilada at the small organization you want to work for. (Ask for "the person in charge.")

- ✔ The department head in the large organization you crave.

- ✔ Most career guides urge you to not contact the human resources department. Because HR doesn't have the power to hire you, career guides argue that it's better to speak with the person who does. My clients have not found this to be the case. Although human resources people don't make hiring decisions, they supervise the hiring process. So they often know who's hiring and what positions are coming up. In addition, by making your inquiry through HR, you eliminate the risk of upsetting a hirer — most of them hate being interrupted by someone inquiring about a nonexistent job. They may also resent your having circumvented standard procedure, which is to contact HR about employment.

"But, you ask, How do I find the names of hirers and human resources people to contact?" Phone the organization. This is the best way, because unlike with directories, you get a currently accurate name, title, address, and, if you're lucky, an e-mail address and direct phone number.

Finding the organization's general phone number is easy. It's almost always at the organization's Web site, and if the organization doesn't have a Web site, simply go to a nationwide online phone directory such as www.whitepages. com, or www.switchboard.com. www.hoovers.com lists contact information for senior officials at 50,000 companies, plus company overviews. Or simply go low-tech: the toll-free phone directory: 1-800-555-1212. Many organizations have toll-free phone numbers.

Getting the phone number of someone in human resources is usually no problem. But what about hirers'? Don Lussier, author of *Job Search Secrets,* recommends this approach: Call the company's general number and say, "I'm updating my mailing list (which you are). Who's in charge of XXXXX (marketing, for example)? How's that spelled? And her title? Her phone number?" If the receptionist asks what it's for, tell the truth. The worst case is he sends you to human resources, which isn't the end of the world.

If you don't get anywhere with the receptionist, call back and ask for the organization's mailroom. It doesn't have gatekeeping responsibility, does have the organization's directory, and often will surrender the information.

Keeping track

Pull out that 8½- by 11-inch three-ring binder you're using to keep track of the want ads you responded to. Or ResumeMaker if you're using the higher-tech approach (see Chapter 13).

Have a separate page for each contact person. At the top, write the person's name, contact information, plus need-to-remember information from conversations and from your research on the organization.

Now get 31 divider sheets, the manila ones with the colored translucent tabs attached. Number each divider from 1 to 31, one for each day of the month. Put them into the three-ring binder.

Place each contact person's page in the correct day's section. For example, if you spoke with someone today and it's the tenth of the month, and you're supposed to follow up in a week, put that page in the section labeled "17."

Finding Out What That Organization Is Really Like

A benefit of targeting just a few organizations is that you have the time to bone up on them before contacting them. An employer likes to see that he's not just one of the 1,000 resumes you scattershot. "I want to work for you because you are a dynamic company," just doesn't cut it.

On the other hand, there's no need to go overboard. Not only is it time-consuming, it could make company officials think you're so desperate for a job that you have nothing better to do than to conduct in-depth research on companies. So just do a modest amount of research. I include many research sources here so you have plenty to choose from, but just pick your favorite few.

The public info

Here's information that's just waiting for the taking:

- ✔ Visit the employer's Web site. You're likely to find everything from the company's plans to the CEO's speeches. But remember, a company Web site is like a new car brochure. It tells you only what the company wants you to know.

- ✔ If it's a public company, your task is easy. Just go to the Wall Street Research Net (www.wsrn.com), enter the company's name, and instantly, you'll get links to valuable information from dozens of sources.

- ✔ Check periodicals. FindArticles.com (www.findarticles.com) enables you to instantly identify every mention of the employer in any of 300-plus periodicals. Willing to part with a few bucks? Factiva (www.factiva.com) will search 6,000 periodicals for articles mentioning your target company. Headlines are free. Full articles are $2.95 each. Links to 10,000 newspapers, magazines, radio and TV station sites are available free at newslink.org. But you have to search them one at a time.

- ✔ The Vault (www.vault.com) and Wet Feet (www.wetfeet.com) have inside information on thousands of U.S. companies.

- ✔ Tell the receptionist of a small company that you're looking for a good organization to work for, have heard good things about this one, but want to learn more about it before inquiring about a job. Can she send you some information on the organization?

- ✔ The Riley Guide offers a gateway (www.rileyguide.com/news.html) to thousands of magazines' and newpapers' Web sites. Many of these allow you to keyword-search their archives. Sometimes, the best strategy is to search the local newspaper where the organization is headquartered.

The inside info

REMEMBER

John Sullivan, professor of human resources at San Francisco State University, wisely advises that visiting a company's Web page is now so easy that it doesn't give you an advantage over many job applicants. What does give you an edge is knowing something about the organization's needs, culture, strengths, and weaknesses — the stuff that doesn't get into print. Here's how to access that information:

✔ Use a search engine (try www.google.com and www.northernlight.com), using the name of the employer as your search term. That may yield unauthorized discussions of the employer: independent product reviews, even rants from disgruntled employees or customers.

✔ Use www.go2net.com's newsgroup search feature, with your target company's name as the search term. It pulls up every mention of your company's name in online discussion groups. It's a good source of dirt.

✔ Ask about the company on an Internet discussion group for that industry. (See www.liszt.com and www.topica.com to find relevant ones.)

✔ Call or e-mail company employees. Start with the people whose job it is to give out information: receptionist, human resources, or public relations. Want more? Talk to someone in your target job. Insider's secret: Speak with a salesperson — they often know a lot about the company and like to talk.

Now you know who you want to work for. Next step: getting them to hire you.

Sam & Mary

Sam loved to write, especially poetry, but the only writing job he could land was as an advertising copywriter. He hated it and, one day, simply quit. To pay the bills, Sam took a job as an unskilled laborer. Because he was brighter than the average laborer, his foreman took a liking to him and taught Sam to be a skilled carpenter. He now supervises a construction crew, makes a good living, and writes poetry in his spare time.

Mary. Although Mary had a pilot's license, she couldn't land a pilot's job. She's an administrative assistant for a major aircraft manufacturer. Nevertheless, she still wanted to fly planes, if only as a hobby. But renting flight time is expensive. So she became an expert at FAA regulations and got freelance jobs flying to remote airstrips to teach those regulations to aspiring pilots. Her instructor's fee more than pays for her flying time. She's still an administrative assistant but feels okay about her day job because she's living her dream after work.

Chapter 13

A Better Approach to the Want Ads

In This Chapter

▶ How much should *you* use the want ads?

▶ Using the Internet to find the right jobs for *you*

▶ Posting your resume on the Internet

▶ The best ads to respond to

▶ The best way to respond to an ad

▶ Want-ad stress savers

I know, I know. You've probably been told, "Don't spend much time answering want ads. You'll answer a thousand before getting one job offer."

That's true for people who don't know how to use the ads, but *you* will. This chapter shows you how to make the most of want ads — a better job search tool than you may think.

Want Ads: The Most Underrated Job Search Tool

The want ads are a more powerful job-search tool than you may have been led to believe.

✔ With literally millions of easy-to-search online job openings to choose from, you can focus on those that really fit. The odds of a networking contact leading to a good-fitting job are much smaller.

✔ It's fast. Respond to an ad today, and you could be hired within weeks or even days. Other job search methods such as networking typically take months.

✔ Ads are a legal cheat sheet for job applicants. Unlike with networking or cold calling, you usually know exactly what the employer is looking for — the job requirements are right there in the ad. So you can tailor your resume, cover letter, and interview to the employer's needs.

✔ Responding to want ads is more psychologically rewarding than networking because:

  • You know you're probably applying for an actual job opening.

  • Responding to want ads is less stressful than asking people to help you find a job, let alone trying to convince an employer who hasn't listed a job opening that she should hire you.

  • Networking and cold calling often involve trying to convince someone to buy something they're not looking for. Unless you're a real sales type, that's not fun.

✔ Using the want ads is an ideal approach for people who work during business hours. "When will I find the time to network and make cold calls?" is a frequent cry of working stiffs. In contrast, you can search for and respond to want ads at night and on weekends, so you don't have to take time off work. And unlike when you're networking, you don't have to worry if you're having a bad hair day.

✔ Using the want ads is ideal if you're looking for a job out-of-town. The Web contains sites with literally millions of instantly searchable job openings all over the world. In fact, want ads should be an especially large part of an out-of-town job search because you probably don't have many faraway networking contacts.

✔ Responding to want ads is ideal for people who write better than they schmooze.

✔ The want ads are a great place to discover employers that are in hiring mode. Even if their posted ads don't fit you, contact them and they may create a job for you.

✔ Want ads can even be useful when you're self-employed. Use them to identify organizations seeking someone to do work that's right up your alley and then propose doing the job on a project-by-project basis.

✔ Most of all, what makes want ads good is how they compare with the other job search tools. Networking works if you have a 500-person Rolodex. Cold-calling dream employers works if you're a terrific self-promoter. Unfortunately, most people, especially those who consult career guides, aren't like that. For the rest of us, responding to want ads feels more doable. Career guidebooks call networking and cold calling the best job-search techniques, but they're useless if you're too uptight to use them. Want ads are a job search tool for the rest of us.

Want ads have long been underrated and networking overrated, but today, that's truer than ever. In the 1980s, when networking first got hot, employers didn't mind getting networked. It was a bit flattering to be asked for advice. Likewise, employers hadn't yet figured out that a request for advice was often a ruse to land a job interview. But now, 20 years later, employers are busier, tired of being networked, and increasingly seeing informational interviews as ploys, even when they're not. So while networking still often works, it is less potent than it used to be.

At the same time, more and more job openings are subject to affirmative action hiring requirements, so fewer jobs are filled from the "inside." To fulfill legal requirements, they must be advertised.

Meanwhile, thanks to the Internet, answering want ads is a job-search method on steroids. Millions of job openings are posted on the Web. You can search through them to find tailor-made jobs from the comfort of your home. You can even have personal electronic job scouts scour the Net for you 24/7, searching through those millions of job openings and delivering the best fits on a silver platter right to your electronic door. All free to you! Now tell me that's not cool.

How Much Should You Use the Want Ads?

Other career guidebooks give everyone the same advice: Use want ads sparingly. But one-size-fits-all advice rarely does fit all. So how much should *you* use want ads? Some people should devote no time at all to scanning the want ads; others should devote more than half of their job search time. Here's how to tell what's right for you: The more of these questions that you answer *yes* to, the more you should use want ads.

- ✔ Are you better at writing resumes and letters than at networking?
- ✔ Are you more likely to answer ads than to network?
- ✔ Do you know only a few people in your field?
- ✔ Are you expecting a salary of less than $70,000?
- ✔ Is your target job in demand?
- ✔ Are you currently employed in or near your target field?

Despite the advantages of want ads, few job seekers should devote all his or her job search time to answering ads. More than half the jobs, in all fields and at all levels, are never advertised. So spend some time contacting target employers even if they have no listed openings and telling people in your personal network what sort of job you're looking for.

That's especially true if you're trying to break into a new field. Employers don't have to advertise to find someone without experience. They can get candidates by asking their current employees, friends, or cousin Poindexter.

Not sure whether the want ads will work for you? Craft good responses to perhaps 20 carefully selected ads. If you get no positive responses, you have your answer.

Making Want Ads Work for You

Okay, here's the meat. This section lifts you from the madding crowd into the group that can reasonably expect to land jobs using the want ads.

While, like every author, I think every word in this chapter is essential, if you want the McVersion, here it is. To use the want ads wisely, be sure to use online as well as print ads. A fine portal to online employment sites is at www.rileyguide.com/jobs.html. Be sure to check out regional and occupation-specific employment sites. Also go to individual dream employers' web sites. When responding to ads, include a cover letter which outlines, point-by-point, how you meet the requirements stated in the want ad. If possible, include a work sample.

Now here's the expanded version of that game plan.

Two easy record-keeping systems

It helps at interview time if you keep the ads you've responded to and the cover letters you've sent.

A low-tech system: Tape each ad to a separate 8½- by 11-inch piece of notebook paper and put it in your three-ring binder along with your cover letter (if customized). Note any supplementary materials you included, for example, a work sample.

A higher-tech system: Get a copy of ResumeMaker software (downloadable for $39.95 from www.resumemaker.com). Not only is it my favorite resume-building software, its job-search manager allows you to note when you responded to an ad, make notes about any employer contact. It also reminds you when to follow up with each.

The best ads to respond to

Most job seekers respond to ads in newspapers and at Web megasites such as www.hotjobs.com but they don't bother with individual employers' sites. That's a mistake. Here's why.

The first place many employers post their job openings is on their own Web sites. Why? Because it's easy, it's free, and respondents to ads at individual sites tend to be higher-caliber and specifically interested in their organization. Because employers aren't inundated with responses to their company-site-posted ads, your e-mail response to one is more likely to get a careful look. A few years from now, most employers will immediately post their job openings on sites such as hotjobs.com. Applicants will then have to compete against the entire world. But we're not quite there yet. So visit your target employers' Web sites and see if they list any openings for you.

Most job seekers think the Net is mainly for tech jobs. Not any more. The Net lists hundreds of thousands of nontechnical job openings.

Developing an efficient way to screen a large number of ads

With all the job listings out there, you need a way to quickly identify your best fits.

Going low-tech

Of course, you can scan your local Sunday newspaper.

You can also consult professional periodicals. In them, you'll find more on-target ads than in general newspapers. If you don't know the professional association for your field, check Associations Unlimited, available in many libraries. Some libraries even allow you to access it online from home.

You can look at your current employer's internal job postings. It should be fairly easy to convince your current employer that you understand your organization's needs.

Using the Internet

The low-tech stuff is all well and good, but, oh the Internet. It contains literally millions of job openings. And though you may be competing against many applicants, the beauty is that you can identify good fits almost instantly.

Sites with job scouts

At many employment Web sites, you submit a resume, create one at the site, or answer multiple-choice questions about the kind of job you're looking for. Then, the site not only searches its thousands of job openings and lists the good fits, but from then on, notifies you by e-mail whenever an employer lists a job that fits you, inviting you to apply. Sign up for that service at a bunch of sites, and you've recruited a team of electronic scouts searching 24/7 through zillions of jobs each day and delivering the best fits to your e-mail address, all for free. Amazing.

Here are major sites offering these electronic scouts: `careers.yahoo.com`, `www.monster.com`, `www.careerbuilder.com`, `www.joboptions.com`, `www.hotjobs.com`, `www.jobbankusa.com`, and `www.nationjob.com`

Or try `www.jobsleuth.com`, which claims to search many job sites' listings and e-mail you the good fits.

Caveats

Note each site's privacy policies. You generally don't want your name or current employer to appear on your posted resume. Not only does that make it easy for your employer to find that you're looking, an unscrupulous headhunter can circulate your resume to thousands of employers so that if you get hired, she gets a big commission. That commission can be just enough to make an employer hire someone other than you. Monster.com has an ideal privacy policy. You can elect to have your resume posted without your name and previous employer. When an employer is interested, it lets monster.com know. Then, monster e-mails you the job ad and lets you know that the employer is inviting you to apply — a perfect arrangement.

RileyGuide webmaster Margaret Dikel warns that electronic job scouts work best for white collar and management jobs. If you're a diamond cutter, don't expect these sites to fill your e-mail box with job listings. Dikel suggests that you submit a few different profiles to see which one yields the best-fitting job openings.

Other mega-employment sites

At other sites, you have to visit the site to see the listings, but it may be worth the small effort. The reason is that it can take an automated site days to send the job listings to your e-mail, whereas if you check these sites daily, they're fresher.

The following sites claim fantastic numbers of job listings, but when I search them, they often report fewer on-target job openings than I expected. But nothing to lose by checking them.

✔ Employment 911 (`www.employment911.com`) claims to list 3.5 million job openings at more than 100 top job sites.

✔ FlipDog (`www.flipdog.com`). Most employment sites function like newspaper want ads — employers pay the site to publish the want ad. FlipDog is different. Its 700,000 job opening are aggregated from 50,000 employers' sites — a big plus because most employers post their openings on their own sites rather than paying other sites to list their jobs. Because FlipDog is free, most of those employers generally agree to post their job listings on FlipDog. So, you'll likely uncover different job openings on FlipDog than on other sites.

✔ Jobtrak (`www.jobtrak.com`) is aimed at new college graduates.

✔ Job Direct (`www.jobdirect.com`) is also aimed at college students and new graduates, including both job listings and internships.

✔ Recruiter Connection (`www.recruiterconnection.com`) permits in-house and third-party recruiters (headhunters) to see your resume.

✔ CareerShop.com (`www.careershop.com`) has won top industry awards. It claims to simultaneously search 41 employment sites, including the U.S. government's.

✔ CareerBuilder (`www.careerbuilder.com`) also aggregates results from many job sites. A CareerBuilder search enables you to screen 3 million jobs.

✔ WantedJobs (www.wantedjobs.com) Aggregates results from 350 job sites. You screen 3.5 million jobs in just a second or two. Truly amazing.

✔ America's Job Bank at `www.jobsearch.org` says it has 1.5 million job listings from 1,800 state employment agencies, mostly in the private sector.

✔ Federal Job Announcement Search at `www.usajobs.opm.gov` posts and updates more than 1,500 *new* U.S. government openings *daily*. Tip: You can speak to someone at the Federal Office of Personnel Management to find out where you might fit. (See your White Pages for a local phone number.)

✔ Federal Jobs Digest (`www.jobsfed.com`) offers a well-categorized list of federal job openings. For a modest fee, it helps you determine which federal job titles and grade levels you qualify for.

✔ For state and local government jobs, see `www.piperinfo.com/state/index.cfm`, and `www.statejobs.com`.

✔ `Govjobs.com` lists positions at all levels of government and government contractors, with particularly rich opportunities in defense and engineering.

✔ For many more links to government employment sites, see `www.rileyguide.com/gov.html`.

It may be worth spending the $49 to have ResumeBlaster (www.resume-blaster.com) or ResumeZapper (www.resumezapper.com) e-mail your resume to thousands of recruiters. Your identity can be suppressed so confidentiality isn't a problem. Just don't put many eggs into that basket. A survey found that a recruiter is least likely to hire someone whose resume came from a mass e-mailing. But occasionally they do, so it may be worth the few minutes and few bucks to do it.

Specialty employment sites

Thousands of regional employment sites exist. Perhaps because fewer applicants are competing, my clients have more often landed jobs using a regional site — www.craigslist.org — than with any national site. A gateway to regional sites is at www.job-hunt.org/states.shtml.

Another way to reduce your competition is to focus on sites that specialize in particular fields. While the masses head to the megasites, you can fly under the radar to these. Some of the entries in this book's Cool Careers Yellow Pages includes an employment Web site specializing in that field. Links to hundreds of other field-specific employment sites are at www.job-hunt.org, dir.lycos.com/Business/Jobs, and www.rileyguide.com/resfree.html. A few examples of specialty sites:

- ✔ Idealist (www.idealist.org) claims to list openings at 20,000 nonprofit organizations. Another great site for nonprofit job seekers is www.communityjobs.org.

- ✔ www.ejobs.org/ lists thousands of jobs in environmental careers.

- ✔ www.dice.com and computerjobs.com are high-tech job seekers' heaven.

- ✔ Absolutely Health Care (www.healthjobusa.com) and Medzilla (www.medzilla.com) offer openings in healthcare fields.

- ✔ www.showbizjobs.com lists a few hundred, you guessed it, showbiz jobs.

- ✔ Online Sports.com Career Center (www.onlinesports.com/pages/CareerCenter.html).

- ✔ The RileyGuide (www.rileyguide.com/intern.html) offers links to 10 major databases of internships.

After you land a job, take your resume off the Net. Don't do it just to keep from getting calls from employers dying to hire you. Your new boss may find it on the Net and think you're already looking to leave.

A word about employment agencies

What's the word? Iffy. Yes, employment agencies can give you access to some jobs you may not otherwise know about, but you pay a price. Agencies typically take 25 percent to 35 percent of what you'd make if you contacted the employer directly. And the employer pays, so the agencies are more concerned about satisfying the employer than ensuring that you find a rewarding job. To boot, the best companies try to avoid employment agencies — especially for their good jobs, they attract enough top applicants without having to pay the agency commission. Sure, if you're well qualified for an in-demand field, it doesn't hurt to include a few *employer*-paid employment agencies on your list of contacts. But focus on going direct to employers. You'll usually find a better job and be paid more for it.

Posting position-wanted ads

Post a "position wanted" request on an Internet discussion group visited by target employers. To find on-target groups, go to www.topica.com and www.liszt.com.

Before posting your ad, check the discussion group's Frequently Asked Questions (FAQs) to be sure you won't get *flamed,* the Net term for "yelled at," for posting a solicitation.

A low-tech option is to place a "position wanted" ad in your professional association's publication or on its Web site. If you're concerned about your boss seeing the ad, place a blind ad — one that omits your name. Respondents send inquiries to the association, which, in turn, forwards them to you.

It's not worth placing "position wanted" ads in general-interest newspapers. Employers rarely read them.

A special way to use the want ads

Most job seekers want to find growing organizations because they hire more people and downsize fewer. Besides, it's fun to work for a place on the upswing. The want ads are a good way to find growing organizations. If an organization is advertising a number of openings, it's probably growing. Even if none of the openings fit you, contact someone there with the power to hire you. For example, if you're looking for a sales manager position, contact the vice-president of sales. Don't know how to find that vice president? Phone the switchboard and ask for the name, phone number, and e-mail address of the most senior person in charge of sales. Ask if they might need someone with (*insert two or three of your attributes*).

Want-ad stress savers

Amid all those ads, all those applications, and yes, all those rejections and no-responses, it's easy to get frustrated. This section's advice can help.

Avoiding intimidation

Intimidating things: Arnold Schwarzeneggar, gangs, the want ads. The want ads? Absolutely. Many job seekers *are* intimidated by the want ads: It seems that every job requires umpteen esoteric skills. The good news is that the ads are misleading.

Employers don't enjoy screening letters from 500 applicants, each of whom claims to be uniquely qualified. So when writing job ads, many employers deliberately beef up the job requirements to hold down the number of applicants, knowing full well that they'll hire someone without all those qualifications. Ken Elderkin, author of *How to Get Interviews from Classified Job Ads*, laments, "It seems that for even the lowliest of positions, applicants are required to leap tall buildings in a single bound." The reality is that most real-world jobs are less demanding than those described in want ads. So relax. Even you can land a job.

Remember that the want ads also represent less than half of all available jobs. The jobs that are advertised tend to require lots of arcane skills — only God has them all. Why? Because an employer can usually fill less-demanding positions without having to advertise them. You can access these easier-to-qualify-for jobs by cold-contacting hirers and by using your personal network — Chapters 14 and 15 show you how. So don't let those want ads intimidate you.

Should you respond to ads for nonprofessional positions?

Don't expect to walk out of your graduation ceremony and into a company car. The everyone-goes-to-college trend produces an ever-growing surplus of college degree holders. So you may well have to start out with a nonprofessional job. Don't worry, they can be launchpads for your professional career. Good if unimpressive entry-level jobs such as customer service or sales assistant are excellent ways to learn about the products and customers' needs.

Don't necessarily jump at ads that say, "No experience necessary" but which don't describe the position. You may find yourself interviewing for a commission-only telemarketing gig or a job cleaning out oil tanks.

What about part-time and temp openings?

Even if your first choice is a full-time permanent job, don't ignore ads for part-time or temporary work. These days, employers are increasingly reluctant to hire full-time employees. Full-timers get benefits, vacations, government-mandated perks and leaves, and — most frightening to employers — strong rights in case of termination. Today in the United States, almost half of full-time permanent terminated women and minorities file wrongful termination claims. Hiring a temp or part-timer enables an organization to employ people only as long as they're needed, and to try out employees before taking the risk of hiring them full time. What this means to you as a job seeker is that if you limit yourself to full-time positions, you'll eliminate lots of jobs, including many that are tryouts for full-time positions.

Temp and part-time jobs may offer you other advantages. They enable you to quickly sample a number of industries and workplaces. They're easier to get hired for, so you may land a position you couldn't get if you were competing against applicants for a full-time position. Temp and part-time jobs may even be a smart choice, long-term. They're more likely to allow you to avoid the long hours and permanent commitment that a full-time job often requires. Temping isn't for everyone, but because it offers advantages to some employers and some employees, it isn't surprising that the number of temps has doubled in the past decade.

 Even temp clerical jobs can be worth a shot — if from minute one, you work to demonstrate that you're someone special; with intelligence and fire in your belly, a person they'd be crazy to not want to add their permanent staff. As soon as you get the sense that you'd like to work there long-term, make your intentions known to the boss. Otherwise, all that effort to show how wonderful you are may go unnoticed.

Major temp agency sites include www.net-temps.com, www.adecco.com, and www.kellyservices.com. www.temp24-7.com lists temp agencies plus temp tales written by actual temporary employees.

When you don't quite fit the job requirements

If you lack up to one fourth of the job requirements listed in a want ad, apply anyway. If you're missing more than that, skip to the next ad. Your chances of landing an interview, let alone the job, are too small. Besides, even in the unlikely event you somehow get the job, you're likely to screw up. Amid the millions of ads out there, with a little patience, you'll find enough well suited ones to apply to.

Sometimes, want ads say little about the job requirements. If a phone number is listed, call and ask for details. If you can't get any, but the ad's few words sound appealing, give it your minimum effort: your generic letter and perhaps your work sample (discussed later in this chapter). If they don't like those, they're unlikely to like you.

Blind ads

Ken Elderkin suggests that you not be turned off by *blind ads* — ads that don't specify the employer. Employers place blind ads mainly to avoid being bombarded by 500 people phoning to find out the status of their applications or to beg for interviews. They're usually real jobs. Don't, of course, respond to a blind ad if you suspect that your employer might have placed the ad.

Whenever you respond to a blind ad, protect yourself against unscrupulous headhunters who want to broadcast your resume to every employer in town. Headhunters add 25 percent to 35 percent to the cost of hiring you. You get some protection by adding this to your cover letter:

> If you are a recruiter, please show my resume only to the employer for this job opening. Contact me before approaching other employers.

Protecting yourself

Don't overestimate the Net, says JobStar.org Webmaster Mary-Ellen Mort. Yes, it's cool; yes it's easy, but remember that you're competing against seven continents of applicants. Mary-Ellen warns, "I get letters from people who sent 6,000 electronic submissions, signed up with every resume site on the Net, got no responses, and feel there's no reason for living. Technology has told them that they're worthless." The reality is that there are zillions of people trying to find jobs by using the Net for the same reason you are — it's easy.

So use the Net, but don't rely on the Net. Invest the small amount of time it takes to see if your dream employers have good-fitting job postings at their sites, sign up for electronic job scouts at employment sites, and once a week, check a few job sites that don't offer a job scout. But think of the Net as only one part of your job search.

When to respond to a want ad

Respond either to fresh ads or to those one to three months old.

Fresh ads are good because sometimes employers want to act fast; they hire the first good person they can get. Generally, these are positions that pay under $45,000. For such positions, respond the first day the ad comes out. For higher-level positions, you probably have a few days — they usually won't start screening until a week after the ad runs or until the advertised deadline.

One- to three-month-old ads are good because, more often than you may think, the hiring process stalls. Perhaps the employer can't decide on a candidate, gets busy with more urgent matters, or already fired the new hire. The employer may be reluctant to call candidates back months after the ad was placed — she's embarrassed that so much time has passed, or imagines that the top candidates have found other positions. Then suddenly, your fresh application appears. Sometimes, the easiest thing is to interview you and if you sound good, offer you the job. Rather than appear like a procrastinator who's just now getting around to responding, send the sort of letter you'd write to a target employer who didn't advertise a job opening — see Chapter 14.

The best way to respond to an ad

Your application must make clear that you:

✔ **Fit the stated job requirements.**

✔ **Are more skilled and have better personal characteristics than the other applicants.** Remember that most ads yield many responses, and only one person gets hired. It really helps to convey your humanity so that you have a chance of making a human connection. If possible, include a work sample — something that demonstrates that you can do the job better than other applicants can: for example, a copy of your stellar performance evaluation or the article you wrote (perhaps just for this job search) on the keys to success in your profession.

Here's how David, a landscape architect, responded to a want ad:

Hello,

I searched through literally thousands of want ads to find the few that really excite me and seem to fit me. Yours, Position 4235J, listed on monster.com, is one of those ads.

Always identify the ad. The employer may be running many.

Your position appeals to me because I've been wanting an opportunity to do more scenic highway restoration. I've done one such major project (restoring the Highway 1 shoreline) and we received an ASLA award for it.

Touting his biggest achievement upfront.

Now, I've been bitten by the big-project bug, and would like to do more. That's why I'm interested in your job opening.

Again, the informal tone conveys good things: enthusiasm, honesty, and that he'd be a nice person to work with.

Not only am I excited about the position, I believe I'm well suited to it as the following table indicates:

The following structure makes it easy even for a clerk to see that you meet the job requirements.

Job Requirement Listed in Ad	Me
Two years experience as landscape architect.	Two years experience as landscape architect.
Experience with technical aspects of shoreline restoration.	Yes, see above.
Knowledge of X-Pro project management software.	Extensive experience with similar project management software.
Negotiating local and regional environmental regulations.	This was a key part of my position.

Note that although David didn't meet one of the requirements (knowledge of X-Pro software), he put the best face on it rather than ignore it.

> Beyond the specific job requirements, my co-workers and boss say that I'm enthusiastic and fun to work with. Of course, those are just words, so I'll be happy to give you my boss's and co-workers' phone numbers.

The previous paragraph again recognizes that personality is as important as skills.

> To give you a sense of what I can do, I'm enclosing a copy of one of my drawings for the shoreline restoration project, the Environmental Impact Statement I wrote, and the before-and-after photos of the project.

That all-important work sample puts him ahead of the pack. Don't just tell them; show them.

> My salary requirement is $45,000 to $55,000 depending on the scope of responsibilities.

This is in response to the ad's request for a salary requirement. The best way to respond is with a fairly wide range plus "depending on the scope of responsibilities."

> Of course, from an ad, it is difficult to see if this position truly is a good fit for me, but it sounds right. I'm hoping that you will choose to interview me, so we can both see if we're right for each other.

The previous paragraph strikes a balance between sounding interested but not desperate.

Sincerely,

David Michaels

Wouldn't you interview David? Even if he didn't include his resume? As it happens, David has been unemployed for a year. By sending a letter and a work sample but not his resume, he increases his chances of landing an interview — even if the ad asked for a resume. Had he sent the resume, his unemployed status might have nixed him.

More ways to boost your chances

Here's a final set of ahead-of-the-pack strategies.

The hide-the-resume game

If, like David's, your employment history is unlikely to be top-of-the-heap, defer showing your resume to employers as long as possible. A surprising number of people get jobs based on a letter, a work sample, an interview, and references, without ever submitting a resume.

Your second-best option is to hold off sending the resume until after your interview. That way, you can customize your resume in light of what you learn in the interview. A third possibility is to bring your resume to your interview. That way, you can explain any weaknesses. So think of it as a game: Hide the Resume. The longer you can keep an employer from seeing your resume, the better.

Remember that a resume is a sales tool. If you sense that your resume won't elevate you over other candidates, don't send it, even if you're asked for it — you don't want your supposed sales tool to kill the possibility of a sale.

Of course, many employers will dump your application if you don't include your resume, but when the day is done, your chances of landing a good job are better if you show employers only the stuff that makes you look better than the competition. Consider omitting your resume especially if you're changing careers, you've a significant gap in your employment history, or if your most recent job was cleaning toilets.

 If your resume is weak, consider using a *bio* instead. A bio is a less-than-one-page sheet summarizing who you are. Traditionally used by authors (mine is at the beginning of this book) and senior executives, a bio often works beautifully as a resume alternative — because of its cachet, because it allows you to include highlights and omit lowlights, and simply because it isn't a resume — resumes are considered among the least truthful of documents.

Don't just tell 'em, show 'em

If resumes are among the least trusted documents, work samples are among the most.

Don't have a work sample to send? You probably do but don't realize it. Teachers can use sample lesson plans; managers, the planning document they created; nurses, a performance appraisal; programmers, their Web site; and artists, photos of their work. If none of these applies to you, how about this? Write a short report titled "Seven Lessons I've Learned About (*insert a topic that is of interest to the target employer*)." Include your bio as the last page. Such a report conveys your expertise in a way that no resume can.

Saving Emotional Energy

Because advertised jobs generate many responses, it isn't worth spending much time on each ad. Crank out your letter, adding a custom-tailored paragraph based on a visit to the employer's Web site, stick in your work sample, perhaps your resume, and send it. Sure, if the job opening is your dream come true, do a bit more research on the employer first. For example, try a search engine such as Google (www.google.com), using the company's name as the search term. But in responding to most ads, it isn't worth your time to do much research.

For ads you're excited about, follow up in two weeks with another letter or phone call. Explain that you're excited about the job and wonder if they've had an opportunity to review your application. (Do not intimate that the employer is a jerk for not having responded. Blame is unacceptable in the job-search game.) You may also ask, "Is there any reason you're hesitant to consider me?" If there is, you may be able to counter the objection. Don't spend a lot of effort on follow-up — just a quick note or phone call.

Have realistic expectations. For every 25 well-done responses to carefully selected want ads, expect a few rejection letters, many no-responses, and one or two requests for interviews. Those two interviews are enough to make responding to want ads well worth your time.

Chapter 14

Getting Hired by Your Dream Employer — Even if They're Not Advertising Openings

In This Chapter

▶ What to write

▶ What to say

▶ Going to the (job) fair

*I*n Chapter 12, I show you how to identify your dream employers. In Chapter 13, I show you how to wow them when responding to their want ads. Here, I show how to land a job at a dream employer, even if no job openings are advertised.

Here's the approach in a nutshell. To a dozen ot two target employers, write a human, honest letter explaining why you're salivating at the thought of working there and what you do and don't bring to the table. Follow up with a phone call. More often than you may think, you impress one of those employers enough to create a job for you, hire you for an unadvertised opening, or give you the inside track on an upcoming position.

This method works so well because you get to be considered for a position without having to compete with zillions of other applicants. And it can work fast — create good chemistry and show up at the right time, and you can get a job offer pronto.

This method works best when searching for entry-level positions and for those at small nonunionized organizations. Larger ones usually require a fully open hiring process. And this method only works, of course, if you make a very good first impression — either in writing or verbally — and if you're not too shy to cold contact employers.

Read this chapter — you may find that it gives you courage and shows you how to reveal your best self. But if this cold-contact method doesn't work for you, no problem. The job-finding strategies in chapters 13 and 15 should work better.

Reading this chapter offers a side benefit. Learning how to cold contact can enhance all aspects of your life. It can help you find out which public schools are best for your child, help you solve your HMO dispute, and even help you find a romantic partner. So give it a shot.

What to Write: Sample Letters

Most job seekers should write a letter first and then follow up with a phone call to hoist their letter off the bottom of the employer's priority list. Writing first allows you to neatly lay out your case for being hired and boosts the chances that the recipient won't have his secretary say that he's in a meeting when you call.

If, however, you're a better talker than a writer, call first and follow up with a thank-you note. A side benefit of that approach is that your thank-you note can focus on the things the recipient cared most about in the phone call.

Include your resume only if it will knock the employer's socks off. Certainly, don't send it if you lack relevant experience. Remember, a resume is a sales tool. If it won't sell you well, don't send it. Better to make your case using a cover letter that enables you to present your best case rather than providing a full recitation of your unimpressive past. If possible, also include a work sample, for example, a report you wrote or an evaluation from an employer.

Also consider including a proposal. Let's say, you'd love to do marketing for your favorite Web site, but the closest you've ever been to marketing is a visit to Safeway. Write a proposal for a marketing campaign for that Web site. Sure, that approach may bomb, but it's more likely to impress an employer than sending a resume than screams "No experience!"

Joyce Lain Kennedy, in *Resumes For Dummies*, recommends that if you e-mail your material, follow up with a hard copy. It demonstrates the seriousness of your interest and reminds the employer about you without your having to nag with a phone call. Send it via U.S. mail, or if feasible, hand-deliver it. If you do, ask the receptionist, "May I give it to him so he can connect a face to the resume?"

What you write depends on your situation. Ellen has no directly relevant experience but knows the sort of work she wants to do. Monica also has no experience but is open to a wide range of options. David has directly relevant experience.

Approach 1: When you don't have relevant experience

Ellen has never sold anything, let alone cable TV programs to cable media system operators (MSOs), but she wants to try it. Here's how she makes the case for why the hirer should let her.

> Dear Ms. Hirer,
>
> After quite a bit of research, I picked out the handful of companies I would most like to work for. Yours is one.

Everyone wants to feel special. If true, say, "You are my dream employer." It's powerful.

> I'm impressed by your relationship with the MSOs, the premium packages you've developed, and the innovative promotions you do, such as inviting buyers to serve as guest hosts.
>
> I thought you might get a sense of what I know and how I think by sending you a white paper that I wrote on a topic you may be interested in: *Seven Lessons On Selling to MSOs.*

Ellen wrote it specifically for her job search.

> Of course, I have only limited information, and no doubt, if I actually were working for you, my ideas would change, but this may give you a sense of how my mind works.
>
> I'm hoping that you'll phone me, ideally with a job lead, but your advice is definitely welcome.

Always request both a job lead and advice.

> My number is 510-555-2578, and the best times to reach me are from 8 to 10 a.m. and 5 to 6 p.m. But I imagine that you're busy, so like any good employee, I won't be passive and simply wait for your response. If I haven't heard from you in a week, I will take the liberty of following up with a phone call.

The previous two sentences have worked well for my clients.

> Sincerely,
>
> Ellen Neiman

Approach 2: When you have no experience and you're open to lots of career options

In this situation, most career counselors say, "You're not ready to contact employers. Go back and figure out what you want to do first." But I've found that many people, despite all efforts, remain open to lots of jobs. They're better off sallying forth and telling the truth. For example:

Dear Mary,

I'm 30 and still trying to figure out what I want to be when I grow up. I have many interests and experiences but no one career stands out. So, I figured I'd tell you a little about myself. If you think I might be of help to you, I'd welcome a call.

Here are some things I've done:

- I helped turn around the shipping department at McFallon's Wholesale Nursery. I developed a new system, hired great people, and created an environment in which everyone — well almost everyone — wanted to work hard.

- I developed the Web site for a little home business — see www.rosefragrances.com.

- I received a grant from Exxon to create a catalog of South Carolina's wildflowers. It was an amazing experience.

I've always loved fragrances. That's why I'm contacting you. (**The company was a perfumery.**) Am I deluding myself into thinking that my lack of experience in your business might actually be a bit of a plus? I had a friend who was a teacher and wanted to join an ad agency's creative team. She successfully argued that *because she came from outside the world of advertising, she would bring a fresh perspective to ad planning meetings.* (**Clever ploy**) I am willing to work my way up from the bottom.

If you think I might be worth interviewing, or you simply have a little advice for me, I'd really love it if you called. My number is 510-555-3888, and the best times to reach me are between 8 and 9 a.m. and 5 and 6 p.m.

Sincerely,

Monica Pataki

An even simpler approach:

> Dear Michael,
>
> I would imagine that someone must have given you your first break. I'm hoping you'll give me mine.

When Martin Schwartz, a world-class stock trader, was looking for a job and a prospective employer said, "Nothing is available," Schwartz responded, "Well, someone must have given you your first break." I'm not sure that one-liner was the main cause, but Schwartz got six job offers within a week.

> I have a lot of experience in the construction trades, but what I'd really love to construct are golf courses. I imagine you must be busy, but could I twist your arm into calling me to offer a little advice about how I can find a good job in the field? My number is 510-555-3637.
>
> Thank you for considering my request.
>
> Sincerely,
>
> Martin Walsh

Approach 3: When you have directly relevant experience

Here's how David, a landscape architect who had burned out and has been unemployed for a year, made his case to Mr. Hirer:

> Dear Mr. Hirer,
>
> I'm a landscape architect who won an ASLA award for a shoreline restoration project for Highway 1 and who would really enjoy doing more highway projects.

Sells his best feature before Mr. Hirer has a chance to toss it in the trash.

> The problem is I don't want a life of installing artificial ponds in people's backyards. I've been bitten by the Big Project Bug.

The informal language conveys honesty, enthusiasm, and a good personality.

> That's why I'm writing to you. I've learned that your firm specializes in highway projects.

This shows the hirer that David has done his homework, yet it took David little time.

> I'm wondering if you need someone with my background, or if not, whether you're willing to offer a few words of wisdom on how I can hook up with a firm that does larger projects?

David was wise to be candid that he's looking for a job, not just advice. Not only is that honest, it's pragmatic. By now, many bosses are wise to the ploy of asking for "advice" when, if a job were offered, the job seeker would probably jump at it.

> To give you a sense of what I can do, I'm enclosing one of my drawings for that project, the Environmental Impact Statement that I wrote, and the project's before and after pictures.

> As I reread this letter, there's something missing. Somehow, I want to convey that my co-workers say I am enthusiastic and fun to work with.

Again informal and therefore attractive and candid, Richard Bolles says that a key to getting hired is telling hirers "what makes you different from the 19 other people who can do the same thing you do."

> Of course, those are just words so I'll be happy to give you my boss's and co-workers' phone numbers.

That shows he's enthusiastic and forthcoming.

> I'm hoping you'll phone me. My number is 510-555-2788, and the best times to reach me are from 8 to 10 a.m. and 5 to 6 p.m.

Always include best times to reach you.

> But I know you're busy, so like any good employee, I won't just passively wait for your call. If I haven't heard from you in a week, I'll take the liberty of phoning to follow up.

> Sincerely,

> David Michaels

Want more sources of inspiration for your cover letter? A Colorado career consultant, Bill Frank, has collected 200 good (if a bit formal for my taste) cover letters at www.careerlab.com/letters/default.htm. They're available in book form as *200 Letters for Job Seekers*.

Off-the-wall ways to make contact

Often, being cutesy bombs, but in fields such as sales, public relations, and in the entertainment industry, one of the following ways to make contact may be worth the risk. They're adapted from Brandon Toropov's *303 Off-the-Wall Ways to Get a Job*.

✔ Send nothing but a hand-written Post-it that says, "You should hire me and I can prove it. Call me at 510-555-2626."

✔ Send a verbal resume: an audiotape in which you recount your accomplishments, and conclude by explaining why the employer should hire you over other people with similar backgrounds.

✔ Attend the company's annual meeting. During a coffee break, introduce yourself to bigwigs you'd never otherwise get access to.

✔ For the truly gutsy: Blow up your resume until it's three feet tall. Get two such enlargements and make them into a sandwich board. From 8 to 9 a.m., stand in front of your dream employer's headquarters wearing the sandwich board, and hand out regular-sized resumes to the employees coming into work. You might even invite the media.

Before Calling

Some successful job seekers do almost no preparation before picking up the phone. They just dial the number, think about their opening line while waiting for the phone to be answered, and wing it from there. That works because it's spontaneous, natural, and doesn't sound scripted. Of course, this works only if you think well on your feet.

Most successful job seekers, however, do some prep work. Three bits of writing can greatly improve your phone calls, not to mention keep you calm. And because you're on the phone, you can always keep those three bits of writing in front of you — a good crib sheet. (No videophones, please.)

Your quick human story

What I call your *quick human story* is your 15-second pitch, what you'd say to a prospective employer you ran into in an elevator. It's what you most want prospective employers to remember about you. It includes:

✔ The job you're seeking

✔ The best thing(s) you bring to the table

✔ Why you're looking

How can you cram all that into a few sentences? Here's Ellen's quick human story:

> I've always been fascinated with cable TV, and people have told me I'm a born salesperson. So now that I've graduated from college and am ready for my first professional job, I thought that selling for the cable industry would be perfect. I would imagine that someone must have given you your first break. I'm hoping you'll give me mine.

Here's Monica's quick human story:

> I've been out of college for a few years and done some interesting things: turned around an inefficient shipping department, created a Web site, and got an Exxon grant to catalog South Carolina's wildflowers. I'm looking for another interesting opportunity and quite open to what that can be. Might there a place in your organization for a person like me?

Here's David's quick human story:

> I'm a landscape architect who recently got to work on my first big project: the restoration of Highway 1, and we won an ASLA award for it. I got really hooked on big projects and would love a job where I can do more of them. Might you need someone with my background?

Once you have your story, you need to present it well. Here are four steps to a great delivery:

1. **Write out your quick human story as a script.**

2. **Write just enough words, perhaps 10 percent of your script, to cue you of its main points.**

   For example, David may have written "first big project, got hooked, want more." Need my background? These are your cue words.

3. **Practice telling your quick human story with just the cue words in front of you.**

4. **On the phone, keep only the cue words in front of you.**

   Tell your quick human story without looking at your cue words but if you're stuck, use them to get you back on track.

This approach not only leads to a natural-sounding presentation, it prepares you for telling your quick human story when you can't have your cue words in front of you — during interviews and in networking. If you're bound to a script, it will probably leach any chemistry from your presentation. Remember, chemistry is key.

PAR stories

PAR stands for Problem, Approach, Resolution: You describe a *problem*, how you *approached* it, and how you *resolved* it. Here's one of David's:

> ✔ **The problem:** We had a problem with the pilings. Although the geologist's report claimed that the earth was solid down to 60 feet, we hit soft stuff at just 18 feet. Everyone thought we'd have to use a drop hammer all the way down to 60 feet, which would have cost an extra $20,000 plus two days of deafening noise for the workers, highway users, and residents.

> ✔ **The approach:** But I checked some print and online resources and found that a project in Maine ran into a similar problem. There they were able to solve the problem by lining the piling with a special sleeve down to only ten feet.

> ✔ **The resolution:** That little bit of research saved us $12,000 and a heck of a lot of noise. It felt pretty good.

You may use only one or two PAR stories, but it's good to have at least three ready, so that you can pick ones that fit naturally into the conversation.

Preparing for likely objections

Here are common objections encountered in a phone call and sample responses. Again, don't use a script. Unless you're a professional actor or TV news anchor, it will sound stiff. (Think of those telemarketers who sound like they're reading. Would you buy from them, let alone hire them?) As with your quick human story, start by writing a script of responses to likely objections to you, then write cue words, practice responding using your cue words, and keep your cue words in front of you while you're on the phone in case you draw a blank. Examples:

Objection: I'm busy and going into a meeting. Can't talk with you.

Answer: I understand. When's the best time for me to call back?

Objection: But you have no experience in this field**.**

Answer: Actually, during my college years, I worked with professors on a number of research projects and was told that I have a knack for it. (*Most candidates have at least some indirectly relevant, if unpaid, experience.*) That's why I'm interested in a marketing research position. I would guess that someone gave you your first break. I'm hoping you'll give me mine.

Objection: You were self-employed. Why would you want to work for a company and lose all that autonomy?

Answer: I've enjoyed it, but Home Depot is making it very difficult for a small hardware guy to survive. Besides, I'm really looking forward to working on a team.

Objection: We don't need anyone with your background.

Answer: I understand. Do you have any idea of what you'd do if you were in my shoes?

After he responds, ask, "Would you be willing to keep your ears open and call me if you hear of anything?" He usually says yes just to get you off the phone. That's fine. If only subconsciously, he will keep his antennae out. You've just recruited a scout! If he agrees to be your scout, make a notation to contact him in a month. At that point, if you're still job hunting, you can call back and say something like: "I'm just calling to check in. I wonder if by any chance you've heard of a job lead that might be appropriate for me or have any other words of wisdom you'd like to pass along?"

The odds are tiny that, at a particular moment, a hirer will have a job for you. However, if you can recruit the hirer as a scout, you'll have weeks of moments during which the hirer could create a job opening or hear of one. So take heart. Even if an employer says "No jobs available," as long as she's willing to be a scout, you've succeeded.

Objection: If you're so good, why are you looking for a job?

Answer: (These are the most widely acceptable answers. If true, choose one.)

- ✔ Looking for more responsibility
- ✔ Want to make more money
- ✔ Tired of the long commute
- ✔ The job ended

One other area to prepare is your voice. You make a hard-to-change impression within the first few seconds of a conversation. Your tone of voice must be friendly and confident without coming on too strong. Yet you must be yourself. Sounds paradoxical, but it isn't. At different times, we all use different voices. Avoid your depressed, I-hate-looking-for-a-job voice. Record your friendly, confident-sounding voice, listen to that tape, and start using that voice more, especially when talking with a hirer. When you pick up the phone, smile — it comes through.

Cold feet?

Before calling an actual employer, role-play a call with a friend. Then call your lowest-priority potential hirers, your throwaways — you're going to mess up on your first few. After you've had a couple of good phone calls, move up to your top-choice employers.

Afraid you'll stumble on the phone? A few mess-ups may actually make you *more* credible. When I started out on radio, to avoid stumbling, I scripted much of what I said. Boy, did I sound perfect — too perfect. Reading a script stripped away the human connection that is so key to a successful interaction. Now, I simply start talking, and only when I get stuck do I look at the few phrases I've written down to remind me of my main points. Now, after many years on the radio, I stumble more than I did when I started, which makes me seem more human, and in turn, actually connects me better with my audience. So relax. Keep your few talking points in front of you to help you when you're stuck, and when you stumble, know that it probably won't hurt you.

The first call is the hardest, so don't just make one call per sitting. Set a goal, for example, "I'll take a coffee break after I've made ten calls." I can hear you protesting, "Ten calls! That will take all day." Remember, if you make ten calls, you'll probably only get through to a few people, so the coffee break will come sooner than you think.

Making the call

Your letter to the hirer or human resources person already laid out all the good stuff about you. You're ahead of the game. The only reason you're following up with a phone call and not simply waiting for the employer to phone you is that unless the recipient happens to instantly need someone just like you, you'll likely be lost in the swamp of higher priorities. For you, your new job is priority one, so it's your place to call.

Getting through to the hirer

One of job seekers' greatest frustrations is being unable to get through to the right person. They can't get past a gatekeeper or through voice-mail jail, and they leave messages that never are returned.

No method always works and prepare to be turned down much of the time (that's no big deal); but each of these strategies increases your chances of getting to speak with the Great and Powerful.

The most important phrase to keep in mind with every contact: *Be persistent but likable.* Please remember this. Those two words are keys to a successful job search: *Persistent. Likeable.*

Getting out of voice-mail (or e-mail) jail

If you get Ms. Hirer's voice mail, don't be disappointed. Voice mail is your friend. It usually means that the hirer gets to hear your quick human story — of course, with your natural, pleasant, and not-stuffy voice. Remember, your first few seconds are key. Here's Ellen's version.

Hi, this is Ellen Neiman. I'm following up on the letter I sent you last week. I'm the new college graduate who's really interested in selling for the cable industry. If you think I might be of help to you or have any words of wisdom on how I might find a job in this field, I know you're probably busy, but I'd love a call back. My phone number is 510-555-2740. (Say it slowly.) That's 510-555-2740. The best times to reach me are today until 5 p.m. and tomorrow from 8-9. Thanks so much.

Getting past a live gatekeeper

Here's a tough scenario. In this case, Ellen didn't write first, so it's a total cold call, and she got the gatekeeper from hell. Here's how she handled it:

Gatekeeper: Mr. Hirer's office.

Ellen: Hi. Is he available? *(The brevity and informal tone suggests that she's not an interloper and increases the chances that the gatekeeper will put her through without an interrogation.)*

Gatekeeper: Who may I say is calling? *(So much for no interrogation.)*

Ellen: Ellen Neiman.

Gatekeeper: May I ask what this is in reference to? *(The dreaded question.)*

Ellen: I could really use your help. *(An opener that has been known to calm even dragon-like gatekeepers.)* I just graduated from college and am very interested in a sales position in the cable industry. I'm sure Mr. Hirer is busy but could I ask you to see if he might speak briefly with me? Even if he can't use someone like me, maybe he might have a few words of wisdom about where I might turn.

Gatekeeper: I'm sorry, Mr. Hirer is unavailable. If you wish, you can leave a message, but there are no positions open.

Ellen: Could you recommend someone else it might be wiser to speak with?

Gatekeeper: No. Would you like to leave a message? I really must go now.

Ellen: Does he have voice mail? Perhaps I could leave him a voice mail.

Gatekeeper: No he doesn't. WOULD you like to leave a message?

Ellen: Thank you, no. I'm tough to reach. When's the best time for me to try back?

Leaving a message, especially with this gatekeeper, is unlikely to bear fruit. Besides, you want to be sure the call happens when you have your notes in front of you. Better to retain control and call back.

Gatekeeper: (Sighs) I don't know. He does stay late occasionally. *(Finally, a morsel.)*

Ellen: Thank you very much.

At least half of gatekeepers are this useless to you — it's their job to protect their boss's time. That's okay. The key is to not let the grinches get you down. Laugh him off as you would a troll in a video game, and move on. Sooner rather than later, a guardian angel is likely to descend.

When to phone back? If the gatekeeper doesn't recommend a specific time, try a *prime time:* a time when the hirer is likely to be at the desk, not in meetings, and without a gatekeeper you'd need to cajole. Prime times are 7:30 to 9 a.m. and 5 to 7 p.m.

If you leave a voice-mail or e-mail message and you don't get a call-back within 48 hours, you probably never will. So maybe try one more time, but after that, the heck with him. If there was any real interest, your mailing and two phone calls would probably have evoked it. Yes, there are stories of job seekers who impressed a boss because they were persistent enough to call ten times, but those are rare except for sales positions. You're better off allocating your time to efforts that are more likely to pay off. However, give any dream employers an extra shot: Try again in a month. Things change.

Try e-mail. Some employers who ignore your phone messages respond to an e-mail because they answer their e-mail at night when they're not as pressured.

Finally speaking with the hirer. Now what?

Ellen has finally gotten Mr. Hirer on the phone. Unfortunately, Hirer isn't much easier to deal with than his gatekeeper from hell:

Hirer: Harold Hirer here.

Ellen: Hi, this is Ellen Neiman. I'm that probably too-eager sounding new college graduate who's interested in selling for the cable industry. *(A bit of mild self-deprecating humor is refreshing, especially from a job seeker. As in every interaction in the job search, the key is to establish a human connection quickly.)* Thanks so much for taking my call. By any chance, might you need someone like me? *(Some career guides advise you to instead ask, "Might you know someone who needs someone with my background?" but that is disingenuous and appears so.)*

Hirer: Ms. Neiman, I really have only a minute. We don't anticipate any openings for the foreseeable future. If you wish, you may send us your resume.

Unfortunately, Mr. Hirer isn't biting.

Ellen: I'll do that. Any words of wisdom on what I might do to get a sales job in the cable industry?

Although her heart sinks, Ellen makes the effort to be pleasantly persistent.

Hirer: I can't think of anything.

Ellen: Anyone you think I might want to talk with, or anything you think I should read?

Hirer: You should get the quarterly *Etamm Monthly.* It's on the CTAM website.

Cool.

Ellen: Thank you. Would you kill me if I asked you to keep your ears open for any other possibilities and to call me if you hear of anything?

Again, humor helps.

Hirer: (Sighs) Well, I'll see.

Ellen: I know you're busy. So if I'm still looking for a job in a month, I'll call you to follow up. Thank you so much.

Hirer: Good-bye.

Hirer may admire her persistence.

Ellen: Good-bye, Mr. Hirer.

This is far from the best conversation. None of the best outcomes happened: Hirer had no interest in considering Ellen for a job. He did not invite her to come in to see how the office operates, nor he did refer her to a specific person. Ellen got only one possibly useful tidbit. Just as in a good treasure hunt, you get a little clue here, a little clue there, and eventually, if you don't give up, you usually hit paydirt.

Of course, every conversation is different. That was an attempt to show you a tough one done well.

Secrets to succeeding in that first conversation

Beyond what Ellen did, here are some other tips that can put you ahead of the pack:

✔ Look for opportunities to build a connection. If the person says something a bit personal, follow with a related comment or question. Typical door openers:

> "We're just finishing up a big project." Follow-up: "Do you want to tell me a little about it?"

> "I'm ready for the weekend." Follow-up: "Are you doing anything special?"

> "I loved Jamal Washington's speech. It was brilliant." Follow-up: "I missed it. What did he say?"

✔ Share interesting information such as a recent research finding or a brief war story.

✔ If Ms. Hirer starts talking about the challenges she's facing, that's a golden opportunity. Play consultant. Ask questions to better understand the problem, perhaps helping the hirer gain clarity about her situation. You may even gently offer a suggestion, worded like, "Obviously, I know just a bit about your organization but in light of what you've just said, I'm wondering if it might help to *(offer solution)*.

✔ Try to get a sense of whether you'd really like to work there. You're not desperate; you're looking for a good match. So if it appears that Mr. Hirer might be interested in you, ask a couple of questions to see if you'd be interested in working at his firm. For example, "What sort of person fits best in your company?" or "Is there anything that makes working at your firm different from working at your competitors?" In addition to helping you decide if you'd like working there, Mr. Hirer's answers offer valuable information to use if you ever get invited for a formal job interview.

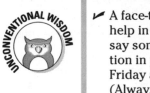

✔ A face-to-face interview is more likely to yield a job offer or substantial help in landing a job. So, if after a few minutes, the chemistry is good, say something like, "You know, I'd be happy to continue this conversation in person. I could be available any time Wednesday morning or Friday afternoon. Do you have a bit of time on either of those days?" (Always give two choices.) This approach is subtly but importantly different from the standard one that implies that you should *always* try to get an in-person meeting with a hirer. Unless an initial conversation gives good reason for optimism, it's not worth your time.

Walking In: Not for the Fainthearted

Walking in unannounced to prospective employers can be effective. When I'm in a TV studio waiting to go on the air, I often chat with the producer and camerapeople. I usually ask them how they got their cool jobs. Frequently, they say that they went door-to-door, from studio to studio, until someone said yes. Similarly, when my wife and I came to California, we got in the car and drove from school district office to school district office. She got three job offers within a week. Colonel Sanders started his career by going from restaurant to restaurant asking the owners to try his chicken.

Richard Bolles advises that walking in without an introduction works best for entry- to mid-level jobs; and for blue-collar jobs, walking in is *the* most effective job-search method.

Always start by telling your quick human story and seeing if you can make an appointment for an interview, or if you're really lucky, get an interview on the spot.

If the gatekeeper says no and you're really gutsy, sit and wait until the boss walks past you. That can easily result in wasted hours, but it has worked. (Or maybe that was a movie.)

Do I Really Have to Write a Thank-you Letter?

It may feel disingenuous to thank someone for putting you through a stressful tryout, but thank-you letters work. In addition to demonstrating that you are thorough, a thank-you letter, done right, can accomplish a lot:

- ✔ The half-life of being in Mr. Hirer's mind is short. A thank-you letter extends it.

- ✔ It allows you to correct screw-ups. ("You asked me about that circuit. On further reflection, . . .")

- ✔ You can say more about things he cares about. ("There is one more thing I think may interest you . . .")

- ✔ You can remind Mr. Hirer of things you said that he liked. ("I'm pleased that you liked my analysis of the trend in optometry away from sports-vision therapy.")

- ✔ You can remind him of your strengths. ("I'm pleased that you think my ability to program in ColdFusion is a plus.")

- ✔ You can remind Mr. Hirer that he committed to being your scout. ("Thanks so much for agreeing to keep your ears open and letting me know if you hear of anything. I know you're busy, so if I haven't heard from you in a month and I'm still looking for a job, I'll call to follow up.")

A model thank-you letter

Here's how one job seeker put it all together.

Dear Marilyn,

Thank you for taking the time to talk with me. I know how busy you are.

I really appreciate your suggesting that I speak with Mike Bergeisen over at Western Maryland High. I've left a message and hope he'll call back.

I thought a bit more about your question, "Why do you use phonics so much even though it seems so boring?" You're right, it's boring to us, but when I watch kids, especially the kids that have trouble learning to read using whole-language, they actually aren't bored at all by phonics. They like it because it's concrete.

Most of all, I appreciate your willingness to keep your antennae out and letting me know if you hear of a teaching position I might be interested in. As you may recall, I'm especially interested in a high school English position at a school with lots of high-achieving kids. I know you're busy, so if I haven't heard from you in a month and I'm still looking for a job, I'll call to follow up.

In any event, thanks so much for your time. Say hi to Sandy for me,

Regards,

Diana Sawin

The worst-case thank-you letter

Even if an employer totally blows you off, it's worth a brief thank-you note.

Dear Ms. Brusque,

I'm sorry I imposed on you with my phone call last week. I understand that you are busy and the last thing you need is to be interrupted by some job seeker.

Sometimes circumstances change, so here's my resume and a work sample. Don't worry. I won't bug you again, but if, in the future, I might be of help to you or one of your colleagues, I'd welcome a call.

Sincerely,

David Michaels

Going to Job Fairs

Imagine a hotel ballroom with dozens of employers, all of whom are happy to talk with you. That's a job fair. You almost certainly won't get hired at a job fair, but it's the only way to get dozens of face-to-face screening interviews within a few hours.

It's also a terrific way to learn about your field: what's new, who the players are, what employers are most looking for, what's salary ranges are, and the best places to train.

Trade shows can serve the same function when you're self-employed and are seeking customers.

Preparing

In advance, see which companies will be attending and do a bit of research on at least some of them: Visit their Web site or call the company and ask for the information they send to prospective customers.

Come with many copies of your introductory letter (and copies of your resume if you think it's strong enough). Have your quick human story ready to fall trippingly off your tongue.

Come with your ego well-protected. Job fairs are usually crawling with job seekers, so employers have to screen you as quickly as possible.

Avoid job fairs if you don't want your employer to know you're looking and if there's any chance he'll find out.

At the fair

Show up early. Things aren't so crowded, and the interviewers' eyes aren't glazed-over. If things are jammed up front, head to the back and work your way forward. (This also works in avoiding long lines at amusement parks.)

When you approach a booth, see if there's a piece of literature about the company. Take it, walk away, read it, and come back with one thing to tell and one thing to ask that would demonstrate that you're a more interesting candidate than others at the job fair.

No matter how promising the conversation, don't spend too much time with one person. No one job fair contact is likely to be worth giving up the many other contacts you could be making. Besides, in excusing yourself after a reasonable amount of time, you come off as confident, not desperate.

To avoid confusion, right after you leave one prospect, make notes on what you learned — perhaps on the back of his business card. If it was a particularly fruitful conversation, jot down what to put in your thank-you note . . . the thank-you note you'll mail that day, right?

Virtual job fairs

The term is misleading. There's no webcam connection between you and each employer. Generally, the term *virtual job fair* just refers to a Web page filled with job listings, sometimes enabling live chats with a company's recruiter. For a portal with links to virtual job fairs: `http://jobsearchtech.about.com/careers/jobsearchtech/msub5-3.htm`.

In the next chapter, I turn to the vaunted personal networking. Are we having fun yet?

Chapter 15

Networking Made Easier

● ●

In This Chapter

▶ How much networking is right for you?

▶ How to network well . . . even if you're not a born schmoozer

▶ How to persuade yourself to network

▶ Less obvious networking opportunities

▶ Networking on the Web

● ●

*H*ere are opinions of networking cited in a recent *Wall Street Journal* article:

Networking is dead.

—William Morin, former chairman of Drake, Beam, & Morin, one of the nation's largest outplacement firms

Networking is a bankrupt concept.

—Michael McGill, chair of the Southern Methodist University Business School

Informational interviews are a pain in everyone's butt.

—Susan RoAne, author of *What Do I Say Next?*

You get a call at work that feels like networking and you want to throw up.

—David Opton, executive director, Exec-u-Net

In the previous chapter, I said that a great way to land a job is to directly solicit your dream employers. Many people think that's networking. No. When you network, you're asking your personal contacts for job information, especially referrals to other people who could hire you.

Through the '80s and much of the '90s, networking was quite an effective job-search technique, but people are increasingly sick of getting networked, while the Internet is making other job-search approaches more effective. Yet career guides continue to urge job seekers to network, network, network.

Today, networking has a good chance of leading to a salaried job mainly when

- ✔ You're naturally good at picking up the phone, asking for, and getting favors *and*

- ✔ Your contact likes you a lot.

- ✔ Your contact knows your work well.

- ✔ Your contact is close with someone with the power to hire you at an employer you want to work for.

- ✔ That hirer is willing to hire you for your target job.

The chances of all five factors occurring simultaneously are about the same as the chances of the publisher of the *For Dummies* books changing the color of its books' covers. And if you're looking for a government job, a union job, or a job with a large company, networking is even less likely to pay off. Their hiring process normally requires extensive open advertising, and decisions are made by a team. Your cousin Agnes' working for an organization is unlikely to be a reason that you to land a job there.

Even when networking results in a job, it usually takes months. Typically, there are many steps between contacting your network and starting your new job: Before someone is willing to go to bat for you, you need to establish a relationship. Even with your existing relationships, you usually must contact umpteen people, only a few of whom are likely to provide you with leads. When things go right, a lead tells you about an upcoming job opening. Typically, weeks or months pass before the job actually opens, you're interviewed (usually multiple times), and, if you're lucky, you land the job. If you need a job fast, networking may not work.

Unless you have a strong personal network, you're better off devoting more of your job search time responding to on-target want ads and cold-contacting dream employers on your own. In addition, many job seekers cringe at the thought of having to network, so they procrastinate. Networking definitely doesn't work if you don't do it.

Then, you ask, why even write a chapter on networking? Because it still can be useful. This chapter shows you when and for whom networking is worthwhile, and how to make the most of it.

How Much Should You Network?

Most people should devote no more than one-third of their job-search time to networking. The more of these statements that are true of you, the more you should network:

- You enjoy networking.

- Your personal network includes many people who can hire you for your target work or refer you to someone who can.

- You're looking for information about the career, not just job leads.

- You want to work for a startup. These companies are often started by a few friends. They end up working long hours and then playing together after work. So startups generally prefer to hire people they know.

- Your best skills are common ones — for example, planning, communication, organization, or management. If you have just those skills, networking is usually a must. Because many people have those skills, employers often offer jobs requiring them to people they already know. So if your best skills are commonly held ones, go forth and network so that you can get to know lots of hirers.

In self-employment, networking probably still is the most effective way to build a clientele — if it's done right. That usually means joining groups and organizations and developing *ongoing* relationships with people who can use your product or service or who can refer you to others who do.

Making the Most of Networking

In essence, the process boils down to making a list of the 10 to 25 people who most like you and most likely know someone who can give you a lead on a job. You call them, trot out your quick human story (that 15-second explanation of why you're looking for work and what you're looking for). They usually tell you they have no leads. You ask them to keep their ears open, and over time, the process usually produces something: if not a job lead, a suggestion of an event to attend, a book to read, and so forth. If you haven't landed a job, you phone back monthly, asking if they've had any ideas. Throughout, you look for opportunities to do nice things for your networking partners so the relationships don't feel one-sided. If you're shy or have few contacts, *e-networking* (joining online discussion groups and joining e-networking sites) can work. E-networking is discussed later in this chapter.

Here's how to make that all happen.

The first step is making your list of networking contacts. Here are your top-choice contacts, in approximate order of desirability:

- People who can hire you for your desired work.

- People who are in your target occupation. If you're a career changer, it's wonderful if you can find someone who has transitioned from your current career into the one to which you aspire.

✔ People who deal with others in your target occupation (customers, colleagues, consultants, and so on).

✔ People in your field's professional association or on-campus professional club.

✔ Wealthy or well-connected people who like you. They know lots of hirers.

✔ Co-workers or supervisors in your current or previous jobs.

✔ Family.

✔ Lovers, past and present (be careful).

✔ Your college's alumni working in your desired career.

✔ Friends, college buddies.

✔ People in the media: journalists, radio/TV, and so on.

✔ College professors, especially those who might know hirers in your chosen field. Look for those who do a lot of consulting or get big research grants.

✔ Your or your parents' lawyer, doctor, financial planner, Realtor, accountant, fitness trainer, landlord, haircutter, and so on. These people know plenty of hirers.

Ten things you can get from a networking contact

Common mistake: Thinking that the only thing you want from a networking contact is a job lead. Actually, if you can get any of the information in the following list from a networking contact, you've succeeded:

✔ The name of someone with the power to hire you

✔ Information about the field or the local situation

✔ The best entry points into this career

✔ Major trends in the field

✔ A suggestion of something to read

✔ A suggestion of an organization to join

✔ A suggestion of an event to attend

✔ The best place to get training

✔ A promise to keep ears open for job leads (important)

✔ A job interview

A high-powered networking strategy

Imagine you were looking to hire an employee and a respected friend said, "I've just heard that Joe Blow may be available. He's terrific. You should try to get him while you can." If you possibly could use Joe, wouldn't you call him in for an interview? So, as a job seeker, ask everyone in your network if they would let a few potential employers know you might be available. You could end up with a quick job search.

Secrets of successful networking by phone

Later in this chapter, I suggest networking methods for people who are too shy to phone, but if you can muster the courage, phoning is usually better than writing and more time-effective than an in-person meeting. You'll be surprised: A reasonable percentage of the people you call are willing to help a job seeker.

An example

Let's make it tough. In this example, David hasn't spoken to Marsha, a fellow student in his landscape architecture program, since college, and she wasn't exactly a bosom buddy back then, nor does she have much time for David now.

David: Marsha, hi, this is David Michaels. I imagine that I'm the last person on earth you expected to hear from.

As important as what you say is how you say it. Your tone should be informal, even playful.

Marsha: Well, that's true, David.

David: I imagine you're wondering why I'm calling. No, I don't need a place to stay.

Again that humor thing. It also subtly makes Marsha grateful that whatever it is David will be asking for it won't be as invasive as him in a sleeping bag on her living room floor.

Marsha, I've just finished a project restoring part of Highway 1, but it was a one-time opportunity. I can live with going back to artificial ponds in people's backyards, but it would be much more fun to find a job where I can do more big projects. Any suggestions for where I might turn?

Marsha: David, I don't have any connections like that.

David: Do you know anyone who might know someone who could connect me with an appropriate person?

Marsha: Well, you could talk with Simon Diaz at A-1 Grading.

David: Great. Know of anyone else by any chance?

Great question. You goal should be to get two names from every networking call. That way you never run out.

Marsha: Can't think of anyone else.

David: That's fine. Would you mind keeping your ears open and letting me know if you hear of anything I should know about? If I'm still looking a month from now, I'll give you a call to follow up.

Marsha (with the enthusiasm of a dental patient when asked if she's ready for her extraction): All right.

That recruits Marsha as a scout.

It's hard for Marsha to say no because keeping her ears open requires no effort. Obviously, Marsha is cool to all this and is unlikely to beat the bushes for David. But if you select the people on your networking list well, they're the types who do hear about lots of things. If Marsha does hear of something, she'll call David, or at least, when he follows up a month later, will pass along the information.

The main purpose of a first networking contact is not a referral to a hirer. The odds of the person having one at that moment are small. The main purpose is to recruit that person as a scout. Once you tell someone, even a casual acquaintance, that you'll be following up with them in a month, they'll be keeping their antennae out for you, if only subconsciously. The result of Round 1 of your networking calls is that you recruited a good number of scouts.

David: Any suggestions about events I should attend, things I should read?

Marsha: I dunno. I'm going to the Northern California Landscape Design conference next month in Monterey. You might want to do that.

David: Good idea. I'll probably go. If I do, can I offer you a ride down there? (Networking is best as a two-way street.)

Marsha: I'm not sure. I may need to come late or leave early.

David: Well, if you think it might work out, feel free to call me. Now that the business part of this call is taken care of, how are you?

Saving the chit-chat for after business is taken care of has two advantages: The chit-chat no longer seems like a ploy to warm Marsha up, and if she's too busy for chit-chat, she can say so and you've already gotten the important part of the call taken care of.

Marsha: David, I'd enjoy chatting with you, but frankly, I've got five things going on here at once. I gotta run.

David: I understand, thanks a lot.

Marsha: Okay, David.

The payoff

If Marsha had given David a little encouragement, he would have tried to make more of the conversation, for example:

- ✔ "Here's what I'm planning to do to find a job. Whaddya think?"
- ✔ "What do you think of my resume?" (or cover letter, or work samples)

Of course, as with direct contacts with potential employers, it's worth sending a thank-you note. (I talk about thank-you notes in Chapter 14.)

Are You a Reluctant Networker?

L. Michelle Tullier, author of *Networking for Everyone,* offers tips for reluctant networkers:

- ✔ Don't assume you're being a pest. Introverts tend to assume they're bothering others if they contact them. In fact, most people enjoy being asked for help and advice.
- ✔ If you're afraid, remind yourself of previously successful conversations. Those recollections may give you the courage to make the next contact.
- ✔ Don't underestimate the power of listening. Networking may seem like it's all about talking, but listening is as important, and it's easier for the introvert.

If you can't get yourself to pick up the phone, write. Here's a letter to a colleague and friend:

Hi Jean,

After we finished physical therapy school, I took some time off to play, but now it's time to grow up, so I'm looking for a PT job. Any ideas on a cool place to work or who I might talk with?

I've enclosed my resume and cover letter in case you have any suggestions on how I might improve it.

If you have any ideas, I'd really appreciate your letting me know.

Thanks,

Chris Hirsch

Extra-Credit Networking Opportunities

Taking advantage of one or more of these opportunities can earn you an A in networking, and more important, it should help you find good work faster.

Attending conferences, trade shows, and workshops

Conferences, trade shows, and workshops are one-stop-shops for training that introduce you to the field, for products that serve the profession, and for meeting people in the profession. You meet potential contacts everywhere: next to you in a session, in the lobby, in the hospitality suites. At conferences, don't forget about the vendors. They can be as useful as attendees. Start by asking about their businesses and themselves. Soon enough, you'll be able to ask for their advice about your career.

Here's a tip just for guys. Thousands of women's organizations have sprouted up: businesswomen's associations, societies of women's engineers, and so forth. These offer invaluable networking opportunities. For reasons too complicated to explore here, few men's networking organizations exist. I recently spoke at an American Women in Radio and TV event. During the networking session, I noticed that the few male attendees were getting plenty of attention from the women, perhaps, in part, because the women admired their bravery at showing up.

Getting active in your professional or trade association

Joining isn't enough. To pay off in a job, you must become an insider. Volunteer for committees (the conference program committee is often excellent for networking), present at conferences, or exhibit at a convention or trade show. Become knowledgeable and meet people in one of your field's hot areas. Speak with the editor of your association's magazine or newsletter. All these contacts can be leads.

To find the right professional association, check *Associations Unlimited,* found at most libraries. Some libraries make it available online to patrons so that they can use it at home or work. If it's not available, try the American Society of Association Executives (www.asaenet.org). Whichever directory you use, visit the association's Web site or phone the national headquarters to get the name and phone number of the president of your local chapter.

Nicholas Lore, author of *The Pathfinder,* suggests that you write an article on a hot topic in your field for your association's periodical. Do some reading first so you don't sound like an idiot, and then interview a few of your field's heavy hitters, especially those with the power to hire you. Make the interview more of a dialogue than an interrogation. Be sure your article accurately quotes them. When the article is published, call your sources, ask if they'd like a copy, and while you're on the phone, ask for a bit of career advice.

Striking up a job-finding conversation at a meeting or party

Gather up a little courage and try this approach when the appropriate situation presents itself:

- ✔ Prepare a five-second introduction, such as, "Hi, I'm Joe Blow. I'm a programmer in the edutainment field." Also, be sure you have your quick human story ready to tell, and any PAR story (see Chapter 14) that might be entertaining.

- ✔ At the meeting, smile and approach a person you'd like to talk with.

- ✔ After exchanging introductions, ask about the person: "What do you do?" Listen well and then dovetail onto something he said. Tell your quick human story, and later perhaps a PAR story. Give yourself a goal: for example, I'll have one of those conversations with at least two people.

Leading a workshop

If you're a good presenter, this is powerful: Offer to teach a seminar attended by people with the power to hire you, yes at a professional association meeting, but even at a Rotary Club or chamber of commerce meeting. At the end of your presentation, if you're looking for a salaried job, mention that you're looking for your dream job, and describe it. If you're seeking clientele, describe what your business offers. This is the equivalent of showing your best stuff to a bunch of potential employers or clients so that they can hire you for your dream career. Not bad.

Networking your way into a nonprofit

One way into a good nonprofit job is to volunteer for the organization's board of directors. You learn how a nonprofit runs from the business side, and you make powerful connections with people who share your ideological passion. Unless you're worth big bucks, the Sierra Club will probably pass on you, but small, local nonprofits are often open to bright, collegial people, especially if someone they know recommends you. Don't have the clout to get onto a board? Some nonprofits have nongoverning advisory boards that are easier to join.

Joining networking groups

These local groups are formed explicitly for networking, usually among businesspeople. They're often sponsored by professional associations, groups such as the chamber of commerce, or minority or women's advocacy organizations. (I'm still waiting for men's advocacy organizations, and, yes, we do need them.) Check local newspapers, especially the business section or events calendar for meeting times and locations.

Build alliances, not shallow networks. *New York Times* career writer Sabra Chartrand advises that instead of chit-chatting and wholesaling your business cards when you meet people who impress you (for example, a speaker at a conference or someone you meet a charity event), ask them to join you in a project or volunteer to join theirs.

A good way to get to know someone is to work with him or her. Volunteer boards of directors are a particularly good place to build alliances, but they can be formed in much less august circumstances — one woman invited all her potential allies to a house painting party.

At group networking activities or in online discussion groups, keep in mind that other people are there because they, too, want to network. They may be as uncomfortable as you. So, if you smile and extend your hand, you'll probably be doing them a big favor.

E-networking

E-networking is a dream come true for people who hate networking. No tough phone calls, which can be awkward even if someone referred you, and no one has to see that you're sweating bullets or that you scripted every word.

At the end of this section, I list a variety of e-networking opportunities, but the rules of the road are essentially the same for all:

✔ Pick one or more participants in each online network.

✔ Send them each an e-mail with the following components (from Nancy Halpern's *E-Networking*):

- How you found the person (for example, on the network, same alma mater, referred by someone).

- Your commonalties (for example, you both worked for the same company, have experience in the same field, have the same career goal).

- A request for further information (for example, information about a particular industry, suggestions of cool employers).

- Something personal that you feel comfortable sharing — it helps create a mutual bond and makes the recipient more at ease.

An example

Dear Bill,

I found you on industryinsite.com and noticed that you're from Washington & Lee, so I figure you can't be all bad. (It's my alma mater too — 1998.) From your profile, I see that you too are trying to land a management consulting job. I'm wondering if perhaps we might compare notes — for example, what you've learned from your interviews. I'll attach to this e-mail my notes following each of my interviews. Perhaps we might even critique each other's resumes.

Hoping to hear from you,

Judy Chandler

If you contact the person via an online discussion group, be sure to e-mail the individual, not the entire group.

Some e-networking sites from Nancy Halpern's *E-Networking* include

✔ *Industry Insite* (www.industryinsite.com). This site helps you create a personal profile of your previous employers, interests, career areas, and so forth. It then tells you how many other members match you on each factor.

✔ **Company of Friends** (www.fastcompany.com/cof). This is *Fast Company* magazine's readers' network. It tends to attract high-powered members.

✔ **Vault.com's message boards. (Go to** www.vault.com **then click on "message boards.")** This offers bulletin boards for dozens of industries and hundreds of major companies. These are liberally laced with rants and raves from insiders.

Freelancers are often your best source of information regarding industry trends and opportunities. Three sites with databases full of freelancers: www.guru.com, www.freeagent.com, and www.elance.com.

Margaret Dikel, author of *Networking and Your Job Search,* is particularly enthusiastic about Usenet Newsgroups and mailing lists. Many professionals use these online discussion groups for networking, discussing recent developments in their fields and asking questions of each other. To find such professionals in your target field, go to www.liszt.com, www.topica.com, or www.egroups.com. You'll increase your chances of getting help if you've first taken the time to read about and then become active in the discussion group. Before posting, read the group's FAQs (Frequently Asked Questions) so you don't violate any local *Netiquette.*

These online discussion groups are ideal for shy people. Before jumping in, you can listen as long as you want without appearing like a wallflower. And because you're writing your contribution, you can take as long as you need to word it just right.

Bonus: Recruiters often lurk amid field-specific networking groups. If they like what you say, you may get a call.

For more on e-networking, see www.rileyguide.com/network.html.

Chapter 16

Interviewing Better

● ●

In This Chapter

▶ Preparing for the interview: Six smart things you can do

▶ Nineteen ways to create chemistry

▶ How to prove — right there in the interview — that you can do the job

▶ After the interview: Where the job is often won or lost

● ●

At its best, a job interview is like a first date: a pleasant discussion in which you're both trying to see if you should get involved with each other. Unfortunately, many interviews are more like The Inquisition. This chapter shows you how to keep things pleasant, maximize your chances of making a good impression, and find out whether you should pursue a relationship.

The keys to a good interview boil down to these:

✔ Show your best self, but be sure it's your real self. Even if you manage to bluff your way into a job, you won't want to or be able to keep up the act forever. You want a workplace that hires you for the real you. Acknowledge your weaknesses as well as your strengths. That brings a side benefit: You come off as honest and not desperate.

✔ Do the little things that create good chemistry; for example, be enthusiastic and keep your answers between 10 and 60 seconds long.

✔ If it feels appropriate, ask questions during — not just at the end of — the interview to discover what the employer's problems are. Explain or demonstrate how you might solve them. If in a particular interview that feels infeasible, consider offering to do a bit of free work, such as write a proposal.

All that is easier said than done. This chapter shows you how to make it easier.

How Chava Triumphed over the Interview from Hell

Chava was applying for her first professional job, but the principles she used apply whether you're a clerk or a CEO.

Chava had been selling women's clothes at Macy's and liked selling, but eight bucks an hour, even with her 20 percent discount on overpriced merchandise, was no life. So she figured she'd try to jump on the Internet bandwagon and try to land a job selling ads for Web sites.

And a phone call came: "Hello, Chava, this is Terry from Justin Crasdale's office at NanoNet. Mr. Crasdale would like to interview you for a sales position here."

Chava: Wonderful! What interview slots are available?

Terry: We'll be interviewing each afternoon next week.

Chava: Could I possibly get the last slot?

A study by Robert Half and Associates found that the last person interviewed gets the job 55 percent of the time. (This sounds too good to be true. Other studies might not yield the same result.)

Terry: Okay. How's next Friday at 4 p.m.?

Chava: Great. Of course, I want to be prepared. In addition to what's on your Web site, is there any other information you can send me that I should look at?

Terry: I'll see what I can find. *(She takes down Chava's e-mail address.)*

Chava: I haven't been to NanoNet's offices. What's appropriate for me to wear for an interview there?

Terry: A nice sweater and pants or skirt will be fine.

Chava: Anything I should know about the company culture or the interviewer that might keep me from putting my foot in my mouth?

Being informal and natural is key to job interview success. You may say, "But this is only the receptionist." Don't kid yourself. Many receptionists are not shy about telling their boss, "That Chava seems like a snob."

Terry: Well, people work hard here, so you might not want to ask about vacations.

Chava: Thanks a lot. Can I get directions? And is parking difficult?

Terry: *(Gives directions and parking info.)*

Chava: Thanks. I'll see you Friday at 4.

Chava got off the phone and yelled, "YESSSSSSSS!" Her next emotion was fear. "Gosh, I want to do well." She channeled her fear into energy to prepare.

"I better learn something about the company. I don't want to be like the applicant for a job at IBM who couldn't answer, 'What does IBM stand for?'" So she visited the company Web site and read the material the secretary e-mailed her.

To calm her nerves, Chava wrote down answers to the questions she was most afraid of: "Why should we hire someone with no experience in the field?" and "Why have you been unemployed for a year?"

She wrote her 15-second *quick human story* (an explanation of what she's looking for and why). Here is Chava's quick human story:

> I've done very well as a salesperson at Macy's, but now I've graduated from college and I'm ready for a real sales job. I've gotten excited about the Internet — I love NanoNet. And I've spoken with one of your salespeople, Jerry Rosoff, and it seems that I could be a great salesperson for you.

Chava tried to put herself in the shoes of the *hirer* (the person with the actual power to hire): "What attributes does Crasdale most want in the person he hires?" "Which of those can I honestly claim?" "How can I prove that my claims are legitimate?" Throughout the interview, she'd stress those things. She decided on

- ✔ Can think on my feet
- ✔ Persistent
- ✔ Good at closing the sale

Chava wrote a few *PAR stories* that prove she has those attributes. PAR stands for a *p*roblem she faced, how she *a*pproached it, and how it *r*esolved. What PAR stories could convince Crasdale that Chava had one or more of the attributes he wanted? Here is one:

> A woman cut in front of my cash register line and asked if we had a dress (a $900 St. John's!) in another color. Dilemma! If I told her to wait her turn, she probably would be angry, but if I took care of her, the other customers would be annoyed. So I compromised. I told her where she could look for the dress and asked her to come back if she couldn't find it. She couldn't, came back, and again cut in front. I stayed calm and said, "I'll be happy to check with the other Macy's stores. If you like, get in line, and I'll help you as soon as you get to the front, or if you prefer, try to find

another salesperson who isn't chained to the register." She decided to wait for me. I checked the computer, found the dress, called the store to verify it was there, and had them ship it to her home. One $900 dress sold, one customer happy.

Chava thought up a few questions to ask, either during or at the end of the interview. "Why has the position opened up?" "What ends up being the key attribute needed to succeed in this position?" "What would you say are the best and worst things about working here?" "Your Web site says that you've started selling video compression solutions. That's interesting to me. Can you tell me a little about that?"

Of course, Chava didn't want to sound scripted. So, after writing all of the above items, she pulled out an index card and wrote a few words to remind her of what to say.

Finally, Chava invited a friend over to role-play an interview, including the questions she was most scared of. Chava even videotaped it. Afterward, they watched the video, putting themselves in the employer's shoes, looking for chemistry as well as content, asking themselves throughout, "Is this making me more or less likely to hire Chava?"

Her final self-calming activity was to remind herself that Crasdale's human too. "We're two imperfect people, trying to see if we can get along. Besides, if he doesn't want me, so what? There's probably a better-fit job around the corner."

The big date

Chava stood in front of her closet, talking to herself. "I really like this dress, but maybe it's too flashy. Hmm. I'll feel confident in this, and it's safer. Oops. I wore it once already. Better be sure it doesn't smell. No faster way to a bad impression! It's okay."

"Easy on the perfume. I know I'm supposed to think of this as a first date, but I don't want to smell like a hooker." (It's safest to pass on fragrance altogether.)

"I'm not going to drive there three hours ahead of time to be sure I don't get lost. If I get there that early, I'll just stew and get more nervous. I'll just leave an extra half-hour.

"All right, let me make sure I have all the stuff I might need:

- My "cheat sheet" index card.
- Copies of my resume. I'll only show it if they ask for it — my resume is unlikely to stand out compared with the competition. Besides, I want to

> focus on what I'll do for them in the future, not what I've done in the past. If they have my resume in front of them, they might ask me mainly about the past.
>
> ✔ Copies of my transcript. Same story here. I'll have it if they ask for it, but I don't want that to be the focus of the interview.
>
> ✔ My work samples: I will bring copies of the evaluations from my supervisor, and a copy of those two nice letters I got from customers."

Chava walks in

She approached the front door of the building. These thoughts ran through her mind:

"I'm going to be myself — my best self — but myself. I have to find an employer who wants me for who I am.

"If I try to enjoy it and create some chemistry, I'll improve my chances of getting the job, and even if I don't, the interview will be more pleasant.

"Unless the interviewer makes it clear that it's a no-no, I'll ask questions during the interview so it's a bit more of a conversation than an interrogation.

"Actually, all we need to know about each other are

> ✔ Can I do the job?
> ✔ Will I do the job?
> ✔ Will we like each other?

"My job in the interview is to help us both answer those questions."

The interview from hell

Chava opened the oak door that read, NanoNet: Technology Made Human. The receptionist smiled, and Chava said, "Hi. I'm Chava Merideau. I'm here for an interview with Mr. Crasdale. Are you the person I spoke with on the phone?"

Terry: Yes.

Chava: Thanks for the material you sent me on NanoNet. That's helpful.

Terry: You're welcome. I'll see if Mr. Crasdale is ready for you. Have a seat.

Meanwhile, Chava reviewed her index card to remember just the big things: "Blue dress PAR story, St. John's dress PAR story, videostreaming question."

Terry: Mr. Crasdale will see you now. This way, please.

Chava entered, unaware that she was about to face the interview from hell. She walked in to find three interviewers.

Chava: Hi, I'm Chava Merideau.

Crasdale: Yes, and I am Justin Crasdale, the sales manager, and these are C. J. Fong from marketing, and Antoine Jackson, our affirmative action officer who will be monitoring the interview. Ms. Merideau, tell us about yourself.

No chitchat, no warming up, just that vague: "Tell me about yourself." Her heart raced but she calmed herself by reminding herself, "If this is a sign of what they're like when they're trying to recruit someone, I don't want to work here."

Chava: Is there any particular information you'd like me to discuss?

She was hoping Crasdale would give her a focus. No such luck.

Crasdale: What in your background suggests you'd be good at this job?

Chava: *(Gives an extended version of her 15-second human story)* When I was in college, I worked in retail sales at Macy's and did well. A customer asking me to show her a dress often left with a blouse and jacket too. I have a knack for sales. As you might imagine, you can't earn a living on the sales floor at Macy's, so I asked myself, "What would I like to sell that could earn me a good income?" That's why I'm here. I love the Internet, I use NanoNet all the time, and when I spoke with Jerry Rosoff, it seemed like I'd do well here. But, as you know, I don't have direct experience selling ads. Do you see that as a serious problem?

Chava's question demonstrates the essence of a good interviewee. She changed the dynamic from adversarial (she's trying to sell us and we're trying to find out what's wrong with her) to collaborative (we're both trying to figure out if we're right for each other).

Crasdale: We're not sure, that's why we're interviewing you. *(Crasdale's as warm as Fairbanks in February.)*

Chava: May I ask, what characteristics make for a successful salesperson here at NanoNet? *(Great question. This helps Chava focus all her subsequent responses, and give her a sense of whether she could do this job well.)*

Fong: In the end, selling is relentlessness and a thick skin. *(Chava cringes. Another sign that this job won't be right for her.)*

Crasdale: May I see your resume? *(Chava gives it to him. Her heart is racing again.)* I see that you have been unemployed for a year. Why is that, Ms. Merideau?

Chava: After graduating college, before starting my career, I figured it was a perfect time to do some things I wouldn't be able to do while working. So, a friend and I drove across country. It was quite an adventure. Mind if I tell you a brief story? *(Half-hearted nods.)* When you're on the road, there are many times you really have to think on your feet. *(One of the attributes Chava thinks is important in a salesperson.)* Our car broke down in the middle of nowhere and when we finally got the car towed to the nearest garage, the mechanic said it was a broken timing chain and it would cost $1,000. We somehow didn't trust that, so I phoned the nearest Toyota dealer, described the problem, and he said that it didn't sound like a timing chain problem. We had AAA tow it to the Toyota dealer. It turned out to be a clogged gas line that cost us $75. That's the sort of problem I faced then. Can I ask you, what's a typical problem I might face as a salesperson for NanoNet? *(Ending a few of your statements with a question helps convert an interview from an interrogation into more of a conversation.)*

Crasdale: Companies can advertise on many sites. So, customers are always saying, "Gee that's expensive. This other site is charging less." *(This warns Chava that perhaps NanoNet ads are overpriced and she might have a hard time selling them.)*

Chava: I understand. I imagine that you'll teach me some strategies for dealing with that sort of problem, but maybe this will give you a sense of the way I think. If a customer said, "Another Web site is cheaper." I'd say something like, "I certainly understand why that would be tempting, but our customers have found that the quality of the ads and the quality of the hits you get on our site actually make us a bargain. Why don't you try us for a trial period and then reassess? We offer special pricing for new trials. Does that make sense?" I was just winging it, but do you think that sort of approach would have a chance of working?

Chava has just done the best thing a job seeker can do in an interview: Project yourself into the job and demonstrate how you'd handle a problem. This is especially true if your past accomplishments aren't terrific — and Chava's certainly aren't: Unemployed for a year, retail sales clerk before that. Note also that Chava again ended her statement with a question. Not only does this convert an interrogation into a dialogue, but that particular question also ensured that she didn't sound like a know-it-all.

Fong: It could. Nothing works all the time. *(Negativity oozes from this place.)*

Chava: Before we get too far, I should get a sense of whether the compensation is in a range I could accept. The job announcement didn't include a salary. What range have you budgeted for the position? *(See the sidebar for why this is a good question.)*

At this point, Chava had asked more than enough questions in a short time, so she let the interviewers ask the rest of the questions. Let's fast-forward to the end.

Crasdale: Do you have any other questions, Ms. Merideau?

Chava: Yes. Could you tell me why the position is open?

Crasdale: The other person didn't work out.

Chava: May I ask why?

Crasdale: He didn't make his number.

Before accepting this job, Chava would insist on speaking with her predecessor. It's appearing ever more likely that the problem is the product and, perhaps, Crasdale.

Chava: What sort of person ends up being happy working for you and vice-versa?

Crasdale: A self-starter. I'm very busy and don't have a lot of time for hand-holding.

Chava: Thank you. I understand. *("I understand you're a bad boss," she thinks. But because she's still not ready to rule the job out, in her best-self voice Chava wraps up.)* Well, I am interested. In light of our discussion, I think that my ability to think on my feet, be persistent, and be enthusiastic about your site means that I can do a good job for you. But of course, you have to make that call. Do you think I can do the job?

"Do you think I can do the job?" is a good concluding question. If the answer is no, you can ask why and counter the objection before leaving, in your thank-you letter, or through your references.

Crasdale: We'll inform you of our decision within two weeks. (He rises. They all rise.)

Chava: *(Friendly tone as always.)* Thank you. I look forward to hearing from you.

Out the door

She keeps her game face on as she says good-bye to the receptionist. When she leaves the building, she finally can relax. "Oh man, I can't imagine working here!"

UNCONVENTIONAL WISDOM

Avoiding uncomfortable questions about salary

Standard advice is to never bring up salary until the job is offered, let alone early in the interview. My clients find the conventional wisdom to be wrong. Typically, somewhere in the interview, the interviewer asks, "What is your current salary?" or "What is your salary requirement?" No answers to that question are helpful to you. It is better to preempt the problem by striking first with a question like, "The position seems to involve *(Insert as high-level a description of the tasks as possible.)* What salary range have you budgeted for the position?"

If they respond, "Well, how much are you looking to make?" Respond, "I'm looking to be paid fairly. What *have* you budgeted for the position?" If they continue to hedge, that's a sign you don't want to work for them. If forced to, offer a wide range, for example, "$55,000 to $65,000 depending on the scope of responsibilities."

The rules are different if you're negotiating as a self-employed person or independent contractor. You don't ask the hirer what he's budgeted. You gather information about his needs, describe what you can do to meet them, and then give the cost. If you've done a good job of this, and priced yourself fairly, the hirer usually will agree to the price.

That is indeed a triumph. Many job seekers are so hell-bent on impressing the interviewer that they don't get enough information to decide if an employer is right for them. Too often, the result is accepting a job they'll be unhappy in. Chava's first-date approach to a job interview prevented an unhappy marriage.

The Key Interviewing Principles

There are things you can do to put yourself ahead of the pack.

Nineteen ways to create great chemistry

Too often, the candidate who wins the job is not the most qualified, but the one who gets along best with the interviewer. Here are potent ways to ensure that you get along.

1: Body chemistry

Let's start with the basics. I wouldn't mention it if it weren't a frequent problem. You can't have chemistry if you have bad breath or body odor. You'd be surprised how many people do.

2: Arrive early

Arrive 20 minutes early. Then find the nearest coffee shop to hang out at for a few minutes. Go over your notes. Walk in to the building five minutes early. Ask where the bathroom is. On the way to and from, get a feel for the place.

Think of the interview as starting the moment you walk into the building and ending when you're on the street again. Why? Slouch into the building and the person walking next to you may be the interviewer returning from lunch. After the interviewer says good-bye, many applicants blow it by letting down their guard and saying something stupid. My wife occasionally asks her receptionist about a job candidate's behavior.

3: Help yourself relax

Think back to a moment when you were confident. In the interview, pretend you're that self and remind yourself that millions of jobs are out there. If you weren't meant to get this one, it doesn't mean you're going to be a bag lady.

If possible, learn something about the interviewer in advance, even if only to ask the receptionist, "What can you tell me about Mr. Crasdale?" Even knowing that Mr. Crasdale just came back from vacation will help you feel more confident, like you have some inside information.

4: The first-date mind-set

Many people think of a job interview as an interrogation. You're sitting there under a bare light bulb, bombarded with questions, many of which you can't answer. After an interrogation-type interview, you're unlikely to know whether you'd like to work for that employer. Not to mention, you've had your worst experience of the week.

Unless it's one of those structured interviews in which every candidate must be interviewed identically, or you get the sense that the interview doesn't want questions, it needn't be that way. An interview *can* be more like a first date, in which each of you has a chance to decide whether you're well-matched, logically and chemically. A first-date mind-set also discourages you from assuming that too-formal, phony-appearing job-seeker persona: "I believe I am well qualified for the position," or "I'm seeking a position with a dynamic organization."

You also make an interview more like a date by asking a few questions during the interview, not just at the end. Your questions can come from your preinterview research about the employer or as follow-ups to what the interviewer said, but here are generic questions:

- ✔ What would people say they like best and worst about working here?
- ✔ What should I know about working here?

> ✔ How many hours a week would I be expected to work?
>
> ✔ To whom would I be reporting? What sort of person gets along best with him?
>
> ✔ How many people have held this position in the past few years? Why did they leave?

Most interviewers are glad to answer a few questions — indeed, they view questions as signs of intelligence and indicators that you're interested but not desperate.

Treat an interview as a first date and you'll both more wisely decide whether to hook up.

5: The most important ten seconds

You make a hard-to-change impression in the first ten seconds you meet someone. How to make a good first impression? It's a sad commentary on human judgment, but all you have to do is follow the advice offered by Gary Ripple, author of *Campus Pursuit*: Smile, offer a firm handshake, look the person in the eye (look long enough that you know what color they are), and pleasantly and confidently say, "Hi, I'm Joe Blow." Wait to be invited to sit down, then lean slightly forward, keep a pleasant look on your face (I said pleasant, not psychotic), and maintain eye contact most of the time. Believe it or not, in just those few seconds, you've given yourself a big boost. Rehearse the above ritual ten times. It's that important.

End the interview similarly. Smile, look the interviewer in the eye, shake his hand, and, if true, say that you enjoyed the interview. If not, thank him for an interesting experience.

6: Avoid turn-off mannerisms

Richard Bolles, author of *What Color is Your Parachute?* urges interviewees to beware of trivial mannerisms that can nix you:

> ✔ You slouch in your chair.
>
> ✔ You fidget in your seat.
>
> ✔ You play with your hair or hands.
>
> ✔ You continually avoid eye contact.
>
> ✔ You're too self-critical.
>
> ✔ You speak quietly as a church mouse or as loud as a wrestling announcer.
>
> ✔ You constantly interrupt the interviewer.

7: When you feel you've gotten off on the wrong foot

If you get off to a bad start, you might get a second chance by interrupting and saying, "You know I think I've gotten off on the wrong foot here. I'm better than I've made myself sound. Could we start over?"

8: Really try to understand the employer's needs

Say you're applying for a position as an accountant. The employer's main priority may be developing a new accounting system, or improving employees' reporting practices, or even a desire to avoid an IRS audit. If you understand the employer's needs and show how you can meet them, you'll have a much better chance of landing the job than if you simply answer the interviewer's questions blind.

Sometimes you can tease out his needs with questions such as, "What sorts of issues are important for your new hire to address?" Other times, you simply need to listen well. The interviewer's questions and statements usually reveal her concerns. Try to show how, if hired, you can address them.

In other words, think of yourself as a consultant, helping the client to identify his needs and then collaboratively figure out a way to solve them. To that end, you may even offer to write a proposal or work on a small project. That can really help you stand out in comparison with the other candidates.

9: Try to have a good time

A good time and a job interview seem to be mutually exclusive, but not necessarily. Enjoy the decor in the reception area. See if you can figure out if the interviewer is nervous. Does her office give clues to what she's like: the family pictures, the golf clubs in the corner, the desk that looks post-tornado. Listen well to the interviewer. Does it sound like she'd rather talk about her upcoming vacation than "What is your greatest weakness?" When you get asked a killer question, answer it quickly and move the conversation to a more pleasant area. Ask the questions you're curious about, the serious and the playful. After you establish some credibility, it may enhance your image as a nice person to ask a human question such as, "What do most people do for lunch?"

10: Be your best self, but be yourself

By being your real self, whether it's quiet, jovial, whatever, you're not that sanitized middle-of-the-road personality that most job seekers try to be. Be yourself and you're more likely to be at the top or at the bottom of the heap than in the middle. Sure, if you're not what they're looking for, they'll turn you down. Fine! Better to show them the real you before you commit to each other than after — just like marriage.

Having said that, I recognize that there are many "real yous": The you drinking beer in front of the TV isn't the same as the you working on your greatest accomplishment. Be yourself, but be your best self.

11: Really listen and watch

Especially in an interview, most people don't listen well. We're so worried about what the interviewer will think of us, and are so busy planning what we're going to say next, that we only half-attend to what the interviewer is saying and showing with body language. That's a shame because there often are crucial hidden messages:

✔ The interviewer may reveal what she's mainly looking for in a candidate.

✔ The interviewer's reactions may reveal what he likes and dislikes about you.

✔ In today's world of frequent job hopping, it probably hasn't been long since your interviewer sat on your side of the desk. Looking out for signs of empathy might relax you.

✔ Perhaps he's nervous because he hired someone before who didn't work out — another bad hire could cost him his job. Being attuned to his nervousness may make it easier to stay positive when he's grilling you.

✔ When you're really listening, you're able to ask questions that follow up on what the interviewer is saying — a great way to create chemistry.

12: Talk the right amount

Most comments should be 10 to 60 seconds long. More than that and you risk sounding egocentric or putting your interviewer to sleep. If the interviewer wants more information, she can ask a follow-up question.

13: Ask one or more power questions early in the interview

"What are you most hoping to find in the person you hire?" "Anything else?" "What are the most important things you'll want me to work on in the first few weeks on the job?" The sooner you can ask these questions, the sooner you can start tailoring your answers to what's important to the employer. It's like getting the answers to the test in advance.

To avoid sounding like you're simply parroting back what the employer wants, be sure to back up your claims with facts or anecdotes. For example, if the boss says he's most looking for someone with fire in the belly, it's not enough to say that you have drive. You need to back it up with a PAR story or other evidence that you go the extra mile.

At the end of the interview, you might ask, "Based on what we've talked about today, I feel good about the position. Do you think I can do the job?" That gives you a chance to counter any objections.

Especially if it's a start-up or other fiscally shaky employer, ask a few questions about the company or workgroup, for example, "What's your burn rate (monthly expenses)? How long will you be able to sustain that rate? With all the dot bombing, any ethical startup will understand that you have the right to ask such questions. Indeed, asking them tends to impress employers.

14: Stay connected with all your interviewers

A panel may conduct your interview. The regular interview rules apply with the following additions. When responding, mainly look at your questioner but occasionally establish eye contact with the others. When asking a question, look mainly at the person you'd like to answer it, but if another panelist seems eager to respond, give that person the nod to go ahead.

15: Bring up one weakness early on

Bringing up a weakness of yours can help you and the interviewer assess whether you're likely to be successful on the job. Chava brought up her lack of experience in the Internet field. In bringing it up herself, not only did it demonstrate her candor — unusual in a job candidate — it allowed an open discussion of how serious a liability that would be. That's good for interviewer and interviewee.

16: Mirror the interviewer

If she's strictly business, you should be too. If he's social and playful, show that side of yourself.

17: Reveal a bit about your personal life

Talk a little about your family, hobbies, and so on. If you get a good response, reveal a bit more.

18: Know the secrets to video interviewing

To save travel costs and reduce scheduling hassles, employers increasingly use video interviewing instead of face-to-face. Increasingly, the employer simply mails the candidate a WebCam. There are only two special things to remember:

- ✔ You look shifty if your eyes avert to the side. You look depressed if your head is tilted downward. The solution: When you're talking, keep your head straight and your eyes trained slightly *above* the camera.

- ✔ A lag exists between the video and audio transmission, so voices can seem out of sync. So before answering a question, wait until you hear the interviewer finish. Don't rely on the video or you risk interrupting the interviewer.

19: (Highly optional) Bring cookies

For most jobs, employers interview many candidates, and after a while, the applicants begin to blend together. Brandon Toropov, author of *303 Off-the-Wall Ways to Get a Job,* offers a way to make yourself memorable: Offer home-baked chocolate chip cookies to the interviewers at the end of the interview. "I thought this might be a nice way to end the interview." Just be sure your cookies rock!

Interview Report Card

Did your face, voice, and body language convey interest?

Did you create a good impression in those crucial first few seconds?

Did you share a weakness early in the interview? Did it seem to help or hurt you?

Did you listen well or were you too focused on what you were going to say next?

Did you describe the accomplishments most likely to impress the interviewer?

Were you able to not just tell but demonstrate that you could do the job?

Did you ask questions during the interview, not just at the end?

Did your questions help you get clearer about whether you want this job?

Did you talk roughly half of the time?

Did your comments rarely exceed one minute in length?

Did you show caring about the people, asking personal questions as appropriate?

Did you show that you care about the organization's product or service?

Did you reveal an appropriate amount about your personal life?

Did you mirror the interviewer's style?

Were you honest enough?

Were you your best self?

Were you able to have a reasonably good time?

Would you hire yourself for this job?

Grading yourself on this report card helps you in subsequent interviews. It's easy to deceive yourself into thinking that you did better than you did.

Don't just say you can do the job — prove it

Many career guides tell job interviewees to focus on their accomplishments — what they did in the past. I've found that interviewees are more likely to score by focusing on the present: by demonstrating — during the interview — how they can help the employer.

Imagine that you're director of sales for a publishing company and are interviewing two candidates for a sales job. Candidate A discussed his previous sales experience, while Candidate B pulled a book off your shelf, pretended she was on a sales call, and sold the book to you. Assuming the candidates were otherwise equal, which one would you hire?

If you're not asked to demonstrate what you can do, consider asking to do so. If that feels inappropriate, say something like: "Can you give me an example of a problem you envision me tackling on the job?" *(Hopefully, you get an answer.)* Then continue: "Can I show you how I might approach a problem like that?" Start by asking the interviewer a question or two about the problem to give you the information you need to craft a plan for addressing it. Then say, "In light of what you've said, might this approach to the problem makes sense? *(Then outline your approach.)* Of course, I'd know a lot more if I were actually working on the project, but this gives you a sense of how I might approach things."

Sometimes, alas, you won't be allowed to do a demonstration. As mentioned earlier, some organizations require that all interviewees be asked precisely the same questions.

Maximize the good part of the interview

Give longer answers to questions you like; give shorter ones to questions you don't. Job seekers frequently do the opposite. They keep trying to dig themselves out of trouble and often just dig themselves deeper, and at minimum, ensure that a larger proportion of the interview is spent on their weaknesses.

Also remember to ask questions to redirect the interview to areas you want to talk about — for example, about the new job and how you'd approach its challenges.

Golden opportunity: Is the employer unsure of the job description?

Often, the employer knows she needs to hire someone but isn't sure how to best use the person. If, in the interview, you can help clarify that the employer needs someone with your strengths, you may well talk your way into a well-suited job.

Early in the interview, ask, "Are the tasks you'd want me to focus on mapped out at this point or do they depend on the candidate?" If there's some play, the interviewer may be grateful for your help. Ask him to tell you about some of the organization's needs. Then gently propose how the position might be structured to meet those needs and how your strengths would be well suited. Example:

> You've identified two key problems: getting the staff comfortable with the new computer program and reducing the backlog in processing claims. That would be fun to tackle. My software training background will help me in getting the staff comfortable with the computer program, and I know I'll enjoy figuring out how to streamline the claims process."

If the job description is fluid, expect that you won't get a job offer right away. The employer probably won't hire until he's settled on what he wants. So, focus on helping the hirer do just that. Offer to do a little homework that might be helpful — for example, write a short proposal or report. That should put you ahead of the competition.

If you sense you're a poor match for this job

Sometimes, you can turn the lemon into lemonade. Try this:

> "In listening to you, it doesn't sound like I'm a good fit for this position but I'm wondering if I might be of use to you in another way. What I bring to the table are (*Insert your best attributes*). Might someone with that background be of help to you?"

This is an example of industrial magnate Henry Kaiser's famous advice to job seekers: Find a need and fill it.

Sometimes, you may think you've done well, but by the end of the interview, you get the sense that you're not going to get the job. It's worth asking, "Is there any reason you'd be hesitant to hire me?" You may tease out an objection that you can successfully counter.

After the interview: Where the job is often won or lost

If possible, right after the interview, head for a coffee shop, and while everything's fresh in your mind, grade yourself on the Interview Report Card, and draft a thank-you note.

Ahead-of-the-pack thank-you letters

If you can draft the darn thank-you letter right after the interview, it's best. Then let it sit overnight, review it with fresh eyes the next day, and mail it out.

A thank-you letter can do more than say thank you. It enables you to

- ✔ Remind the interviewer of the things he was most impressed with. "I'm pleased you think my experience managing stevedores would be valuable."
- ✔ Give a better answer to a question you flubbed. "I've given further thought to that question you asked about retrograde transmission."
- ✔ Say more about things the interviewer cares about. "There was one more thing I thought you might be interested in."
- ✔ Reiterate your interest in the position.

Here's a letter that accomplishes all of the above:

> Dear Nadine,
>
> I really enjoyed the opportunity to interview with you. The dyslexia project is generating some impressive results. I am pleased that you think my background in pathology would be helpful and look forward to the possibility of joining your staff.
>
> You asked a question that got me thinking. You asked what sort of study I think would be the most valuable next step. On reflection, I think we'd get valuable information from doing PET scans of dyslexic children of different ages to better understand how cerebral structure and function change developmentally. That could point us to the best times to provide educational as well as physiological interventions.
>
> I am excited about the prospect of working for you.
>
> Sincerely,
>
> Allan Gold

A question I'm frequently asked is, "Should I send my thank-you note via e-mail?" It depends on the recipient. If it's a high-tech sort of person, e-mail is fine. If it's someone who would seem to value a hand-written note more, do that.

References

Don't get too compulsive about your references. Many employers treat references cursorily. They know that, for a variety of reasons, recommendations can be invalid. A boss can sing the praises of a lousy employee to avoid the risk of a lawsuit. Or she can sound lukewarm about a top employee to avoid the new employer suing her if perchance that employee doesn't work out. Don't sweat recommendations much.

However, do ask potential references if they're willing to serve. That can avoid surprise bashings. Try this wording: "I was hoping to use you as a reference. Do you feel you're in a position to provide a strong one?"

When a prospective employer is ready to call your references, you call them first. Explain the ways that you're well suited to the job and the issues you'd like your reference to address.

If you are employed, ask hirers to defer contacting your references, especially your current employer, until ready to hire you. You don't want your current boss to find out you're looking if you don't actually get a job offer.

Even if you're excited about a possible job, be careful not to tell anyone who may tip off your current employer. Hot prospects often turn cold. The career battlefield is littered with people who talked about their next job too soon and got shot down by their current boss who didn't want an employee he couldn't count on. Hold off until you and the new employer have actually signed a job offer. Trust me on this one.

The end game

Often, this is where the game is won and lost. Most employers appreciate polite persistence.

A few days after you mail your thank-you letter, call to ask where you stand. If you're not the front runner, ask, "Is there anything that makes you hesitant to hire me?" If a concern is raised, explain why it is unjustified (if it is), have a reference do so, or offer to provide a work sample — a report, proposal, or one-day trial, for example. End the call by affirming that you're eager and confident that you can do the job. If it doesn't feel too pushy, you might offer to continue the discussion by saying, for example, "Of course, we only scratched the surface in our discussion of *(insert topic)*. If you might find it useful, I'd be happy to explore *(insert topic)* with you further." Send a follow-up note reiterating all of this.

If it's a job worth using up some of the goodwill of one of your references, ask him to phone the hirer to say how wonderful you are.

Two weeks later, if you haven't heard anything, you can send a letter such as, "You and I discussed *(insert topic)*. I came across this article and thought you might be interested. Speaking of interested, I still am interested in the position and hope to hear from you soon."

Today, when it has become extraordinarily difficult to dismiss a full-time employee, expect multiple interviews and possibly employment testing. Three or four rounds of interviews are common for mid-level positions. This is especially likely when the job description is fluid. Keep trying to help the employer develop that job description and you'll likely be the candidate who gets it.

You Got the Job Offer!

Congratulations. It's a great feeling to be offered a job, but don't sound too eager. At minimum, it will hurt you when negotiating the terms of your employment. I've even know a case in which excess enthusiasm resulted in a retracted job offer. The employee was so ecstatic that it made him appear desperate. That motivated the employer to check his references more closely than he otherwise would have, whereupon the employer developed buyer's remorse and offered the position to another candidate.

The right response to a job offer that you'd consider is a moderately enthusiastic, "That's great. Can we set up an appointment in a couple of days to discuss salary and other terms of employment?" Then it's time for a bit of homework. See Chapter 17.

Someone Else Got the Job: All's Not Lost

If the job is offered to someone else and you're in mourning about it, phone the employer and say something like, "I'm disappointed. I believe I could have done a good job for you. Might I ask what made you hesitant to hire me? Anything else? (That follow-up question often generates something valuable.) I want to know if there's something I need to work on." Close with, "If by any chance your situation changes, I hope you'll keep me in mind. Would you mind if I phoned you back in a month to follow up? And is there anyone else you think I should talk with?"

Sometimes, the employer may like you, but not for that position. Don Lussier, in *Job Search Secrets,* suggests that you ask if one or more of the following are options:

- ✔ Considering you for another opening
- ✔ Considering you for an upcoming opening
- ✔ Creating a temporary opening
- ✔ Creating an opening by releasing a problem employee
- ✔ Offering you a consulting assignment
- ✔ Recommending you to another employer
- ✔ Doing a project as a volunteer. Even if that project doesn't turn into a paying job, you can still list that first-rate organization on your resume as your most recent work experience.

Facing Rejection

Despite all efforts, even the best candidates get rejected a lot. The successful job seeker learns from it, doesn't allow himself to get frustrated, and moves on to the next constructive task.

A rejection after you've told your true human story is often a blessing. Wouldn't you really rather hold out for someone who wants you for who you are?

Chapter 17

Negotiating a Cool Deal (Even If You're Dealing with Scrooge)

· ·

In This Chapter

▶ The argument for and against negotiating

▶ Preparing: Where the game is often won or lost

▶ Getting the boss excited about you

▶ Twelve things every negotiator must know . . . and most don't

▶ Negotiating tips for the self-employed

▶ When to say yes

· ·

*N*egotiating is worth the effort. The minutes you spend negotiating the terms of your employment can not only earn you more money but can also gain you more respect. Most employers admire people who value themselves enough to hold out for what they're worth. If you accept the first offer, you may make the boss think that you're desperate, which lowers your perceived value.

On average, my female clients are less willing than my male clients to negotiate their salaries. Most accept what is offered. I wonder if that may explain some of the male/female disparity in salaries. So, if you're a woman and don't like being paid less than men, do your part. Negotiate!

You may want to read this chapter even if you're not ready to negotiate your compensation. Remember that life is a negotiation — from who gets the bathroom first in the morning to reacting to your parents' pleas that you don't phone home often enough.

Having just endorsed negotiation, let me cop to the fact that I've personally stopped negotiating *vigorously* and stopped encouraging my clients to do so. Here's why.

I've studied many books, articles, and tapes on negotiation. I've counseled countless clients on how to negotiate. I have negotiated hard all my life, and people say I'm an excellent negotiator. Yet in looking back, I've come to the conclusion that *extensive* negotiation isn't worth it. Often, you get little more than what you could have gotten had you simply proposed an alternative to the first offer and accepted the counteroffer. Beyond that, people rarely get enough, after taxes, to improve their lifestyles. Extensive pre-employment negotiation also can distract you from more important factors:

- ✔ Will you enjoy the job: the tasks, its people, and its ethics?

- ✔ Will you learn a lot, especially things that can enhance your career long-term?

- ✔ Is it a growing organization? Not only does that make you more downsize-resistant, it's also more fun to work for a place on the upswing.

- ✔ Would a few grand more in salary (minus taxes) compensate for lifestyle decrements such as a two-hour commute or 60-hour workweek?

So, while this chapter includes all the effective negotiation strategies that I know, ask yourself whether, in your situation, it's wiser to just accept the employer's response to your first counteroffer.

Note: In public sector or unionized workplaces, even modest negotiation may not be possible. You may, however, be able to get your position classified upward or be hired as a consultant, so you're not limited to the standard salary.

Good negotiation boils down to

- ✔ **Preparation.** This starts with a little research to be sure you really want the job. If you do, then get ammunition that makes the boss more likely to pay you well. This ammunition includes upgrading the job description so the boss can justify paying a higher salary, showing what people in similar positions earn, calculating the big bucks your efforts will generate for the employer, and building good feelings between you and the boss to maximize the inclination to be generous. Probably the highest-caliber ammunition is to generate a competing job offer.

- ✔ **Firm, not-scared negotiating.** Ask for what you want. Make clear that you won't be taken advantage of. Show your ammunition. Noncash parts of the compensation package can be more important than salary — often they're tax-free and easier for the employer to concede on. Rule: Be hard on the issues, easy on the person. Be nice but resist giving in until the last minute. When you feel you've gotten as much as is reasonable from the boss, end with, "All right, if you'll agree, I'm willing to accept _____."

The rest of this chapter shows you how to make all that happen.

Chava Negotiates with Scrooge

In Chapter 16, Chava was savvy enough to triumph over the interview from hell. At the end of an interview with another employer, she heard the magic words: "We'd like to hire you. Let's talk compensation." Here's the story of Chava's next triumph: negotiating the terms of her employment.

The end of the interview

To protect the guilty and to make sure I don't get sued, I'll just call the boss Scrooge. Right at the end of Chava's interview, Scrooge wanted to sew her up.

Scrooge: Chava, we'd like to offer you the job. Let's talk turkey.

Chava wasn't biting.

Chava: Fine. Can we set up an appointment a couple of days from now to do that?

That lets Scrooge know, in a nonconfrontational way, that Chava won't accept just any offer. It also gives her time to prepare.

Scrooge: Are you sure you wouldn't like to talk salary now?

Chava: Thanks, but if it's okay with you, let's meet a couple of days from now. By the way, do you have any written material to help me learn more about the company or the projects I'll be working on? Also, I'd like to talk with a couple of the people I'd be working with to get a sense of the job. Would you give me their names and phone numbers?

Chava prepares

The first thing Chava did after the interview with Scrooge was to contact other potential employers: "Hi, I just received a job offer. Before accepting it, I wanted to contact you because I'm quite interested in your firm." A second job offer dramatically improves her negotiating position.

Next, she contacted the co-workers Scrooge told her about. Yes, they were hand-picked to be pro-Scrooge, but going behind his back to query more representative employers is too risky. She asked, "What's it like to work here?" "What's the typical workweek expectation? How would you describe the corporate culture — suits or sweaters? Boxers or briefs? — just kidding. What's most important to Scrooge: the bottom line, relationships, his image, risk-avoidance?" The latter question helped Chava craft her justification for a higher salary. One of her contacts seemed forthcoming, so she asked, "What do you think is an appropriate salary for me to ask for?"

She got answers that convinced her to take the job. She also learned that Scrooge was very concerned about the bottom line — he owned a lot of stock options and so if the company did well, he did very well.

Chava also came up with a higher-level responsibility that she was capable of taking on, hoping that might convince Scrooge to boost her salary.

Finally, she role-played the negotiation with a friend so that she wouldn't feel like a total novice going up against a pro.

The negotiation meeting

In addition to her chart of comparable salaries, Chava brought her most confident self. Employers rarely concede much to a scared negotiator.

Scrooge: Come in.

Chava: Thank you. I imagine you must have done dozens of these salary negotiations.

Knowing that even Scrooges may soften a bit when there's a human relationship, Chava starts with a bit of chitchat.

Scrooge *(Smiling wryly):* More than dozens.

Chava: Do you like doing them?

Scrooge: To tell you the truth, I don't.

Chava: Well, let's see if we can make this easy for both of us.

Scrooge: As long as you give in on everything.

Scrooge knows that humor doesn't cost him a dime and often softens the opposition. Chava laughs and then, before turning to the actual negotiation, does one more important thing.

Chava: I read the material that you gave me and I'm wondering: If I were to accept the position, might it be helpful if I set up a database that merged all the sales reports? That way, we'd all have access to great data on what works with what kinds of customers.

Note that she threw in a confident "If I were to accept the position." She doesn't want Scrooge to think she'll accept just any offer.

Scrooge: That does sound like it might build the bottom line. We'll see.

Chava has raised her perceived value. This is the time to pop the question.

Chava: So what do you think is the highest salary that's fair *(the most powerful word in a negotiation)* of me to expect?

Scrooge: There's no salary. It's commission only. *(Hardball negotiators often make a low-ball "take-it-or-leave it" offer. They know that intimidates most people. If the candidate rejects the offer, they can always come back with, "Well, let me see what I can do.")*

Chava: I checked a Web site that reports salary surveys, and here are the averages. *(She shows Scrooge her chart of comparable salaries.) Note that Chava simply ignored Scrooge's low-ball offer and proceeded to make her point. Sometimes, ignoring is wiser than confronting.*

Scrooge: Well, what would you accept?

Chava: What is the most the company is able to give?

It's generally better to try to let the number come from the employer. (But see later in the chapter for another point of view.)

Note also that she asked what the company — *not what* he — *is willing to give. It's a subtle reminder that it isn't the boss's money, so he shouldn't be so tight with it.*

Scrooge: I don't play those games. Let's hear your bottom line.

Chava: Okay. As you can see from the comparables, the average salary for a new salesperson is $40,000 base, with a commission structure that yields the average salesperson $60,000. You chose me because I'm above average, so I need a $50,000 base.

Scrooge: We have *never* paid a new salesperson that much.

Chava: Nevertheless, as you can see, I deserve that.

And she waits. Silence is powerful. Finally, Scrooge appears to blink.

Scrooge: I'll see if I can get you a $40,000 base with a commission structure that, if you're any good, should yield you $60,000. I'll talk with the sales manager. If he says okay, you've got a deal.

Chava: I'll consider that.

Unfortunately, naive Chava doesn't realize that Scrooge is using two hardball techniques on her. First, he's icing her: He raises her hopes of getting a good offer, and then puts her on ice while he ostensibly consults a higher authority. Scrooge deliberately waits a week before calling her back, knowing that will make her antsy and more likely to accept a low offer. And at the meeting, he pulls hardball technique number two: the higher authority ploy, the oldest trick in the book.

Scrooge: Chava, I am so sorry. I'm shocked. I did everything I could to convince the sales manager, but he absolutely refused. He said that giving you that much would alienate the other salespeople. The best I can do is a $20,000 base, but with commission, you should end up with $35,000.

Chava now summons her courage. She reminds herself that most employers (perhaps not as doggedly as Scrooge) try to get employees to work for as little as possible, but if pushed, will pay market value. Otherwise, a company is left only with employees willing to work for peanuts — which usually means a weak workforce. And Chava must remember that if Scrooge Online is one of those foolish companies, she doesn't want to work there. **She must retain the power to walk away.** *This is the time to be tough. She remembers the old negotiating maxim: Be tough on the numbers, easy on the person. That means be nice, even playful with your opponent, but stand quite firm on the terms. Chava also knows that, if possible, she shouldn't make a specific counter to his $20,000 offer. That would be a concession without getting anything in return. Here's how Chava puts it all together:*

Chava: This may not work. I need to be paid fairly. *(There's that powerful word again.)* And I do have other irons in the fire.

Having other options is the most potent negotiating tool. That's why you need to pursue as many job leads as possible even when you think you're likely to accept a position.

You chose to offer me a job because I am above average. It would feel wrong to accept below-average pay. Scrooge, I'm sure that while trying to get a good deal, you also want to be fair. You can count on my giving you more than your money's worth. For example, I am open to doing projects like developing that database. *(Now do you see why it's important to propose a high-level project?)* Do we have any chances of working this out or do we need to part company here?

Scrooge: Okay, enough. $30,000. Final answer.

Chava: Let's put salary aside for a moment and discuss benefits?

They discuss benefits, and Chava is able to extract a couple of things that benefit her yet actually build Scrooge Online's profits. She gets permission to work at home one day a week. That saves her commute time and Scrooge office expenses.

She also gets Scrooge to spring for $1,500 a year in continuing education. Chava benefits because she gets to stay up to speed, and Scrooge gets an employee better able to build the bottom line. Now, having come to some agreements and having had a tension-reducing break from the salary issue, Chava returns to the sticking point.

Chava: Well, we still have one point of contention: the salary. I understand that you need to keep your costs down. On the other hand, I deserve to be compensated fairly. What are we going to do?

Scrooge: Okay. Let's get this done. $35,000. That is absolutely it.

Chava: All right, on one condition: I get a bonus of 1 percent of gross sales for sales above my quota. That way, I'm only rewarded for bringing you more than you expected.

Scrooge: Half of 1 percent.

Chava: Okay.

Chava challenged Scrooge and did fine. Her previous wage was $8 an hour for her job at Macy's. Now she has a $35,000 annual base with a commission schedule that should result in a total salary of $50,000.

Relax. Most negotiations won't be this tough. This chapter, though, shows you everything you need to hold your own, even against Scrooge.

What Would Convince You to Give a New Employee a Fat Salary?

Imagine you're the boss. Which of these would convince you to give an employee as much as you can?

- You see a list of comparable salaries at similar organizations that justifies a higher salary.
- You're afraid of losing the candidate to another employer.
- The employee can take on more responsibility than was originally envisioned.
- The employee is likely to build the bottom line more than anticipated.
- The quality of the employee's work is likely to be better than his peers'.
- You like the person.

Right. All of the above can boost your chances of getting a good deal. Now, I show you how to make each of those happen.

Before the Negotiation Session

The most powerful way to improve your negotiating position is to have more than one job offer in hand or in the offing. It discourages Scrooge from low-balling you. And you gain the confidence of knowing you have other options. So even if you're scheduled for a salary negotiation, keep trying to get other job offers.

But even if Scrooge Online is your only option, there's still much you can do. Be sure you've followed the advice on how to interview in Chapter 16, asking what salary range has been budgeted for the position and seeing whether you can have the job molded to your strengths and upgraded.

What are you worth?

If you haven't upgraded the position during your interviews, you still have another chance. Think back on what you learned about the organization's needs from your interviews and preparation for interviews. If necessary, do a bit more research on the organization: visit its Web site or talk with an employee at that organization or at a competitor. What higher-level tasks can you propose to do that management may perceive as worth a higher salary?

A fair way to counter a low offer is to show that other employees in similar positions are better paid. How do you get this information? Start with employees in your target organization, and perhaps a competitor. Possible sources include:

- ✔ **The human resources department.** Some organizations make salary information public.

- ✔ **The boss.** Say, "To get a better sense of what seems fair, might I ask what my peers in the company earn?"

- ✔ **Other company employees.** It's appropriate that you talk with company employees to help you decide if you want the position. Don't worry; you shouldn't get in trouble for doing that. In such a conversation, you might ask, "This is a bit awkward, but I'm at that moment of truth. I've just been offered a job at the company and am meeting with the boss tomorrow to discuss salary. I'm not sure how much to ask for. Any advice?" You might also ask, "Any advice about how to handle a negotiation with *(insert the boss's name)*?"

> ✔ **Your local unemployment office.** Most such offices post all your state's civil service job listings, including salaries. Pay may be similar in the private sector. The unemployment office may also have local salary survey data.
>
> ✔ **A local headhunter specializing in your field.** To find one, visit `www.recruitersonline.com` or call the human resources department of a large local company in this field and ask, "When you hire a headhunter to fill a position as *(insert your job title),* whom do you usually use?"

The results of national and regional salary surveys are often less applicable but more accessible:

> ✔ `www.rileyguide.com/salary.html` and `www.salary.com` contain hundreds of salary surveys, covering most major professions. Salary.com is particularly good for finding local data — if it has your job title in its database.
>
> ✔ Salary surveys often appear in the magazines of trade and professional associations. Don't know the name of yours? Find it at `http://info.asaenet.org/gateway/Onlineassocslist.html` or at the more extensive *Associations Unlimited,* available in many libraries.

The temptation to show the boss only those positions with the highest salaries is understandable, but I recommend against that. Impress your boss with your integrity. Who knows, maybe that in itself will incline the boss to raise the offer. (I can't seem to shake that youthful idealism.)

To reduce your chances of being skewered by the higher authority ploy that Scrooge used on Chava, ask to negotiate with the person with final decision-making power. This won't always work. The negotiator may say, "Mr. Power asks me to handle negotiations and to consult him only if there's a problem." But there's no harm in asking.

A dress rehearsal

Your boss is probably a more experienced negotiator than you are. A bit of rehearsing can help level the playing field. After reading the next section, role-play the negotiation. Have a friend play the boss. Then switch roles, with you playing the boss. That can help you understand the employer's perspective.

The Negotiation Session

Here's how to make your preparation pay — literally.

Building chemistry

I know you're anxious to get down to business but it's worth taking a few minutes for small talk. Even if the boss suspects it's a technique, it usually softens his and your fervor to pinch every penny. Besides, this is your first project with your boss. Start out on a human basis.

A common mistake is to be friendly and pleasant during the small talk and then, as soon as the actual negotiation starts, to get deadly serious. Throughout, your tone should be informal; the conversation should be sprinkled with humor and little breaks for a light comment or anecdote.

Getting ammunition

During the initial small talk, you want to find out how badly the employer wants you and what she likes best about you. Ask these innocent-sounding questions:

- ✔ **"I'm curious. How long was the job open?"** If it was open for a while, it means that the employer had a hard time finding someone. You can be a tougher negotiator.

- ✔ **"Was I clearly the person you wanted?"** If there wasn't a close runner-up, you can be a tougher negotiator.

- ✔ **"What made you choose me?"** If she says, for example, "Your ability to train people on databases," you can stress that in making your case for a higher salary.

Yes, there's a slight risk that asking these questions may make you sound insecure, but if you ask them in a confident tone, they'll probably just seem like questions you were curious about.

Getting the boss excited about you

Before starting the actual negotiation, you might spend a few minutes discussing the job. The goal is to get the employer excited about what you can do. It also gives you an opportunity to try to upgrade the job.

Popping the question

At the moment when the boss seems most enthusiastic about the prospect of your working for him, pop the question: "What's the highest salary you think is fair of me to expect?"

No matter what number he throws out, wait a second, then repeat the number questioningly — for example, "$45,000?" Then count to five in your head. If the employer feels the offer is low, he may perceive your silence as incredulity and raise the offer without your having to utter another word. If so, that's the highest income per second you'll ever earn.

If the salary offer is lower than those on your list of comparable salaries, say something like, "I'm not looking to make a killing. I just want pay that's similar to that of others who do my work." Then show your boss your list of comparable salaries and wait.

To keep the wait from feeling so agonizing, count to ten in your head. A better offer may be forthcoming.

If no better offer comes, calmly ask for 10 percent to 20 percent more than the minimum you'd accept: "Scrooge, I know you want to be fair. Looking at the comparables and what this job entails, don't you agree that $XX,000 is fair?"

Dear reader, I know it's scary to ask that, and that there is a tiny chance that the boss will say, "That's way over our budget. If you want that much, you'll be an unhappy employee if you took less. Thanks for your time." The vast majority of the time, though, your request will yield a better offer or at least make the employer feel he'd be getting a bargain if you came on board for the salary he originally offered you.

If you think the employer's offer is just barely acceptable, don't rush to close the agreement. It makes you seem desperate. At impasse, consider a statement like, "Why don't we put salary aside for a moment and talk about the benefits." Or if benefits are not at issue, say, "I think I need to take some time to think about this." (The "I think" gives the boss room to make another offer.) As I said earlier, however, a good argument can often be made for accepting the boss's second offer.

Negotiating with an employment agency

When an employment agency tells you how much a job pays, it may not be cast in stone. Aim for 75 percent of the *bill rate*. The bill rate is the amount that the employer is willing to pay for an employee, including the employment agency's fee. The agency may try to get you to work for 50 percent to 60 percent of the bill rate, pocketing the difference, but you often can do better — if you know what the bill rate is. Ask, and if the agency won't tell you, try the employer's human resource department.

Benefits

Benefits are particularly desirable because they're usually tax-free. Here are some unusual ones:

- Reporting to a higher-level or otherwise more desirable boss
- Moving expenses
- The opportunity to work at home at least one day a week
- Reimbursement for education (that training course in Hawaii, for example)
- Flexible benefits: you can spend the dollars on whatever benefits you choose
- Tech stuff: a computer, laptop, or cell phone
- Association dues
- Health club memberships
- A company car
- A desirable office
- Your title
- The timing of your next salary review

Some employers are particularly likely to grant requests that benefit your family:

- Alternate work hours (so you can avoid the traffic or be home when your kids get home from school, for example)
- A job, or at least job counseling, for a family member
- That your vacations be timed to coincide with your children's vacations

Stock options

A *stock option* is the right, at some time in the future, to buy a share of the company's stock at a specified price. So if a share of stock is selling at $10, and you have the option to buy it at $5, you've made five bucks.

When negotiating for options, be sure you know the value of the options being offered. Try to get options with *current* value of 25 percent of your salary.

Of equal importance is the option's _strike price:_ the price at which you'd be able to buy shares. If the current share value is $2 and the strike price is $4, having the option to buy $2 shares for $4 is probably worthless — even if it goes up in the future, it's unlikely to double. Of course, the more bullish you are on the company's management, product, and funding, the more confident you can be that its stock price will rise.

Finally, be sure your vesting period is reasonable: you should be allowed to exercise 25 percent of your options after one year of employment and 25 percent more each year for the next three years. Occasionally, you can even negotiate for immediate vesting of some options, or that all your options become exercisable if the company is sold.

How much are those options worth? Get an estimate from Robert's Online Options Pricer: `www.intrepid.com/~robertl/option-pricer1.html`.

It is true that the few hundred people who got in on the ground floor of Yahoo! made zillions. But for every Yahoo! winner, countless employees of other companies feel like yahoos, holding stock options that are worth zippo, nada, zilch. Stock options are like lottery tickets. They're good to have but not worth giving up salary for.

The days of the handshake agreement are pretty much gone. So, at the end of the negotiation, offer to write a note summarizing the terms of agreement. She who writes the agreement gets the gray areas.

Twelve things every negotiator must know . . . and most don't

Here are my favorite under-the-radar negotiation strategies:

1. **Be your most confident self.** Both parties are scared in a negotiation, but if your counterpart smells your fear, it will cost you. To feel more confident, remember that if you turn the employer down, he must justify to his boss how he let you get away. And he'll have to live with his second-choice candidate.

2. **Sense if the boss is more fact- or emotion-driven,** and make your appeals accordingly. If the boss is mainly fact-driven, justify your salary requests with facts — for example, "I see three ways that I am likely to build the bottom line: _(Give them.)_" If your boss is emotion-driven, use feeling-based appeals such as, "I sense that we'd really get along, but I need to feel like I'm being paid fairly."

3. **Sense if the boss is fast-paced or slow-paced.** Do you sense that the boss wants you to get to the point or prefers a more leisurely approach? Act accordingly.

4. **Know how to respond to "How much are you looking to make?"** Answer: "I want to be paid fairly. What is the range you've budgeted for the position?"

   If you have to give a number, make it high but flexible. So if your research suggests that the position is worth around $50,000, say, "I'm looking to get a common salary for this sort of position, in the 50s."

5. **Know how to respond to "What's your current salary?"** If your current salary is below what you're hoping to get, chuckle and say, "Not enough! I was willing to accept that job as an investment in my future. What's the salary range that's budgeted for this position?"

   But what if your previous job *wasn't* an investment in your future? Let's say you were slinging hash for seven bucks an hour because you were still "finding yourself." You can honestly explain away even that: "I took an interim job to give me time to figure out what I really want to do. Now I've found it. What's the salary range budgeted for this position?"

   If your current salary is at market rate, say, "It's $XX,000, but to make a move, I need more than that."

   If your current salary is above market rate, just tell the boss your salary. If he blanches, calmly explain, "I was paid that because *(Insert two to three reasons why you're worth big money.)*"

6. **Use the power of being heard.** When the boss says something you don't like, start by restating her position. That lets her know you understand her stance. This is a great tool for all discussions, especially when fighting with a family member.

   For example, the boss says, "We're under real pressure to cut costs, so we can't pay anywhere near that much." Your response: "I understand. I know you have to keep your superiors happy, yet you want me to come aboard and feel okay about it. So what do you think is the most that the company can pay?"

7. **Should you make the first offer?** I used to always follow the traditional negotiation advice: Get your opponent to make the first offer. However, lately I've had successes making the first offer, 10 percent to 30 percent over my bottom line. On reflection, that makes sense. You come off more confident by saying, "I need $XX,000." than if you say, "Mr. Employer, what have you budgeted for the position?" Worst case, if the employer says, "No. Next candidate," you can always backtrack: "Depending on the position, I would take less." So don't be rule-bound. Decide, case-by-case, whether to make the first offer.

8. **Avoid making counteroffers.** If your boss makes an offer, say something like, "I can't accept that." Sometimes, that generates a better offer — without your having to reveal what you'd be willing to accept.

9. **Make a concession only if you get something in return.** To appear like a nice person, it may be tempting to give something away: "Okay, I'll give up *(insert concession)*." But that makes you seem desperate and can inspire the boss to get you to make other concessions without giving anything in return.

10. **Perhaps offer to do less for less money.** If the boss says that no more money is available, rather than lowering your salary demand, consider offering to work four days a week for 4/5 of your desired salary.

11. **Don't seem too pleased with a concession the boss makes.** Don't say, "Gee, that was great of you." Save the thank-yous for the end, at which point you might say something moderate such as, "Well, that seems fair. I look forward to working with you." If you're too gushy, it makes the boss feel he was too generous.

12. **Don't get caught up in the game.** The goal is a fair agreement, one that leaves both people feeling satisfied. If you manage to extract every last dime, you may cause resentment, which can hurt you more than the extra dough helps.

For each negotiating item, ask yourself, "Would King Solomon think it's fair of you to ask for this?" If yes, that builds your confidence in making the request. If no, drop it.

If you're self-employed

Not surprisingly, similar rules apply to self-employed persons.

✔ **Do your homework.** Ask what your customer has budgeted. Find out what your competitors charge. Check out if there's a public record of what they've paid for similar services in the past — common among government contractors.

✔ **Be at ease in talking about money.** Practice if necessary. Don't be too eager. Customers are more willing to pay a fair fee to people who are in demand. Generally, self-employed people charging by the hour can make only a middle-class living if they charge at least $75 an hour, more if they have high overhead. Here's why: From the $75, you must subtract taxes (usually 30 percent to 50 percent if you count federal, state, self-employment, disability, and so forth), liability insurance, cost of setting up and maintaining your office, travel time to clients, equipment, books, accounting fees, marketing costs, business license fees, training costs, vacations, sick leave, health insurance, and retirement. And don't forget: you probably can't bill 40 hours a week. Most small business owners must spend much time on nonbillable activities: marketing, administrative work, acquiring new skills and so forth. The average one-person business bills only for 10 to 15 days a month. You only want customers that will allow you to earn at least a middle-class income.

✔ **Get a concession for a concession.** If you must lower your price, reduce, in some way, what you're doing.

✔ **If your customer doesn't have a form contract, be the one to write up the agreement.** Get a written agreement, even if it's just a brief note or a purchase order. If there is a form, don't hesitate to negotiate its terms.

After the Negotiation

Puhleeze, before accepting the job, talk with people to find out about what it's really like to work there. Otherwise, you may find yourself miserable and looking for another job.

Learning about your new job

How to check out an organization? Talk with peers, prospective boss, and supervisees. Ask questions, such as

✔ Why did my predecessor leave?

✔ What does it take to be successful here?

✔ What's the best and worst things about working here?

✔ What should I know about this place that wouldn't appear in print?

✔ What sort of person is happiest here?

✔ What sort of hours are we expected to work?

✔ Is it expected that I'll ask for a fair amount of support, or am I expected to work pretty much on my own?

✔ Is the firm in growth mode, downsizing mode, or steady-state?

You may also want to use the research tools for learning about a company outlined in Chapter 14.

Nine signs of a job that's right for you

You angle for an extra thousand. You pitch for the chance to work a day per week at home. Amid all the machinations, it's easy to lose sight of what's really important in deciding whether to accept the job offer. These questions can bring things back into perspective:

✔ Will you find the work interesting?

✔ Does it use your skills?

✔ Is it an important job?

✔ Will you receive useful training?

✔ Will you enjoy working with the co-workers, especially your boss?

✔ Is the workload expectation reasonable? (including the commute)

✔ Is your workgroup likely to be in growth rather than downsizing mode?

✔ Are the salary and benefits fair?

✔ Does this organization make the world a better place?

If your answer to most of these questions is yes, congratulations! You've found a cool job.

Part IV
Customizing Your Career

The 5th Wave   By Rich Tennant

@RICHTENNANT

PSYCHIC
HOTLINE

NOW HIRING

"We don't care where you see yourself in five years, as long as you can see where our clients will be."

In this part . . .

You buy a suit. Off the rack, it probably looks just okay. To really look terrific, you need to tailor it and accessorize it. The same is true with your career. In this part, I show you how to customize an off-the-shelf career so you're maximally likely to be happy and successful. For example, I show how to get your assigned tasks changed so that they match your strengths.

Another way to customize your career is to be your own boss. In this part, Paul, Sarah, and I show you how to become successfully self-employed, even if you're not a born entrepreneur.

Chapter 18

30 Days to a Good Job

In This Chapter

▶ What to do, hour-by-hour

▶ Whom to contact

▶ What to say

▶ What to do when you have no experience

There are, of course, no guarantees. If you're ability-free and personality-impaired, your job search can take years. That's also true if your current job consumes 50 hours a week on top of wiping the noses of your two babies and one spouse. But for many people, finding a good job within 30 days is a realistic goal — if you spend those 30 days wisely. Here's how.

No single approach works for everyone, but this should be a reasonable model to work from. I've tried to keep things as simple as possible without impeding the effectiveness of your job search.

Before getting started, tell a good nudge (lover, mother-in-law, older brother, priest, rabbi, shrink, and so on) about this 30-day blitz. Then arrange to see your nudge at least every few days. The terror of answering that inevitable question, "Well??!?" will keep you on the program.

Day 1

8 a.m. Decide if you're going to do a *focused* or a *diffuse* job search. In a focused search, you identify a specific job target, for example, information miner for a dot-com located less than a half-hour from home. In a diffuse search, you're willing to accept a wider range of jobs, for example, any job within a half-hour's commute that requires good research skills.

8:10 a.m. Pull information from the Internet about your target industry or profession. You may want to start at www.wetfeet.com or www.vault.com. They provide free capsules on many industries and companies. Next, search on the industry's or profession's name using a top search engine such as www.google.com or www.ixquick.com. Find professional and trade associations' Web sites at http://info.asaenet.org/gateway/onlineassocslist.html. Find relevant online discussion groups at www.topica.com and www.liszt.com. Need more? A portal to industry information is at www.rileyguide.com/trends.html. Or search on your profession's name at www.amazon.com. You'll find books on your field. Plan on spending only an hour or two on all this research. More than that is usually overkill.

9:20 a.m. Create a resume using ResumeMaker (downloadable for $39.95 from www.resumemaker.com). Create two versions of your resume, one fully formatted for printing out and the other in plain text to paste directly into an e-mail or onto a job-hunting Web site. (I'll give addresses of those later.)

Note: Developing a resume is a few-hour, not a few-day activity. Some job hunters spend weeks primping their resumes when they could be doing the more productive job-search activities that I'll recommend. Just be sure to show a draft to a couple of respected reviewers before sending it out.

12ish: Lunch

1 p.m. Using the contact-tracking feature of ResumeMaker, list the name, main local phone number, and if available, the Web address of your 30 to 50 most desirable employers — the ones most likely to hire you for a job you'd gladly accept. Don't forget about nonprofits and government agencies. You'll need more names if you're looking at small organizations, fewer if you're looking at large ones.

There's a compendium of "best" employer lists at www.rileyguide.com/busrank.html. If the Internet and your Yellow Pages don't provide enough on-target employers, head to a public or college library with a good business section. The librarian can help you. In addition to responding to ads at these organizations' Web sites, you're going to try to get a hirer with these organizations to create a job for you or give you the inside track on an existing or upcoming opening.

If you're no superstar, and especially if you're trying to make a career change, you need to find hard-up companies — for example, those racing a new product to market or having just received a pile of venture capital — that need to hire NOW. How do you find those desperate firms? Sure, ask your network, but you can also scan print and online want ads to find companies advertising many positions, look at ads for job fairs — they list attending companies, and find mentions of fast-growing companies in newspapers, the *Business Times,* at startup sites such as www.startupzone.com and in trade publications.

3 to 5 p.m. Assuming you didn't have to go to the library, start gathering information on those 30 to 50 target employers. Use the organization's name as the search term on www.google.com or www.ixquick.com. You'll probably find the employer's Web site and other sites mentioning the employer. Again, avoid overkill. At this point, just get a bit of information on each organization. Of course, you'll want to enter it into your file on that company in ResumeMaker.

Day 2

8 to 11 a.m.

Continue with the research on your target organizations.

11 a.m. to noon

Create a cover letter. Make it short, simple, human, and honest. Sample letter:

> Dear Mr. Jameson,
>
> I'm a new college graduate with a liberal arts degree. People say that I'm a good problem solver and that I have excellent people skills.
>
> I'm looking for a place to start my career. I'm interested in working for your organization because: (Insert a sentence or two based on the company or industry research you did yesterday.) I imagine someone must have given you your first break. I'm looking for someone to give me mine.
>
> I enclose my resume. If you might need someone like me or would be kind enough to suggest where I can turn, I'd welcome a call. The best times to reach me are (insert times).
>
> Sincerely,
>
> Diane Woods

Noon to 1 p.m.: Lunch

1 to 5 p.m.

Phone each organization's main local number and say something like, "Hi, I'm updating my mailing list *(the contact tracker you created)*. What's the correct spelling of your marketing manager's *(or whoever you think would be your target boss)* name? And what's his or her direct-dial phone number? And their e-mail address? Can you connect me with *(insert the first name he gave you)*? If the switchboard operator asks what it's in reference to, explain that it's complicated and that you'd prefer to explain it to that manager or leave her a voice mail. When you get the hirer or her voice mail, say something like:

> Hello, Mr. XXXX, I'm a high school teacher who's doing well — my principal gives me top evaluations — but I'm ready to move on to a job where I can spend time with adults, not just teenagers. If you need someone who's quite able to explain things simply and is well organized, I'd love a call. My phone number is 510-555-7457. That's 510-555-7457. The best times to reach me are between 8 and 10 a.m. and 4 and 6 p.m. Thank you.

If you get the hirer on the phone, give the same sort of pitch. If he asks more than two questions (questions are signs of interest), say something like, "You know, it sounds like we may have something to talk about. I'd be pleased to come in so you can connect a face to the voice if you think it might be helpful." A face-to-face meeting increases your chances of getting a job. If the employer isn't interested in you, end the conversation by asking, "Is there someone else you think I should talk with, an event I should attend, or something I should read?

After each call, e-mail your resume, cover letter, or thank-you note as appropriate.

If your resume is likely to be weak in comparison with likely competitors for a job, don't send it. Just send a thank-you note. Here's a sample:

> Dear Mr. Johnson,
>
> Thanks for taking my call yesterday.
>
> I am pleased that you think my background is marketable. I do think that my year doing e-commerce marketing taught me a lot that would be valuable to an employer.

And, of course, I appreciated your willingness to keep your ears open for a position that may be appropriate for me.

I've already followed up on your suggestion that I contact Jamal Washington. I just called and left a voice mail.

Work aside, it was fun hearing about your new sailboat.

Best regards,

Harry Moskowitz

Day 3

8 to 11 a.m. Finish phoning your 30 to 50 target employers.

11 a.m. to noon

Again, using the contact tracker in ResumeMaker, create records for the 10 to 25 people most likely to know someone who can hire you for an acceptable job. This is your personal network. And yes, you do know 10 to 25 people. Think about your former employers, co-workers, friends, professors, lovers, relatives, family friends, family lawyer, accountant, doctor, and others, even the person who cuts your hair — haircutters chat with dozens of people each week.

Noon to 1 p.m.: Lunch

1 to 5 p.m.

Phone all 10 to 25 people in your network. Don't get out of your chair until you've had conversations with all of them — yes, voice mail counts. (And okay, I'll permit a few bathroom and coffee breaks.) Whether you get the person or voice mail, leave a message similar to the one I recommended (on Day 2) leaving on a target hirer's voice mail:

Hi Maria, this is Harry Moskowitz. I imagine I'm the last person you expected to be calling. Here's why I'm phoning. My job has become rather repetitious (or some other true but minimally denigrating reason why you're looking for another job). So, if you know a good company that needs an energetic e-commerce marketing person, I'd appreciate it if you'd pass their names along to me or even make a call on my behalf. And might you be willing to keep your ears open in case you hear of something?

Save the chitchat for the end of the conversation. If you start chatting up front, your motive for friendliness may be suspect. Also, by saving the small talk for the end, if your contact needs to cut short the conversation, you'll have already taken care of the important part of the conversation.

You should be able to complete 25 phone calls, including chitchat, by the end of the day: 20 three-minute voice mails (including dialing time) equals one hour. Five phone calls averaging 12 minutes equals one hour. Allowing a half-hour's worth of breaks during the afternoon brings you to just 3:30!

Today and during the next few days, from those 30 to 50 contacts with hirers and 10 to 25 with your personal network, you'll probably receive 5 to 15 returned phone calls. Right after you get a return call, send a thank-you note, and if you think it will help, your resume.

Day 4

8 a.m. to 10 a.m.

If you haven't done so already, finish sending the notes and resumes.

10 a.m. to 5 p.m. (with a break for lunch)

Hundreds of employment Web sites are on the Internet. Pick out a few on-target ones from this portal: www.rileyguide.com/jobs.html. Focus primarily on sites that are regional or specific to your field.

At each employment site, do one or more of these:

- ✔ **Search its job listings.** In minutes, you can screen truly fantastic numbers of ads by keyword and geography.

- ✔ **If the site offers a "job scout" service, sign up for it.** That will get you an e-mail notifying you whenever a new job is listed that meets your criteria. Talk about a lazy person's approach to landing a job!

✔ **Post your resume at the site.** Only post on sites that allow you to hide your identity — that way your boss won't know you're looking and unscrupulous headhunters can't broadcast your resume to millions of employers, which would make it 25 percent to 35 percent more expensive for any of them to hire you. That 25 percent to 35 percent may well be enough to motivate the employer to hire someone they unearthed themselves.

✔ **Blast your resume.** E-mail your resume to thousands of targeted job sites, employers, and recruiters for under $50 at www.resumeblaster.com or www.resumezapper.com.

Alas, the previous four steps are sometimes not as helpful as they may seem. This is especially true for career changers and for people fresh out of school. No one should put all their job search eggs in those baskets. You should also do the other things I recommend in this chapter.

Day 5

8 a.m. to noon

Respond to on-target want ads in local newspapers and trade publications. Your cover letter should include a section with two columns: On the left side, list the job requirements; on the right side, explain how you meet each requirement.

Don't waste your time responding to ads for which you don't meet most of the qualifications. Few employers go through the cost and hassle of openly advertising a job if they were willing to accept someone who lacks a third of the stated qualifications. If an employer were *that* flexible, he'd probably have hired his cousin, Rufus.

Noon to 1 p.m.: Lunch

1 to 5 p.m.

If you're seeking a job for which you have previous experience, contact a recruiter, also known as a headhunter. To find an appropriate one, visit www.recruitersonline.com/match/search.phtml or call the human resources department of a target employer and ask, "I'm looking to submit my resume to a recruiter for a *(insert type of job)* position. When you use one to find that type of employee, who do you use?" Don't consider a recruiter who asks you for money — the fee should be paid by the employer.

If you're looking for an entry-level position or are a career changer, forget about headhunters. You may, however, spend an hour or two contacting employment agencies. Look in your Yellow Pages to find on-target ones. Again, if they ask you for money, hang up. The employer should pay the agency.

Unlike other cover letters, include your salary requirement in a cover letter to an agency or headhunter. State it as a range such as "$48,000 to $58,000 depending on the nature of the position." You also need to explain that you don't want your resume sent to an employer without your permission. If it was an employer you were planning to contact anyway, it's better if you contact them directly — if the agency does it, the employer has to pay a fat fee.

Day 6

Make follow-up phone calls to all employers to which you sent written material. Whether you get voice mail or a person, say something like, "I'm Harry Moskowitz. I'm the e-marketing specialist who phoned and then sent you a resume last week. I'm just calling to follow up to be sure you received it — I know how things can get buried. If you haven't received it or would like to talk with me, the best times to reach me are between 8 and 11 a.m. and 2 and 5 p.m. My phone number is 510-555-3434. That's 510-555-3434. Thanks."

Days 7 to 28

Continue to respond to on-target want ads, both those in the newspaper and those sent to you by the electronic job scouts you signed up for.

Twice a week, revisit any other employment sites that had on-target listings the last time you were there.

Of course, follow up on any callbacks from your personal network or the dream employers you tried to get to create a job for you or tout you for an upcoming opening.

You know your job search is on track if you have at least six live prospects. That means, for example, someone who doesn't have a job opening now but asks you to check back in a month.

If you've done what I suggest on days 1 through 6, you should have lined up multiple interviews on days 7 through 28. Tips for job interviews:

- Before the interview, go back and more thoroughly research that employer. If it's a public company, go to the Wall Street Research Net (www.wsrn.com), enter the company's name, and instantly, you'll get links to valuable information from dozens of sources. If it's a private company or other type of organization, call the receptionist, explain that you have an interview scheduled and wondered if there's any printed material about the organization that's not on its Web site that could help you prepare.

- With a company, you may also ask to speak with a salesperson — they're often forthcoming. Explain that you're interviewing for a job and want to find out a bit more about the company so you don't come off like a dunce. Ask questions such as: "What's the company known for? Is there anything I should know about the company that wouldn't appear in official publications? Any idea about what the company is focusing on these days?"

- Have a few PAR stories ready: A *p*roblem you faced at work, how you *a*pproached it, and its positive *r*esolution.

- Early in the job interview, ask a question or two that helps guide your responses throughout the interview, such as: "What attributes end up being most crucial on this job?" or "What's an important task I'm likely to be asked to do in the first few weeks on the job?"

- Ask if the job description has been fully mapped out or if it depends on the candidate. If it's the latter, it's a golden opportunity: Play consultant and see if you can identify employer's problems that you could solve. That could encourage the employer to recast the job description in your own image.

Some employers, especially in unionized environments, require all candidates to receive the identical interview, so you may not be allowed to ask questions until the end. Don't force it.

- Especially if your job history suggests that you are underqualified for the job, try to move the discussion away from your past and on to what you might be asked to do on the job. Explain how you might tackle those tasks.

- E-mail a thank-you note the same day.

- Follow up three days later, saying something like, "I'm quite interested in the job, so I'm calling to follow up. May I ask where I stand?" If it isn't number one, ask if there's anything that makes them hesitant to hire you. Offer to submit additional material, for example, a short proposal outlining how you'd address a problem the organization is facing.

Days 29 and 30

Negotiation. When you get the call offering you a job, don't negotiate terms on the phone. Make an appointment for a day or two later. That subtly makes clear that you won't accept just any offer. If you've done all the preceding steps, chances are you have multiple irons in the fire. That improves your negotiating position. Prepare for the negotiation by creating a list of comparable salaries for the position. You can often get these from `www.rileyguide.com/salary.html`, from trade publications, or from local employment agencies that specialize in your field.

No one model works for everyone, but having worked with 1,500 clients, I've found that this chapter's approach helps the most people land a good job quickly.

Secrets to a Smooth Career Change

Because so many of this book's readers don't have previous experience in their target jobs, I want to be sure that they have a step-by-step approach outlined just for them, all in a couple of pages. Here it is.

You're a new college graduate. Or you're a teacher and you want to go into high-tech sales. Or you're a high-tech salesperson who wants to become a teacher. How do you convince an employer to hire you rather than someone with prior experience in the field?

- Take a crash course so you sound knowledgeable about the field: visit Web sites, read a book and articles, attend a seminar.

- If you were a good term paper writer in school, try this. To demonstrate your interest in and knowledge of your desired job, don't just rely on a cover letter and resume. The resume simply documents your lack of experience. Consider writing a short paper — for example, "Thoughts on what it takes to be a great TV news reporter."

    Of course, no matter how much you learn before getting hired, you're not going to be fully competent in your target job — after all, it's a new field for you. That's okay. Be honest with employers about what you can and can't yet do. Someone will give you an entry-level job.

- Think about all the abilities and experiences you've had in previous work — paid and unpaid — that may help you do your target job well. Stress all of that in your inquiries about a job.

- Spend only a small fraction of your job search time responding to want ads. If an employer were willing to hire someone with no experience, he wouldn't have wasted his time and money placing an ad and screening a zillion resumes. He would have hired his wayward sister.

✔ Forget about using recruiters/headhunters. Companies pay headhunters big bucks, but they won't pay that for a candidate without any experience.

✔ Focus your job search on these four methods (concentrating mainly on the first two):

- **Networking:** Make a list of the 10 to 25 people in your personal network most likely to know someone in a position to hire you. Pitch each of them: "I'm looking for an entry-level position in the environmental field that allows me to work outdoors and offers reasonable prospects for advancement. Know anyone in a position to hire me?" If not (probably), ask if they'd keep their ears open for you, and if in a month you're still looking, whether you can call back to follow up.

- **Cold-contacting 30 to 50 dream employers:** E-mail or phone them with a message that basically says, "Someone must have given you your first break. I'm looking for someone to give me mine. I have been a *(insert current employment or that you've been a student)*, and I'm now looking for a job to begin my new career. My dream job would be *(insert something like, "An opportunity to help the environment in which I use my ability to deal well with people and to be organized")*. I would deeply appreciate any advice you may have — not to mention a job offer!"

- **Employment agencies**. If you don't have personal referrals to good ones, pick out a half-dozen from the Yellow Pages of your phone book. Remember: never pay a fee — employers pay. Temp jobs offer you an opportunity to shop many employers to find one that fits you well. If you like a particular workplace, let the boss and others there know that you'd love to make it your permanent home.

- **New college graduates may also want to attend job fairs.** See Chapter 14.

✔ Please, please, expect negative responses to most of your inquiries. The response to your phone or e-mail query will likely be something like: "Sorry, we're not hiring." "We're downsizing." or "We need people with three years of experience." Even more often, you'll get no response. But enough hirers will respond positively to make it worth your while. Remember, you need only one good job offer.

✔ If you're interviewed, move the discussion from the past to the future. That means, instead of letting the interviewer focus on your background (which will highlight your lack of experience in the field), move the discussion to the future — ask about what it really takes to succeed on this job. Ask what sorts of tasks you'd be asked to do. If true, enthusiastically explain that you believe you can do them well.

Even better, if possible, *demonstrate* that you can do a key task — for example, for a sales position, demonstrate how you'd try to sell the product. If you're applying for a training position, demonstrate how you'd teach a concept. Providing a job sample can convince many employers that you're capable of doing the job even though you have no experience.

✔ If necessary, agree to be hired on a temporary basis, as an intern, or even as a volunteer, if only to help out during a brief crunch time. Try-before-you-buy reduces the employer's risk.

✔ Don't expect your first contact with an employer to lead to a job. Unless the employer is truly desperate, it is irrational for him to hire someone with no experience. The primary way you can get an employer to make an irrational decision is by building a relationship with him.

So if the hirer turns you down, ask, "If by chance I'm still looking in a month, would you mind my following up to see if you have heard of a lead for me?" Call back in a month re-explaining that employer is your dream employer. But don't burn yourself out. After three negative attempts with a hirer, the heck with him.

✔ Keep the faith. If you've followed these ten steps, you're miles ahead of most job seekers. You should land a cool job.

Chapter 19

Making Any Job Better

In This Chapter

▶ Molding the job to fit your strengths

▶ Optimizing your work environment

▶ Becoming a star without becoming a workaholic

▶ Staying fresh

▶ Moving up, moving out

Vou've completed the first two of the three steps to a satisfying work life: You've selected a career and you've landed a job in that career. Now I turn to what may be the most important step: making the most of that job.

How Chava Turned an Okay Job into a Cool Career

In previous episodes, Chava triumphed over the interview from hell in Chapter 16 and the salary negotiation with Scrooge in Chapter 17. Now, she tries to sculpt her okay job into a masterpiece.

Getting the lowdown

Before taking a chisel to her job, Chava needed to know what she was working with. She started by asking her Scrooge Online supervisor Kelly for information she might read about the company, for example, its strategic plan or a consultant's report. She also asked Kelly and co-workers: "Anything special I should know about how to succeed here? Who are the computer whizzes? Who are the veterans who really know the politics?" She asked customers, "Truthfully, how do we compare with our competitors?"

Starting the sculpture

After reflecting on what she learned, Chava came back to Kelly.

Chava: I want to get off on the right foot, so could you give me an idea of what you expect from me in these first few weeks?

Kelly *(a little embarrassed):* To tell you the truth, with all the other stuff I'm doing, I haven't had a chance to think much about it. *(A common condition among supervisors.)*

Chava: Well, in talking with Judy and Ping *(two of the other salespeople),* and in thinking about what I do best, I wonder if I might make a proposal. Your salespeople mostly do outside sales, but I'm best on the phone. On a trial basis, can I start half outside and half inside to see which works better?

Tailoring the job to your strengths greatly boosts your chances of liking your worklife.

Kelly: I'm worried that the other salespeople will resent that you get to stay inside while they have to traipse all over the city.

Chava: I trotted the idea by Ping and Judy, and they didn't object.

Kelly *(feeling magnanimous, as bosses tend to feel during a new employee's honeymoon):* Well, I'm not crazy about it, but go ahead and try it.

Chava: Here's an idea you might like better. I read the division plan you gave me and noticed that retailers are one of your target markets. As you know, I worked at Macy's before coming here. So can I get some retail accounts?

Kelly: That's no problem.

That was as much as Chava could ask for in one sitting, but she wasn't finished sculpting her job. Fast-forward a month.

Chava: I'm a little nervous you won't be thrilled with my next proposal, but I really want to ask you about it.

Kelly: Okay, I'm bracing myself.

Chava: Kelly, I'm a single parent with two kids. I'd love to be home when they come home from school. Can I do my by-phone sales work at home?

Kelly: Chava, I don't think so. If I let you do it, all the other parents will want to work at home too.

Chava: Maybe they should be allowed to, but at least with regard to the other salespeople, it's not an issue. They do outside sales, so they can't work at home.

Kelly: There's another reason I want to say no. I can't imagine you getting the same amount of work done with two kids pulling at you.

Chava: I can understand why you'd worry about that, but I know my kids and I know me. Can we try it for a few weeks? If my sales numbers are good, fine. If not, the experiment stops. That would make me very happy.

Kelly *(nervous about whether he's hired a problem, but feeling slightly stuck):* Well, we'll try it for one week, but I want an ongoing log of how you spend your time.

Chava: Deal. Thank you. The bottom line won't suffer, I promise, and my kids and I will love you!

Kelly: Well, is that all? Next you'll want the penthouse office.

Chava *(grinning):* That's next week. For today, the last thing is something I think you won't find objectionable. I'd like to do some extra work.

Kelly: Now you're talking my language.

Chava: Could I assemble a booklet of tips and tricks that the salespeople have used successfully? That will teach me a lot, it will help me get to know the other salespeople, and maybe I'll create something that will help everyone.

Chava also picked that project because it's something she can point to at promotion time and something she'd find fun.

I can hear you protesting, "Doesn't that force Chava to do extra work for no pay? She was hired to be a full-time salesperson, and now in addition, she's taking on this big project." Chava was too savvy to fall into that trap. She looked for places to cut corners. She did the minimum paperwork and got a college intern to make cold calls to generate warm leads. She also avoided being roped into low-payoff activities such as chairing the holiday party committee. Chava knew where to focus her efforts: on the things that are both important and fun. As you'll see, she also recruited an all-star support team that made her life easier.

Kelly: Sounds okay. Write me a one-pager outlining what you plan to do.

Chava: Fine. Can we meet for a few minutes each week until we're both comfortable that I'm on track?

Kelly: Okay, as long as you don't decide that next, you want a spa in the lounge.

Chava: Only a masseuse. Oh, and between meetings, if you have any feedback for me, please let me know.

Kelly: Okay, Chava. Good-bye.

Chava used up a few chits with Kelly, but it was worth it. She took that piece of marble called an off-the-shelf job and already has done a lot to sculpt it in her own image.

Recruiting her all-star team

Chava's next order of business was to cultivate relationships with people she could call on for assistance: knowledge gurus to help with technostuff; wise old souls to help her craft strategies for getting her ideas implemented and making sure she gets credit for them; plus fun folks — she recognized that all work and no play makes for a dull Chava. A company's all-stars usually are in demand by many people, so Chava knew she needed to do things to curry their favor. So, early on, she asked key players out for lunch, stopped by to say hello, and heaven forbid, even flirted a little.

Staying fresh

Sales can feel as repetitious as emptying a full swimming pool with a bucket. So Chava knew she needed to add variety to her job. Of course, there was her salespeople's tips and tricks booklet, but she did more. For example, she figured out how to incorporate her photography hobby into her job — she took her camera on sales calls and asked her customers if she could photograph them for the collage on her office wall. She promised to send customers copies of their pictures. Every one wanted a picture taken, and you can bet that the picture, an ongoing pleasant reminder of Chava, didn't hurt her sales numbers.

Another key to staying fresh is to keep learning. Wisely, Chava didn't focus on improving her weaknesses. For example, she is a poor reader. Many people would work on that. But Chava recognized that if she was a weak reader after 16 years of schooling, it's unlikely that more reading instruction would help much. Instead, Chava took additional sales training — something she was naturally good at and therefore more likely to profit from.

She was too busy for college-based courses, so she did her learning the efficient way. In the car, when she didn't feel like vegging out, she listened to Tom Hopkins' tapes on how to sell. A social animal, Chava joined an association of Internet ad salespeople. At the local chapter's get-togethers, she traded war stories and found out what works and what doesn't. Her membership also got her monthly newsletters, which, alas, soon started to pile up. Well, you can't do everything.

Moving up

Chava didn't want to turn into Willy Loman, unhappily selling until she dropped. So she did what was necessary to be promoted. Her mantra: **Even if you're a clerk, think like a CEO.** That means keeping your antennae out for big ideas: a new profit center, a way to streamline a process, or a method to make workers' lives easier. So Chava frequently asked questions of co-workers, customers, and suppliers, finding out what was working and what wasn't. And she brainstormed solutions, which she found to be fun.

Some bosses try to steal workers' ideas but not from Chava. When she came up with an important idea or special work product, she'd first run it by a trusted colleague to make sure it wasn't stupid. Then she'd "ask for feedback" either at a staff meeting or by broadcasting an e-mail message. That way, everyone knew the brainchild was hers.

Moving out

Despite doing everything right, promotions sometimes just don't come. The company may be in downsizing mode, the bosses could be too entrenched, the chemistry between you and management may be wrong. Chava knew that the world has changed — patience, with regard to promotions, is no longer a virtue. After a year in sales for Scrooge Online, Chava was starting to feel stale, and despite doing everything right, when she asked about a promotion to sales manager, all she heard were hollow noises: "You're doing really well, Chava. Give it another year and I could see you getting promoted." She looked around and saw that almost no one was moving up. The company's sales figures were stagnant. She was not at the right place at the right time.

Chava's response was to announce to her friends at the Internet ad salesperson's association that she was ready to move out and up. She also whipped out e-mailed queries to senior managers at competitors' companies. It was easy to impress them because, thanks to those special projects she always was cooking up, Chava could prove that she was no run-of-the-mill salesperson. Within two weeks, she got a sales manager job offer. Good-bye, Scrooge Online.

Chava took her off-the-shelf job and sculpted it into quite a piece of work.

Seven Steps to Making the Most of Your Job

Most people who love their jobs appreciate seven things about it:

- ✔ A good boss and co-workers
- ✔ Work that isn't too hard
- ✔ Work that's interesting
- ✔ A moderate quantity of work
- ✔ Moderate stress
- ✔ Winning at office politics
- ✔ Fair salary

Chapter 17 covered salary. This section shows how to maximize your chances of having the other six.

Making the most of your boss (and co-workers)

Do you change readily? Neither do bosses. So it's best if you can start out with a good one. How to maximize your chances of that? Job search vigorously so you get multiple job offers and can pick one with a good boss. Other chapters in this book urge you to ask questions during the interview and after being offered the job to avoid the clinkers. But let's assume it's too late for all that.

And let's assume it's the worst case: You've been assigned to the boss from hell. Even if it's your first day on the job, if even a remote possibility for a better option exists, request the transfer right away. It's often easier to change bosses before everything is cast in stone.

No dice? Try these fixes for dealing with a bad boss or making the most of a good one.

✔ **Train your boss.** Yes, in the first week or two, you may need to work longer hours to get up to speed. But as soon as possible, try to get down to a workweek you're willing to sustain. If, in the beginning, to impress your boss, you work 70-hour weeks and later start to slow down, your boss may think you've lost interest in the job. Occasionally, we all have to give up an evening or weekend, but if you want moderate work hours, start conditioning your boss to accept that early on. Compensate by keeping her aware of all your accomplishments.

✔ **Give your boss a suggestion or two for tailoring the job to fit you.** Do you think any of the following can make your life better?

- **A revised job description that capitalizes on your strengths and minimizes your weaknesses.** For example, a programmer who's good at troubleshooting but lousy at design may offer to trade roles with another programmer who's the opposite.

- **A piece of equipment.** An architect's life can be made easier by getting his own CAD terminal.

- **Changed work hours.** Working from 7 a.m. to 3 p.m. instead of 9 to 5 avoids traffic jams and allows you to watch your kid's Little League games.

- **Autonomy.** A manager at a dot-com got permission to take full charge of a new part of the site, from design to marketing.

- **A new challenge.** A biotechnician got the okay to use a cutting-edge technique for his next experiment.

- **More feedback.** Feedback junkies enjoy being kept apprised of how they're doing.

- **More time in the field or in the office.** A salesperson was supposed to spend most of his time in the field, but on many appointments, felt unprepared. So he requested more time in the office to learn more about his client before the appointment. It was granted.

- **Change who you work with**. A manager had worked well with an employee in another unit. She got that person transferred to her department.

Developing excellent communication skills

Are you trying to get something from your boss (or co-worker or lover)? Needing to get out of trouble? Communication skills are key. Most people think they're terrific communicators — but few actually are. These tips may help:

✔ **Learn your boss's decision-making style**. It boils down to two questions: Is she fact-driven or emotion-driven? Fast- or slow-paced? Respond accordingly. If you have a slow-paced, emotion-driven boss, you'd be foolish to barge into his office saying, "Hi, Al. If we do A, B, and C, I think we can generate big bucks. Whaddya think?" Yet the same approach can work with a fact-driven, fast-paced boss.

✔ **Curious, not convince.** When you're annoyed with your boss (or a co-worker, or a loved one), it's tempting to try to convince them of the error of their ways. Alas, that rarely results in future improvement. Think back to the last time you tried that. Did it help?

Here's a better approach. Rather than trying to *convince* the other person that he's screwed up, recognize there's usually another side to the story. So ask questions demonstrating your *curiosity* about that other side. Remember this mantra: *Curious, not convince.* Try starting your next tough talk with a sentence like, "I'm unhappy because *(insert perceived wrongdoing),* and I'm wondering if there's something I'm not understanding." Then really listen to the other person's perspective. That requires 100 percent of your attention — there's no room for judging or devising solutions. There's time later for solutions. When the person stops talking, and you sense more could be said, just wait, say "mm-hmm," or ask a question that encourages him to say more.

✔ **When your protagonist makes an accusatory statement, paraphrase it back.** Doing that shows that you've really heard it, forces you to better understand his perspective, and usually serves as a more helpful response than your first instinct: "You jerk!" So when he says, "You've been slacking off," you might respond with, "I can understand why you'd think that. I *have* been taking long lunches." Then, he may be more open to hearing your explanation, for example, "I've been having a hard time working in this room with all the noise. So, from noon to 2, I've been going to a coffee shop to work. I get a lot more done. Can I show you what I've been accomplishing?"

✔ How do you feel when someone says, "You should do XXXX"? Chances are, your internal reaction is, "No!" Few of us like to be told what to do. The key to getting someone to change is to try to **get him to come up with a solution.** Ask questions that make that possible, such as: "So it sounds like our inventory database is causing the problem. Any sense of what should be done?" If your counterpart gets stuck, and you want to propose a solution, say, "Jane, would you mind if I suggest something?" Getting his permission makes him more likely to feel some ownership of the idea.

✔ **Conclude by asking the other person to summarize what's been agreed to** and, if true, by thanking him for making a difficult conversation easier.

If the boss is a hothead

Don't take it personally. The louder she yells, the sorrier for her you should feel, but don't dismiss everything she says. Just because the tone is off-putting doesn't mean the feedback is invalid. Try to judge what's said on its merits and not its tone. If you want to discuss a criticism with a hothead, be sure to use those excellent communication skills.

If you find yourself continually having to endure tirades or passive-aggressive attacks, get a transfer or quit. You deserve better.

If your boss is a micromanager

Use a Zen approach. Fight back by not resisting. Keep your boss as informed as possible. For example, offer to e-mail him an update each day. There's a decent chance that after your boss sees that you're someone he can trust, he'll redirect his micromanaging to less trustworthy types. And remember, sometimes a supervisor micromanages because you do need a lot of guidance. Before resenting the close supervision, ask yourself whether you might benefit from it.

If the boss is lazy or incompetent

You won't change these. Work hard at accepting her as she is. Just as you wouldn't be furious at a developmentally disabled child's inability to perform, you must react that way with an incompetent or lazy boss. As you plan, of course, don't count much on her. Ask only for the most crucial things. If you need support, look for it elsewhere.

Keeping your job interesting

Sometimes, all you need is a **special project.** During a tour of my friend Pat's house, I noticed a wall of awards she had received from her various employers. I asked her, "What's the secret of your success?" not really expecting an answer. To my surprise, she offered one: "On every job, I propose a special project that I'd find fun and that would please my boss." What project could you propose that would inject some pleasure into that humdrum job of yours?

No time for an additional project? See if you can make a lateral move. A biologist had spent years on karyotype analysis but saw that another division of the company was working on a cool mouse gene project. He pitched his boss and the mouse-project boss, and got his transfer into a whole new job. *Note:* You're more likely to get to do new work within your current organization, where you're trusted. An outside employer is likely to hire you to do what you've been doing.

More often than you might think, you can **incorporate your hobby into your job**. Ann Flexer, who works at the Edelweiss jewelry store in Berkeley, California, plays the guitar when business is slow — it passes the time while attracting customers. Way back when I was a teacher, I felt out of place with the mostly female faculty. In the break room, conversation typically centered around such matters as Cuisinarts and toilet training — not high on my interests list. One of my hobbies is breeding roses. One day, I brought a bouquet into the faculty room to the oohs and ahhs of the teachers. From then on, I brought in a fresh arrangement each week. Before long, I developed a reputation as the school romantic and became a favorite of the teachers and the principal. Can you think of a way of incorporating a current or past hobby into your worklife?

Build cool avocations into your after-work life. One of my clients, a Fortune 500 manager, during his lunch hour, works on a screenplay he hopes to sell to Hollywood. Another client takes an hour during most workdays to hit a bucket of golf balls. "It makes me feel like I have a great job — I can go to the driving range in the middle of the day."

Keeping the workload moderate

Your perfectly good job can become miserable in a hurry when there's too much work or it's too hard. Here are ways to cut your workload down to size:

- ✔ **Use the one-minute struggle.** Rarely does struggling with a problem for more than a minute result in a solution. It usually results in more frustration. So when you reach a roadblock, struggle for no more than one minute. At that point, decide that your imperfect solution is good enough, that you need help, or that you can complete the project without solving that problem.

- ✔ **Adjust your quality standards to suit the task.** Ask yourself whether you're doing some of your tasks too perfectionistically.

- ✔ **Find an intern.** You're already managing time well: you prioritize, you try to be efficient, you even caved in and bought a Palm. Yet you rarely catch up. One solution: an intern. Have him do tasks you dislike but aren't too routine — that would be unfair to the intern. After clearing it with your boss, post a position announcement at a local college's internship office.

- ✔ **Ask the most efficient person you know to watch you work** for a half-hour and then have her offer suggestions for how you can improve.

- ✔ **Get your job tasks realigned.** Once you've done this, you spend maximum time using your strengths and minimum time using your weaknesses. A lawyer was great at drafting documents but a paralyzed wimp in the courtroom. He arranged to trade tasks with another of the firm's lawyers who was the opposite.

Learning the smart way

Staying current keeps you competent, confident, and increases your employability. But with the information explosion, staying current isn't easy. Before going back to school for a course, let alone a degree, see if these just-in-time learning approaches can help:

✔ **The Hey Joe School.** When you're stuck, simply ask someone in your office, or by phone, "Hey Joe. How do I . . . ?" This simple approach can be powerful. Unlike in a class, where you're amassed with information with no real-world opportunity to apply it, at the Hey Joe School, you learn what you need when you need it.

Most organizations have experts at various things — for example, the computer wizard or the nut who can recite all your company's product specifications in his sleep. Because they're so good, they're likely in demand. If you expect them to return your phone call within the decade, go out of your way to help them when you can. And when they help you, a thank-you note or little present doesn't hurt.

✔ **The tutor.** For most people, the best way to learn something complicated, such as a computer program, is not a course but a tutor. Who might tutor you? A savvy co-worker in your office, a community college instructor interested in moonlighting, someone from www.tutor.com. Set up your tutoring this way: Keep track of all your questions and use that as the basis for the next tutoring session. Ask if you can call your tutor for help in-between sessions.

✔ **The mentor.** Find a respected person in your field and agree that you can call for counsel. Or create an online version: Form an e-mail group with colleagues in which each member can post questions for the group's consideration. Simple software for such a group is available free on www.egroups.com.

✔ **The article.** Articles are wonderful — they offer condensed expertise on virtually any topic at minimal cost and requiring minimal time. And thanks to search engines such as www.google.com, article archives such as www.factiva.com, or links from your professional association's Web site, it's easy and fast to find on-target articles.

✔ **The book.** How terrific to have a large quantity of an expert's best thoughts, available 24/7 for the cost of a large pizza, or free from the library. And you can search Amazon.com's database of 3,000,000 books to find precisely the title you're looking for, often including reviews by readers and experts.

✔ **The electronic discussion group.** Of the hundreds of thousands of electronic discussion groups, almost assuredly, at least one is related to your career. Use www.topica.com or www.liszt.com to find the best fits.

✔ **The workshop.** Professional associations and university extension programs put on workshops that focus on the basics or cutting-edge issues. Ask your colleagues which workshops they've found most useful. For online databases of seminars, check www.alx.org, www.seminarfinder.com, and www.seminarinformation.com.

✔ **Certifications.** In thousands of specializations, you can earn a respected certification by taking a few courses or via self-study. Find on-target certifications at America's Learning Exchange (www.alx.org) and Brainbench (www.brainbench.com).

✔ **How good of an employee are you, really?** I have counseled hundreds of fired employees. Barely a handful said it was their fault. My sense is that many of them had good self-esteem but in fact were weak employees. Could you be one of them? A way to find out is a *360-degree evaluation:* asking people all around you (for example, boss, supervisee, peer, customer, vendor), "As part of my professional development, I'd like some feedback. What would you say are my strengths and weaknesses?" It is scary to request a 360-degree evaluation but perhaps less scary than a stalled career.

✔ **The world's fastest self-improvement strategy.** On your refrigerator, desk, or computer monitor frame, write, "I need to stop (*insert something*). I need to start (*insert something*). I need to continue doing (*insert something*)." Every time you drink something, read those words aloud to keep your goals front and center.

✔ **Continual self-improvement . . . give me a break!** A client of mine says that he can be in ongoing improvement without being overwhelmed by remembering a Japanese car company's motto. Instead of, "How can I improve?" he asks, "How can I be just a little bit better?" Sometimes, I wonder whether we all deserve an even easier approach — giving ourselves a total rest from self-improvement. Is there not a point at which, at least for a while, we deserve to say, "I'm good enough!"?

Moderating your stress

Conserve your *emotional energy units*. You can often reduce your job stress by being conscious of how you expend your emotional energy units. Every day we start out with a full supply, but if we expend our energy units too rapidly, we're burned out before the end of the day. Susannah, a home health nurse, came to me complaining of burnout. On questioning, it was clear that most of her burnout was caused by just three of her 30 patients. Those three refused to cooperate and their families were unhelpful, often loudly drunk. I asked her to consciously try to conserve her energy units while visiting those patients. A few days later, Susannah called and excitedly told me that simple technique reduced her burnout enough that she no longer felt a need to change jobs.

As you feel stress, ask yourself, "Am I expending my energy units wisely?"

A deep breath or a stretch is an easy and fast way to reduce stress. I have a Post-it on the frame of my computer monitor that says, "Breathe. Stretch." I need the reminder.

In our ever-more-pressured workplaces, without a fun person to break things up, we can gyrate ourselves into whirling work dervishes. The funmeister offers badly needed respites: a joke he pulled off the Internet, gossip about who's seeing whom, or a recipe for Last-Request Chocolate Cake. **Recruit a funster** onto your all-star support team.

Many people feel less stress if they **have an attractive workspace**. Even all cubicles aren't alike. Want one near the window with the view? Far from the elevator? Near the chatterboxes? Away from them? Even if your cube is run-of-the-mill, would your job feel a bit less stressful if you decorated it to suit you? I recall one cubicle with an Oriental rug on the floor and oil paintings on the walls.

My favorite stress-buster: **Get permission to bring your dog or cat to work.** Fourteen of Vermont's Small Dog Electronics' employees bring their pets to work. And to boot, the employer pays 80 percent of their veterinary insurance. Workers and management rave: Not withstanding the occasional piddle, flea visitation, and dog-phobic employee, pets at work reduces stress, increases employee loyalty, and saves employees the time and cost of a pet sitter. Pet perk — a great idea. www.dogfriendly.com lists hundreds of employers with pet-friendly policies. See if your boss will bite.

Be in the moment. When writing my first book, I focused on getting it done. I lived for the moment when I could see the book finished. That looking-forward orientation gave me one moment of pleasure but deprived me of thousands of good moments during the writing process — most work is filled with many little interesting problems to solve. Since then, I strive to stay *in the moment,* trying to derive pleasure in whatever I'm doing that minute. I find that makes work less stressful . . . sometimes.

Making the most of telecommuting

Of course, many people wouldn't want to work at home. They'd miss the office chitchat, find it too tempting to goof off, or discover they live next door to someone who practices the drums all day.

For many others, though, telecommuting, for at least part of the week, reduces stress enormously. I work at home, and I work relaxed — no worry about someone looking over my shoulder. And I am much more efficient. When I used to work in an office building, I was faced with nonstop meetings and interruptions such as "Let me tell you about my daughter's sweet sixteen." Now, when I want to work, I work. And when I want to socialize, I chat on the phone or invite someone to lunch. Between clients, I get to play the piano or with my cat. My normal writing attire: underwear. Try that in an office! I don't have to waste time getting dressed for success — unless you call Jockey shorts and uncombed hair dressed-for-success — and I have a ten-second commute.

Here are keys to keeping your boss and yourself happy as you merrily work at home:

- ✓ **Reassure your boss.** Many bosses are control freaks. They're afraid that if you're out of sight, your work will be out of mind. They have visions of you sleeping 'til noon, watching soaps 'til 3, and squeezing in a smidge of work before your kids come home at 3:30. Offer to document how you used your time to stop her from losing sleep over that sybaritic lifestyle she thinks you're living on company time.

  Remind your boss that he's saving on office space and that you'll be a more effective employee now that you can start work each day without hours worth of makeup, hair-doing, and a draining commute. Besides, he'll have an employee who's happier, and therefore less likely to bolt for a job paying a few pesos more.

- ✓ **Set limits.** Your boss may at least be partly right. Work at home and there are endless temptations: morning tennis, housecleaning, a call to your girlfriend, and, yes, the refrigerator — telecommuting can be a diet killer. And, of course, there's the biggest impediment to a successful telecommuting day: kids. If you have young children, it may be worth getting childcare so you can work in peace.

- ✓ **Be your own OSHA inspector.** In most workplaces, especially larger ones, the employer takes steps to ensure an ergonomically reasonable workplace. Telecommuters also are entitled to one. Be sure your chair is adjustable, the keyboard is placed so your wrist needn't strain, and if you use the phone much, you have a headset. Yeah, I know they look dorky, but they feel wonderful.

- ✓ **Try to get compensation for telecommuting.** If you're working at home, your employer saves office space, furniture, utilities, phone, computer costs, and so on. Why should you have to pay for that?

- ✓ **Stay in the loop.** Telecommuters often are passed over for promotions — out of sight, out of mind. Especially if you're telecommuting more than a day a week, be sure to stay in the loop — phone and e-mail colleagues frequently, and don't miss the company picnic.

For a portal to articles about telecommuting, see `telecommuting.about.com`.

Winning at office politics

Employees often complain, "I can't take the politics," when they really mean, "I can't win at the politics." Here's a top-ten list for keeping your star rising and your back unstabbed.

1. **Be powerfully placed.**

   Here's the ideal: You're in a department that's central to the organization, well-funded, involved with a core or hot product, and led by a rising star boss. If not, can you angle for a transfer?

2. **Get tasks that are high-priority and visible.**

3. **Even if you're a clerk, think like a CEO.**

   Think of a way to streamline a procedure, build the bottom line, or make employees' lives easier.

4. **Don't wink in the dark. Cautiously self-promote.**

   To get ahead, higher-ups must know how good you are. How do you let them know without press releases? Career coach Kate Wendleton recommends having a one-sentence message ready. For example, when your boss's boss sees you in the elevator and asks, "How are you, Sam?" instead of the usual, "Fine, Ms. Moneybags, how are you?" occasionally try something like, "Great. I just closed a deal with Astrogel." As writer Angela Durden says, when you work hard without promoting yourself, "it's like winking at a girl in the dark — you know what you're doing, but no one else does."

   Be sure no one takes credit for your brainchild. When you come up with a good idea or have drafted an impressive document, run it by a trusted colleague to be sure it isn't stupid. If it passes muster, bring it up at a staff meeting or e-mail the staff "to get feedback" on the idea. That way, everyone knows the gem was yours.

   Don't rub your good work in co-workers' faces, especially those of weak employees. They can be saboteurs. Instead, keep a record of everything good you do — useful at salary review time or if enemies try to build a case against you.

5. **Make your boss look good.**

   Support him where you can. When you do a project, be sure to give due credit for your boss's assistance.

6. **Use those keys to excellent communication** (described earlier in the chapter).

7. **Get feedback.**

   Ask co-workers how you're doing. Anything they wish you'd improve? Early feedback gives you time to fix things before you're a marked person.

8. **Befriend a wise old soul.**

   It really helps to have a confidante who knows the political ropes. Often these wise old souls no longer are interested in climbing the ladder, but instead enjoy playing an avuncular role, passing on words of wisdom to the next generation.

9. **Make friends in low places.**

   Often, employees such as receptionists and janitors know what's going on, and may be more likely than higher-ups to give you the inside scoop.

10. **Perform non-random acts of kindness.**

    Bake cookies for the office, look for legitimate reasons to compliment others, or throw a TGIF office party. Not only will doing such things help you politically, you'll enjoy your job more.

The survivor scenario

All that is well and good, but in the real world, even if you play positive politics perfectly, employees can gang up on you: They may be threatened by you or dislike you, if only because you dress funny. Let's say that, as in the *Survivor* TV series, three officemates decide, if only subconsciously, to form an alliance against you. They do plenty to make you look bad: keeping you out of the information loop, never supporting your proposals, not prioritizing getting your project done, never offering to help you. And they bad-mouth you: "That Chava. She really gets more credit than she deserves." And if you dare show even a hint of frustration with them, they run to your boss complaining that you have a bad attitude that is destroying office morale. Even though you're a good employee, you can see that their machinations can get you kicked out of the Outback. What should you do?

Assuming you prefer not to quit, in addition to positive politics strategies:

- ✔ **Store your ammunition.** Keep a list of everything you've done to try to build relationships with alliance members — from helping them out when they were overworked to those brownies you bring in. Brownies are potent political weapons.

- ✔ **Try to neutralize your enemies.** Ask them about things they're interested in, take coffee breaks with them, and so forth.

- ✔ **If those tactics fail, *gently* confront the group.** Convene a formal meeting with them. Recount your efforts to work well with them. Ask what *you* can do to improve the office environment. Don't expect them to offer to change anything. That's okay. Often, over the next few weeks, they'll cool down. Don't threaten to go to the boss; it's implicit that you might, and making it explicit can motivate them to go to the boss first. That could force you onto the defensive.

✔ **If that fails, have one of your powerful allies intervene.** Perhaps your wise old soul or other respected employee can gently let the alliance know that top management likes you, and that if they continue to mess with you, they — not you — will suffer.

✔ **If that fails, go to your boss, perhaps with your ally.** Show your documentation of your peacemaking efforts, and if necessary, evidence of your on-the-job accomplishments.

✔ **If that fails, decide that you can accept the status quo or go to your boss's boss.** This rarely works, so you should also start looking for a new job.

Will You Get Ahead?

Up isn't the only way. In fact, many higher-ups wonder if the extra salary is worth the extra headaches. But for many people, getting ahead is a way to make a career better. How likely are *you* to get ahead? After you've been in your new career for a few months, hopefully having followed the above principles, try this self-test. Or take it now to give you goals to shoot for. Many of these items are from a *Fortune* magazine inventory.

_____ 1. Compare your work with that of your peers. If you think you've added more value, give yourself 1-3 points. If you've been less productive, take away 1-3 points.

Can't figure out how valuable you are? Think about, or even ask, your peers, suppliers or customers, how much they value what you do.

_____ 2. Do you play a leadership role in tasks and projects central to the organization's success? If so, give yourself 1-3 points.

_____ 3. Do you perform a worker-bee task that is so crucial to the organization that they can't afford to promote you from there? If so, subtract 3-5 points.

_____ 4. If at least one of your suggestions for improving the organization has been adopted and you've gotten credit, give yourself 1-3 points.

_____ 5. If your organization or department is ripe for downsizing, subtract 1-3 points.

How do you know? Here are some clues:

• Your department's product stacks up poorly against others in the organization or among your competitors.

• Morale is low and office politics high.

• You're involved in cutting costs rather than building market share or creating new products.

———— 6. Are you known for your enthusiasm? Give yourself from minus 3 to plus 3 points.

———— 7. Do you have long-term career goals and specific strategies to achieve them? If so, give yourself 1-3 points.

———— 8. If you've already received a promotion, give yourself 4 points.

———— 9. Are you pampered? For example, if you still need a secretary to do your word processing, you look like a dinosaur and a high-maintenance one at that. Subtract 2 points.

———— 10. Do co-workers and bosses frequently seek your counsel? Give yourself 1-3 points.

———— 11. If your co-workers and bosses were polled, would at least three-quarters of them say they like you? Give yourself 3 points.

———— 12. Have you cultivated important allies in and outside your department? If so, give yourself 1-3 points.

———— 13. Do you regularly ask friends and colleagues for feedback on how you're doing? If so, give yourself 1 point. If, you've then improved, give yourself 2 more points.

———— 14. Are you actively upgrading your skills in areas valued by employers? If so, give yourself 1-2 points.

———— 15. Do you build your reputation by writing articles, speaking at industry events, or being active in your professional association? If so, give yourself 1-3 points.

———— 16. If you lost your job today, could you tap a network of people for advice and job leads? If so, give yourself 1-4 points.

———— 17. Do you have portable skills such as technical or management know-how? If so, give yourself 1-3 points.

———— 18. Listen to your boss during a performance review. If she talks to you about your role in the organization's big picture, give yourself 1-3 points.

———— 19. Is your boss's star rising or in a death spiral? Give yourself between +2 and -2 points.

———— 20. Do you dress like someone in the position to which you aspire? If so, give yourself between -2 and +2 points.

———— 21. If you were the boss, would you hire you? If yes, give yourself 3 points. If no, subtract 3 points.

———— 22. If you were the boss, would you promote you? If yes, give yourself 5 points.

Think twice before aspiring to management

In the past, it made sense to want to go from worker bee to manager, because it meant more money, prestige, and a launchpad to even more prestigious job titles. Things have changed. The hierarchy is flatter so fewer opportunities for promotion exist. Senior management demands ever more productivity at the same time as new laws make it tougher to fire incompetents. In the book *Gig*, Chad Finlay, a video game designer turned manager, said, "When I first got into games, you're making stuff and you get to read cool reviews about it . . . . Now I'm walking around, 'How's this going? Are you getting this done? I need this by Friday.' It got old."

When you're promoted to manager, your camaraderie with your former peers tends to decline. Your credibility with your former peers also is also likely to slide because it's hard to stay current when you're a manager. For example, few programmers have the time to keep up with the latest programming languages when their full-time job is now to manage other programmers.

Even more dangerous, management requires different skills than those required of worker bees. The Peter Principle often raises its ugly head — the great classroom teacher may not be a great principal.

And let's not forget about money. Managers usually work longer hours than worker bees, and because managers don't get paid for overtime, they often earn less per hour than the people they supervise! With a 40 percent to 60 percent marginal tax rate, the after-tax benefit of a promotion to management probably won't improve your lifestyle.

The final kibosh: At a time when most people wish they had more spare time, managers work long hours.

An often smarter move than aspiring to management: a lateral move to one of the company's cool areas.

A highly unscientific scoring system:

10 or less: You may be downsizing material. Is this a wake-up call to start working on some of the above items? Would you be more motivated to do so in a different job? In a different career?

10-25: You may be safe . . . for now.

25-35: Star potential

35-45: Superstar potential

46+: Send me your resume.

Chapter 20

The Six Musts of Successful Self-Employment

In This Chapter

▶ Taking the Self-Employment Test

▶ Finding *the* idea

▶ Putting your toe in

▶ Creating your mini business plan

▶ Keeping the cash flowing

▶ Getting business to come to you

*W*hat if you know what your perfect career is, but no one's hiring? Or what if you'd love your job but only if you could do it your way, on your time schedule, in the locale of your choice, with the kind of people you like working with?

Many of the coolest careers are those we create for ourselves. So if you can't find a job pursuing the career of your dreams, consider creating your own.

Who's going to give you a salary to be a ghost hunter, peacock farmer, prairie preservationist, collector of antique furniture, musical instrument maker, horror aficionado, nature poet, Mediterranean culinary historian, backcountry adventurer, boot maker, video biographer, surfing photographer, or Web cop? These are only a few of the thousands of cool careers people have created for themselves by becoming their own bosses.

We're not talking about building an elaborate business, as a classic entrepreneur might. If you were one of those, you probably wouldn't be reading this book. We're simply talking about creating a job for yourself in which you find customers willing to pay you to pursue your cool career. You don't need to have employees unless you want them and can afford them. You probably won't need to get bank loans or venture capital. You may not even need to shell out the big bucks for an outside office. Many self-employed people do just fine, thank you, working from home.

But What about the Downsides?

People contemplating self-employment often get teased: "So you're considering trading job security for the freedom to work 70 hours a week with no benefits?" Or "Being self-employed is being on a perpetual job search." Or "When you're on your own, you only have to work half-time — whichever 12 hours a day you want." With a little luck, and if you follow the advice in this chapter, you have a good chance of enjoying the freedom and control of self-employment while providing yourself with the perks of a job: good benefits and reasonable vacations, plus at least as much job security as you can get in a so-called real job.

Job insecurity

Many people equate being your own boss with job insecurity. Fact is, self-employment, *well done,* offers a good shot at a lifelong paycheck. No one can fire you on a whim. You'll never be merged, purged, right-sized, or downsized. And with the average job lasting only 3.5 years now, isn't job security more nostalgia than reality?

Insane hours

Conventional wisdom says that the self-employed work harder and longer than anyone else. Yet corporate managers routinely work more than 50 hours a week. In fact, many dot-commers think a 50-hour week is for shirkers. Remember also that a 50-plus hour corporate workweek doesn't even count the ever-lengthening commute time. For people working in offices of 100 or more, 73 percent must work on weekends, and to make ends meet, many people are forced to request overtime or to take a second job. The savvy self-employed often needn't work longer, especially if they're working from home.

You're on a perpetual job search?

If being on your own feels like a perpetual job search, you're probably not doing it right. At first, yes, you'll be busy lining up clientele, but stay with it for a while, and if you're good and you listen to your customers, business will start coming to you.

So you may be wondering: "If all this is true, how come not everyone is self-employed?" The answer is that many people aren't suited to or interested in being their own boss. However, many people would do just fine in self-employment if they only knew how. That's what this chapter is about. We give you a chance to discover whether creating your own job is a good decision for you and show you what it takes to maximize your chances of succeeding at it.

The Self-Employment Test: Is Independence for You?

No need to study for this test. Just look inward and try to be honest about yourself.

1. Do you like being in charge?

Do you love running the show and hate having someone tell you what you can and can't do? When you're your own boss, you make all the decisions — from which color iMac to buy to whether to take on a lucrative but risky project. To stay motivated when on your own, it helps if you crave one of the main benefits of being self-employed: control.

2. Are you flexible?

Planning is valuable when you're on your own, but often, you have to throw out your plan and reinvent. If you're looking for a relatively fixed job description, you'll do better in a salaried job. But if you like the idea of continually reshaping what you do, self-employment feels good.

3. Can you get things done?

Are you unusually productive? Ideas and dreams are a dime a dozen. The key to turning them into reality is implementation. As they say, success is 5 percent inspiration and 95 percent perspiration. If you're easily distracted from work, you'll have problems.

4. Are you good at solving real-world problems quickly?

Think of the stumbling blocks you recently faced at work and at home. Did you overcome most of them reasonably quickly, or did you stay bogged down? When you're your own boss, there's always a thorny issue to address. The successfully self-employed solve their problems quickly, by themselves or with inexpensive help.

5. Are you persistent?

Even the successfully self-employed face many setbacks, but they don't sulk. They quickly move to develop a new strategy. (Of course, that doesn't preclude an occasional private rant or cry.)

6. Do you communicate well?

As the front person, you must make a good first impression, orally and in writing.

Today, much of how we communicate occurs by computer. To succeed in most businesses, you must be able to quickly draft e-mails, find information on the Internet, and perhaps set up your own Web site. The latter has become easier with do-it-yourself Web site-creation software such as `store.yahoo.com`, `www.freemerchant.com`, or `www.homestead.com`.

7. Are you willing and able to market and sell?

No matter how much you enjoy doing your work, you won't get the chance to do it as your own boss unless you can find a way to let others know what you can do for them.

You probably don't have to make cold calls to get customers. In this chapter, I show you other ways to get business to come to you.

Scoring

If you couldn't honestly answer yes to all seven questions but are still eager to be self-employed, consider working as an assistant to a successfully self-employed person. You'll either acquire the skills and mindset you need to be successfully self-employed, or realize that you'll be happier employed by someone else.

Perhaps the most important determinant of your success in creating your own career is how motivated you are to do it. If, on a ten-point scale, your desire to create your own career is less than an eight, don't do it.

Six Musts for Hiring Yourself

Entire books have been written about how to become successfully self-employed. Indeed, Paul and Sarah have written 12. Yet, when the three of us really think about it, the keys to success reduce to only six things.

A good idea

People think the key to a successful business is coming up with *The Idea.* Actually, that's the easy part. Good ideas are everywhere:

- Chapter 2 (The Cool Careers Yellow Pages) lists dozens of our favorite self-employment ideas.

- Your own regular Yellow Pages phone book lists virtually every kind of business. Scan its index and in the space of an hour, you'll be exposed to hundreds of business ideas that actually are up and running. Find one you like? Visit a few businesses of its type, incorporate their best features into your version of the business, and aim yours at a particular geographical location, age group, or ethnic/gender market.

- Think about your current work. Is there a problem that you frequently hear co-workers or customers complaining about? Could you start a business that would solve it?

- Do you believe in a product or service that you might like to sell?

    All things being equal, service businesses are safer than product businesses. Service businesses have no costly inventory, no theft problem, and no spoilage. Plus, service businesses usually are easier to run from your home, which saves you commute time and thousands of dollars in rent.

- A franchise. See suggestions in Chapter 21.

- Paul and Sarah's book *The Best Home Businesses for the 21st Century* profiles more than 100 of their favorite home businesses.

    An easy way to refine your idea is to use a search engine such as www.google.com. For example, thinking of starting a wedding-cake-baking business? Search on "wedding cakes." You'll learn lots.

Don't be tempted by advertised get-rich-quick schemes. You probably won't get rich, and it certainly won't be quick. Whatever they're selling will take time, energy, and money, just like whatever it is you really want to do. So don't fall into the trap of thinking, "Well, I'll just buy their envelope-licking business 'opportunity' until I make plenty of money and then I'll do what I really want to do." Instead, save time and figure out how you can make money doing what you really want to do in the first place.

Two of the top ten scams on the Internet involve work-at-home offers and business opportunities. Be extra skeptical of e-mail solicitations. The old saying "If it sounds to be good to be true, it is" has never been truer. If you're still interested, check with the Federal Trade Commission (www.ftc.gov/ftc/complaint.htm), the U.S. Postal Inspector's office (www.framed.usps.com/websites/depart/inspect/emplmenu.htm), and the Better Business Bureau on its national Web site (www.bbb.org/library/searchBySubject.asp). The bureau offers more than 50 online publications on specific scams.

One more caveat: Just because nothing is reported about a business offer doesn't mean that it's legitimate. Most people do not report being scammed; they're embarrassed or think it's they're own fault. Internet career expert Margaret Riley Dikel adds, "If you have to pay to work, you're being screwed."

Putting your toe in the water

A business idea may sound great, yet in practice, it's a flop.

Sometimes an idea may, indeed, be great, but you may not have the ability to make it succeed. To reduce that risk, watch someone in your prospective business. For example, if you're thinking about being a Web site designer, watch one for an hour or two. Could you see yourself, with training, doing that 40 hours a week? If so, try to learn a bit of the necessary material — for example, HTML — on your own or with a tutor. Are you catching on quickly? If so, chances are you'll develop the skills needed to succeed.

Other times, a business succeeds only because of Herculean effort — an owner willing to work 80 hours a week or invest a fortune to ensure its success. Last time I looked, you didn't look like Hercules, nor did you have a fortune to invest.

Still other times, the idea was good, but its heyday is over. Open yet another bagel shop in your city and you'll face a double whammy — a market that's already saturated, and you're buying into a fad that's fading. A risk-reducer: Catch people in front of a store, call people out of the phone book, arrange a get-together of friends, whatever. Describe your product or service and ask them how likely they would be to buy it. Beg them to be brutally honest — "Better to know now than after I've opened the business." Ask them what they'd comfortably be willing to pay for your product or service and how the product or service could be enhanced so they'd pay more.

Your mini business plan

Preparing a simple business plan will help you decide whether to be self-employed. Don't be intimidated by the term *business plan*. It simply demonstrates that a market is out there for your product or service, describes what you'll do to reach that market, includes a rough budget for the first year, and says where you'll get the money. That marketing survey we just recommended will be key to developing a valid business plan. Want more guidance? Go to www.bplans.com. It offers a wizard to help you create a mini business plan, model business plans for all sorts of businesses, articles on how to create a business plan, and links to other resources, such as the federal government's Small Business Development Centers.

After developing your business plan, look at it. If you were an investor, would you invest in this business? Your answer may make it clear whether you should open up shop or look for a salaried job.

If you decide to go out on your own, don't compromise your cool career by making either of these two waffling mistakes:

- **All Things to All People.** George had a lot of management experience but had been downsized three times in ten years. He decided he could make more money and have greater security as a management consultant. Being his own boss was a real boost to his morale and confidence, but he worried about whether he could line up enough business to support his family. So he decided he wouldn't be picky. He told prospective clients that he'd work with any business on any sort of problem. To his dismay, he's finding few takers. What should he do?

  Answer: Find a niche, a specialty that makes him stand out from the crowd of other management consultants. He might, for example, specialize as a restaurant franchising consultant or an optometry practice adviser.

- **Jack and Jill of All Trades.** Connie wanted a career creating gourmet wedding cakes. She had always loved cooking, and all the wedding cakes she'd made for family and friends received rave reviews. So she left her job and, working out of a rented kitchen, began marketing her wedding creations. Business was slow coming in, though, so when a friend asked Connie to join her as a partner in her desktop publishing business, she agreed. But there wasn't enough business yet to keep them both busy, so when a cousin urged Connie to get involved in her multilevel marketing skin care business, Connie bought in. Now she had three businesses, three business cards, three business names, but of course, not enough time or money to make the most of any one of them. What should Connie have done?

  Answer: Stuck to building her wedding cake business.

Have an entry plan that keeps the cash flowing

You shouldn't need a lot of money to launch your independent career. The myth that you need a bank loan, venture capital, or rich friends and family keeps far too many people from becoming their own boss. Creating a job for yourself is not like starting a traditional business. The average person starting a business spends under $5,000, according to the Small Business Administration. Today, much of that money goes for a computer and office equipment — which you may already have, and the costs of which keep going down. Most of the self-employment opportunities listed in this book's Cool Careers Yellow Pages require only a small investment. Before spending big, think hard about ways to launch your business less expensively. If you can't, before getting into hock, consider another business.

Keys to controlling costs

The old axiom "It takes money to make money" may be true in big business, but we've found that in creating your own little business, it actually helps if you're a cheapskate. You're going to make errors in the beginning. So if you have low monthly costs, you're more likely to survive those errors without going bankrupt.

- ✔ **Start your business at home.** You can save literally thousands of dollars a month in rent and other costs. If you need to meet with clients and your place is a pigsty, offer them the convenience of meeting at their place, at a quiet restaurant, or at a rent-by-the-hour office in an executive center.

- ✔ **Provide a service rather than a product.** Products must be produced or bought, and usually require you to maintain thousands of dollars of inventory.

- ✔ **Learn how to be a businessperson**. The small-business battlefield is littered with former business owners who had a great idea but lacked the knowledge or willingness to run it, and especially to market it hard and smart. Unless you love techno-minutiae, don't bother getting technical expertise; you can always hire that. *You* learn how to run a business. That's a skill that never goes out of style, that many people find doable and more fun than learning endless arcana, and that opens the door to making serious money. In contrast, most technical types work long hours to earn just a moderate wage.

  How should you learn business? Volunteer or work for successful businesspeople. Don't try learning it in school. If those professors were such good businesspeople, they'd probably be running a business, not teaching. Remember that most professors are hired based on how well they do theoretical research, not how good of businesspeople they are.

✔ **Avoid the temptation to buy expensive stuff.** Office furniture, state-of-the-art techno-equipment, and pricey ads all cost money. You need that cash for more important things like your training, business phones, a computer, marketing, and perhaps a Web site.

✔ **Avoid hiring help.** If you need help, see if you can hire other self-employed people on an as-needed basis. Not only does that avoid the ongoing overhead of employees, but it also saves you from paying hefty payroll taxes.

✔ **Consider using a small business incubator.** These are sets of adjacent offices that allow you to share equipment and secretarial services, and provide a professional environment. With more than 900 in the United States and 3,000 worldwide, one is apt to be near you. Beyond the cost-savings, the presence of other budding entrepreneurs seems to inject a pioneering spirit among everyone. A University of Michigan study reported that 87 percent of businesses incubated by "mature incubators" still were in business after five years. To find an incubator, look in your Yellow Pages under "executive suites" or at the National Business Incubator Association Web site: www.nbia.org.

Transition plans

Here are common ways to transition into self-employment:

✔ **The Moonlighting Plan.** Keep your full-time job and develop your business as a sideline. When it takes off, you can go whole-hog. Be sure to work at least eight hours a week on a sideline business, and don't save all eight hours for Saturday.

✔ **The Part-Time Plan.** While you're building up the business, work a part-time job to provide a base income. When your business equals the base, drop the part-time job.

✔ **The Spin-Off Plan.** Turn your previous employer into your first major customer or, when ethically possible, take a major client with you from your previous job.

✔ **The Cushion Plan.** Of course, there are obvious cushions like savings, divorce settlements, or severance packages, but think about less obvious assets. Benjamin funded his new business by selling his grand piano, saying, "I wasn't playing it anyway. It was just a very expensive piece of furniture." Your cushion should be large enough to cover your expenses for the cash-poor start-up phase, typically six to 12 months.

✔ **The Leave Plan.** Start your independent career while on sabbatical or leave.

✔ **The Piggyback Plan.** If you have a working spouse or partner, cut back your expenses so that you can live on one salary until your business gets going.

✔ **The Key Client Plan.** If you have sufficient stature in your field, line up one or more retainer contracts with clients for the first year to provide you with assured revenue in exchange for a discount rate.

Smart pricing

Of course, when you're first starting out, charging top dollar is unfair, but consider charging at least mid-range if only because many prospective clients will be turned off if you charge too little. They believe you get what you pay for.

Many new businesses charge too little, either because they're desperate for customers or because they fail to take into account all the costs of doing business. In setting your pricing, start by figuring out what yields you a reasonable annual income. On top of that, you must factor in all your costs — for example, setting up your office, your Web site, training time, equipment, materials, travel to clients, phones, accounting fees, utilities, marketing costs, your benefits, and the 30 percent to 60 percent you'll pay in federal, state, local, self-employment, Medicare, disability, business license, and other taxes.

Do you lament that employed people get benefits but the self-employed don't? You simply have to build the cost of sick leave, vacation time, retirement, and health insurance benefits into what you charge. Web sites such as www.quotesmith.com and www.insweb.com make it easy to find good insurance values. Sites such as www.nase.org, www.bizbuyer.com, onvia.com, ebdirect.com, www.freeagent.com, and www.freeagentnation.com link you to all sorts of services for the self-employed: insurance, legal services, even potential customers. Also check with your state's health insurance commission for special programs for the self-employed.

Don't base your fees on the assumption that you'll be able to bill out a 40-hour week. It's the rare person who can. How many billable hours you can expect to generate each week depends not only on how much business you can line up but also on the nature of the work. A medical transcriptionist might bill 40 hours a week, while a consultant may average no more than 15. Talk to others about the norm in your field, but soon, your own experience will be your best guide.

Finding money

Okay, we've done what we can to keep you out of debt, but sometimes it's unavoidable. If you really need to borrow money to get underway, here's the straight scoop on the most often considered sources of start-up funds:

✔ **Banks.** Banks are eager to give loans to small businesses and self-employed individuals for expansion. The problem is, they're looking for a two- to three-year track record.

✔ **Equity loan.** Here's where a bank can help — if you have equity in your home.

✔ **Friends, relatives, and other personal contacts.** This is probably your best bet, but before hitting up ol' Uncle Albert, consider what would happen to your relationship with him if, somehow, you aren't able to repay.

✔ **Credit cards.** Usually the easiest but an expensive approach, unless you're careful. Here's how we'd do it. Get at least two cards while you still have a job: one for personal use and one for your business. Find cards with low interest rates. They are available as low as 5 percent or 6 percent for the first six months or year. After that, you can switch cards for a new introductory rate.

✔ **Venture capital.** Generally forget about it. Venture capitalists want to invest at least hundreds of thousands of dollars for a piece of some action that promises them millions. They're not interested in helping someone create a great career. Okay, so you're curious about venture financing? www.vfinance.com has lots of articles, plus links to 700 venture capital firms and 85,000 *angels*. (See below.)

Beware of firms offering to find you venture financing for a four-figure fee. They rarely work. If you need help tweaking your business plan, hire a consultant for an hour or two.

✔ **Angels.** Say you're not established enough for a bank loan, too small for a venture capitalist, without friends and family, and holding too many maxed-out credit cards. Maybe you need to be touched by an angel — a financial angel, that is. *Angels* are individuals looking for projects to invest in. How to find one? Light a candle and pray at these sites: www.angelnetwork.com, www.vfinance.com, www.ace-Net.org, and universityangels.com. Just be sure you have an irresistible one-to two-page summary of your business plan and a compelling 30-second verbal summary ready to go.

✔ **Small Business Administration loans.** An SBA loan is a possibility, especially if you're a minority or a woman. To find out more, visit www.sba.gov/financing, or phone 800-827-5722.

✔ **Other sources.** *Inc.* Magazine does an annual feature on financing your small business: www.inc.com.

Acting like the CEO you are

When you're self-employed, you suddenly go from subordinate to CEO. To succeed, you have to act like the chief executive. Here are common no-nos:

- **Never use a resume.** Prepare a bio, brochure, and/or portfolio. Have professional-looking letterhead, business cards, and stationery and per-haps a Web site.

- **Never refer to yourself as a freelancer.** If you want to command good fees, don't represent yourself as less than the head of your own com-pany. Freelancers routinely get paid less and are paid last. Also, never put the word *just* in front of what you do — for example, "It's just a home business" or "I'm just a one-man shop." Be proud of your one-person operation. After all, your clients never have to work with an underling. They get the personal attention of the firm's principal.

- **Never ask for an interview.** Interviews are for jobs. *You* are getting busi-ness, lining up customers, serving clients. Therefore, you arrange for a meeting, offer to make a presentation, make a bid, provide a quote, or submit a proposal.

- **Never ask what someone pays.** Tell people what you charge. However, don't announce your fees first thing, even if that's the first thing they ask for. Explain that you need to better understand their needs before you can quote a price. That gives you the opportunity to learn their needs and explain how they'd benefit from your work. Build value for what you do before announcing the price, and customers are more likely to be relieved to hear that your fee isn't higher.

- **Never work without an agreement.** Before you begin working with a new client or customer, get an agreement in writing as to what you'll be doing, the price, payment arrangements, and so on. Depending on the nature of your work, your agreement can be a simple order form, a purchase order, or a letter of agreement (a less intimidating word for a contract).

You will often be the one to provide the agreement, but large organiza-tions usually have their own standard forms. Beware when you get one of those babies — their attorney probably wrote it to benefit them. If you're nervous, it may be worth hiring your own legal eagle to review it. And remember that even though those corporate contracts look official, they're not set in stone. Don't hesitate to negotiate.

When extending credit, remember that it's always a privilege, no matter how big, well-known, or established the customer. Take the time to check credit references. Big companies go bankrupt, too. Remember that Macy's went Chapter 11.

✔ **Never complain.** Your customers have enough problems of their own. That's probably part of why they want to work with you. So don't add to their problems. If you're having business or personal difficulties, commiserate with family and friends if need be, but don't moan and groan to clients. Ever hear a CEO complain to a customer?

Getting business to come to you

It's every new businessperson's biggest question: How do I get customers? Eventually, if you're good, repeat business and word of mouth may largely sustain you, but for now, you've got to get the word out. People have to know not only what you do but also how you're different from others who do similar work.

The good news is that there are plenty of ways to market, and you need to choose only the method(s) that you feel comfortable with. If cold calling makes you sweat, pick something else. Chances are, you won't do a marketing activity you hate. Here are several of the quickest, most effective marketing activities. They're also low-cost.

✔ **Schmoozing.** Otherwise known as networking, schmoozing is the most popular way for self-employed individuals to get business. You can schmooze at professional and trade association meetings, in business organizations and Chambers of Commerce forums, and through formal networking groups like Business Network International (`www.bni.com`), which has chapters all over the United States.

If business gatherings aren't for you, schmooze by phone with colleagues, friends, and associates. Or browse Web sites and user groups, leaving helpful information along the way. Add a tag line to your online signature so that people know what you do and can reach you by e-mail.

✔ **Cross Referrals.** Figure out categories of businesspeople you can cross-refer with: "I'll send you mine if you'll send me yours." In my case, as a career counselor, I'd target psychotherapists. I'd attend a local conference of shrinks and, during breaks, chat with people until I found at least one to whom we both felt we could honorably refer clients.

✔ **Conduits.** *Conduits* are people whose business puts them in contact with lots of people who need what you offer. Make a list of everyone your potential customers do business with. These are your conduits. For example, if you have a cleaning service, commercial real estate agents can be conduits for you because their clients need property cleaned before sales. Let all relevant conduits know about you and what you offer. Sometimes, referrals from one or two good conduits can keep you busy full-time.

✔ **Sampling.** Your work can be your own best sales force. Let people see what you do. Give them a taste, a sample. Whet their appetite for more. You can provide samples of your work through your Web site, photos, portfolios, brochures, business cards, demonstrations, tapes, free consultations, speeches, and seminars or by passing out actual samples. Or be even more creative:

- **Get interviewed on a talk show.** Especially on small stations, getting on the air is easier than you may think.

- **Post flyers where your target customers will see them.** If I were looking for new clients, I might post flyers near a college's career center saying,

  Want more career help?

  I pick up where career centers leave off.

- **Write an article for a trade publication or have someone write an article about your business.** My favorite clients are doctors, so I might write a piece for the local medical society's newsletter called "When Doctors Need a Career Transplant."

- **If you're a consultant, try posting your availability on these sites:** www.monster.com, www.elance.com, www.guru.com, www.monster.com's Talent Market, and www.freeagent.com.

Please, as long as you need more customers, whenever you're not doing paying work, make marketing your number one priority. This may be the most important sentence in this chapter.

But What If I Fail?

If you fall on your face, corny as it may sound, force yourself to congratulate yourself for having had the courage to try, regroup, and put together another plan for crafting your cool career. Winston Churchill once said that success is moving from failure to failure with grace, composure, and confidence. Being more optimistic than that, we would add: until you get the hang of it. If you're willing to learn from your experiences, you probably will get the hang of it; you will find a way to make your cool career work.

If you have trouble finding the winning combination of what people will pay for, Paul and Sarah provide hundreds of examples of unique businesses people have created for themselves in their book *Finding Your Perfect Work.*

And of course, it's perfectly okay to decide at any point that being your own boss is not for you. As you can see in the Cool Careers Yellow Pages, there are plenty of great salaried careers.

You're Not Alone

It can feel scary to go off on your own. Remember, just because you're on your own doesn't mean you are alone. Limitless support resources are available. For example, are you a parent trying to run a home business? www.en-parent.com. Looking for a little inspiration? Read Rieva Lesonsky's book *Young Millionaires*. It tells the stories of nearly 100 small-timers who made it big. And the portal at www.about.com/smallbusiness will connect you to more support, written and human, than anyone could possibly use.

And that's not counting another incredible resource: the literally millions of other people who are living their dreams in an independent cool career, many of whom would love to talk with you.

Marti, Susan, John & Joanne

Marti was a cat lover. So when her friends went on vacation, they'd ask if Marti would care for their cats. They so appreciated being able to board their kitties in a private home rather than at a kennel that Marti wondered if this couldn't turn out to be a business. So she started Kitty Bed-and-Breakfast. Marti recruited "aunties" willing to temporarily board cats. Is Marti making a living at this, or does *she* have to eat cat food? She laughs, "I'm doing fine, plenty of cats. I just need to keep finding aunties."

Susan found out that she had lost her job while driving to work. The radio announcer said her company was closing. Susan got out of her car and cried in the street. She thought about how she had given so much that "there was no time to clean my house. My mail went unopened. My bills went unpaid." That gave Susan an idea: Why not help busy people with the tasks of daily life? She placed an ad in the paper, "Don't agonize, organize. The modern concept for handling your busy life: a personal assistant." That launched Susan's new career.

She now resides in California's Marin County, which is among the nation's most expensive places to live.

John worked at a computer manufacturer for 23 years. As a child, he had delivered newspapers on a unicycle but gave it up "the day I got my driver's license." 25 years and 25 pounds later, he got back on a unicycle. He found that bike shops couldn't meet unicyclists' needs, so he started Unicycle.com. Within eight months, his monthly income from the site was higher than his paycheck from his job.

Joanne was an administrator at a Bay Area university when suddenly her position was eliminated. Her favorite part of her job was developing and analyzing surveys, so she decided to make that the focus of a new business: The Survey Company. She provides her services to market research firms and to universities, including the one that let her go! In just three years, she's making 300 percent more than she did at the university.

Part V
The Part of Tens

In this part . . .

Many good ideas don't require long explanations. So, I plunk every good idea that's self-explanatory into this part. Five-hundred-plus good careers not enough? I show you at least ten ways to find thousands more. Suffering from the heartbreak of procrastinitis? Stall no more. I give you ten (all right, 48) extra-strength cures. Don't miss The Part of Tens.

Chapter 21

Ten (Plus Five) More Sources of Cool Careers

· ·

In This Chapter

▶ How an index can be your best friend

▶ Internet hot spots

▶ Potent places in periodicals

▶ Finding your career while watching TV

▶ Capitalizing on who you know

▶ Creating your own cool career

· ·

You scoured this book's Cool Careers Yellow Pages (see Chapter 2). Nothing sounds good. You've wracked your brain. Nothing. If you hear advice from one more person, you'll explode. Yet you still can't find a career that turns you on. Here's hope: easy ways to find literally thousands of additional cool careers.

A Special Note

When you've reviewed a zillion careers and still nothing jumps out at you, your problem may not be resolved by looking at a zillion more. Could the problem be:

   ✔ That you're waiting for a sure thing, something that, up front, sounds fabulous, something you're sure you'll succeed at? That rarely happens. Usually you don't know a career is right for you until after you've been in it, tailored it to fit you, and succeeded at it. Sitting on the sidelines makes you much less likely to succeed.

   ✔ Perhaps your career is fine, but you're not as good at your current job as you need to be. Should you bone up? Or scale back your career goal?

✔ Is your problem not that you make too little money but that you spend too much?

✔ Could it be that your career is fine but that you need different co-workers?

✔ Maureen realized she wanted to be loved by her boss. She didn't need a new career; she needed a lover.

✔ Are you asking too much of a job? Some people refuse to accept that work *is* work. Talk to people, even the ones with dream jobs such as actors and journalists, and most of them will admit that their jobs are rarely as fun as play.

Many people who come to career counselors end up realizing that what they need is to tweak their current careers, not dump them. So before going on to the rest of this chapter and digging up more careers, ask yourself whether you need to look more closely at what you're already considering or doing. If you want to tune up your current job, see Chapter 19.

That said, some people do need to be exposed to even more careers than the 500-plus in the Cool Careers Yellow Pages. This chapter shows you how to find them.

Lists of Careers

Had Eric not skimmed his local Yellow Pages index, never in a million years would he have thought of becoming an acid dealer (industrial acid, not LSD, you Deadhead!). Had Patricia not browsed the index of the *Occupational Outlook Handbook,* she never would have considered being a zookeeper. After scanning the College Board's *Index of Majors and Graduate Degrees,* Justin knew he wanted to be something he had never heard of before: a textile scientist, someone who develops new fabrics. Your library has many directories that list careers. A little scanning can expose you to thousands of options.

Variation on the theme: Hundreds of career books contain descriptions of many careers. A few titles to whet your appetite include:

✔ Leonard Mogel's *Careers in Communication and Entertainment.*

✔ *Environmental Careers in the 21st Century.*

✔ *O*Net Dictionary of Occupational Titles.* Just the facts on 1,122 occupations, covering 95 percent of the United States workforce. (Available free online at `http://online.onetcenter.org`.)

VGM Career Horizons publishes such titles as:

✔ *Careers for Homebodies*

✔ *Careers for Talkative Types*

✔ *Careers for Courageous People*

✔ *Careers for Animal Lovers*

✔ *Careers for Good Samaritans*

✔ *Careers for Environmental Types*

✔ *Careers for Self Starters*

✔ *Careers for Computer Buffs*

✔ *Careers for High-Energy People*

✔ *Careers for Born Leaders*

✔ *Careers for Sports Nuts*

✔ *Careers for Bookworms*

✔ *Careers for Culture Lovers and Other Artsy Types*

Paul and Sarah Edwards have written two books you may want to look at. *Best Home Businesses for the 21st Century* profiles 100 outstanding home businesses. *Finding Your Perfect Work* describes hundreds of novel careers that people have crafted for themselves.

College catalogs and Web sites usually contain lists of careers; look in the section describing each major. Especially look at community college and *college extension* catalogs/Web sites. They describe short programs in new and locally in-demand careers. **Note:** Community colleges often offer programs suitable for people who already have college degrees.

Wet Feet (www.wetfeet.com) and The Vault (www.vault.com) offer great information on dozens of popular industries and careers, including insider reports and real-person profiles.

Want a megalist of careers you can prepare for quickly? America's Learning Exchange (www.alx.org/cert_search.asp?usertype=user) offers a database of programs that award certification within a year or two. Registered biological photographer, anyone?

The biggest career list of all is the want ads, especially the online listings. You're almost guaranteed to run into many careers that you never even knew existed — there are tens of thousands of different careers, each in at least 31 flavors. Sure, browse the want ads in your local Sunday paper, but for the ultimate lists, check out Internet employment sites such as Career Builder (www.careerbuilder.com), which lists 3 million job openings. To keep you from being overwhelmed, the ads are categorized and keyword searchable. Want more focused employment sites? There are hundreds. For example, www.dice.com is for computer types. www.ejobs.org lists environmental jobs, and www.usajobs.opm.gov offers government gigs. For more, see www.rileyguide.com/jobs.html.

Create a Vision

Are you ready for a more intuitive — some would say California — approach? Turn the lights down. Keep taking deep breaths until you're about as relaxed as you're going to be. Now, let your imagination go a little wild. What would be the coolest career you could imagine? On the set with Steven Spielberg? In a lab curing cancer? Where would you work? In your PJ's at home? In a gorgeous office building? In the wilderness? In Japan? Who would you work with? Brilliant, fast-paced people? Children? By yourself? Now picture the perfect workday from the morning's first groggy awareness to your heavy-lidded fade into sleep. Does any of this suggest an even somewhat realistic career goal? You may never get all the way to that dream career, but sometimes the journey is more important than the destination.

Develop a Third Eye

As you go through your day, keep a third eye out for careers you encounter, especially oddball careers — those most career-seekers would never think of. Walking down a street, I see a scaffold with a sign, "Turner Scaffolding." Hmm: run a scaffolding service. Listening to a cool commercial: hmm, commercial copywriter. Playing basketball: hmm, gymnasium floor salesperson. Hearing the annoying sound of an airplane overhead: hmm, soundproofing specialist. While driving, noticing a sign on a truck, "Napa Drayage." What's *drayage?* (Trucking heavy loads.) Lamenting your bad memory: hmm, memory coach.

Right now I'm writing this while on a plane. While waiting to take off, I noticed beautiful Asian-influenced music playing. Who created that? Who sold it to United? A few minutes ago, I looked at the person across the aisle from me. He's reading a training manual for a platform lift — machinery that enables skyscrapers to be built. Many people have careers with the company that makes those. Later on the flight, I started a conversation with the guy sitting next to me — he's an actor who now makes his money training people to be mock patients used in medical schools.

Once you develop that third eye, you may never run out of career ideas.

Be Where You Want to Be

Sometimes, no one career goal stands out, but you know there's an environment or two you'd love to work in. Perhaps it's a university, or a Fortune 1000 company, working around young smart people, or rich old ones. Put yourself in that environment as much as possible. Want to work at a university? See if you could volunteer on a research project. Like to work in Silicon Alley?

Attend a meeting of the New York New Media Association. Want to work among the landed gentry? Become active in the local Junior League. Put yourself in your desired environment and good, often unexpected, career opportunities emanate.

The Media

You hear a radio interview with a range scientist, a person who manages grazing pastures. Sound like a cool career to you?

You watch a TV segment on some new gizmo. Want to sell it?

At a career Web site, you read a profile of a flower importer. Wanna smell the roses on a full-time basis?

You spot a newspaper article in which a company was found guilty of maintaining a hostile work environment because it didn't have a written harassment prevention plan. That will scare companies fast. Want to develop those plans for a living?

Keep your antennae out. There's an ongoing, easily accessible gold mine of ideas coming at you from the media 24/7. Especially fertile media outlets are

- ✔ **The Discovery Channel.**

- ✔ **A newspaper's or magazine's business, career, and science sections.** Sometimes, an article's career implications are obvious, but often it requires a little thought. You read an Election Day article on a school construction bond that just passed. That should mean a boom for construction companies that specialize in schools. A magazine article reports on the trend to interracial relationships. Want to be a counselor specializing in multicultural couples? The general principle is that when you see a feature on something new, ask yourself, "What kinds of problems will this cause? Do I want a career that would solve them?"

- ✔ **Trade and professional magazines.** These are treasure troves of cool careers and trends, written by leading insiders. Don't ignore the advertisements. You can learn about companies' latest and greatest products. Want to work for one of those firms?

The next three career sources are for people who suspect, deep down, that they're not going to find a career they're passionate about. They just want a career that pays reasonably, that they can succeed at, and that doesn't require breathing toxic fumes or listening to clanging equipment.

Personal Connections

Personal connections are particularly helpful if you don't have extensive formal credentials. Make a list of everyone who likes you who might hire you or know someone who could. Then phone each person and describe what you're looking for. You may need to say no more than, "I've just graduated from college and don't really know what I want to do. I just want to find a decent place to start my career." You never know what might turn up. You may never have thought about working for a food brokerage. Heck, you never even knew that food got brokered. But if your cousin told you that you could get an entry-level management job in food brokerage, especially if you didn't have extensive credentials or a burning passion, mightn't you go for the interview? Asking your personal connections for career leads can turn you on to careers you never would have thought of.

Isaac was a schizophrenic whose medication finally got him under control. He was ready for a job, any job. I asked him to list everyone who cared about him. Outside of his parents, he could list only one person: his therapist. (Schizophrenics don't have lots of friends, let alone friends in a position to hire them.) I told Isaac to ask his therapist for career advice. She referred him to the manager of a mental health advocacy group, and Isaac got an internship there. His goal now is to become a spokesperson for schizophrenics. Not a career he would have otherwise thought of.

Often, your connections will only help you get a short-term or part-time job. That's okay. That can turn into a full-time position, a reference for another job, or even the first step toward going into business for yourself.

The Dream Industry

The same sort of people who, despite all efforts, can't really narrow down their career goals, are sometimes clearer that they'd like to work in a particular industry. Shane knew he wanted to work in baseball even if he had to pick weeds in the outfield. And that's exactly what he did. Even though he had a college degree, he took a job as a minor league assistant groundskeeper — translation: he mowed the grass and picked weeds — and he was happy, but that's not the end of the story. One game, when staring at the scoreboard, he realized that someone had to be running all the fancy video equipment that creates the between-innings entertainment. Shane had worked in his college's TV studio, which gave him the background for that job, and volunteered to assist in the scoreboard room. Before long, Shane had a cool career as scoreboard operator, a career he never would have known existed.

The Dream Organization

Some people care more about which employer they work for than what they do there. Kathy felt that way about Estée Lauder. She loved their products, was intrigued that it remained a family-run business despite being so big, and simply wanted to work there. Short of sweeping the floors, she would do anything. It took her two years. Kathy kept contacting their human resources department month after month, visiting its Web site, writing letters to the president, the whole deal. Finally, a sales manager was impressed with her persistence and offered her a position as a manufacturer's rep. For Kathy, a cool career — one she wouldn't have thought of.

Internet Searches

Go to a state-of-the-art search engine such as `www.google.com` or `ixquick.com` and try these search terms. They can uncover career ideas you wouldn't have thought of:

✔ (something you're interested in) plus "careers". For example, photography careers.

✔ (something you're interested in) plus "trends". For example, publishing trends.

✔ New career(s)

✔ Best new career(s)

✔ Hot job(s)

✔ Hot career(s)

A directory is an alternative to a search engine. Just click on categories until you narrow down to what you want. The three leading Web directories are `www.dmoz.com`, `www.looksmart.com`, and `yahoo.com`. Or simply play around at virtual career libraries such as `www.rileyguide.com`, `www.acinet.org`, or `www.uhs.berkeley.edu/CareerLibrary/links/careerme.htm`.

An excellent career-finding questionnaire linked to hundreds of careers is at `http://cbweb9p.collegeboard.org/career/html/searchQues.html`.

Imitate a Successful Business

Many aspiring business owners think they need an original concept. If they see a similar business, they're discouraged. The smart reaction is to be pleased. If a similar business has been around awhile, it means it's reasonably successful. If you'd like to run that sort of business, go for it. Check out a number of businesses of that type, incorporate the best features of each, and open your business in a prime location. Sometimes prime doesn't mean downtown. Jon enjoyed training corporate employees in team building and communication skills but found the U.S. market saturated. He went to Poland, where, following the fall of Communism, corporations are now just ramping up. Jon is now a wealthy man.

A franchise offers the opportunity to copy a business with the steps laid out for you. But don't think it's pure cookie cutter; inevitably there are local problems to solve. Pick a franchise that's been around for at least five years and has at least 50 franchisees so that there's a track record. You don't want the franchiser to use you as a guinea pig. Before buying, ask at least five franchisees chosen *at random* if they're happy with the franchise. Hundreds of franchises are described at the International Franchise Association Web site: www.franchise.org. Every January, *Entrepreneur* magazine uses a quantitative model to pick its Franchise 500. See this year's picks at www.entrepreneurmag.com. Bison (www.bison1.com) is a portal to tons of information on franchising.

These franchises are top-rated by *Entrepreneur* or *Success* magazine, and strike me as having a future and likely being pleasant to run. Pillar to Post (home inspection), Kumon Math (tutoring), Proforma (personalized tee shirts, cups, and so on), American Leak Detection (find gas/water leaks), Great Clips (haircuts), Handyman Connection (residential repairs), We the People (paralegals helping people complete basic legal documents), Jackson Hewitt (computerized tax prep). Use www.google.com to find their Web sites.

Ten Ways of Creating Your Perfect Cool Career

These prompts can help you come up with a career that capitalizes on your passions:

1. Do what you love.

2. Provide a service to others who do what you love.

3. Teach others to do what you love.

4. Write about what you love.

5. Speak about what you love.

6. Create a product related to what you love.

7. Sell or broker what you love.

8. Promote what you love.

9. Organize what you love.

10. Set up, repair, restore, fix, or maintain what you love.

Combine Two of Your Features

An accounting expert whose hobby is magic tricks? Incorporate the tricks into workshops for accountants. Computer programmer with a thing for young women? Program for a young women's magazine. Parent of a develop-mentally disabled child and love sports? Work for Special Olympics.

Peter is an engineer who spends his free time hiking and taking wilderness photos. As he explored how he could combine these, his thoughts returned repeatedly to memories of the many evenings his family enjoyed reviewing the photo albums from their wilderness trips. That gave him the idea. His target customers are wilderness adventure companies who want to enhance their customers' experience by providing a video or still record of their trip. He created Peter's Wilderness Adventure Video Memories.

Okay, Tiger. Let's do it. What are two or three of your key and perhaps unusual features? How could they be combined into a cool career?

Seven Career Fantasies

These fantasies are provided by Arlene Hirsch, author of *Love Your Work and Success Will Follow*. They may trigger a custom career idea for you.

- **Hitting the open road.** Be like the Illinois scientist who gladly gave up his life of the mind to drive a big rig.

- **Risking it all.** For example, take on a physical challenge.

- **Letting your creative juices flow.** Become an artist or performer.

> ✔ **Embracing a tropical paradise.** Let yourself be motivated by place and by a calmer, less stressful existence.
>
> ✔ **Benefiting society.** Help others while shunning the profit motive of big business.
>
> ✔ **Returning to your roots.** Embrace life's basic ingredients, such as growing your own food or living in a small town.
>
> ✔ **Staying close to family.**

Find a Need and Fill It

New laws and regulations create opportunities. For example, Jane is an attorney whose best skill is translating legal mumbo jumbo into plain English. At a meeting of the Society of Technical Communication, she found out that the Securities and Exchange Commission had just started requiring all mutual fund prospectuses to be converted from legalese into plain English. Right up Jane's alley. What new law or regulation has been passed? What career opportunity could that create for you?

Randomness

A message behind this and most how-to books is that planning is good. Yet, sometimes — probably more often than we like to acknowledge — things just happen. Marilyn Maze, career software designer for ACT, tells about her cousin, Grace (name changed) who was a biology major in college. After graduating, Grace took an entry-level position in a bank. She had never even considered a banking career but saw it as a temporary solution when the job market for biologists was depressed. Now she's vice president of a bank and very happy. Marilyn said, "Yes, people should make some effort to decide if they have a true vocation, but many people don't, so they should take advantage of opportunities that present themselves."

Serendipity is more likely to happen where you're around successful people. Go to parties and other events with successful people. Let them know you're contemplating a job change and are open to a wide range of options. You may learn of some opportunity you never would have thought about.

Chapter 22

Ten (Okay, 48) Extra-Strength Procrastination Cures

In This Chapter

▶ When it's okay to procrastinate

▶ What causes *your* procrastination? Custom-tailored cures

▶ All-purpose cures

*L*et's come back to this chapter later. (Just kidding.)

Does Your Procrastination Really Need Curing?

Sometimes procrastination, like pain, is a warning that something is wrong. Just as the ouch when you touch a hot stove tells you to stay away, procrastination can be your brain telling you to stay away from a task.

For example, you could be "procrastinating" the start of your job search. Sometimes, that's your mind, having factored in everything — the benefits, the risks, the hassle — calculating that the job search isn't worth doing. Great. That's your brilliant self saving you from a lot of unnecessary work.

When is your brain correct in telling you to procrastinate? Here is a test to find out. Write down your answers to these questions:

✔ What are the likely benefits of doing the activity you're procrastinating about?

✔ What are the likely benefits of *not* doing the activity?

Okay, Tiger, now look at what you've written. Decide to do the activity or drop it forever. If you need more information before deciding, give yourself a deadline — "By this date, I will decide, one way or the other."

Other people are fully aware that procrastination hurts them. They know it's like a credit card: fun when you use it, but painful when the bill comes in. Nevertheless, they suspect they'll never change. They accept their procrastination as an immutable weakness, much as a blind person knows he has an impediment. Most procrastinators I've worked with fit into that category. If you're confident you can't or won't change, perhaps the best advice I can give is for you to just accept yourself and stop feeling guilty. We all have flaws.

So You Want to Stop Procrastinating

Let's say you're in that minority that really wants to stop procrastinating. This chapter contains 48 ways to help you. That sounds good on first blush, but having many choices can be overwhelming, especially to a procrastinator. So, as you read, just checkmark the few cures that you think you'd like to try.

My System for Curing Procrastination

So you don't want to bother reviewing 48 options? Try this one-page system. It amalgamates the strategies that have worked best for the largest number of my clients.

Step 1. Decide whether you really want to do the task. Maybe its benefits aren't worth the effort. If you decide you want to do the task, do you want to do it now or schedule it? Consciously choosing makes it more likely that you'll actually complete the tasks you decide to do.

Step 2. Procrastinators tend to repress thoughts of doing the dreaded task. **So, build in a reminder:** Write an alphabet letter on your hand, set a timer to go off when you should be starting the task, or simply schedule the darn thing on your calendar.

Step 3. Identify the moment of truth: The moment when you're about to procrastinate will occur when you realize you should do the dreaded task or when you reach a hard part. At that moment, say aloud, "Stop!" Literally pinch yourself for sliding back into your wicked ways, and gin up the energy, the discipline, to get started. This is the moment of truth, the moment when you have to believe that "Right now, it's in my interest to be productive rather than to have fun." After starting, you'll find it easier to continue. If that doesn't work, proceed to Step 4.

How Marty Nemko controls his procrastination

I try to stay in the moment. I don't think about what fun thing I could be doing instead, or how much work is ahead of me. I try to stay focused on whatever my next few-second (literally) task is. When I feel a compelling urge to play instead of work, I usually indulge it — guilt free. For example, take a few minutes to surf the Net or grab a snack, but I try to keep the play short so there's plenty of time to get my work accomplished.

Step 4. Ask yourself, "What is making me reluctant to do the task?" Your response, for example, may be: "It's going to be hard," or "I'd rather do something fun."

Step 5. Come up with a solution for Step 4. For example:

✔ Let's say you're afraid the task will be hard. Remind yourself that you can divide it into small bites, and when you reach a tough part, you need struggle only for a minute before deciding to get help or that you can complete the task without making any more progress on that hard part.

✔ If you're afraid to ask for a job because you believe you're not qualified, ask yourself if that's rational. If so, get training or change careers. If it's irrational, recognize that and make the darn phone call.

✔ If you're tempted to do something fun instead of the task, ask yourself whether the short-term relief is worth the long-term consequences. Your call.

Step 6. Commit to a small amount of effort, for example, three phone calls.

Work at being efficient during that small amount of effort. Frequently ask yourself, "Is this the straightest line to getting the task done?"

Step 7. Look back and ask yourself whether it was worth the effort to get the task done.

Step 8: Block out some time for pure, unadulterated, guilt-free fun.

Cured? If not, read on.

Cures for Excuse-Making

Some procrastinators can be helped by a cure tailored to their particular excuse for procrastinating.

The Live-for-today Excuse: "Searching for a job is yucky, no fun at all. I always find something I'd rather do."

The cures:

Remember that you'll actually have more fun if you don't procrastinate. When you procrastinate, you suffer in many ways. You suffer ongoing guilt: Even when you're watching your favorite TV show, a little voice whispers in your ear, "You should be working on getting hired." You also suffer from staying in the same miserable situation that made you want to find a cool career in the first place: the low pay, the lousy work, your lack of success. Plus, you must endure your family's searing questions: "When *are* you going to find yourself, Melvin?" If you truly like pleasure more than pain, the key is to get your work done as efficiently as possible so that maximum time is left for pleasure without guilt or negative consequences to spoil the fun.

Make the task as pleasurable as possible. As you're doing the task, keep asking yourself, "What's the fun way to do this?" If, for example, you know you need to cold-call prospective employers, ask yourself, "How can I make these phone calls fun?" That can simply be a matter of not taking it too seriously if a hirer blows you off: "Screw him. There are plenty of others I can call."

Beware of focusing only on the fun parts or of creating fun side activities that you rationalize are necessary. For example, many job seekers spend hours playing with the format of their resume or researching companies on the Net, rather than contacting potential employers. Solution: As you're working, keep asking yourself, "Is this the most direct path to my goal? Or am I fooling myself?"

Make a deal with yourself. For example: "Okay. I've decided it's in my best interest to do this miserable good-for-nothing task but I want a reward. So, here's the deal: If I work on it for 15 focused minutes, I'll take a few minutes to answer that e-mail from my girlfriend."

Accept that you have an addiction. Like drug addicts, live-for-today procrastinators accept a damaged life in exchange for the momentary relief of deferring work. Are you finally willing to say, "That's it. I'm ready to kick my addiction. I'm ready to be moderately disciplined; I'll be happier if I make myself value productivity more than fun during the workday"? A client of mine, Dave, in his early years was a procrastinating nonachiever. One day he simply decided he had enough. Today Dave is a successful fundraiser, having won literally dozens of achievement awards, and is a happy guy.

The Spacey Procrastinator's Excuse: "I just can't seem to focus."

Spacey people often have big ideas but can't stay focused enough to accomplish even little things.

The cures:

Become more time-aware. Many spacey people are oblivious to time. Set a timer to go off every three minutes. Each time it buzzes, ask yourself, "Is this the most direct approach to achieving my goal?"

Be alert to early signs of spacing out. When you feel yourself *starting* to fade out, laugh aloud, "Okay, focus!"

Pick a productivity place and time. Is there a place you're least likely to procrastinate? Is there a time? Use that place and time when you have an important task you're likely to procrastinate.

Ritalin. If you've had a long-standing inability to focus, even on important things, a trial course on this drug may be worth considering. Originally used with children, Ritalin has more recently been found to help some adults. Of course, before taking any prescription drug, discuss it thoroughly with your physician.

The Fear-of-failure excuse: "I'm afraid of failing."

The cures:

Of course, sometimes fear is a sign you shouldn't tackle a task. But if you think it's probably in your interest to do a task but are too scared to try, one or more of these tactics may help:

Remember that not trying usually means greater failure. If you don't try, you're a guaranteed failure. If you give it a shot, there's at least some chance you'll succeed, and at minimum, you'll learn from your failure. You'll also gain self-respect and the esteem of others. People who try and fail are respected more than people who don't try at all.

Think less and do more. As a child, I'd lie awake worrying about dying. As a young adult, I interpreted every twinge as a sign of an impending heart attack. Doctors tried to reassure me that nothing was wrong, while therapists tried to find the cause of my hypochondria. But nothing worked. I was a worrywart.

But at age 30, I suddenly stopped worrying. Who cured me? My wife. "Martin," she ordered, "the more you think about your health, the more in knots you are. From now on, every time you get a hypochondriacal thought, force yourself to think of something else." Within two weeks, I was cured. That was 20 years ago. Of course, now I worry about little green men from Mars coming to destroy the earth. Just kidding.

Why am I telling you this? Because too often, people procrastinate taking action by thinking a problem to death — *analysis paralysis.* This, of course, usually leads to a worse result than if they had tried something, even if it ended up not working. If you stay at the source of a river until you figure out the precise route to its mouth, you'll never arrive there. Most successful people do minimum planning, try something and then revise, revise, and then revise again. Start down the river and then make mid-course corrections.

Avoiding analysis paralysis is particularly important for career searchers. Rarely can you make progress just sitting there and thinking. Write something, phone someone.

I have found analysis paralysis to be a particular problem with clients who have been in psychotherapy that focuses on the childhood roots of their problems. Many of these people appear *more* paralyzed as a result. They seem stuck in the past, more interested in talking yet again about their childhood woes than in doing something to get unstuck.

Stop your downward spiral. Fear is usually better and worse at different times. Often, what makes things worse is momentum: One unproductive thought triggers another, which triggers another, and before you know it, you're overwhelmed. The key is to stop unproductive thinking before it builds momentum — it's easy to stop a rock that's just starting to roll down a hill, but if it gains speed, it can knock you over. So, as soon as you recognize an unproductive thought, for example, "I'm too dumb," just say *Stop!* to yourself and do something productive. That sounds simplistic, but it often works.

Do NOT wait until you feel more confident. It works the other way around. The more you do, even if it isn't very successful, the better you'll feel. The less you do, the worse you'll feel.

The Perfectionist's Excuse #1: "It takes me a long time, but I want to get it right."

The cure:

Know when okay is good enough and when you need to be perfect. It usually takes a long time to get from good to perfect, so you only want to spend that time when it's worth it — for example, in crafting a good answer to "Why have you been unemployed for the last nine years?" In nearly every other task in a career search, shooting for perfection is time that can be more valuably spent.

I've seen many clients waste weeks agonizing over the fine points of their resumes, the design of their business cards, or their cold-call script. Their job prospects would be better if, instead, they started contacting employers. One reason people are perfectionists about such things as their resume is that it's more comfortable to fiddle with inanimate things than to risk embarrassing yourself. Be aware of that tendency. Ask yourself, "Is this the most direct route to achieving my goal?"

Advice from Tiger Woods

Golf requires an extraordinary degree of perfection. Mis-hit a ball by a tenth of an inch and it can end up in the woods. Tiger Woods is arguably the most perfect golfer in history, and even he doesn't strive for perfection. He aims for what he calls "professional excellence," a competent effort on every shot. If it's good enough for Tiger, maybe it's good enough for the rest of us.

The Perfectionist Excuse #2: "I'd rather not do it than do it poorly."

The cures:

That high-minded talk coming from a career searcher can be fear talking. Such career searchers are afraid that if they make a mistake, others will think they're stupid. The fact is, most successful people don't let fear of mistakes stop them. They dive in, make errors (sometimes appearing stupid), and learn from them. Unsuccessful people are much more likely to plan, plan, plan, hoping to get it perfect and giving up before implementing much of their plan. Or if a project *has* to be done, they find themselves at the eleventh hour, forced to crank out something far worse than what they would have produced if they hadn't procrastinated. Sometimes a procrastinator's motive is to protect his ego: "I could have done it well if I had taken the time." For that cold comfort, they pay a huge price. Sure, brain surgeons and diamond cutters must be perfect, but career searchers needn't be.

Another difference between winners and losers lies in how they react to failing. Winners don't waste time on self-pity. They focus on learning from their failure so they can succeed the next time.

The Fear-of-Imposing Excuse: "I don't want to contact them because I don't want to impose."

The cures:

- *Recognize that you may not be imposing.* Many people enjoy giving advice. Plus, if you're phoning for a job and the employer happens to need someone like you, you'll be doing him a favor. If not, you'll have wasted ten seconds of his time. Big deal.

- *The karma concept:* Even if you *are* imposing, recognize that it's okay to ask for help as long as you remember to be kind to job seekers who ask you for help.

The Fear-of-Success Excuse: "I'm not sure I want to succeed. If I do, I'll pay a price."

The simplest cure for fearful procrastinators

If rationally, you believe that the potential rewards of doing the task justify the risk, do as author Susan Jeffers says, "Feel the fear and do it anyway."

The cures:

Remember that you can set limits. Accepting more pressure than you want is unnecessary. For example, many successful executives have decided that the stressful 70-hour weeks aren't worth it no matter how high the salary, and quit to do something low-key like teach college. Others who are strongly committed to family usually, with persistence, find a family friendly job that allows them to preserve most of their evenings and weekends.

Be aware of the martyrdom tendency. Some people avoid succeeding because they're afraid their spouse or parent will feel inferior in comparison. You shouldn't sacrifice yourself to protect someone's ego.

The Adrenaline Addict's Excuse: "School got me into the habit of waiting until the last minute to do assignments. I was able to get good grades even though I didn't start working until the night before."

Unfortunately, except in dead-end jobs, last-minute work usually doesn't cut it in the real world. Fine, blame the schools, but now you have to cure your adrenaline addiction.

The cures:

Realize that adrenaline addiction is dangerous. It's bad for your health and leaches pleasure out of every task.

If you're not ready to kick your addiction to adrenaline, try these palliatives:

Create an artificial deadline. For example, say, "I am going to create a networking list by 9:00." Set a timer. If you're excessively perfectionistic, try giving yourself an absurdly short deadline. For example, "It's 11 a.m. and I want to have lunch at noon. Let's see if I can write a draft of my resume by then."

A client of mine who supervises a cancer clinic was overwhelmed by the task of creating his annual budget. I told him: "You have three minutes. Draft a budget." The absurd time limit forced him to focus only on its key components and to identify the fuzzy areas. Three minutes later, he had written a ton about the budget and was eager to fill in the blanks.

The high-potency version of this cure: Hand a friend $100. If you don't finish the work by the agreed-on time, he keeps your hundred bucks.

The Resent-Authority Excuse: "You're not going to make me do that."

The cure: You're right. Neither family nor societal pressure can make you do anything, but *recognize that if you make the choice not to succeed, you, not the authority, will suffer.*

The Don't-have-time Procrastinator's Excuse: "I can't get started on my career search until I clean my desk (or get my divorce finalized, quit my job, whatever)."

The cures:

Realize that these are delaying tactics. Yes, they are also legitimate problems, but millions of people with piled-high desks, doing full-time jobs, and yes, even in the throes of divorce, have found new careers. Often, the search for a better career actually provides rays of hope and distraction from the stresses of a breakup. If you wait until all the stars are aligned, you'll never get started.

A career- or job-search does take time. Starting now, as you contemplate beginning an activity (including turning on the TV), ask yourself, "Should I be working on my job search?"

Pull out your appointment book or Palm Pilot, and schedule blocks of time to devote to your search.

All-Purpose Procrastination Cures

Those excuse-specific cures often help, but some general ones can also be of real benefit. Pick out a few that might work for you.

Ask yourself, "If I were my grown-up self, what would I do?"

Create a to-do list that you check throughout the day.

Pick a specific time to start on your task. Put it on your schedule, just as you might a doctor's.

Do short tasks now. You save the time it takes to put them on your to do list; you avoid adding to the many tasks hanging over your head like Poe's pendulum in the pit. Doing them now tends to make you not be overly perfectionistic about them, and you avoid procrastination — you've gotten it done. So instead of the guilt, you'll start hearing from others, "Wow, thanks for the fast response!" That feels so good.

Use a few-second task to get you rolling. Before you start or when you reach a hard part, it's tempting to grab a soda, call your friend, or trim your nails. That's when you have to force yourself to get working (on the task, not your nails). Ask yourself, "What's my next few-second task?" For example, "I have to open my address book to see whom I need to call." Many of my clients and I have found the few-second task strategy helpful.

Be aware of the moment of truth. When tempted to procrastinate, you face a moment of truth when you're still not over the edge, like when you're on the brink of losing your temper. At that moment, you can consciously suppress the desire to procrastinate. When you feel that temptation arise, gin up your energy, your discipline, and ask yourself, "What's my next few-second task?"

Recognize that choosing to procrastinate says, "Even during the workday, I value fun more than being productive." Do you really want to define yourself that way?

Attach a sense of urgency to the task: "I *have* to do this."

Think of your workday as a series of two-minute blocks. That mindset proffers many advantages. Many two-minute blocks go wasted — for example, the two minutes before lunch or before a meeting. You'd be amazed how much work can get done in two minutes. Work during those two-minute periods and you may wring an extra half-hour out of your day without putting in any overtime. Another benefit of the two-minute mind-set is that it keeps you from being too perfectionistic or becoming overwhelmed by the size of a task. After all, you can do only so much in two minutes.

Don't think about how much work you have ahead of you. That can overwhelm you into procrastination. Instead, think like a mountain climber. Just put one foot in front of the other, and when you get to the top and look down, you'll be amazed at how far you've gone.

Before I began to write this book, I knew 400-plus pages lay ahead of me, but I never let myself think about that. It would've felt overwhelming. As soon as those thoughts entered my mind, I immediately replaced them with, "What's my next few-second task?"

The one-minute struggle. If you find yourself stuck, give yourself just one minute to get unstuck. If you haven't made real progress by then, chances are you won't solve the problem. Long struggles, of course, frustrate you and make you want to procrastinate on the whole project. So, if you're stuck after a minute, see if you can complete the project without solving that problem. If not, get help.

Remind yourself of the benefits of not procrastinating. Examples: When you find a job, you can support your family, feel useful, afford that vacation you've fantasized about, and rid yourself of the guilt that you're letting life pass you by. How do you keep your key benefit in mind? By writing it on your palm. For example, John wrote "GWOMB" It stood for "Get Wife Off My Back."

Think back to times you've procrastinated. What were the consequences? Has it hurt your career? Your relationships? Your self-esteem? Sometimes, looking at the price you've paid for procrastinating can make you angry enough with yourself to say, "I'm tired of sabotaging myself. I am not going to let this happen again."

Think back to a time you *didn't* procrastinate on an unpleasant task. What kept you from procrastinating then? A rigorous schedule? Someone nagging you? Does that give you a clue as to how to beat your current procrastination?

How will you feel tomorrow about having procrastinated on a task today?

Remember: the less you accomplish, the less you want to accomplish. Conversely, the more you accomplish, the more you want to accomplish.

What would you say to get your twin to quit procrastinating?

Figure out *where* you're least likely to procrastinate. If at home you play too much with your dog or take too many coffee breaks, consider working somewhere else.

Figure out *when* you're least likely to procrastinate. Block out that time as career-search time. Write it in your datebook just as you would an appointment with a friend. You wouldn't fink out on your friend. Maybe you won't fink out on yourself.

Some people become energized when listening to music. Might you?

Draw a thermometer and tape it to your desk. Instead of numbers on its side, write the little steps you need to do to get the task done. Every time you complete a step, color in that part of the thermometer. This technique helps churches raise lots of money. My wife says it was the key to her getting her Ph.D. dissertation done.

Focus on small changes. We underestimate the effects of small changes. A client of mine, Dianne, lived wracked with guilt because she paid little attention to the accounting part of her photography business. I said, "Commit to 15 minutes a day working on your books." She did that and what a relief! Next session, she said, "Fifteen minutes isn't a big deal but it turns out to make a big difference, psychologically as well as practically."

The Scarlet P. This tactic is a bit draconian, but what the heck. Write the letter "P" (for procrastinator) on the outside of your hand so that everyone can see it. Unlike in Hester Prynne's case, no one's forcing you to do it. That P, which follows you everywhere you go, is an ongoing reminder that curing your procrastination is Job One. The P is also embarrassing, so it may motivate you to overcome the problem so you can honorably remove it.

Just do it. Do it now, even if you don't feel like it. If you only work on your career when you feel like it, you won't feel like it often enough. Don't expect it to be fun. That's okay. As those obnoxious but correct people say, "No pain, no gain." Fight through the discomfort and just do it. Think how good it will feel to have put in a good hour. Think of the benefits you'll derive. Then make yourself start working.

Find someone to check in with. Some career seekers can go it alone, but many, especially procrastinators, find it helpful to have someone to check in with. Regular check-in is a key to the success of Weight Watchers and 12-step programs.

Some people prefer one-on-one support. Find a friend you can phone every day. Richard Bolles, author of *What Color is Your Parachute?,* suggests finding a "loving taskmaster," someone who can meet weekly with you, giving you a gently dispensed hard time if you've been a slacker during the week. I allow procrastinating clients to e-mail me nightly to report their progress. One client said, "Knowing I'll have to report to you each night makes me feel like Marty Nemko is at my side all day urging me on."

Would you prefer group support? Ongoing groups are available in most large cities. For example, the 5 O'Clock Club has branches in New York City; Washington, DC; and Chicago; plus virtual branches — online groups (www.fiveOClockclub.com). Also consider Forty Plus: Visit www.fp.org/chapters.htm to find your nearest chapter. To find other local job-search support groups, visit the Riley Guide's collection of job clubs (www.rileyguide.com/counsel.html), check with your chamber of commerce, college alumni association, church, or unemployment office.

You can even start your own support group. Here's an approach adapted from Barbara Sher's *Wishcraft*. Recruit members by asking friends, relatives, or colleagues, or by placing an ad in a local newspaper. Just write, "Forming a career-search support group. For information, call *(insert phone number)*." Your group should have four to six members. Meet weekly or at least monthly. At each session, each person gets ten minutes in the hot seat. That member starts by telling the group her career/job-finding goal(s). Then group members offer advice on objectives for the next week. Before moving out of the hot seat, each person ends by saying what she commits to accomplishing by the next meeting. Consider using this book as the group's "textbook." That helps ensure that all members are knowledgeable about career issues.

Members of job support groups generally do well. They feel accountable to the group and come away with ideas and encouragement from group members, as well as inspiration from seeing people arrive unhappy and leave with better work lives.

Fall in love. I'm not sure why it works, but a number of lifelong procrastinators report being cured after falling in love or having a baby.

Our Best Thoughts on How to Have a Happy Work Life

*H*ere, we thought we would take the liberty of speaking as individuals.

Marty Nemko's Thoughts

Although I hold some conventional views about work, why waste space. Here are some of my unconventional yet deeply held beliefs about work. Before reading them, I invite you to remember the old aphorism, "We find comfort among those who agree with us; we find growth among those who don't."

Think twice about following long-shot dreams

Many career guides tell you to do what you love and the money will follow. They're filled with stories of starving artists who no longer starve, aspiring novelists who no longer have to aspire.

Those books don't tell you that for every person who achieves his long-shot dream, dozens don't. Talented artists still starve; terrific actors and novelists still wait tables.

Here is more realistic advice: If you believe that your life will feel empty unless you pursue a long-shot career full-time, then do it, but give it no more than a fixed amount of time — say, a year. If, after a year, you don't have clear signs that you'll make even a modest living at it, the odds are great that you never will. You still have plenty of time to start another career.

If you can see yourself having a good life even without that long-shot career, please turn that long-odds dream into an after-work activity. You dramatically increase the chances of accomplishing your long-shot dream if you don't insist that you get paid for it.

The fact is, there are plenty of miserable artists, writers, and actors and plenty of happy teachers, electricians, and programmers. For most people, career happiness, in the end, comes from doing something that you're good at and that you think is worthwhile, having co-workers who appreciate you, working ethically, and making a reasonable living.

Consider choosing an *under-the-radar* field. It seems that half my clients want to enter one of just a few fields: the arts, the media, or nonprofit work. Good jobs in these fields are tremendously competitive, and even if you land one, the pay is often unconscionably low. Desirable internships are even more unfair. After graduation, my daughter, who won an award as UCLA's outstanding student, got to work in the White House. However, because the position was in such demand, she was expected to work 13 hours a day for almost a year, yet she didn't receive one thin dime.

Remember that for most people, job satisfaction largely depends not on the particular career but on the tasks being moderately challenging, having a good boss and co-workers, and helping to provide a worthwhile product or service. No one ever grew up saying, "I want to be an office manager at the local water utility," yet I know someone in that job who thinks she has a cool career and makes more than you'd think — $57,000 — simply because that job is not on most career seekers' dream list.

In praise of the anonymous achievers

Who gets the media's attention? Answer: the performers, athletes, politicians, and society's have-nots. My hero is the anonymous achiever. The smart, hard-working people who make the world run and get few rewards for it. These days, we're not allowed to say that one person is better than another, but I believe those *are* our better people. The smart geologist who labors in anonymity trying to find oil reserves. The restaurant owner who's out buying fresh produce at four in the morning and who works into the night to provide fresh meals at fair prices. The Social Security eligibility worker who ensures that people get the help they need while simultaneously protecting our taxpayer dollars. It saddens me that these bulwarks of our society, thanks to a 40 percent to 60 percent state/federal marginal tax rate, sometimes even with a second income, cannot afford to buy even a modest home in a safe neighborhood. We spend a lot of time admiring entertainers and athletes — people who make millions for doing something nonessential. I would love to see the media pay attention to the real contributors, the anonymous achievers without whom our quality of life would be decimated.

Balance is overrated

I believe that some people are wise to work long hours rather than embrace the vaunted work/play balance. How can I assert such heresy? After all, since the days of Aristotle, the golden mean has been revered. Today's women's movement deifies work/play balance. We ridicule people who work 60-plus hours per week as *workaholics* — people whose lives are out of balance. Yet I believe that, in certain circumstances, balance is overrated. I believe that if you choose a meaningful career, you may be more satisfied with your life and do more good if you work long hours.

I'm not saying that everyone should work 60-plus hours per week. My goal here is simply to encourage you to consciously decide how much you want to work rather than be swept along by the popular consensus.

Want to succeed? Consider lowering your self-esteem

Many people would be more successful if they *lowered* their self-esteem. American students score near the bottom on achievement tests among industrialized nations, but are number one in self-esteem. Conversely, Asian students score highest yet have the lowest self-esteem. Within the United States, African-American achievement is below average while their self-esteem is above average.

These are not coincidences. If you have more than moderate self-esteem, you believe you're wonderful, which takes the edge off feeling that you need to work hard. In contrast, if your self-esteem is only moderate, you are at least a little scared that your work won't turn out well. Your only chance, you believe, is to work hard. Most successful people I know, when beginning a project, usually are a little fearful it won't come out well. This is even true of icons of success we'd think were brimming with self-esteem. For example, after his election to the presidency, George Washington wrote in his diary: "About 10 o' clock, I bade adieu to Mount Vernon . . . with a mind oppressed with more anxious and painful sensations than I have words to express, and set out for New York . . . with the best disposition to render service to my country, but with less hope of answering its expectations." Worry motivates us to work hard. Of course, we can't be so afraid of failing that we don't even start a task, but we must be a little worried. I was a little anxious as I started every chapter of this book, and although I've been host to a radio show for years, I'm still a bit nervous before every show. If I went into preparing for a radio show thinking, "I'm great, I can do this, no problem," the work wouldn't be as good. I wouldn't work as hard. Instead, I worry a bit. It's ironic that self-esteem, so often promulgated as the cure for low achievement, can cause it.

Many people blame their problems on low self-esteem. Often that's a face-saving way to avoid the harder-to-accept truth that they have poor intellectual or social ability. Such people don't suffer from low self-esteem; they're accurately portraying themselves. Low self-esteem exists only when a person's self-appraisal is worse than the reality. So, next time you blame your problems on low self-esteem, ask yourself whether your problem really is low ability. If so, instead of trying to boost your self-esteem, you may make more progress by scaling back your expectations or working to improve your skills.

The Tough-Love Lecture

We avoid calling people "lazy," at least to their face. We can call them procrastinators or fearful, but "lazy" is seen as too much of a putdown. But the unvarnished truth is that some people *are* lazy. Some of my lazy clients have been helped by my tough love lecture:

> People who always find excuses for not doing what they should are losers. Yes, losers. They fail at work and usually in their relationships. And you're well on the path toward becoming a permanent loser. The good news is that there's still time to change — if you're willing to face the fact that right now you are a loser, and that all the introspection, self-pity, and therapy won't take the place of just doing it — work before play, no excuses, no working on peripheral, easier tasks when there are central ones waiting. Every time you reach the moment of truth — when you're deciding whether to work or goof off — you're taking a step toward being a winner or a loser. It's your choice.

Work is work

Many career searchers want to hold out for a job that's fun. They fantasize about leaping out of bed each morning rarin' to start the day, but the fact is, few people — even those with carefully chosen careers — leap regularly.

Despite what many career guide authors and motivational speakers tell you, work is generally work. Even an ostensibly glamorous job such as writing a book for a fine publisher or playing host to a radio show, for the most part, is work.

Of course, if your boss is continually oppressive, the workload is crushing, or your co-workers are asinine, change jobs. But a key to a contented worklife may be to not expect work to be play; that's why they call it work. Appreciate being able to work: that you can do something useful, and get paid for it to boot. I embrace work and concentrate on trying to make the most of each working *moment.* I find that when I do that, the work actually feels more pleasant.

Up is not the only way

Climb the ladder — it's the American way. Earn more so you can buy more stuff you don't really need.

If high income is important to you, fine, but it's easy to shoot for a high-income job without really thinking about the tradeoffs. This section merely asks you to make that decision consciously.

With a 40 percent to 60 percent marginal tax rate for many American middle income earners, it's usually difficult to raise your standard of living significantly without plenty of extra hours at work and time away from the people and things you love. You may well have to spend a lot of effort on something you don't really believe in. You may have to do a lot of apple polishing, maybe some ethical compromising.

And what are the likely benefits? Material. Is it really worth those compromises so you can drive a nice car rather than a functional one, live in an upscale place instead of an adequate one, fly to a faraway vacation spot rather than drive to a nearby one?

Imagine what would happen if you agreed to trade away some income for work that required fewer compromises with your values.

Sixteen years ago, I said goodbye to the university, where I was essentially forced to pass prospective teachers I wouldn't allow to teach my own child, where I was forced to teach theoretical constructs that my students didn't need to know, where I was forced to write journal articles that would do nothing for the world.

Now I spend my time telling my truth and helping others find their truth. I feel alive.

Here are some decidedly low-paying but potentially rewarding careers that you might consider, at least for part of your employment:

- Lead wilderness tours. Over the campfire, talk about life.
- Write grant proposals for important things.
- Train babysitters.
- Teach people how to use the Internet.
- Tutor children — or grown-ups.
- Help people manage their money. Be amazingly honest with them.

> ✔ Become a parenting coach.
>
> ✔ Paint murals on ugly concrete walls in the community. If you don't know how to paint, find children that do.

I ask you to consciously consider whether the upsides of climbing the ladder are likely to be worth the price — for you and the others you affect.

Paul & Sarah's Thoughts

Having traded in livelihoods that sapped our energies and literally made us ill, for careers that feed our bodies, minds, and souls, we hold strong beliefs about making a living.

If play is child's work, why cannot work be adult's play? It's possible. On our weekly radio show, which we've broadcast since 1987, we've interviewed thousands of people in many different businesses. From these exchanges, and the hundreds of interviews we've conducted in writing our books, we know that many people would continue to do the work they do even if they won the lottery. Sure, they'd delegate out the parts they dislike, but they would continue doing the work they enjoy.

For some, work means even more. It means making a difference, leaving the world a bit better. We believe that these values, along with loving and being loved, are what matter most in life. And we firmly believe that it's realistic to find a career that provides plenty of this kind of sustenance. It's a choice we can make.

Sometimes, the key is choosing to tackle something big, maybe even something so big that it feels scary: to go beyond your comfort zone, stretch yourself, and strive to surpass what you and others expect of you. Consider approaching your career in the spirit expressed by President John Kennedy in the early '60s when he said that we choose to go to the moon in this decade, not because it is easy, but because it is hard.

Especially if you are self-employed, but even if you are not, you can be the artist of your life. You hold the brush in your hands. The events that life presents are your watercolors, your dreams are your guide, and your canvas is the 24 hours that lie ahead. If you don't like the color, the texture, and form of your life, you can usually change it until you get something more to your liking.

There is no need to compare your canvas to that of others. The good life means different things to different people. Only you know what it is for you. Courage is being willing to take a stand for what *you* want and to get busy creating it from the realities at hand. For us, that's what livelihood is all about.

Appendix

The Cool Career Finder

· ·

*H*ere are 16 special lists of careers: from those likely to impress your family to those too much fun to be work. You can read about each career on the page listed next to it.

Make a big difference

Biological Weapons
   Deterrence Specialist, 30
Biologist
   (molecular/genetic), 28
Book/Magazine/Website
   Acquisitions Editor, 41
Computer Security
   Programmer, 35
Environmental Attorney, 79
Environmental Engineer, 108
Film Director/Filmmaker, 112
Fundraiser, 24
Journalist, 40
Librarian, 42
Lobbyist, 73
Non-Polluting Car Developer,
   108
Nurse, 112
Photojournalist, 104
Physician's Assistant, 120
Plant Geneticist, 29
Producer, 25
Talk Show Host, 67

Easy-to-transition-into careers

Abstractor, 43
Coffee Cart(s) Owner, 76
Customer Support Specialist,
   83
Debt Collection Specialist, 66
Dispensing Optician, 99

Emergency Medicine
   Technician, 121
Fundraiser, 24
Grant Proposal Writer, 89
Home Stager, 98
Information Retriever, 42
Locksmith, 54
Manager (work-family/
   telecommuting/associa-
   tion), 61
Massage Therapist, 100
Online Marketer, 90
Personal Chef, 55
Personnel Recruiter, 21
Photographer (newborn,
   industrial), 104
Sales, 23
Specialty Consultant, 93
Telecommunications
   Equipment Installer, 51
Victim Assistant, 19
Web Indexer, 43
Web Writer/Copy Editor, 39

Too much fun to be work

Advertising Planner, 65
Background Vocalist, 73
Dating Coach, 18
Fashion Designer, 103
Flavorist, 32
Foley Artist, 47
Filmmaker/Director, 112
Game Programmer, 35

Garden Designer, 102
Graphologist, 44
Holographer, 47
Image Consultant, 18
Incidental Music Composer,
   73
Makeup Artist, 100
Matchmaker, 22
Muralist, 46
Newborn Photographer, 104
Perfumer, 48
Personal Historian, 81
Pet Photographer, 104
Photojournalist, 104
Polygraph Operator, 75
Product Tester, 56
Professional Speaker, 68
Pyrotechnician, 56
Rock Band Photographer, 109
Soundtrack Sound Designer,
   72
Special Effects Artist, 45
Special Occasions Cake
   Baker, 44
Sports Announcer, 67
Sports Statistician, 32
Textile Designer, 46
Trend Spotter, 91

Impress your friends and family

Administrative Law Judge, 80
Architect, 122

Attorney, 77
Biologist, 28
Biological Weapons
  Deterrence Specialist, 30
Book/Magazine/Website
  Editor, 41
Brewer, 110
Cinematographer, 47
City Manager, 62
Clergy, 71
Coroner/Medical Examiner, 94
Cryptanalyst, 33
Curator, 122
Dentist, 98
Engineer, 106
Enologist, 110
FBI Special Agent, 117
Fashion Designer, 103
Filmmaker/Director, 112
Foreign Service Officer, 82
Game Programmer, 35
Investment Banker, 87
Journalist, 40
Landscape Architect, 98
Lobbyist, 73
Management Consultant, 92
Mediator, 14
Meteorologist, 30
Non-Polluting Car Developer,
  108
Photojournalist, 104
Physician, 118
Plant Geneticist, 29
Political Campaign Manager, 64
Portfolio Manager, 37
Producer, 25
Professional Speaker, 68
Professor, 89
Radio Guide Publisher, 44
Radio/TV News Reporter, 66
School Administrator, 63
Soundtrack Designer, 72
Sports Announcer, 67
Sports Information
  Director, 88

Talk Show Host, 67
Trend Spotter, 91
Venture Capitalist, 88
Veterinarian, 120
Web Designer, 83

Express yourself
Actor, 71
Architect, 122
Artist/Graphic Designer, 45
Attorney, 77
Cinematographer, 47
Engineer, 106
Ethicist, 44
Exhibit Designer/Builder, 47
Fashion Designer, 103
Filmmaker/Director, 112
Garden Designer, 102
Home Stager, 98
Interior Designer, 97
Industrial Designer, 109
Inventor, 109
Journalist, 40
Landscape Architect, 98
Makeup Artist, 100
Newsletter Publisher, 35
Photographer, 103
Producer, 25
Professional Speaker, 68
Professor 89
Public Relations Specialist,
  80
Radio/TV News Reporter, 66
Special Occasions Cake
  Baker, 44
Specialty Seamstress, 55
Sports Announcer, 67
Sports Information Director,
  88
Talk Show Host, 67
Teacher, 69-70
Video Yearbook Publisher,
  118
Web Designer, 83
Writer, 39

Could lead to big bucks
Actuary, 36
Attorney, 77
Computer Security
  Administrator, 115
Dentist, 98
Engineer, 106
Executive Recruiter, 21
Idea Generator, 92
Investment Banker, 87
Management Consultant, 92
Physician, 118
Portfolio Manager, 37
Producer, 25
Securities Trader, 88
Trial Consultant, 27
Venture Capitalist, 88
Veterinarian, 120
Web Designer, 83
Webmaster, 84

I have no degree, but I want a good career and I want it fast
Computer Tutor, 74
Employment Interviewer, 21
Farrier, 54
Food Cart Owner, 76
Home Stager, 98
Locksmith, 54
Mobile Auto Detailer, 53
Nanny, 20
Neon Sign Maker, 47
Notebook Computer
  Repairperson, 50
Paramedic, 121
Personal Assistant, 20
Personal Chef, 55
Sales, 23

For the brainy
Accountant, 85
Acoustics Specialist, 94
Actuary, 36
Architect, 122

Attorney, 77
Biological Weapons
  Deterrence Specialist, 30
Biologist, 28
Business Plan Writer, 93
Computer Programmer, 33
Coroner/Medical Examiner,
  94
Cryptanalyst, 33
Economist, 36
Editor, 41
Engineer, 106
Executive Coach, 18
Exercise Physiologist, 115
Filmmaker/Director, 112
Geographer, 95
Geologist, 96
Idea Generator, 92
Information Technology
  Manager, 60
Inventor, 109
Investment Banker, 87
Journalist, 40
Librarian, 42
Management Consultant, 92
Mediator, 14
Meteorologist, 30
Network Administrator, 115
Oceanographer, 95
Operations Research
  Analyst, 84
Patent Agent, 106
Physician, 118
Plant Geneticist, 29
Political Campaign Manager,
  64
Portfolio Manager, 37
Producer, 25
Professor, 89
Program Evaluator, 90
Proposal Writer, 89
Psychotherapist, 15
Software Engineer, 83
Statistician, 32
Systems Analyst, 84

Thesis Completion
  Consultant, 89
Toxicologist, 29
Trial Consultant, 27
Venture Capitalist, 88
Veterinarian, 120
Web Designer, 83
Webmaster, 84
Writer, 39

Employers are begging
Automotive Technician, 52
Biologist (bachelor's level),
  28
Bioinformatician, 29
Catholic Priest, 71
Computer Programmer, 33
Database Administrator, 84
Engineer, 106
Forensic Accountant, 86
Information Technology
  Manager, 60
International Accountant, 86
Nanny, 20
Nurse (master's lever), 112
Operations Research
  Analyst, 84
Patent Attorney, 79
Physician's Assistant, 120
Software Engineer, 83
Software Trainer, 68
Supply Chain Manager, 85
System/Network
  Administrator, 115
Systems Analyst, 84
Teacher, Science, Math,
  English as 2nd Language,
  70
Technical Support Provider,
  83
Telecommunications
  Technologist/Installer, 51
Web Content Finder, 42
Web Designer, 83
Webmaster, 84

Little-known but great
Accent Reduction Specialist,
  74
Audiologist, 120
Child Life Specialist, 19
Biological Weapons
  Deterrence Specialist, 30
Biomedical Visualization
  Specialist, 46
College Student Affairs
  Admin., 59
College-Bound Athlete
  Counselor, 74
Cryptanalyst, 33
Doula, 18
Enologist, 110
Family Historian/Biographer,
  81
Flavorist, 32
Genomics/Proteomics, 124
Ghostwriter, 40
Graphologist, 44
Home Stager, 98
Hydrologist, 30
Idea Generator, 92
Indexer, 43
Information Retriever, 42
Lighting Designer, 47
Muralist, 46
Money Counselor, 15
Newborn Photographer, 104
Non-Polluting Car
  Developer,108
Nurse Midwife, 113
Orthoptist, 57
Pedorthist, 49
Perfumer, 48
Personal Chef, 55
Physician, Infectious
  Diseases, 119
Physician's Assistant, 120
Plant Geneticist, 29
Private Practice Consultant,
  93
Proposal Writer, 89

School Computer Coordinator, 116
Shyness Coach, 17
Social Science Analyst, 43
Soundtrack Sound Designer, 72
Special Occasions Cake Baker, 44
Sports Information Director, 88
Succession Planning Consultant, 65
Surgical Technologist, 97
Troubled Teen Consultant, 74
TV/Radio Community Affairs Director, 62
Victim Assistant, 19
Video Yearbook Publisher, 118
Volcanologist, 31

Maximum security

Accountant, 85
Attorney, Patent, 79
Automotive Technician, 52
Biological Weapons Deterrence Specialist, 30
Computer Programmer, 33
Database Administrator, 84
Dentist, 98
Electrician, 52
Engineer (computer and electrical), 107
Fundraiser, 24
Geographic Information Specialist, 95
Government manager, 60
High-Tech Repairperson, 50
Military Officer, 65
Nurse (master's-level), 112
Occupational Therapist, 75
School Administrator, 63
Social Worker, 19
Software Trainer, 68
System/Network Administrator, 115

Systems Analyst, 84
Teacher, 69-70
Telecommunications Technologist/Installer, 51
Web Designer, 83
Webmaster, 84

Good with your hands?

Artist, 45
Cartographer, 110
Conservator, 46
Die Maker, 48
Diver, 56
Electrologist, 101
Engineering Technician, 109
Exhibit Designer/Builder, 47
Holographer, 47
Inventor, 109
Locksmith, 54
Massage Therapist, 100
Makeup Artist, 100
Muralist, 46
Musical Instrument Repairer, 49
Neon Sign Maker, 47
Orthotist/Prosthetist, 49
Pedorthist, 49
Photo Restorator, 104
Physician, 118
Specialty Seamster, 55
Special Occasions Cake Baker, 44

The leading edge

Biological Weapons Deterrence Specialist, 30
Biologist, 28
Biomed Visualization Specialist, 46
Computer Security Programmer, 35
Distance Learning Teacher, 70
Ecotourism Tour Operator, 38
Engineer, 106

Flying Car Developer, 108
Geographic Information Specialist, 95
Green Architect, 122
Idea Generator, 92
Inventor, 109
Non-Polluting Car Developer, 108
Online Marketer, 90
Patent Agent, 106
Patent Attorney, 79
Planetary Geologist, 96
Space Lawyer, 79
Special Effects Artist, 45
System Administrator, 115
Systems Analyst, 84
Toy Designer, 110
Trend Spotter, 91
Virtual Reality Programmer, 34
Web Programmer, 34
Web Designer, 83
Wireless Device Programmer, 34

Kick-back careers

Archivist, 94
Brewer, 110
College Student Advisor, 16
Cosmetologist/Makeup Artist, 100
Dispensing Optician, 99
Enologist (winemaker), 110
Foley Artist, 47
Foreign Language Translator, 82
Garden Designer, 102
Gemologist, 54
Graphologist, 44
Historic Preservationist, 111
Home Inspector, 101
Home Stager, 98
Image Consultant, 18
Massage Therapist, 100
Matchmaker, 22
Muralist, 46

Musical Instrument Repairer, 49
Neon Sign Maker, 47
Perfumer, 48
Personal Coach, 16
Personal Historian/Biographer, 81
Relocation Consultant, 27
Restaurant Menu Creator, 112
Specialty Seamster, 55
Thesis Completion Consultant, 89
Trend Spotter, 91

My favorite shoestring businesses

Business Plan Writer, 93
College-Bound Athlete Counselor, 74
Computer Programmer, 33
Electrician, 52
Food Cart Business Operator, 76
Garden Designer, 102
Home Schooling Consultant, 75
Home Stager, 98
Image Consultant, 18
Indexer, 43
Money Counselor, 15
Newborn Photographer, 104
Parking Lot Oil Change Business Operator, 77
Personal Coach, 16
Proposal Writer, 89
Specialty Seamster, 55
Succession Planning Consultant, 65
Thesis Completion Consultant, 89
Trial Consultant, 27
Tutor, 74
Web Developer, 83

Supercool careers (the best of the best)

These careers scored highest overall on my criteria: make a difference, enjoyable to many people, good pay, ease of entry, little-known, and good job prospects.

Adoption Specialist, 78
Audiologist, 120
Biological Weapons Deterrence Specialist, 30
Biologist (bachelor's level), 28
Biomedical Visualization Specialist, 46
Book/Magazine/Web Site Editor, 41
Business Plan Writer, 93
Business Home Economist, 123
Case Manager (nurse), 114
Computer Security Programmer, 35
College Admission Consultant, 74
College Student Advisor, 16
College Student Affairs Administrator, 59
Education Software Programmer, 34
Electrician, 52
Fundraiser, 24
Garden Designer, 102
Home Inspector, 101
Home Stager, 98
Idea Generator, 92
Interior Designer, 97
Journalist, 40
Landscape Architect, 98
Librarian, 42
Lighting Designer, 44
Locksmith, 54
Mediator, 14
Money Counselor, 15
Musical Instrument Repairer, 49
Newborn Photographer, 104
Non-Polluting Car Developer, 108
Nurse Anesthetist, 113
Optometrist, 57
Patent Agent, 106
Personal Coach, 16
Physician (infectious diseases), 119
Physician's Assistant, 120
Plant Geneticist, 29
Political Campaign Manager, 64
Proposal Writer, 89
Prosthetist/Orthotist, 49
Radio/TV News Reporter, 66
School Computer Coordinator, 116
Social Marketer, 91
Social Science Analyst, 43
Speech-Language Therapist, 73
Sports Information Director, 88
Succession Planning Consultant, 65
Surgical Technologist, 99
Systems Analyst, 84
TV/Radio Community Affairs Director, 62
Tutor, 74
Venture Capitalist, 88
Veterinarian, 120
Virtual Reality Programmer, 34
Web Designer, 83
Web Content Finder, 42
Work-Family Manager, 61

Index

• Numbers •

200 Letters for Job Seekers, 272
303 Off-the-Wall Ways to Get a
  Job, 273

• A •

abilities, 137–138
  final decision and, 163, 165
  generic, 138
  proving during interview,
    313–314
  specific expertise, 138
  tailoring job to, 352–353
About.com, 186
accomplishments, 142
accomplishments in ad
  responses, 263
accomplishments, resume,
  226–231
  soft, 227
  transferable attributes, 228
  unpaid work, 228
accusatory statements from
  boss, 358
admission to college, 193–196
  prestigious colleges, 195–196
  professor's opinion, 196
  student's contribution to
    school, 195–196
  test preparation, 195
Adrenaline Addict,
  procrastination and, 408
advancing, 367–369
  management, 369
adversity, career choice and,
  139
advisors, college, 200
agencies, 258
  negotiation and, 329
agreements, self-employment,
  382
Amazon.com, 155
America's CareerInfoNet Web
  site, 155
America's Learning Exchange,
  183, 186
American Society for Training
  & Development's Seminar
  Agent, The, 186

American's Learning Exchange,
  391
ammunition during
  negotiation, 328
anger, career choice and, 140
apprenticeships, 183, 210
arrival time for interview, 308
article writing, self-
  employment, 384
assistant positions, 169, 210
Associations Unlimited, 295
attire, interviews, 300, 302, 307
attitude, 213–216
  fear of rejection and, 217
  playfulness, 214
authenticity, questions and, 137
authority resentment,
  procrastination and, 409
authors' career changes,
  168–170
awards, resume, 232

• B •

bad start to interviews, 310
being in the moment, 215
benefits
  large companies, 240
  negotiation and, 330
*Best Home Businesses for
  the 21st Century, The*,
  13, 154, 375, 391
bill rate, agencies, 329
biographies
  in lieu of resumes, 265
  self-employed, 382
biography, 222
blind ads, 261–262
body chemistry, 307
bosses
  accusatory statements from,
    358
  hotheads, 359
  incompetent, 359
  making most of, 356–359
  micromanaging, 359
  self-employment and, 373
  work hours, 357

• C •

Career Builder Web site, 391
career change, advantages/
  disadvantages, 167
career change tips, 348–350
career musts
  questions for, 135–137
  questions to ask, 146
  suggestions of other careers,
    146–149
  values, 136–137
career planning, 7–10
CareerInfoNet Web site, 155
careerwriter.com Web site, 237
casual tone with contacts, 207
categories
  Cool Careers Yellow Pages, 12
  self-employment, 141–142
certificate programs, 183
certifications, new job and, 362
chemistry with interviewer, 307
  body chemistry, 307
  negotiation and, 328
chronological format, resumes,
  224
client meetings, self-
  employment, 378
co-workers
  making most of, 356–359
  networking and, 290
  relationships at new job, 354
cold calls, 267–285
  directly relevant experience,
    271–272
  e-mail, 279
  job fairs, 284–285
  letters, 268–272
  networking and, 343–344
  no experience, open to
    options, 270–271
  no relevant experience, 269
  off-the-wall, 273
  PAR stories, 275–276
  preparation, 273–282
  quick human story, 273–274
  resumes, 268
  role-playing, 276–277
  thirty-day plan and, 339–350
  voice mail and, 277
  walk ins, 281–282

college catalogs, 391
college extension programs, 185
  prestigious schools, 193
college graduates, Web sites for, 257
colleges
  admission, 193–196
  admission, test preparation, 195
  advisors, 200
  alumni network contacts, 290
  benefiting from, 198–200
  financial aid, 196
  financial aid, comparing, 198
  job market and, 179
  prestigious, 192
  prestigious, admission, 195–196
  salaries and, 192
  selecting, 192–193
  student's contribution to school, 195–196
  tuition, 196–197
committing to choice, research and, 163
communication
  developing skills at new job, 357–358
  self-employment, 374
  tone, 207, 214
community involvement, resume, 232
company culture, interviews and, 300
Company of Friends Web site, 298
competition in specific field, 398
complaints, self-employment, 383
computers, necessity of, 208
concessions, negotiation, 333
conduits, self-employment, 383
conferences, 160
  networking and, 294
cons of self-employment, 372–373
consulting, 229
contact information, resume, 222
contacts, 155–158
  cold calls, 342–343
  connection building, 281
  locating, 247–248
  networking and, 289–290

off-the-wall, 273
  recordkeeping, 248
  ResumeMaker, 343
  ResumeMaker software, 340
  what to say, 156–158
contracts, self-employment, 382
control, self-employment, 373
conventional job search techniques, 205
Cool Careers Yellow Pages, 11–133
  icons, 13
cost control, self-employment, 378–379
costs of degree programs, 191
counseling, virtual career counseling, 147–148
counter offers at negotiation, 333
course work, college extension programs, 185
cover letter, 341
  repeating information in resume, 231
creativity, career musts and, 136
curious, not convince mantra, 358
current position, tweaking, 170
customer support, 210

• D •

daily examples of careers, 392
deep breathing, stress and, 215
degrees. *See also* education
  certificate programs, 183
  convincing employers about, 182–183
  doctoral, rate of award, 179
  enthusiam of professor, getting caught in, 190
  incompetence despite having, 177
  MBA, rate of award, 179
  mentors, 180
  payoffs, 177–179
  program, choosing, 189–191
  program, quality, 190–191
  program cost, 191
  program official materials, 191
  psychological barriers of not having, 177
  reasons for getting, 175–176
  successful people without, 177
  universities' awareness of job market, 179

You University, 179–180
diffuse job search, 339
Directory of Private Career Schools and Colleges of Technology, 190
discussion groups online, 155, 246, 259
distance learning, 186–187
doctoral degree, rate of award, 179
dot-com businesses, 241
downsides of self-employment, 372–373
dream employers, 206
  industry, 394
  organizations, 395
dressing for interview, 300, 302

• E •

e-classes, 185
e-networking, 2, 206, 289, 296–298
e-mail
  cold calls and, 279
  employer's address, 223
  hardcopy follow-up, 268
  resume attachments, 235–236
education. *See also* degrees
  About.com, 186
  America's Learning Exchange, 186
  American Society for Training & Development's Seminar Agent, The, 186
  apprenticeships, 183
  benefiting from, 198–200
  certificate programs, 183
  college admission, 193–196
  college extension programs, 185
  e-classes, 185
  Globewide Network Academy, 187
  Hungry Minds Web site, 187
  learn2.com, 186
  lifelong learning, 188
  mentors, locating, 184–185
  Mindedge.com, 187
  online seminars, prestigious colleges, 184
  Peterson's Guide to Distance Learning, 186
  prestigious colleges, 192
  school selection, 192–193
  Small Business Administration, The, 187

Thomas Edison State College, 194
tutors, 187
Yellow Pages, 12–13
education section of resume, 231–232
electronic resume, 235–236
emotion-driven bosses, negotiation and, 331
emotional energy units, 362
emotional investment in want ads, 266
employers
  contacts, 247–248
  degree, convincing to hire without, 182–183
  highlighting previous, 229
  inside information, 250
  internal job postings, current employer, 255
  locating, 244–248
  needs, interview and, 310
  public information, 249
  Web sites, 255
employment agencies, 258
  negotiation and, 329
employment Web sites, 344–345
ending interview, 306
entertainment industry, Web sites, 258
enthusiasm
  at offer, 317
  during negotiation, employer's, 328
  professor's, getting caught in during coursework, 190
entry-level positions, non-advertised, 267
Environmental Careers in the 21st Century, 390
environmental careers, Web sites, 258
excitement level, 149
excuse-making, cures, 403–409
expectations of new job, 351

● *F* ●

fact-driven bosses, negotiation and, 331
family, networking and, 290
family opinion, 142
fast-based bosses, negotiation and, 332

fear of failure, 165–167
  procrastination and, 405
  self-employment, 384
  status quo and, 167–168
fear of rejection, 217–219
  attitude and, 217
  curing, 219
  library book attitude, 217
  rejection as blessing, 218
  skills and, 217
  worst case scenario, 218
feedback on resume, 235
fees
  degree program, 191
  self-employment, 382
final decision on job
  abilities and, 165
  indecision in, 164–165
  market existence, 164
  multiple, 169
  research and, 163
  skills and, 165
  training and, 165
  trial period, 169
financial aid, 196
  comparing deals, 198
Finding Your Perfect Work, 384, 391
first date interviews, 206
first impressions, 309
  bad, 310
flexibility, self-employment and, 373
focused job search, 339
follow-up
  hardcopy after e-mail, 268
  thirty-day plan, 339
food items at interview, 312
formal tone in communications, 207
formatting resume, 223, 225
Fortune magazine, 245
franchise purchase, 187, 396
fraternal organizations, scholarships and, 197
freelance workers, networking, 298
freelancers, 382
friends
  contacts, 156
  networking, 290

● *G* ●

gatekeepers, passing, 277–279
get-rich-quick schemes, 376

Globewide Network Academy, 187
good enough resumes, 221
Good Idea, self-employment startup, 375–376
government jobs, 242–243
  career musts and, 137
  Web sites, 257
grad school selection, 192–193
grade point average, 231
graduation, expected date, 231
groups, networking, 296
growing organizations, want ads and, 259
Guerrilla Tactics in the Job Market, 218

● *H* ●

hardcopy follow-up to e-mail, 268
head hunters. *See* recruiters
healthcare field Web sites, 258
Hey Joe school, 361
highlights of resume, 233–235
hobbies, incorporating into new job, 360
hothead bosses, 359
human story. *See* quick human story
Hungry Minds Web site online courses, 187

● *I* ●

icons in Yellow Pages, 12–13
icons used in book, 4
ideas, avoiding stolen, 355
imperfect work history, 229–231
imposing on others, procrastination and, 407
incompetence despite degree, 177
incompetent bosses, 359
indecision regarding choices, 164–165
Index of Majors and Graduate Degrees, 390
Industry Insite, Web site, 298
Industry Link Web site, 155
industry, dream industry, 394
informal style in ad response, 263
initial feelings regarding career choices, 164
inside information on employers, 250

Internet
  discussion groups, 246
  number of people using, 262
  online searches, 155
  scams, 376
  searches, 206, 339, 395
Internet access, 208
internships, 160
  mentors and, 184
  Web sites, 258
interrogations, avoiding during
      interview, 299–318
Interview Report Card, 313, 315
interviews
  arrival time, 308
  attire, 300, 302, 307
  bad start, 310
  chemistry with interviewer,
      299, 307
  company culture, 300
  dress, 302
  empathy, 301
  employer's needs,
      understanding, 310
  ending, 306
  ending with food items, 312
  first dates versus
      interrogations, 206,
      299–318
  first impressions, 309
  food items, 312
  hirer's point of view, 301
  job description, employer
      and, 314–315
  listening skills, 311
  mannerisms, 309
  mirroring interviewer, 312
  note card cues, 302
  panel interviews, 312
  PAR story, 301
  persistence after, 317
  personal life, 312
  poor match, 315
  post interview questions, 313,
      315
  producing resume during, 265
  proving abilities, 313–314
  questions, answer length, 314
  questions, lost job, 318
  questions, when to ask, 311
  questions during, 299
  quick human story, 301
  real self during, 310
  references, 316–317
  rejection, 318
  relaxing, 308

  researching prior to, 301
  role playing and, 302
  salary, 305, 307
  scheduling, 300
  self-employment, 382
  self-talk, 303
  talking during, amount, 311
  thank you letters, 315–316
  timing, 300
  tone, 207, 312
  video, 312
  weaknesses, 312
investigating career choices,
      151–160
  contacts, making, 155–158
  employer visits, 158–159
  reading, 153–155
  reading materials, 154
  seminars, 160

• J •

job fairs, 206, 284–285
Job Finder book series, 246
job market, colleges and, 179
job offers. *See also* negotiation
  enthusiasm at, 317
job openings not advertised,
      267–285
job requirements. *See*
      requirements
Job Search Secrets, 248
job search, self-employment,
      372–373
job security, self-employment
      and, 372
job target, 223
job-hopping, 229
juggling all options, 215

• K •

key client plan, self-
      employment startup, 380

• L •

large companies, advantages
      of, 240
lateral moves within company,
      359
lazy bosses, 359
learn2.com, 186
learning on job, 361–362
leave plan, self-employment
      startup, 379
legal issues, large companies,
      240

letters
  cold calls, 268–272
  cover letter, 341
  directly relevant experience,
      271–272
  job fairs, 284
  no relevant experience, 269
  reference, 227
  thank you letters, 282–283
libraries, online searches and,
      154
library as resource, 154
library comparison, 217
lifelong learning, 188
  Thomas Edison State College,
      194
likeability, persistence and, 277
listening skills, 311
lists of careers, 390–391
locating employers, 244–248
location of job, 147
  career musts and, 136
lovers, networking and, 290

• M •

management, advancing to, 369
managing stress, 362–363
mannerisms during interview,
      309
market, existence of for sales,
      164
marketing, self-employment
      and, 374, 383–384
MBAs, rate of award, 179
media, exposure to different
      careers, 393
mentors
  apprenticeships, 183
  locating, 184–185
  new job, 361
  tutors, 187
  You University, 180
micromanaging bosses, 359
Mindege.com, 187
mirroring interviewer, 312
mission statement, 137
model resumes, 225
moonlighting plan, self-
      employment startup, 379
Myjobsearch.com, 155

• N •

narrative resumes, 231
needs, seeing and offering
      solutions, 398

negotiation, 319–321
  ammunition, 328
  benefits, 330
  chemistry with hirer, 328
  concessions, 333
  counter offers, 333
  emotion-driven boss, 331
  employment agencies, 329
  fact-driven, 331
  fast-paced bosses, 332
  highest salary to expect,
    328–329
  post session work, 334–335
  preparation, 320–327
  self-employed persons,
    333–334
  slow-paced bosses, 332
  stock options, 330–331
  summary of agreement, 331
  thirty-day plan, 339–350
  worth, 326–327
networking, 143, 206
  by phone, 291–293
  cold calls, 343–344
  conferences and, 294
  contacts, 289–290
  conventional techniques, 205
  definition of, 287
  e-networking, 206, 289,
    296–298
  freelancers and, 298
  groups, joining, 296
  how much to, 288–289
  information from contacts,
    290
  nonprofit organizations, 296
  opinions on, 287
  personal connections, 394
  professional associations,
    294–295
  reluctance, tips for, 293–294
  ResumeMaker contacts, 343
  self-employment, 383
  social situations, 295
  strategies, 291
  trade associations and,
    294–295
  trade shows and, 294
  workshops, teaching, 295
  workshops and, 294
*Networking and Your Job
  Search*, 298
Networking for Everyone, 293
new job
  communication skills,
    357–358
  expectations, 351

getting ahead, 367–369
  hothead boss, 359
  lateral moves, 359
  learning at, 361–362
  making most of, 356–367
  mentors, 361
  micromanaging bosses, 359
  special projects, 359
  tutors, 361
newspapers, 255
  thirty-day plan, 339–350
  want ads, 206, 251–253
niches, 398
No BS Marketing Newsletter, 209
nonprofit businesses
  career musts and, 137
  locating, 247
nonprofit organizations, 241
  networking and, 296
nonprofit Web sites, 258
note card cues, 302
note taking, job fairs, 285

• O •

*O*Net Dictionary of
  Occupational Titles*, 390
O*Net web site, 155
observing daily life for ideas,
  392
Occupational Information
  Network, 155
*Occupational Outlook
  Handbook*, 13, 154, 390
offers, enthusiasm at, 317
office politics, 365–367
official materials, degree
  program, 191
old want ads, 262
online courses, 186–187
online discussion groups, 155
online searches, 155, 206
  library, 154
  search engines, 155
organizations
  dream organization, 395
  selecting, 139
  size, career musts and, 137

• P •

panel interviews, 312
PAR (Problem, Approach,
  Resolution), 227, 301
  cold calls and, 275–276
part-time plan, self-
  employment startup, 379

part-time positions, want ads,
  260–261
passions/interests, 139–142,
  149
  adversity, 139
  anger, 140
  persons to work with, 141
Pathfinder, The, 295
people skills, 227
people to work with, 147
perfectionists, procrastination
  and, 406–407
persistence, 277
  self-employment, 374
personal connections, 394. *See
  also* networking
personal information, resume
  and, 232
personal life, interview and,
  312
personality parts, 399
personality showing in ad
  response, 264
persons to work with,
  passions/interest and, 141
*Peterson's Guide to Distance
  Learning*, 186
piggyback plan, self-
  employment startup, 379
playful attitude, 214
politics, office, 365–367
portfolios, 222
position requirements. *See*
  requirements
position wanted ads, 259
positions not advertised,
  267–285
Post-It note as cold call, 273
preparation time, 208
  cold calls, 273–282
  job fairs, 284
  negotiation, 320–327
presentation kits, 222
prestige, career musts and, 136
previous experience, 228
pricing, self-employment
  startup, 380
*Princeton Review Guide to Your
  Career, The*, 154
prioritizing job search
  activities, 216
problem solving, self-
  employment and, 373
procrastination
  Adrenaline Addict, 408
  all-purpose cures, 409–412

procrastination *(continued)*
   authority resentment and, 409
   curing, 402–403
   excuse-making, cures, 403–409
   fear of failure, 405
   fear of success, 407
   imposition, fear of, 407
   perfectionists, 406–407
   reasons for, 401–402
   time issues, 409
productivity, self-employment, 373
professional affiliations, resume, 232
professional associations
   Associations Unlimited, 295
   meeting attendance, 156
   mentors and, 184
   networking and, 294–295
   networking contacts, 290
   publications, 154
professional attendance, publications, 156
professional excellence, procrastination and, 407
professional periodicals, want ads, 255
program, degree
   choosing, 189–191
   cost, 191
   official materials, 191
   quality, 190–191
promotions, 355
psychological barriers of not having degree, 177
public information on employers, 249
publications, 154
   professional periodicals, 255
   professional publications, 154

• *Q* **•**

questions
   abilities, 137–138
   accomplishments, 142
   career musts, 135–137, 146
   family opinion, 142
   interview, 299
   interview, answer length, 314
   interviews, when to ask, 311
   lost job, follow-up, 318
   mission statement, 137
   organizations to work for, 139
   passions, 139–141

persons to work with, 141
post interview, 313, 315
self-employment categories, 141–142
skills, 137–138
who you know, 143
quick human story, 301
   cold calls, 273–274

• *R* **•**

randomness in job search, 400
reading about career, 154
real self, 214
   interviews/letters, 207, 299, 310
reality of career choices, 165
Rebecca Smith's model resumes, 225
recorded resume, 273
recordkeeping
   contacts, 248
   want ads, 254
recruiters
   networking groups, 298
   thirty-day plan, 345–346
   Web sites, 257
reference letters, 227
Reference Service Press, 197
references, 316–317
referrals, self-employment, 383
regional Web sites, 258
rejection, 318
   fear of, 217–219
relationships with co-workers, 354
relaxing prior to interview, 308
repeating information in cover letter, 231
requirements
   ad response and, 263
   not quite fitting, 261
research
   committing to choice and, 163
   final decision and, 163
   online searches, 154
   prior to interview, 301
   reading materials, 154
resentment concerning job search, 219
resources
   library, 154
   lists of careers, 390–391
responding to want ads, 262–265

response styles to want ads, 263–265
response styles; want ads, 263
Resume Maker Web site, 237
ResumeMaker software, 254, 340
   contacts, 340
   networking contacts, 343
resumeplace.com Web site, 237
resumes, 206. *See also* biographies, portfolios, presentation kits
   accomplishments, 226–231
   awards, 232
   biographies instead of, 265
   cold call letters and, 268
   community involvement, 232
   contact information, 222
   education section, 231–232
   electronic, 235–236
   employers and, 222
   feedback, 235
   formatting, 223, 225
   good enough, 221
   highlighting previous employers, 229
   highlights, 233–235
   job fairs, 284
   job target, 223
   model, 225
   narrative, 231
   personal information, 232
   previous experience, 228
   producing at interview, 265
   professional affiliations, 232
   recorded, 273
   repeating information in cover letter, 231
   self-employed, 382
   time spent, 221
   time spent preparing, 340
   vague language, 230
   work samples in lieu of, 265
Resumes For Dummies, 268
right job for you, nine signs, 335
Riley Guide, The (web site), 155
risking failure, 166
role playing
   cold calls and, 276–277
   interviews and, 302

• *S* **•**

salary. *See also* negotiation
   career musts and, 136
   college and, 192

highest to expect, 328–329
interview discussion, 305, 307
reasons for large, 325–326
requirements discussion in
    ad response, 264
worth, 326–327
sampling, self-employment, 384
scams, Internet, 376
scheduling interviews, time
    slots, 300
scholarships, 192
    fraternal organizations and,
        197
    Reference Service Press, 197
SCORE (Service Corps of
    Retired Executives), 184
screening want ads, 255–259
search engines, 155
self-employment, 243
    agreements, 382
    articles, 384
    behaving as CEO, 382–383
    biographies, 222
    career musts and, 136
    categories, 141–142
    client meetings, 378
    communication, 374
    complaints, 383
    conduits, 383
    cons, 373
    contracts, 382
    control, 373
    cost control, 378–379
    created careers, 371
    downsides, 372–373
    fear of failure, 384
    fees, 382
    flexibility and, 373
    franchises, 396
    full-time job as well, 377
    get-rich-quick schemes, 376
    Good Idea, 375–376
    increasing business, 383–384
    initiating successful business,
        396
    job search, 372–373
    job security, 372
    marketing, 374, 383–384
    multiple businesses at once,
        377
    negotiation and, 333–334
    networking, 383
    persistence, 374
    pricing, 380
    problem solving, 373
    productivity and, 373

questions testing suitability,
    373–375
referrals, 383
sampling, 384
scams, Internet, 376
startup funds, 381
success tips, 375–384
vague services, 377
working hours, 372
Yellow Pages, 12
self-expression, career musts
    and, 136
self-talk, interview prep, 303
selling yourself, 207
seminars, 160
shopping comparison, 213
sideline job to get started, 168
skills, 137–138
    fear of rejection and, 217
    final decision and, 163, 165
    generic, 138
    incorporating multiple in job,
        397–399
    specific expertise, 138
    tailoring job to, 352–353
slow-paced bosses, negotiating
    and, 332
Small Business Administration,
    The, 187
small companies, advantages
    of, 240–241
social situations, networking,
    295
soft accomplishments, 227
software, ResumeMaker, 340
special projects, 359
spin-off plan, self-employment
    startup, 379
stability, large companies and,
    240
start-up businesses, 241
    locating, 246–247
status quo and fear of failure,
    167–168
stock options, negotiating,
    330–331
stolen ideas in the workplace,
    355
strengths, tailoring job to,
    352–353
stress management, 362–363
stress, deep breathing and, 215
strike price, stock options, 331
student contribution to school,
    admission and, 195–196
Success Without College, 177
success, fear of, 407

successful people without
    degrees, 177
successful self-employment,
    375–384
supervisors, networking, 290
support, 206, 215
survivors of office politics,
    366–367

● *T* ●

tailoring job to your strengths,
    352–353
talking during interviews, 311
technology, large companies
    and, 240
telecommuting, 363–364
temporary positions, 210
    want ads, 260–261
test preparation, college
    admission, 195
thank you letters, 282–283,
    315–316
The Budget of the United
    States Government, 246
The Teaching Company Web
    site, 180
The Vault Web site, 391
third eye observance, 392
third party callers, 211
thirty-day plan, 339–350
Thomas Edison State College,
    194
time issues, procrastination
    and, 409
tone of communications, 207,
    214
top-choice careers,
    discovering, 146–149
trade shows, 160
    networking and, 294–295
training
    career musts and, 136
    final decision and, 164–165
    large companies and, 240
transferable attributes, 228
transitioning to new career, 1
transitioning to self-
    employment, 380
trends, 398
trial period, 169
truth option, 214
tuition, 196–197
    degree program, 191
tutors, 187
    new job, 361

• U •

U.S. Government Manual, 246
unemployment, 229
unpaid work, accomplishments and, 228
upbeat attitude, 213–216

• V •

vague language in resume, 230
values, career musts and, 136–137
vault.com, 298
verbal resume (recorded), 273
VGM Career Horizons publications, 390–391
video interviewing, 312
virtual career counseling, 147–148
virtual job fairs, 285
visualization, 392
voice mail, cold calls and, 277
volunteer positions, resume and, 230
volunteering, 160, 210

• W •

walk-ins, 211, 281–282
want ads, 206, 251–253
  best to respond to, 255
  blind ads, 261–262
  emotional investment, 266
  growing organizations, 259
  identifying specific ad, 263
  intimidation, 260
  job requirements, not fitting, 261
  jobs not advertised, 267–285
  nonprofessional positions, 260
  older, 262
  part-time positions, 260–261
  percentage of total plan, 253–254
  position wanted, 259
  recordkeeping, 254
  recordkeeping and, 254
  responding to, 262–265
  response styles, 263–265
  screening, 255–259
  temporary positions, 260–261
  thirty-day plan, 339–350
  Web sites, 255–259
weaknesses, interviews, 312

Web sites
  About.com, 186
  Amazon.com, 155
  America's CareerInfoNet, 155
  America's Learning Exchange, 183, 391
  American's Job Bank, 257
  Career Builder, 391
  CareerBuilder, 257
  careerbuilder.com, 247
  careers.yahoo.com, 247
  CareerShop.com, 257
  careerwriter.com, 237
  CMGI, 247
  college graduates, 257
  Company of Friends, 298
  Employment 911, 257
  employment sites, 344–345
  entertainment industry, 258
  environmental careers, 258
  Federal Job Announcement Search, 257
  Federal Jobs Digest, 257
  Flipdog, 257
  Govjobs, 257
  health care, 258
  high tech jobs, 258
  Idealist, 258
  individual employers, 255
  Industry Insite, 298
  Industry Link, 155
  investigating careers, 151
  Job Direct, 257
  Jobtrak, 257
  Kathryn Troutman, 237
  learn2.com, 186
  Mindedge.com, 187
  Myjobsearch.com, 155, 246
  nonprofit jobs, 258
  O*Net, 155
  Occupational Information Network, 155
  precautions, 256
  PriceWaterhouseCoopers Money Tree, 246
  Rebecca Smith, 225
  Recruiter Connection, 257
  regional, 258
  Resume Maker, 237
  resumeplace.com, 237
  Riley Guide, The, 155, 258
  scouts, 256
  show business, 258
  specific fields, 258
  Startup Network, 246
  Startup Zone, 246
  Susan Whitcomb, 237

The Teaching Company, 180
The Vault, 246, 391
Thomas Register, 246
Top Startups, 246
vault.com, 298
Venture Wire, 247
want ads, 255–259
WantedJobs, 257
WetFeet, 246, 391
WetFeet Web site, 391
work environment, career musts and, 136
work history, imperfect, 229–231
work samples, 222, 266
  ad response, 264
  in lieu of resume, 265
working hours, 357
  self-employment and, 372
workload, new job, 360
workshops
  networking and, 294
  new job, 362
  teaching, 295
worst case scenario, fear of rejection and, 218
writing articles, self-employment, 384

• Y •

Yellow Pages, 11
  additional sources, 390–391
  categories, 12
  education, 12–13
  icons, 12–13
  self-employment, 12
You University, 179–180
  lifelong learning, 188
  mentors, 184–185
Young Millionaires, 385

Index of Careers

• A •

accent reduction specialist, 74
accessory designer, 103
accident reconstructor, 105
accountant, 85–86
acoustician, 94
actor, 71–72
actuary, 36
acupuncturist, 121
administrative law judge, 80
adoption specialist, 78
adventure travel organizer, 38
advertising executive, 131
agent, literary, artist's, or
        performer's, 19
aging parents, 129
agricultural scientist, 31–32
animator, 45
anti-aging research and practice,
        125
appraiser, 39
arborist, 54
architect, 122
archivist, 94
area specialist, 95
artificial intelligence, 126
artist, 45–46
association manager, 61–62
athletic coach, 70–71
athletic team trainer, 98
attorney, 77–80
auctioneer, 25
audiologist, 120
automotive technician, 52–53
avionics technician, 50

• B •

background vocalist, 73
banker, commercial, 87
biographer, 81
bioinformatics, 29
biological weapons deterrence
        specialist, 30
biologist, 28–29
biomedical equipment
        repairperson, 51
biomedical visualization
        specialist, 46
biometrics, 124
botanist, 29
brewer, 110

broadcast technician/engineer,
        110–111
business developer, 92
business equipment
        broker/lessor, 101
business home economist, 123
business loan broker, 88
business plan writer, 93
business valuator, 86

• C •

cake baker, 44–45
cancer registrar, 33
car detailer, mobile, 53
car developer, 108
cardiovascular technologist, 99
career coach/counselor, 16–17
car mechanic, 52–53
cartographer, 110
case manager, 114
casting director, 22–23
celebrity Web chat listing
        service, 44
chef, 131
chemist, 131
child-care provider, 20
child life specialist, 19
chiropractor, 131
cinematographer, 47
city manager, 62
clergy, 71
client prospecting specialist, 93
clinical trials coordinator, 114
cloning, 124–125
college administrator, 59
college admissions consultant, 74
college admissions recruiter, 24
college financial aid counselor, 66
college financial aid officer, 85
college student advisor, 16
commercial banker, 87
commercial debt negotiator, 66
communications specialist, 80–81
community affairs manager, 62
computer chip layout designer,
        48
computer programmer, 33–35
computer repairperson, 50–51
computer security administrator,
        115
conference taping specialist, 50
conservator, 46

consultant, 123
consultant, specialty, 93–94
convention planner, 26
convergence, 127
coroner, 94
corporate concierge, 21
corporate identity consultant, 92
corporate intelligence officer, 66
cosmetic surgeon, 119
cosmetologist, 100–101
court administrator, 59–60
court reporter, 131–132
credit risk manager, 37
criminalist, 111
cryonic suspension, 125
cryptanalyst, 33
curator, 122
cytotechnologist, 95

• D •

database administrator, 84
debt collection specialist, 66
debt negotiator, commercial, 66
demonstrative evidence
        specialist, 46
dental hygienist, 99
dentist, 98–99
development specialist, 24–25
diagnostic medical sonographer,
        76
die maker, 48
dietitian, 58
director, 112
dispensing optician, 99–100
diver, 56–57
dog trainer, 55
doula, 18
drafter, 53
dream-career trainer, 68
driving instructor, high-security,
        49

• E •

e-commerce, 128
economist, 36
editor, 41
elder mover, 103
electrician, 52
electrologist, 101
electro-neurodiagnostic (END)
        technician, 76

employee assistance professional, 19
employee background checker, 117
employee trainer, 68
employment interviewer, 21
engineer, 106–108
engineering technician, 109
enologist, 110
entomologist, 32
environmental analyst, 30
environmental manager, 62
ethicist, 44
event planner, 26–27
executive recruiter, 21–22
exercise physiologist, 115
exhibit designer/builder, 47
expense reduction consultant, 36
expo planner, 26
expo/show producer, 26
export agent, 38–39
exporter, 38

• F •

facilities manager, 61
farrier, 54
fashion designer, 103
FBI special agent, 117
filmmaker, 112
financial planner, fee-only, 65
firefighter, 132
flavorist, 32
focus group leader, 91
Foley artist, 47
food operations owner, 76–77
food scientist, 32
foreign language interpreter, 82
foreign service officer, 82
friend finder, 22
fundraiser, 24–25
funeral director, 75–76

• G •

garden designer, 102
gemologist, 54
gene therapy, 124
genetic counselor, 58
genomics, 29
geographer, 95
geographic information specialist, 95–96
geologist, 96
geophysicist, 31
geriatric care manager, 14
golf course superintendent, 102
golf seminar instructor, 69
government manager, 60
government procurement consultant, 36–37

graphic artist, 45–46
graphologist, 44

• H •

headhunter, 21–22
healthcare administrator, 62–63
heart/lung perfusionist, 48–49
health educator, 69
hearing officer, 80
historian, personal, 81
historic preservationist, 111
holographer, 47
home inspector, 101–102
home remodeling contractor, 102
home schooling consultant, 75, 128–129
home stager, 98
hospital research director, 119
hotel manager, 132
human resources manager, 63
hydrologist, 30

• I •

idea generator, 92
image consultant, 18
incidental music composer, 73
indexer, 43
industrial designer, 109–110
infant mental health counselor, 15
infectious diseases, 119
infertility specialist, 120
information abstractor, 43
information retriever/ independent search specialist, 42
information technology manager, 60
interior designer, 97–98
Internet trainer, 42
inventor, 109
investment banker, 87–88
investor relations specialist, 81
irrigation system specialist, 49

• J •

journalist, 40–41

• L •

labor relations specialist, 64
landscape architect, 98
laser technician, 109
legal transcript digester, 44
librarian, 42
lighting designer, 47
lobbyist, 73
location expert, 95
locksmith, 54

• M •

makeup artist, 100–101
management consultant, 92
manager, 58–63
marketer, 90–91
market rationalization, 128
massage therapist, 100
mass customization, 129
matchmaker, 22–23
mediator, 14
medical examiner, 94
menopause counselor, 114
men's therapist, 15
meteorologist, 30–31
microscopist, 94
middleman, 132
military officer, 65
millwright, 52
mobile audio repairperson, 53
mobile car detailer, 53
money counselor, 15
muralist, 46
musical instrument repairperson, 49
musician, 72–73

• N •

nanny, 20
nanotechnology, 125
neon sign maker, 47
network/system administrator, 115
newsletter publisher, 35
noise control specialist, 52
non-polluting vehicles, 129
nonprofit manager, 62
nurse, 112–115
nurse legal consultant, 115
nurse practitioner, 13, 113
nutritionist, 58

• O •

occupational medicine, 119
occupational therapist, 75
oceanographer, 95
online education and training, 126–127
operations research analyst, 84
optician, dispensing, 99–100
optometrist, 57
organizational developer, 92–93
orthopist, 57
orthotist, 49
overseas careers, 130, 132

• P •

packaging designer, 110
paralegal, 14, 80

paramedic, 121
parking lot oil change business
    operator, 77
park ranger, 102–103
patent agent, 106
patient discharge planner, 114
pedorthist, 49
performance artist, 132
performing arts manager, 60
perfumer, 48
personal assistant, 20–21
personal care facility owner, 27
personal chef, 55
personal coach, 14, 16–18
personal historian/biographer, 81
personal organizer, 18
personnel recruiter, 21–22
pet sitter, 56
pharmacist, 57
photogrammetry technician, 96
photographer, 103–105
photojournalist, 104
photo restorator, 104
physical therapist, 121
physician, 13, 118–120
physician's assistant, 13, 120
physicist, 132
piano technician/tuner, 50
pilot, 97
planetary geologist, 96
planner, 116
plant geneticist, 29
police officer, 132
political aide, 73
political campaign manager,
    64–65
politician, 132
polygraph operator, 75
portfolio manager, 37
precision agriculture, 96
pre-employment tester, 116
private investigator, 117
private-practice consultant, 93
private school founder, 64
producer, 25–26
product manager, 61
product tester, 56
professional speaker, 68
professor, 89
program evaluator, 90
project manager, 61
proposal writer, 89
prosthetist, 49
psychotherapist, 15–16
public health administrator, 63
public relations specialist, 80–81
purchasing specialist, 85
pyrotechnician, 56

• **Q** •

quality assurance specialist, 116

• **R** •

radio guide publisher, 44
radio/TV news reporter, 66–67
real estate salesperson, 133
regulation compliance
    consultant, 82
relationship acceptance
    therapist, 15
relocation consultant, 27
respiratory therapist, 115
restaurant menu creator, 112
resume writer, 41–42
retail buyer, 133
retail manager, 133
reunion planner, 26
risk management specialist,
    117–118
robotics technologist, 51

• **S** •

salesperson, 23–24
school administrator, 63–64
school computer coordinator, 116
school guidance counselor, 20
school psychologist, 16
school-to-work coordinator, 22
seamster, specialty, 55
securities analyst, 37
securities trader, 88
security system consultant, 94
seismologist, 31
silviculturist, 96
small business consultant, 93
social science analyst, 43
social worker, 19
software architect/engineer/
    developer/designer, 83
software trainer, 68
solar and wind energy
    technologist/installer, 51
soundtrack sound designer, 72
speaking coach, 68
special effects artist, 45
speech-language therapist, 73–74
sports agent, 78
sports announcer, 67
sports information director, 88
sports psychologist, 15
sports referee/umpire, 103
statistician, 32–33
student travel service, 38
stunt person, 106
succession planning, 65
supply chain manager, 85
surgical technologist, 99

surveyor, 53
system/network administrator,
    115
systems analyst, 84

• **T** •

talk show host, 67
teacher, 69–70
technical illustrator, 46
technical support specialist, 83
telecommunications specialist, 51
telecommuting manager, 61
temp agency owner, 27
textile designer, 46
thesis completion consultant, 89
tile setter, 54
time management coach, 17
toxicologist, 29
toy designer, 110
trade show planner, 26
translator, 82
transplant coordinator, 113
travel agent, 133
trend spotter, 91
trial consultant, 27
troubled teen consultant, 74
tugboat operator, 48
tutor, 74
TV newswriter, 41
TV/radio news reporter, 66–67

• **V** •

venture capitalist, 88
veterinarian, 120
veterinary technologist, 120–121
victim assistant, 19
video yearbook publisher, 118
violence prevention/resolution,
    123
viral defense, 123
virtual assistant, 20–21
virtual reality, 126
viticulturist, 96
volcanologist, 31

• **W** •

Webcasting technician, 111
Web commercials, 124
Web content finder, 42–43
Web designer, 83–84
Webmaster, 84
Web site evaluator, 90
Web store owner, 37–38
wedding planner, 27
wellness coordinator, 114
wireless telecommunication,
    127–128
work-family manager, 61
writer, 39–40, 132